ENCOUNTERING
MISSIONARY LIFE
AND WORK

A. Scott Moreau, *series editor*

Also in the series:

Introducing World Missions: A Biblical, Historical, and Practical Survey
  A. Scott Moreau, Gary R. Corwin, and Gary B. McGee
*The Changing Face of World Missions: Engaging Contemporary Issues
  and Trends*
  Michael Pocock, Gailyn Van Rheenen, and Douglas McConnell

ENCOUNTERING MISSIONARY LIFE AND WORK

Preparing for Intercultural Ministry

TOM STEFFEN AND
LOIS McKINNEY DOUGLAS

Baker Academic
a division of Baker Publishing Group
Grand Rapids, Michigan

Published by Baker Academic
a division of Baker Publishing Group
P.O. Box 6287, Grand Rapids, MI 49516-6287
www.bakeracademic.com

Printed in the United States of America

Library of Congress Cataloging-in-Publication Data
Steffen, Tom A., 1947–
    Encountering missionary life and work : preparing for intercultural ministry /
Tom Steffen and Lois McKinney Douglas.
        p.   cm. — (Encountering mission)
    Includes bibliographical references and index.
    ISBN 978-0-8010-2659-1 (pbk.)
    1. Missions. 2. Missionaries. 3. Christianity and culture. I. Douglas, Lois
McKinney, 1931– II. Title.
    BV2061.3.S75 2007
    266—dc22   2007045046

From Lois McKinney Douglas: To the memory of Ross Alan Douglas

Our six years of marriage became a honeymoon as we shared our lives and activities together, among them the initial stages in the development of my chapters for this book. My prayer is that the tears that became intermingled with the writing process after God took you home will be transformed into joy for readers as they begin their missions journey.

Contents

Preface

WHY THIS BOOK?

Two popular and significant textbooks on missionary life and work have spanned the twentieth century: Arthur J. Brown's *Foreign Missionary* (1907, 1932, 1950) and J. Herbert Kane's *Life and Work on the Mission Field* (1980).

Arthur J. Brown (1856–1963)

Arthur J. Brown served as the administrative secretary of the Presbyterian Board of Foreign Mission for thirty-four years (1895–1929). Throughout his adult life, he had continuing leadership roles in international missionary conferences and made frequent overseas trips to mission fields, including two long tours to Asia. He insisted on the importance of missions being centered in the national church. During his 106-year life span, he authored fourteen books, among them *The Foreign Missionary*. This work appeared in three editions, the first in 1907, the second in 1932, and the third—with extensive revision—in 1950 (R. P. Johnson 1998, 94).

He states the purpose of his book as being "to describe the missionaries who incarnate this great work, who and what they are, their motives and aims, their policies and methods" and praises the foreign missionary as "the incarnation of the worldwide mission of the Christian Church" (Brown 1950, xiii):

> Whether one sympathises with that mission or not, no thoughtful person can be indifferent to a movement of such magnitude and character. Statistics do not adequately express its significance. Exact figures are soon

out of date. Suffice it here that there are approximately 30,000 foreign missionaries and 153,000 native workers. Evangelists are preaching the Gospel of Christ in hundreds of languages and in every part of Asia, Africa and Latin America. Educators are teaching in 55,000 schools of all types from kindergartens to universities. Physicians and nurses are ministering to the suffering in 1,100 hospitals and 2,300 dispensaries. There are asylums for lepers and the insane, special schools for the blind and for deaf-mutes, homes for rescued girls and hundreds of orphanages. Boys and girls are taught useful trades and household duties in industrial schools. Young people are trained for Christian service in their own country in theological seminaries, medical colleges, nurses' training schools, teachers' normal schools, and agricultural colleges. The Bible and Christian books are translated and widely distributed. (ibid.)

In his introduction to the same volume, Samuel M. Zwemer reminds readers of the dramatic changes in the missions world that occurred between the 1907 and the 1950 editions. In 1907, Brown noted, nearly "one-half of Asia, ten-eleventh of Africa, and practically all of the island world are under nominally Christian [colonial] governments" (1907, 264). By 1950, Zwemer comments,

Nearly all of Asia and large areas in Africa are independent. Nationalism is in the saddle and Imperialism has lost its hold. . . . Politics are in confusion but people are still there. The Church is still very much alive and Christ is still on the field of battle.

It is therefore not less, but more, important and urgent to understand the foreign missionary's tasks; what his qualifications are, what he is trying to do, what difficulties must be overcome and what are the human conditions for that success in the realm of the spirit where, in the last analysis, all depends not on man's device or wisdom but on the power of the Holy Spirit. (viii)

J. Herbert Kane (1910–1988)

Born in Canada and naturalized a US citizen, Herbert Kane and his wife sailed for China with the China Inland Mission in 1935. There they worked in the Anhwei province until they were forced to evacuate in 1945, after staying during most of the Japanese occupation. They returned to Anhwei in 1946 and had to evacuate again in 1950, nineteen months after the Communist domination of the country. After returning to the United States, Kane taught missions at Barrington College, Lancaster Bible College, and Trinity Evangelical Divinity School. He has been described as having an encyclopedic knowledge of missions (Covell 2000b, 534) and as one of the most productive and influential American evangelical missiologists of his time (G. H. Anderson 1998, 353–54).

Kane authored several books that have been used extensively as missions texts, among them *Life and Work on the Mission Field* (1980). His insights related to missionary preparation and meeting the demands of missionary life and work were filled with practical suggestions related to raising financial support, keeping in touch with the home church, adapting to the culture, maintaining health on the field, educating children, coping with loneliness, and other important topics.

ABOUT THIS TEXTBOOK

Writing this text was a double challenge. The two textbooks we described above were written by missions giants of the twentieth century, and there was no way that we could replace or substitute their work. Rather, we have tried to stand on their shoulders, build on their insights, and incorporate their passion for missions into this new textbook. The second challenge was to help prospective missionaries prepare for their life and work in the midst of so much change, so many options, and so much uncertainty. The world is in constant flux, new missions strategies are continually being developed, and prospective missionaries are changing as well.

How, then, could we write a book that would not be obsolete before it got into print? How could we be certain that we were aware of newer issues arising even while we were trying to wrap things up? It is encouraging to remind ourselves in the midst of such disequilibrating change that there are still constants. God has allowed us to participate with him in what he is doing in the world through his church. However much the world is changing, it still needs Jesus Christ. We are his messengers to that world. Regardless of how disorienting changing contexts may be, these eternal truths are still our compass.

When we began collaborating on this textbook, we soon discovered how different our personalities, perspectives, and experiences were. Tom was of German descent; Lois's ancestors were Irish. Tom's field experiences were mostly in tribal areas in the Philippines; Lois had worked largely in urban contexts in Portugal and Brazil. Tom's thinking style was more linear, analytic, low context, and time-oriented. Lois was more global, intuitive, high context, and event-oriented. Tom was making significant academic and field-based contributions to the development of missions strategies; Lois was celebrating fifty years of active ministry in theological and missions education. Tom was rooted in the Southern California missions culture; Lois was immersed in the missions culture of the Midwest.

We shared our insights and celebrated our differences as we worked together in the development of this textbook. Our prayer is that God will use our efforts to help you prepare spiritually, personally, and vocationally for missions in a changing world, and that he will fill your hearts with joy and peace as you follow and serve him in the years to come.

ACKNOWLEDGMENTS

From Tom Steffen: I would like to express my heartfelt appreciation to a number of people for helping make this book become a reality. First, Baker Academic deserves a big hand for their collective wisdom in recognizing the need to update foundational missions textbooks for the twenty-first century. My colleagues at the School of Intercultural Studies, Biola University, also deserve special thanks. Thank you Marla Campbell, Katrina Green, Doug Hayward, Judith Lingenfelter, Kitty Purgason, and Dean Doug Pennoyer for your continual encouragement, wise insights, and tolerance of my sporadic appearances on campus. I would be remiss not to mention my dear coauthor, Lois. Losing her loving husband, Ross, during the writing of this book slowed the process but produced a stronger, more spiritual woman. Thank you, Lois, for your friendship and scholarship. Last, I would like to thank my lovely wife, Darla, for all her patience as this book took shape as well as the hours of library research she conducted on its behalf. I could not have done it without you.

From Lois McKinney Douglas: I am grateful to my colleagues Tom Steffen and Scott Moreau for their encouragement, patience, and helpful suggestions throughout the book-writing process. The active involvement of the editorial team at Baker Academic is also appreciated.

Special thanks are extended to the students in my DME 842 "Intercultural Communication" course at Trinity Evangelical Divinity School during the fall semester of 2005. Since many of my assigned chapters were also topics in this course, interacting with them as they were being developed became an important class activity. Many of the suggestions growing out of these discussions have found their way into this book. I am especially grateful to David Ngaruiya, who spent long hours in the Trinity library tracking down bibliographical information for me, and to Jennifer Stadelmann, who helped me to bridge the language and culture gap as I (a septuagenarian!) was attempting to write for missionaries in the twenty-first century. Both David and Jennifer contributed personal insights and field experiences that helped to enrich this textbook.

My thanks are also extended to my patient friends and colleagues in Brazil, who so graciously accepted my long absences from my ministries there while I was in the United States immersed in this book. My wish is that it will soon be adapted and translated into Portuguese for them. Last but not least, special thanks are due to my Doberman, Jeannie, who gave me such warm welcomes each time I returned home and stayed beside my desk while I was writing.

xii

Introduction

As you surf the Internet, turn on the TV news, or glance at newspaper headlines, you may have the sensation that you are gazing into a constantly shaking kaleidoscope. The shapes and colors shift so rapidly that you are unable to follow them or make sense of them. Or, to change the metaphor, you may feel as if you are on an amusement-park ride that keeps whirling faster and faster until you are afraid the G force will spin you off.

Welcome to the twenty-first century, where disorienting changes such as the information explosion, movements of peoples, crises of all sorts—poverty, natural disasters, pandemics—and a fundamental worldview shift toward postmodernity are keeping us all in a whirl.

Information Explosion

When missionaries waved good-bye to friends and family from the deck of a ship fifty years ago, they were also leaving instant communication. Letters could take six weeks or more to reach their destination. Newspapers and magazines could take just as long. Signals from shortwave radio faded in and out; cable TV and satellite signals were still in the future; electric typewriters were just becoming available. The popularized use of computers, the Internet, and e-mail were still more than thirty years away.

Today, except in the most remote areas of the world, communication is instant. If we want to get in touch with a friend or send a report to a mission agency or church, we can telephone, send a fax, write an e-mail message, or log on to the Web for chatting and conferencing. If we find yesterday's newspaper or last month's professional journal too dated, we can go to their Web sites for news as it is happening today. If we want information about unreached peoples, religious movements, regions of the world, or mission agencies, it is available to us with just a few clicks of a mouse (see, for example, www.mislinks.org).

Movements of Peoples

From the fifteenth to the nineteenth century, migration was largely from European countries as people left to settle and colonize the Americas, much of Africa, and large portions of Asia. Now the flow has reversed. Asians and Africans are migrating to Europe. A steady flow of Latin American immigrants is entering the United States and Canada. The massive Chinese diaspora has created opportunities for missions among these dispersed people and missions participation through them as well (Wan 2003, 35–43). Add to these the all-too-frequent forced displacements through wars, famines, natural disasters, and the like, and it is easy to see why we are living in the midst of the most confusing and complex patterns of migration in human history (Conn 2000, 626).

Simultaneously, Africans, Asians, and Latin Americans are migrating in large numbers from rural areas to urban centers.

> The number of city dwellers in 1985 was twice as great as the entire population of the world in 1800. Africa's urbanization rate is the most rapid. Its urban population, 7 percent in 1920, more than quadrupled by 1980. Asia's urban population will likely hit 40 percent by 2000, a 665 percent growth over 1920. Seventy-four percent of Latin American and Caribbean populations lived in urban areas by 1997.
>
> A unique feature of this urban wave is the trend toward ever larger urban agglomerations. In 1900 there were 18 cities in the world with populations over one million; thirteen were in Europe and North America. At the turn of the twenty-first century, that figure will surpass 354. And 236 of the total will be found in developing countries. In 1991 there were 14 so-called mega-cities (exceeding 10 million inhabitants). Their number is expected to double by 2015. (Conn 2000, 993)

These trends toward ever-larger agglomerations of peoples and the movement of the center of gravity of the world's populations from the northern to the southern hemisphere are extremely significant for missions. The growth of non-Christian and anti-Christian populations in the cities of the southern hemisphere, along with the concentrated populations of the poor who live in the slums and shantytowns surrounding these urban areas, have set the stage for evangelism and social outreach in the twenty-first century (Conn 2000, 993–94).

Conflicts and Crises

Throughout the history of the church, missionaries and other faithful Christians have served Christ in the midst of poverty, pandemics, natural disasters, and violence. Today's missionaries are no exception. They are surrounded by crises created by malnutrition, starvation, deforestation, pollution, and diminished water supplies. They can find themselves in the middle of tsunamis, floods, hurricanes, earthquakes, volcanic eruptions, and other natural disasters. Pandemic outbreaks of HIV/AIDS, influenza, and other diseases occur constantly. Violence in all its forms—from global terrorism to rape, murder, and abuse within families—is rampant in some parts of the world in which missionaries witness and serve. Security checkpoints, gunfire in the distance, disruptions of church services by authorities, and searches of their homes and workplaces may have become a part of their daily lives. Evacuations, kidnappings, or even murders are possible. Burnout or posttraumatic stress disorder (PTSD) occur, and missionaries and other Christian workers need help and support to face them.

Postmodernity

Changes in our world are not only external. A fundamental shift in the way people look at their world has also occurred. We are moving from the "modern" paradigm toward the paradigm of "postmodernity." Modernity viewed human reason as the beginning of all knowledge. Scientific objectivity, inductive reasoning, and the manipulation of the physical world were emphasized. Modernity was guided by cause and effect assumptions and tended to be deterministic. Scientific knowledge was considered factual and value free. Religion—at least in those cultures embedded in the modernist paradigm—was relegated to the private world of opinion and divorced from the public world of facts (Bosch 1991, 264–67).

In contrast, postmodernity sees truth as relative and subjective. What you believe and what I believe are regarded as equally valid. Our unique feelings and differing viewpoints are valued and communicated through our relationships and experiences.

Postmodernity offers both support and challenges for missions. Its emphasis on whole persons encourages the spread of a holistic gospel and the transforming work of the Holy Spirit in lives and relationships. The missions challenge is to respond "to the nihilism, relativism, pluralism, and the loss of the concept of truth and sense of purpose that mark the foundationless character of postmodern society" (Van Engen 2000, 773–74).

MISSIONS IS CHANGING

In the fall of 1949, students in a Bible college were gathered for a solemn chapel service. The People's Republic of China had taken over the nation, and missionaries were being forced to evacuate. Tears flowed and sobs were heard as, slowly, one by one, on a large world map scattered with lights representing missionaries who had studied at the school, the lights in China were turned off. The missionaries were gone. The church would die. Only later, when encouraging news began to leak out, did the missions world begin to realize that the work of God in China not only had survived; it had even thrived without an expatriate missionary presence. What was dying was an era of colonial, Western-dominated missions (McKinney Douglas 2002, 174).

The demise of colonialism was spawned with the rise of independence movements in former colonies, and this in turn led to the development of nationalism. Within missions circles, this meant missionaries began developing national leaders and working ourselves out of a job. We were a temporary scaffolding; the future of missions within the country belonged to the national church. Lois recalls her own involvement in the leadership development and nationalization process in Brazil from 1974 to 1978:

> When I returned to Brazil in 1974, I became deeply immersed in teaching and developing a master's program at the Faculdade Teológica Batista de São Paulo, directing Brazil's nation wide TEE [theological education by extension] association, and launching a graduate-level training program for educators and writers for TEE. . . .
>
> Four years later, in 1978, when I was due for home assignment again, I realized that [the masters' program], the TEE association and the internship program were able to function well under capable national leadership. This realization gave me an ecstatic sense of fulfillment. "Father," I prayed, "I'm ready to go home to be with you. If you give me a long life with more ministry opportunities, I want to be faithful to you, but I cannot ask you for any more than you have already given me." (McKinney Douglas 2002, 175)

God did have more ahead. Before another decade had passed, nationalization was giving way to globalization. Missionaries were going from all the world to all the world. The mission fields were becoming a missions force.

> In 1987, I was back in São Paulo as a North American delegate to COMIBAM (a Spanish/Portuguese acronym for Ibero-American Missionary

Cooperation). The gathering was a celebration of Latin American and Iberian missions coming of age or, as the conference theme put it, of the two regions emerging "From a Mission Field to a Missions Force." The opening night was dedicated to recognition of expatriate missionaries who had brought the Gospel to their regions. During a standing ovation the auditorium reverberated with the sounds of clapping, cheering and shouting. The ecstatic sense of fulfillment that the nationalization of Brazilian programs had brought me had turned out to be penultimate. God had allowed me to climb an even higher mountain from which I could see and hear this celebration of globalization and partnership. I felt as if the hosts of heaven were cheering and clapping with us. (McKinney Douglas 2002, 177)

This movement toward globalization has of course not been limited to Latin America and the Iberian Peninsula. It has become boundary-less. Sidebar I.1 provides statistics showing that, even though the majority world missions movement is still much smaller than that of the Western world, it is growing at a much faster rate (Jaffarian 2004, 132).

Other globalizing efforts are in progress as well. International partnerships are being created among sending agencies; efforts are being mobilized to reach immigrants next door as well as people groups within the 10/40 window, and former sending countries are being seen as needy mission fields. One example of this kind of focus on "reverse mission" is the Gospel and Our Culture Network, which is engaged in research on the "encounter of the gospel with North American culture and encouraging local action toward the transformation of the life and witness of the churches" (Hunsberger 2002, 402–3; see www.gocn.org).

In spite of the overwhelmingly positive impact of such globalization, missionaries from the United States, for whom this textbook is primarily written, will find some of the fallout from the process disturbing. They may find that in many parts of the world American missionaries are not welcome. The only way they will be able to enter will be through creative access strategies. Even when they serve in countries where they can be open about their missionary intentions, they are likely to encounter anger and hostility directed toward political policies and interventions of the United States. These attitudes will be spread through the media, encouraged through mass demonstrations, and sometimes even directed toward them as individuals because of their American nationality. Unfortunately, these tensions in United States–host country relationships can even filter down into the Christian community. There they are reflected in stereotyping, prejudice, and uncomfortable relationships between missionaries and their national colleagues. Holy Spirit–generated attitudes of humility and servanthood are required if US missionaries are to be faithful witnesses in such situations.

SIDEBAR I.1
PROTESTANT, INDEPENDENT, AND ANGLICAN MISSIONARIES
IN 1990 AND 2000

Sources: Johnstone (1993, 643); Johnstone and Mandryk (2001, 747)

REGIONS	MISSIONARIES IN 1990	MISSIONARIES IN 2000	GROWTH RATE (%)
Africa	1,669	3,126	87
Asia	3,476	13,607	291
Latin America	1,489	3,837	158
Majority world total	6,634	20,570	210
Europe	15,701	16,077	2
Northern America	43,554	50,720	16
Pacific	3,672	3,526	-4
Western world total	62,927	70,323	12
Total	69,561	90,893	31

MISSIONARIES ARE CHANGING

A century ago, white male missionaries from North America or northern Europe waved good-bye to their families and friends at the dock as they took their wives and children aboard a ship with them to sail off for faraway lands with no thought of returning home. There many of them spent their lifetimes trekking along jungle paths, wearing pith helmets for protection from the sun, as they took the gospel to remote unevangelized villages. In stark contrast, today's missionaries are both men and women, both young and old. They come from many nations, ethnic groups, and Christian traditions and serve in a broad spectrum of ministries and roles.

Long-term, career missionaries still provide the backbone for this global missionary force. They are going from all nations to all nations, proclaiming the Word, planting churches, nurturing Christian growth, and developing church leaders. Medical missions, schools, and community development projects are also an integral part of their witness and outreach. These longer-term missionaries are no longer alone. They have been joined by short-termers, professionals, retirees, tentmakers, and other newcomers who are participating in global missions in creative ways.

Overwhelming numbers of new missionaries are short-termers. They usually travel as teams to participate in disaster relief, sports evangelism, musical groups, study and vision tours, and other assignments. According to the 2004 *Missions Handbook*, North American mission agencies reported sending 346,225 short-term workers in 2001. This is likely to be a small fraction of the total since it does not include those who were sent directly from local churches or who went on their own (Moreau 2004, 33).

Another important group of missionaries is professionals who intersperse missions assignments with their responsibilities at home by taking leaves or sabbaticals. A librarian may help a theological school to set up its library, a consulting psychologist may provide on-site psychotherapy for hurting missionaries, or a high school teacher may take a sabbatical to teach in a missionary children's school. These and many other professional skills are useful and needed in missions contexts.

As people are leaving their full-time work earlier and living longer, retirees are finding fulfillment in missions-oriented ministries abroad. As these older missionaries serve in a variety of missions roles and activities, the maturity, insights, experience, and skills they bring to their ministries enable them to make significant contributions to missions teams.

With Christian missionaries no longer welcome in many places in the world, bi-vocational workers, or tentmakers, have become a significant part of the world missions force. They enter hard-to-reach areas as teachers of English, professors in universities, medical workers in hospitals and clinics, employees in multinational firms, developers of local business enterprises, and through a variety of other vocational roles. In some of these contexts, they may be able to work discretely with local groups of believers. In others, direct contact can cause harm to the group and perhaps even lead to the missionary's expulsion from the country. Regardless of how open or closed the situation may be, the primary witness of these tentmakers will be through dedication to their professions, developing friendships with those with whom they work, and, once trust is established, sharing their faith in Jesus Christ.

The list above does not exhaust the options available to today's missionaries. Their roles can be as varied as their creativity allows and the situations demand.

FLOW OF THE BOOK

The book is divided into four parts, each focusing on elements that all missionaries can expect to face as they seek to follow God's prompting to bring Christ to those who do not know him. The appendix also lists a number of useful Web sites on many of the major topics discussed in the book.

The Changing Scene

In part 1, we present important missionary figures from the past and draw lessons from their lives for today's cross-cultural workers. We also discuss key ideas and important terms that are crucial for understanding missions in the twenty-first century.

Home-Front Preparations

In part 2, we cover the part of the missionary life cycle that includes all the preparation necessary for healthy cross-cultural service. This includes issues such as understanding God's will and the call of God, the spiritual formation of the missionary, competencies that are necessary for personal and ministry effectiveness, the avenues people use to cross cultures for Christian service in our globalized world, ways for you to find your own personal niche in the total work of God's kingdom, and the development of a personal journey plan that will help you express the ways you sense God is leading you and keep you on task as you prepare for service.

On-Field Preparations

In part 3, we explore the realities of learning how to live well in a new culture. A critical building block in that process is understanding culture itself—what shapes it and how it grows and changes—as well as how every person grows and develops as a member of a particular culture. Knowing what culture is will make your job of adjusting to your new culture easier, which cannot be done without the processes of learning the language and the culture as well as bonding with the people for whom that culture is home. We explore what this bonding involves in terms of intercultural communication and relationship development. We also examine the obstacles to successful adjustment, such as culture shock and culture stress.

Missionaries and Their Lives

In part 4 we work through issues that today's missionaries and other cross-cultural workers can expect to face once they have adjusted to their new homes and are engaged in ministry.

The fact that women comprise at least two-thirds of the total missionary force, and that conservative Christians have often offered only subordinate roles to women, calls for focused attention. Understanding the perspectives—both biblical and cultural—on their status and role is central to the completion of the Great Commission.

Missionaries who are married bring with them not only their spouses but also children. The family lives of missionaries are an important topic to consider, as care for children (and more recently for aging parents) plays an important role in the success or failure of missionaries. We explore the issues involved, including such things as schooling of children, helping the whole family handle cultural and adjustment issues, and facing home assignments together.

In addition to the normal ebb and flow of typical missionary life, missionaries also must be ready to face crises. These range from health issues (physical or psychological) to traumatic events (wars, insecurity) to the reality of the stresses of relating to people who are not of your culture, and even disagreements with other missionaries. No one in our fallen world ever lives a crisis-free life, but dealing with crises far away from home without your normal supports can be a daunting task. We offer helpful thinking and preparation for that reality in missionary lives.

One of the realities of successfully transitioning from your home culture to a new culture is that home never quite feels the same again. From the relatively less severe trauma of coming back for several months to a year for deputation to the more challenging adjustment of coming home for good, we explore the realities of what it is like to cope with reentry stress and shock. Realizing that this is a normal part of missionary life plays an important role in the adjustment process, and we help you prepare for the realities.

In our final chapter, we offer glimpses of several trends in missions and the implications they have for those who serve God in cross-cultural settings. Like Esther, we anticipate that many of you will find yourselves living in "such a time as this" (4:14) with unparalleled and unprecedented ministry possibilities. Our hope is that this book will prepare you to meet the challenges in ways that glorify God and enable those around you to more clearly see Christ living through you.

PART 1

The Changing Scene

Remembering the Past

Scripture and history are saturated with the fingerprints of our missionary God.

Alicia Britt Chole (2000, 59)

Remembering the past, both distant and near, provides explana-
tion and instruction for the present and the future. Thus, in this
chapter we briefly highlight some of the more recognized missions players, as well as those who have not received as much attention,
noting some of their bright spots as well as their blemishes. Some were
strategists; some were strategist-practitioners; some were practitioners.
Some placed the task over human and spiritual relationships, some the
work over family, and some their family over work. Some finished well,
while others left behind destroyed families. Some suffered physically
for Christ; some were martyred, while others only experienced verbal
abuse. Even so, the hand of God is evident throughout the careers of
these servants of God as they attempted to live and work as co-laborers
with him in very different and often difficult places. What can twenty-
first-century cross-cultural Christian workers learn from our predecessors
about the total ministry package, that is, the walk and the work? How
should their lives influence our lives?

Today's cross-cultural Christian workers will do well to reflect on those who have walked, or are presently walking, the missional path. These individuals can help us to better understand the life and times of today's missionaries. Given the numerous cross-cultural Christian workers since the first century, we must be selective. The chapter begins with Luke, moves from Constantine to Luther and Count Nikolaus Ludwig von Zinzendorf. From there we shift our focus to more contemporary figures: William Carey, Eleanor Macomber, J. Hudson Taylor, Charlotte ("Lottie") Diggs Moon, Ralph D. Winter, Joanne Shetler, Luis Bush, Omar Gava, Natasha, and Martin and Gracia Burnham. Drawing from their lives, we identify some of the implications for twenty-first century missionaries in relation to Holy Spirit–directed living and practice.

LUKE

Luke, a well-traveled medical doctor, a good friend of Paul, an outstanding researcher, writer, missionary-theologian, and the only Gentile author in the New Testament, highlights the expansion of the Jesus movement (called "the Way") in two volumes we know as Luke and Acts. Better thought of as a single unit, Luke-Acts features a selective collection of stories that comprise two-fifths of the New Testament, covering approximately seventy years. The stories found in Luke-Acts introduce a varied cast of human characters—Peter, John, Barnabas, Stephen, Philip, Cornelius, James, Paul, Lydia, Priscilla, Drusilla, Bernice. It also includes spiritual characters, God the Father, Jesus, the Holy Spirit—and the enemy of humanity known as Satan. Unquestionably the dominant spiritual character in Luke's stories is the Holy Spirit.

The Holy Spirit provided the young followers of the Jesus movement the power to expand God's kingdom (Acts 1:3, 5; 8:12; 14:22; 19:8; 20:25; 28:23, 31) in Jerusalem, Judea-Samaria, and to the far-flung corners of the then-known world (Acts 1:8). Through a combination of signs and wonders, oral communication of the gospel, suffering, and persecution, churches were born, multiplied, and matured throughout the Mediterranean. The gospel crossed ethnic boundaries, creating a universal church composed of Jews and Gentiles. Luke documents the expansion of God's reign as the gospel penetrates the barriers of ethnicity, gender, generations, geography, nationality, politics, and broken relationships with the Creator.

The Holy Spirit also provided direction to his coworkers (Acts 10:10–20; 13:2; 16:1–40). Desiring to take the gospel to the East, the Holy Spirit kept the Pauline team "from preaching the word in the province of Asia" (16:6). At a later date the team concentrated on Ephesus (19:1–41), thereby strategically reaching all of Asia, including the seven churches

4

SIDEBAR 1.1
WOMEN NOTED IN LUKE-ACTS

The following women are noted in Luke's two accounts in the New Testament. As you look through the list, choose those you do not know very well and read their stories.

LUKE	ACTS
• Mary and Elizabeth (1:24–2:35)	• Sapphira (5:1–11)
• Anna (2:36–38)	• Widows (6:1)
• Herodias (3:19)	• Candace (8:27)
• Widow of Zarephath (4:26)	• Dorcas (9:36–41)
• Simon's mother-in-law (4:38)	• Widows (9:39, 41)
• Widow of Nain (7:11–12)	• Mary, mother of John Mark (12:12)
• Sinful woman (7:36–50)	• Rhoda (12:13)
• Mary Magdalene, Joanna, and Susanna (8:3)	• Lydia (16:13–15)
• Jesus's mother (8:19–20)	• Slave girl who predicted future (16:16–18)
• Mary and Martha (10:38–42)	• Leading women (17:4)
• Unnamed women (11:27–28)	• High-standing Greek women (17:12)
• Queen of the South (11:31)	• Damaris (17:34)
• Woman with spirit infirmity (13:10–17)	• Priscilla (18:2–3, 18, 26)
• Woman who lost coin (15:8–10)	• Four unmarried daughters who prophesied (21:9)
• Lot's wife (17:32)	• Drusilla (24:24)
• Widow (18:1–8)	• Bernice (25:13, 23; 26:30)
• Poor widow (21:1–4)	
• Maid (22:56–57)	
• Women who mourned for Jesus (23:27)	
• Women from Galilee (23:49, 55; 24:10)	

REFLECTION AND DISCUSSION

1. How many of the stories of these women do you know?
2. Given the number of women mentioned in Luke-Acts, why do we not hear more of them in missions history?

referenced in Revelation. In the meantime, the Jesus movement marched west through the continents of Europe and northern Africa. How different the church history books would be today if the Holy Spirit had led the Pauline team east toward China rather than west.

Acts ends abruptly, leaving the impression that the job of expanding God's reign has yet to reach completion. Many questions remain unanswered. Why does Luke end his narrative with Paul in jail? Why does Luke make Paul's arrival in Rome so anticlimactic? Was Paul eventually released? Did he ever reach Spain? Did Luke plan to write a third volume? What happened to Peter and James after Acts 15? What happened to Barnabas? Perhaps the message of Acts is much larger than the monumental roles played by Peter, James, Barnabas, and Paul in the Jesus movement. Luke's message is more about the unstoppable power of the Holy Spirit and the Word of God to expand God's kingdom globally than about the enemy's ability to thwart key leaders within the Jesus movement.

Although the Jesus movement documented by Luke was not without significant theological and cultural differences and challenges (Acts 15), persecution, and martyrdom, it did gain a unified and legitimate identity. Although tied historically to Judaism, the new movement slowly became distinct from it, moving beyond Palestine. Through "word and deed" the people of "the Way" would eventually advance to Italy, Europe, North America, Latin America, Africa, and Asia. But we get ahead of ourselves.

CONSTANTINE TO MARTIN LUTHER

After years of sporadic persecution of the faithful followers of Christ, the fourth century saw the emperor Constantine take a public stand for Christianity. Persecution slowed, as did aggressive evangelism. State-sponsored religion driven by creeds, church buildings (in contrast to house churches), politics, and colonial imperialism slowly replaced vibrant followers of Christ with nominal Christians. Even so, over the coming centuries God continued to send dedicated workers to expand his kingdom, including Ulfilas to the Goths, Patrick to the Celts, Willibrord to the Vikings, Augustine to England, and Leif to Greenland. The dark days for Christendom would return again during the bigoted Crusades (1095–1600s), dividing the Eastern and Western church and increasing hatred between Muslims and Christians. But spiritual light would again burn brightly during the Reformation.

Luther, Calvin, Zwingli, and a spate of others challenged a decadent papacy. Through their courageous efforts, first-century understanding of justification by faith replaced the then-current misunderstandings of a works-oriented salvation. A revival began that would change the course of history. Even so, mission theology and practice received little if any attention. Kenneth Latourette provides five possible reasons for this: (1) the apostles had already fulfilled the Great Commission; (2) they were preoccupied with "home" work; (3) political authorities were responsible for public worship; (4) there was no general awareness of the non-European world; and (5) Luther believed the world was near the end (1939, 3:23).

Donald McGavran (1988, 3) expands on Latourette in explaining Protestant seminary training from 1550 to 1800. Sealed off by Muslim armies to the south and the east and Spanish and Portuguese navies to the west, the Reformers believed that their job was to Christianize the masses of Roman Catholics swept into the Reformation. He argues that this led to a "maintenance mentality" that was reflected in seminary curricula and church practice. Sadly, this orientation remains to this day. The Reformation focused on improving adherents' understanding of Christianity within existing churches rather than planting and multiplying new ones. Maturation was more important than multiplication.

COUNT NIKOLAUS LUDWIG VON ZINZENDORF

German Count Nikolaus Ludwig von Zinzendorf (1700–1760) became the father of the Moravian missionary movement and, on a broader scale, laid the foundation for Protestant global missions. Growing up under the influence of Pietism—a movement during the late seventeenth and mid-eighteenth centuries that emphasized the blending of Bible doctrine, individual piety, and faithful practice—he practiced what his grandmother and aunt had modeled. When religious Protestant refugees from Moravia appeared unexpectedly, he offered them a place to stay on his land at Herrnhut, Germany. When they continued to come, his door remained open in spite of strong family opposition. On August 13, 1727, revival spread through the growing group of Moravians at Herrnhut, resulting in a great passion for missions. Through Zinzendorf's vision and contacts and Christian David's tireless efforts to bring refugee believers from throughout Europe to the count's estate, the Moravians began a monumental movement that would take the good news of Jesus Christ to the unreached world. The first Moravian missionaries went to the Virgin Islands in 1732, sixty years before William Carey. Others followed God's call to the West Indies, Asia, Africa, Russia, North America, and other places around the world. From the 1500s to the 1700s, the Moravians sent out more missionaries than all other Protestant groups combined.

The Moravians were the first Protestants to practice their duty as a church to evangelize "the heathen." William Danker claims, "No church better illustrates the total apostolate" (Pierson 2000, 660). Forged out of persecution, this small group of refugees fled to Zinzendorf's estate, where they began a community that integrated faith and economics. From this humble start would come "over half of the Protestant missionaries in

7

the eighteenth century" (ibid.). Their purpose in going out was twofold: to reach the unreached and to renew faltering churches.

Comprised of called clergy and laypeople, male and female, married and single, and expected to work to support themselves, the Moravians set out for the far corners of the world, where they formed self-supporting communities. Their for-profit model helped the Moravians identify with the community, taught those they reached the dignity of labor, and provided funds for the support and expansion of missions. For-profit business found its basis in the Moravians' philosophy that regarded "the working day as just as holy as Sunday; work is never meaningless, because Jesus works for us" (Danker 1971, 71). For Danker, the Moravians' most important contribution was the belief that every Christian was considered a missionary and should witness daily within his or her specific vocation (73).

The Moravians' dedication to God's call did not come without cost. Families were left behind while husbands ventured to unreached areas of the world. Even the sometimes arrogant Zinzendorf would eventually regret taking for granted his first wife (Erdmuth) and family while he traveled extensively for Christ. In spite of such over-dedication, the Moravians' influence, work ethic, and humility did not go unnoticed by another major missionary hero, William Carey.

> *Our method of proclaiming salvation is this: to point out to every heart the loving Lamb, who died for us . . . by the preaching of His blood, . . . never, either in discourse or in argument, to digress . . . from the loving Lamb: . . . to preach no commandment except faith in Him; no other justification but that He atoned for us; no other sanctification but the privilege to sin no more; no other happiness but to be near Him, to think of Him and do His pleasure; no other self-denial but to be deprived of Him and His blessings; no other calamity but to displease Him; no other life but in Him.*
>
> Count Nikolaus Ludwig von Zinzendorf (Adams n.d.)

WILLIAM CAREY

While Martin Luther focused on theological correctness in relation to justification by faith in the West, and Nikolaus von Zinzendorf began the Moravian mission movement that went global, the Calvinistic William Carey (1761–1834) would challenge the Protestant church to change its position on the idea that missions ceased in the first century. His classic book *An Enquiry into the Obligation of Christians to Use Means for the Conversion of the Heathen* (1792) argued that the role of the apostles

SIDEBAR 1.2
ADDITIONAL RESOURCES

Here are some of the more important resources on mission history, which provide greater depth and breadth:

- Kenneth S. Latourette, *A History of the Expansion of Christianity*, vol. 3 (Zondervan, 1971).
- Samuel H. Moffett, *A History of Christianity in Asia* (Orbis, 2005).
- C. Stephen Neill, *A History of Christian Missions* (Penguin, 1975).
- Andrew Walls, *The Missionary Movement in Christian History* (Orbis, 1996).
- Ralph D. Winter, *The Twenty-five Unbelievable Years, 1945 to 1969* (William Carey Library, 1970).

For a focus on the people of missions, see:

- Gerald Anderson, ed., *Biographical Dictionary of Christian Missions* (Eerdmans, 1998).
- Gerald H. Anderson, Robert T. Coote, Norman A. Horner, and James M. Phillips, eds., *Mission Legacies: Biographical Studies of Leaders of the Modern Missionary Movement* (Orbis, 1994).
- Ruth Tucker, *From Jerusalem to Irian Jaya: A Biographical History of Christian Missions* (Zondervan, 2004).

continues, requiring that missionaries be sent globally in every generation. This proposal, as well as his life activities in the coastlands, would demand application of his most famous quote: "Expect great things from God; attempt great things for God." It would also begin what has been called the "Great Century of Missions" (1792–1910).

Probably incorrectly crowned the "Father of Modern Missions," Carey conducted missionary exploits that nevertheless are dizzying. A fictive quiz of India's brightest students captures the breadth of this multitalented person: Who was William Carey? All hands shoot up simultaneously. One says: "William Carey was a Christian missionary. . . . And he was also the botanist after whom Careya herbacea is named." Another responds: "William Carey introduced the steam engine." Still others chime in:

He introduced the idea of savings banks, was the first to campaign for the humane treatment for India's leprosy patients, is the father of print technology, founded India's Agri-Horticultural Society, was the first to translate . . . great Indian religious classics, introduced the study of astronomy, pioneered . . . lending libraries, wrote essays on forestry, was the first man to stand against both the ruthless murders and the widespread oppression of women, transformed the ethos of the British administration from indifferent imperial exploitation to 'civil' service, revived the ancient idea that ethics and morality were inseparable from religion, is the

9

father of the Indian Renaissance of the nineteenth and twentieth centuries (Mangalwadi 1999, 17–25).

Amazingly, all of these accomplishments are correct! To them could be added, among other things, Carey's wedding of for-profit business with missions, challenging of widow burning and infanticide, and advancing evangelism in the workplace as well as among expatriate Europeans.

The "consecrated cobbler" was not without help to accomplish all of the above. Known as the Serampore Trio, Joshua Marshman, William Ward, and William Carey set the standard for effective missionary teamwork.

Even so, Carey's family suffered because of his overly demanding schedule and his lack of firmness with his sons. With an overextended father and a mentally disturbed mother (Dorothy), the Carey children benefited from Hannah Marshman's intervention, which compensated for some of their father's laxity. A man of multiple talents, flaws, and friends, Carey influenced followers of Christ in India, England, and America, which resulted in the continued expansion of global missions.

ELEANOR MACOMBER

Eleanor Macomber (1801–40) became the first single female supported by the Baptist Mission Board of the United States. At a time when many considered missions a man's work, certainly not something for the "weaker sex," the American missionary board of the Baptist Church sent Macomber to teach Ojibwa Indians at Sault Sainte Marie, Michigan, in 1830. This location was at least close to her home, although working conditions may have been more difficult than at some missions abroad. Eddy depicts well the mood at the time concerning the role of women in missions: "Almost all the heroines who have gone forth from the churches of America to dot heathen soil with their lowly graves have been attended by some stronger arm than that of weak, defenseless woman. Many of them have had husbands on whom they relied for support and protection, and to whom they could turn with the assurance of sympathy in hours of anguish and gloom" (Eddy 1854).

After four years of faithful ministry and failing health, Macomber returned home. Two years later (1836), she sailed to Burma to serve in the Karen mission. Mr. Osgood accompanied Macomber to remote Dong-Yahn, a community of "brutal, drunken . . . heathen barbarians," some thirty-five miles from Maulmain. Not allowed to stay with another missionary couple, as the Burmese would interpret this as a polygamous household, Macomber was on her own. After "a flood of tears," she pulled herself together and began learning the language. In a matter of months, her preaching in broken Karen resulted in over twenty believers. Strong persecution followed from the Buddhist priests and local authorities, including several attempts to burn her home. Undeterred, she posted the times for group prayer and praise in her home and began a "training school that attracted a dozen willing pupils." Baptisms, however, would have to wait until "brother Osgood came up again" because the ordinance of baptism was restricted solely to males (Tucker 1988, 91).

Determined to reach beyond Dong-Yahn, Macomber began training the young converts. She then sent them to neighboring tribes, sometimes accompanying them as her goal was to visit all the families who lived within six or seven miles of Dong-Yahn at least twice. It was on one of these trips that Macomber contracted jungle fever. Nine days later, at the age of thirty-nine, she succumbed to the disease.

J. HUDSON TAYLOR

J. Hudson Taylor (1832–1905), a disciplined, self-educated, nonordained person with great organizational skills, a strong confidence that God would supply for all his needs, and a desire to take the gospel to the interior of Asia (in contrast to Carey who went to the coastlands), gave his life to reach China for Christ. As a researcher, Taylor identified several provinces in China without a Christian witness. The unreached frontiers became his passion. In time, they also became the passion of a host of new missionaries and agencies that would follow his vision.

Taylor became a devoted follower of Jesus Christ at the age of seventeen. Four years later he sailed to China following God's call on his life. Fighting homesickness and depression brought on by culture shock and stress, he eventually learned the language.

Taylor then left the missionary coastland compounds behind, moving to the interior of the country, where the gospel was still unknown. While this move raised the eyebrows of many in the missions community—they felt much work remained on the coastlands—his next acts would earn their outright condemnation.

Challenging traditional Protestant missionary precedent, the humble, conscientious, formally uneducated Taylor contextualized his appearance by wearing Chinese clothes, shaving his head, and dying his sandy pigtail black. He did not want to look like a foreigner as he attempted to reach a whole nation for Christ. Taylor would eventually meet Maria Dyer, herself a child of missionaries living in China, who became his wife and partner in ministry.

Failing health for both Hudson and Maria resulted in a return to England. During this time Hudson continued his studies in medicine, and they revised the Ningbo New Testament translation and founded the China Inland Mission (CIM) (1865), now the Overseas Missionary Fellowship. The agency, with no connections to a denomination, offered the working class possibly the only channel at that time for participation in missions. Single women were welcome, since they would be readily accepted by Chinese women. Wives and husbands were both considered missionaries. Evangelism was stressed, rather than the planting, developing, and multiplying of churches, because the return of Christ was considered imminent.

The agency did not solicit funds because Taylor was convinced that God would supply for all needs. Incoming funds were shared equally among everyone, including the general director, as all members were to live by faith. Character, not one's formal education, determined membership. For these emphases Taylor is now known as the father of faith missions. Driven by prayer and dependency on God, but certainly not without team conflict, CIM became the largest mission agency in the world at that time. By 1934 it had over thirteen hundred missionaries.

While CIM missionaries were often looked down on by missionaries outside the agency because of their lack of formal education and blue-collar background, CIM prepared the way for a host of other faith missions, such as Africa Inland Mission (AIM), Christian and Missionary Alliance (C&MA), New Tribes Mission (NTM), Sudan Interior Mission (notice the emphasis on interior; now called Serving in Mission [SIM]), and The Evangelical Alliance Mission (TEAM). Taylor also laid the foundation for training institutions such as Biola University, Gordon College, Moody Bible Institute, and Prairie Bible College. Indeed, Taylor's legacy lives on.

The Boxer Rebellion (1900) resulted in the martyrdom of seventy-nine CIM missionaries and their children, the largest loss incurred by a Protestant agency in China. Taylor was devastated. Even so, he refused his right to submit claims for government compensation. After losing two wives and four children, Taylor again returned to his beloved China in 1905, where he died the same year.

CHARLOTTE ("LOTTIE") DIGGS MOON

Charlotte ("Lottie") Diggs Moon's (1840–1912) almost four decades of ministry in China would challenge the mission world in a number of areas, leaving behind a legacy matched by few. Her upbringing no doubt contributed to this legacy. Born to wealthy Baptist aristocrats, Moon, along with four sisters and two brothers, grew up on a fifteen-hundred-acre plantation with the largest number of slaves (fifty-two) in the county. She was thirteen when a river accident claimed the life of her father. Her deeply religious mother took over the plantation, modeling independence and strong will, which did not go unnoticed by her children. Her older sister, Orianna, went on to become the first woman to earn a medical degree in the South. Lottie, although small in stature (4 feet 3 inches), was large in vision. She eventually became one of the first women in the South to receive a master of arts degree.

Unlike her mother, Moon had little time for religion. During college days a friend invited her to church. While the "precocious and irreverent child" went off to scoff, her friend returned to her room to pray all night. A later service led by Reverend Headden changed Moon forever when he talked about ripe harvest fields and the lack of laborers. Dissatisfied with her teaching career and sensing a call from God,

> *If I had a thousand lives, I would give them all for the women of China.*
>
> Lottie Moon
> (Christian History Institute 1996)

Moon headed for China to join her younger sister, Edmonia. She left for Tengzhou, China, in 1873, disregarding the concerns of some that a girl coming from wealth and power could reside in such poverty.

Moon began her ministry in China teaching young children. As in the United States, she soon tired of teaching "unstudious" children, desiring instead to evangelize and church plant among the Chinese people. Moon's sister had great difficulty adjusting and relating to the Chinese, which eventually resulted in her premature return to the United States. During the same period, Lottie almost married her fiancé, Dr. Toy, but his pro-evolution view made it impossible to tie the knot. These events left her totally dedicated to reaching the Chinese for Christ. But with whom and where?

Moon soon found herself embroiled in a deeply embedded gender issue related to missions. She wanted to be involved in ministry beyond a few women and children. Clashing with male field leadership, Moon worked with those men who requested her assistance. Although one senior female missionary colleague referred to her as "lawless[ly] prancing all over the mission lot" (Hyatt 1976, 104), Moon believed that women missionaries who came to China wanted "free opportunity to do the largest possible work" (Hyatt 1976, 104). They desired and demanded "perfect equality" (Hyatt 1976, 105) with the male missionaries in policy making and ministry opportunities. Moon saw herself not as an ardent feminist but rather as a pragmatist trying to come to grips with God-given talents and spiritual gifts entrusted to women, with ample global opportunity to use them. Her broad vision was to raise up a group of mature Christian women to place in mission stations that would link the north and south of China.

13

Moon eventually learned the Chinese language and came to understand the culture, thus endearing herself to the people. While living in rural P'ingtu, she wore the traditional dress. Moon believed that "we need to make friends before we can make converts" (Hyatt 1976, 109). This approach seemed revolutionary to most missionaries in that era. It was also revolutionary that an unordained, single, female missionary, by herself, would be instrumental in the development of more than thirty indigenous churches led by Chinese in the area.

Moon used the power of the pen to challenge mission tradition, recruit new workers, and solicit funds. Through her prolific writings she advocated adapting to the lifestyle of the people, taking two years to learn culture and language before beginning major ministry. She helped broaden the ministry role of single female missionaries and women in general. She was among the first to suggest that furloughs (now called home assignments) taken every ten years would help keep workers from burning out and took her own furloughs in 1892 and 1902. She wrote an article for the *Foreign Mission Journal* proposing that a Christmas offering be collected for missions. The collection was instituted the following Christmas and yielded over $3,000, sufficient to send three new missionaries. In 1918, it was renamed the "Lottie Moon Christmas Offering for Foreign Missions." The annual offerings have since raised over $1.5 billion for missions, financing approximately 50 percent of the entire annual Southern Baptist missions budget.

A severe famine followed the Boxer Rebellion and the Nationalist overthrow of the Qing Dynasty (1911), resulting in thousands of Chinese starving to death. Working by herself from morning to evening in remote P'ingtu, a lonely and desperate Moon wrote home requesting funds from an already indebted agency, but to no avail. She voluntarily cut her own food intake, sharing it with needy Chinese, and gave of her monthly salary and later of her inheritance. Eventually, she paid the price physically and mentally.

Alarmed missionary friends sent someone to accompany their depressed, malnourished colleague back to the United States. While docked in Kobe Harbor, Japan, a mere fifty-pound Lottie Moon, following Chinese culture, raised her fists together to meet her Savior on Christmas Eve. Following Japanese law, her seventy-two-year-old body was cremated before being returned to waiting family members in Virginia. Although her death certificate states the official reason for death as dementia, the epitaph on the marble marker placed at her grave by a Virginia woman captures her life ministry: "Faithful unto Death" (Howard n.d.). The *Foreign Missions Journal*, reflecting on Moon's ministry that impacted not only the Chinese but also the role of single women in missions, honored her by calling Lottie Moon "the best man among our missionaries" (Allen 1980, 280).

RALPH D. WINTER

Ralph D. Winter (1924–), a preeminent twentieth-century missiological thinker, historian, theologian (BD from Princeton), statistician, engineer (BS from Cal Tech), visionary entrepreneur, prolific writer, and beloved husband and father, culminated his formal studies with a PhD from Cornell. Leaving behind a promising future in engineering (his father oversaw the development of the Los Angeles freeway system), Ralph and first wife and full ministry partner, Roberta, left for Guatemala, where they spent ten years (1956–66) as Presbyterian missionaries among the Mam Indians.

During that decade, Ralph Winter, along with Raymond Buker, Jim Emery, Ross Kinsler, Ted Ward, and others, played a major role in the development of the Theological Education by Extension (TEE) movement. His edited volume *Theological Education by Extension* (1969) documents the early philosophy and practice of the movement. The goal of TEE was to take schooling to the settings where the greatest numbers of potential, tested leaders resided. This was thought to be much better than drawing to a city-based seminary a few untested, free from responsibility, youth who after graduation were more likely to stay in the city than return to their home areas. This decentralized schooling idea spread from Latin America to Africa and Asia. Seldom accepted by the formal academic academy, particularly in the United States and the Philippines, the movement eventually evolved into a number of different approaches, one being distance education. Although it never became the massive movement initially envisioned, cries for its reestablishment— not as a competitor with but as a complement to formal education—can be heard today.

In 1966, Winter received an invitation from Donald McGavran to join the faculty of the Fuller School of World Mission in Pasadena. There he spent a decade in a centralized educational environment influencing hundreds of new and veteran missionaries. Winter's impact on mission history and leadership development made a significant contribution to the school. But within ten years God began stirring Winter's heart yet again.

Leaving behind a secure salary at a prestigious seminary, the Winters began the U.S. Center for World Mission (USCWM) in 1976. Envisioned as a "Pentagon for missions," the USCWM drew numerous mission agencies together in one place to provide a "think tank" for reaching the remaining "hidden" (unreached) people groups. Many spin-offs would follow, including William Carey International University (an international undergraduate and graduate extension program), William Carey Library (which publishes and disseminates key missions texts at reduced costs;

15

www.WCLBooks.com), the International Society of Frontier Missiology with its journal, the *International Journal of Frontier Missions*, and Adopt-A-People. Although Winter is not without his critics, his fertile mind and ministry have nevertheless positioned him as one of the premier missionary statesmen of the twentieth century.

JOANNE SHETLER

Joanne Shetler (1936–) grew up a shy farm girl in Paso Robles, California. With little exposure to the outside world, she dreamed of what she already knew: a large, beautiful farmhouse with a white fence, a nursing career like her mother's, closeness to family members, and cows roaming the hillsides. She met Christ at the tender age of eleven when a Bible club teacher told her the good news of Jesus Christ, the best news she had ever heard. This new relationship would result in new dreams.

> *I argued with God. What about my dream farmhouse, the rolling hills, the nursing? What have I gotten myself into? I fought. I told him over and over, "You must have the wrong person—I can't do this. I don't even know what a missionary is." But God seemed as unimpressed as my father had been when I told him I couldn't drive the pickup. God wouldn't accept my inadequacies as an excuse.*
> Joanne Shetler
> (Shetler with Purvis 1992, 22)

During a Sunday morning service, Shetler heard a missionary state that 90 percent of the mission force concentrated on only 10 percent of the world's population (Shetler with Purvis 1992, 21). With so few workers concentrating on the remaining 90 percent, Shetler decided to be a missionary even though she had no clue what one was. Further challenged by a summer camp missionary speaker, she began to pray that God would send her to people who would believe the gospel. Then she was off to Biola University to study Christian education. There Shetler learned more than just Christian education. Through the help of a friend she also began to overcome her shyness.

After hearing about a course on language learning at the University of Oklahoma, Shetler enrolled, knowing that she would have to learn a foreign language to be a missionary. This led to her connection with the Summer Institute of Linguistics and Wycliffe Bible Translators. Her first experience in a village setting in Mexico was a total disaster. Questions flooded her mind: *"Why can't I trust God? Why am I so afraid? . . . What if I can't do this?"* (Shetler with Purvis 1992, 27). To Shetler's astonishment, however, Wycliffe did not give up on her and assigned her to work

16

with a couple in the mountains of Guatemala. Ken and Bobbie Williams taught her through word and deed that Bible translation and disciple making go together.

Shetler then received a request from her like-minded friend Anne Fetzer to work with her in a high-priority field for Wycliffe, the Philippines. Reluctantly, she agreed to go to that *"isolated sandbar. . . . That flat hot place"* (Shetler with Purvis 1992, 29). She soon discovered, however, that their assignment would be in a remote mountainous area of central Luzon among the Balangaos. It was there that she would find the answers to her daily prayers since high school. For example, Ama came to Christ, Tekla longed to know about God, and many other Balangaos proved ready to follow the Creator rather than the created.

When the two missionaries arrived among the Balangaos, Ama marched into their home declaring that he would be their father because they needed protection. While reluctant at first to accept Ama's offer, Shetler and Fetzer soon realized that this man's wisdom and insight would help them avoid or gracefully recover from all too many cultural faux pas. After initially rejecting Christianity, Ama eventually became a strong believer and a helper in moving the Balangaos to Christ and beyond. When the aged Ama "stepped into heaven," the earth shook, awaking all the Balangaos in the area.

Shetler and Fetzer learned that the Balangaos believed the spirits had power to make people sick, even kill them, and that these spirits pursued the Balangaos relentlessly. The newcomers also learned to pray to confront the spirits. One Balangao who received a lot of prayer was Tekla. Tekla, who was thought to be the "daughter of a spirit" (Shetler with Purvis 1992, 51), refused to sacrifice to the spirits, even when her children were sick. Instead, she threw sand in the eyes of the "black monstrous dogs or wild beasts" (52), but they kept coming back. After countless hours with Shetler and Fetzer, Tekla became a follower of Jesus. But she paid a high price for her decision. Others gossiped about her relationship with the outsiders and all the gifts and money she must have received from them. Shetler and Fetzer decided to distance themselves from Tekla to relieve the pressure. Ama was soon on their doorstep to tell them that this was an unwise move. Nor would Tekla pull away. Family trumped all criticisms and circumstances among the Balangaos.

Missionary life was much more than Bible translation. In fact, it was difficult for Shetler to find time for translation. After Fetzer left to marry her fiancé, she was without a partner. Medical work was constant, and Shetler became a midwife, saving the lives of countless mothers and babies. When a Filipino doctor suggested that they build a hospital, Shetler was ecstatic. The medical needs of the Balangaos would be met, freeing her for translation. But it was not to be. The helicopter loaded with cement and construction materials crashed on landing, killing the doctor and seriously injuring Shetler.

After much discussion and delay, the Balangao believers decided to host a Bible conference for neighboring tribes, with the purpose of multiplying the impact of Bible teaching through multiple Christian teachers. This conference would be a first, requiring hours of planning and work.

The Balangaos gathered food and firewood. Abundant meat, fish, vegetables, and rice for their guests would be necessary so that the hosts would not be shamed. Even so, head-hunting stories abounded. How would those coming from different areas without established peace pacts respond? Ama captured the outcome well when he addressed the excited but leery attendees: "You say you're looking for a miracle? . . . You'd like to see God's power? Well, look at it. Those Antipolo men walked all the way here through enemy territory, safe and unafraid. That's a miracle. Here are people from Sagada, Batad, Hamal, Amganad . . . all of us together. When in history did this ever happen before? We've never met before except to roll heads. Brothers and sisters, you are witnesses—this is God" (Shetler with Purvis 1992, 128).

> *I simply had to resign as the manager of God's glory.*
> Joanne Shetler
> (Shetler with Purvis 1992, 103)

The conference nonetheless got off to a rocky start. The guest speaker—whose address had to be translated into multiple languages—was a dismal failure. Nevertheless, discussions, singing, and praying continued into the wee hours of the morning in the various houses. The Antipolo Ifugaos, like other groups, returned home to tell anyone who would listen that they were not the only followers of Christ in Luzon. The impact of Bible teaching was felt by everyone who had attended the conference. Because of this success, annual intertribal Bible conferences were instituted among the Balangaos, a model followed by other tribal groups throughout the Philippines.

In 1982, after twenty years of intensive, tedious preparation, the Balangao Bible was dedicated. During the two-day dedication celebration, Shetler recalled the questions that she had struggled with long ago: "How can I be a missionary? How will I know when I'm done? What could I do that would last forever? What if all anyone ever knew about God was what I taught them?" (Shetler with Purvis 1992, 156). The shy farm girl from California is now a sought-after conference speaker and missionary trainer. God has transformed not only a people group but also the messenger who, with others, faithfully helped bring the Balangaos the gospel.

LUIS BUSH

Born in Argentina and raised in Brazil by loving Protestant parents, the affable, enthusiastic, vision-casting Luis Bush (1946–) became a gang leader on the streets of São Paulo. His brother, John Bush, along with Howard Hendricks, Warren Wiersbe, and others, would challenge him to rethink the direction of his spiritual life. Bush now uses his organizational abilities to lead God's gang in a host of endeavors to expand the kingdom.

Leaving behind a systems analyst position with Arthur Andersen, Bush entered the ministry, where he assumed several influential roles: senior pastor of Iglesia Nazaret in San Salvador, mission mobilizer with COMIBAM, international president of Partners International (1986–92), international president of AD 2000 and Beyond (1992–2002), and presently international director of World Inquiry. In his current position, Bush represents an ongoing trend in global missions: the internationalization of mission leadership.

One of Bush's major leadership roles was international president of AD 2000 and Beyond. The genesis of this organization occurred not in a vacuum but against a backdrop of monumental change. The Soviet Union was crumbling; Communism was in shambles; the end of the second millennium was approaching; and a new openness to spirituality in secular settings was emerging. With the International Congress on World Evangelization (1974, Lausanne) providing the impetus for reaching people groups rather than countries, and the International Congress on World Evangelization (1989; Lausanne II in Manila) acting as a springboard for its organizational structure, the AD 2000 and Beyond movement was born in 1989. It would end in 2001 as required by its corporate by-laws. The purpose of the movement was to "motivate and network men and women church leaders by inspiring them with the vision of reaching the unreached by the year 2000 through consultation, prayer efforts, and communication material" (Bush 2003, 32).

From AD 2000 a number of related efforts were spawned, such as Global Consultation on World Evangelization '95 (Korea) and '97 (South Africa), where reconciliation took place between Eastern and Western leaders (a prerequisite to a church-planting movement); books, such as *Praying through the 100 Gateway Cities of the 10/40 Window*, that helped facilitate a prayer movement of over forty million people; and the Joshua Project 2000 and Project II. According to the Joshua Project II, 10,900 unreached people groups (UPG) remain to be reached for Christ. They define "people group" from an ethnocultural perspective as "the largest group within which the Gospel can spread as a church planting movement without encountering barriers of understanding or acceptance."

19

They define an "unreached people group" as "a people group among which there is no indigenous community of believing Christians with adequate numbers and resources to evangelize this people group." Any people group with less than 2 percent evangelical Christians or less than 5 percent Christian adherents (e.g., Protestant, Roman Catholic, Orthodox) is considered unreached. Such definitions have influenced some churches to support only those Christian workers who minister within the 10/40 window. They have also provided strategic input for churches and agencies regarding where to place practitioners who can address spiritual and social needs.

Often credited with originating the term "10/40 window," Bush attributes the concept to his wife, Doris. As a group was gathered in a living room discussing possible ways to conceptualize the unreached areas of the world, the idea of a box emerged. Looking out the window and seeing a beautiful tree, Doris countered with the notion of a window through which they could see the unreached parts of the world. Doris won the day, and window replaced box as a means to visualize where the majority of the unreached people groups reside. The window covers North Africa, the Middle East, and Asia; 10/40 refers to an area from ten degrees north of the equator to forty degrees north of the equator. Within the window live two-thirds of the world's people, with the majority of the sixty-one nations represented remaining unevangelized. This part of the world has the most poverty, over 50 percent of the world's youth, and is the birthplace of all the great religions of the world—including Christianity. It has the greatest persecution of Christianity and the majority of unreached peoples, many of whom live under governments that oppose Christianity. Unfortunately, only about 20 percent of the mission force focuses on this target. While the 10/40 term has been helpful in identifying unreached peoples and creating urgency, Bush recognizes that an overemphasis on any geographical area can hinder God's global plan. While Bush's leadership tenure with the AD 2000 and Beyond movement has ended, the influence of the organization will be felt for years to come.

OMAR GAVA

Between 1914 and 1918, when the world was waging World War I, many Christians suffered because of their beliefs. One of them was a young Yugoslavian man, Esteban Gava (we are indebted to Kimberly Gava for this story). Esteban was a deeply committed Christian who believed that no person had the right to take another person's life. Therefore, when he was sent to the front lines to fight in Serbia, he refused to take up arms. Because of this act of defiance, which he considered an act of faith, the government sentenced him to six years of imprisonment. During this time his young wife, Zivana, was awaiting their first child, which made the situation even more painful. During those difficult years the Lord tried the family's faith in a number of ways. Even so, there were bright spots. One of the most exhilarating experiences Esteban had was on the day he received a Bible along with permission to hold Bible studies in prison. God's hand was undoubtedly upon him.

After Esteban had been imprisoned for five and a half years, the queen celebrated the birth of her baby by offering amnesty to all prisoners, providing the Gava family the opportunity to leave the country. With Abraham-like faith, they took the first ship they could board, not knowing where it was bound. Esteban and his family would later learn that it was headed for Argentina, a country they knew nothing about. Little did they realize God's future plans for them and their extended family.

Years passed, and out of this young couple's love eleven more children were born in the buoyant province of Buenos Aires. Number eleven, born in 1946, was Omar Gava, a recognized mission leader in Latin America today. Presently he is involved in missionary training and leadership roles serving the Lord through Recursos Estratégicos Globales (REG; www.reg.org.ar), the International Missionary Training Network (IMTN; www.missionarytraining.com/contact.htm), and Cooperación Misionera Iberoamericana (COMIBAM; www.comibam.org). His faithful ministry career dates back to 1966, when Omar accepted Jesus Christ as his Savior and surrendered all his life, plans, and dreams to him. He immediately started witnessing door-to-door with the Bible as his powerful and only companion.

At that time evangelical Christians represented only 0.5 percent of the total population in Argentina. Most Argentineans regarded them as heretics and greatly despised them for their faith. In this context the Lord prepared Gava to know what it meant to suffer for his name, experience hardship, yet maintain his faith in God. Gava was able to do this, inspired by the example set by the first Christians in Acts, his father, and the torture and murder of his brother Daniel by the ruling military regime in 1955.

When Omar was twenty the Lord moved him and his brother Juan inland to the province of Entre Ríos, where a major missionary movement developed. In 1971, he married Stella, a young Argentinean whose father was a Yugoslavian immigrant. She joined him in his work to spread the gospel to unreached people groups throughout Argentina and neighboring countries. He then founded and directed PENIEL, a unique Bible School in Argentina where hundreds of Christians from around the world received missionary training, taking God's Word from Patagonia to the Brazilian forests, from Paraguay to Germany, and from Bolivia to Canada.

21

Gava has always believed in teamwork as a biblical principle in ministry. Over the years he has built strong bonds and working relationships with other committed Christians from different nations, adding breadth and depth to the training in REG, IMTN, and COMIBAM. He continues to devote his life to communicating the gospel to the entire world by training Latinos for missions.

Omar and Stella have four daughters who have participated in the family's ministries in various ways, always supporting these ministries and their parents. Another generation now living in the province of Córdoba follows in the footsteps of faith modeled by grandparents and parents alike.

NATASHA

Natasha (a pseudonym; we are indebted to Mike Matthews for this story) was born into a Christian family in the breadbasket of the USSR, the Ukraine, in the 1950s. She grew up in the days when the persecution of believers was as common as borscht (Russian soup made of beets and cabbage) in the former Soviet Union. From an early age Natasha wanted to serve God as a missionary. For her, this meant attempting to be light and salt in the harsh gray world of Communism.

After high school, Natasha enrolled in medical college, believing that this would place her in a position to help people with scars and sicknesses, leading eventually to spiritual healing. Never an "underground believer," Natasha did not conceal her viewpoints about God from her classmates and instructors. This resulted in daily ridicule and abuse from students and teachers alike. And once a week, Natasha endured the "psychology ethic," which consisted of two hours of relentless grilling by a KGB agent—all calculated to convince Natasha that she had been brainwashed by her parents into believing "this God stuff."

Besides the daily harassment, Natasha was informed near the end of her studies that she would not be given a diploma unless she "changed her mind about certain things." The ridicule and coercion were not easy to endure, but the idea of working for several years and then not receiving a diploma was particularly oppressive. It would not be easy for Natasha to get a job under any circumstances. Without the diploma it would be practically impossible.

As graduation day neared, the president of the school paid a visit to Natasha's home. He saw the potential in this especially bright student and felt compelled to "talk some sense" into the heads of her parents. In typical Soviet fashion, he began attacking Natasha's belief in the supernatural. He was just getting warmed up when Natasha's mother interrupted him: "Why are you doing this? Do you think you are fighting against this girl? You are fighting against God!"

It was crystal clear to the president he was confronting something much larger than he had anticipated, and for some unexplained reason he changed his mind. When graduation day came, he secretly gave Natasha her diploma.

After medical school, Natasha was sent to Volgograd, where she served as a health worker for a remote railroad construction crew of more than one hundred people. These men worked hard and drank harder. When they drank, they fought. When they fought, they got hurt. And that is where Natasha came in, bandaging and caring for men who cut and beat one another.

Even though Natasha dressed the men's wounds, she was no more popular with them than with the students and teachers at the medical college. The men wanted her to drink with them. When Natasha repeatedly refused, they became infuriated. So they devised a plan to get even. On Saturday nights Natasha would ride the train into a nearby city to attend a small church on Sunday, returning to the construction site Sunday evening. On one particular Sunday evening, she was especially tired. As usual she slept during the ride, and as usual she had prayed God would awaken her before her stop as he had always done. But when she awoke, she was well past the construction site. She disembarked at the next stop and spent the rest of that cold, dark night in an empty train station until a train going in the opposite direction arrived. Not until she reached her living quarters did she learn that a band of angry men had been waiting the previous evening at the train station to kill her.

After leaving this job, Natasha heard about the need for missionaries in out-of-the-way places of Siberia. Communism had fallen by this time. Travel was still difficult, but there was a new openness in the country to share Christ. Natasha wanted to do just that in places where there were no or few believers and churches. She heard about the needs of such people groups as the Yakutian, the Evenki, and the Chukchi. With her church's and her family's blessing, she headed east to the capital city of the Republic of Yakutia. Here Natasha teamed up with other national missionaries from various parts of the former Soviet Union and a few local believers to do evangelism and discipleship in this large republic (more than double the size of Alaska). Natasha was a gifted singer and had taught herself to play the piano when she was younger. With these gifts, solid Bible teaching from her church and parents, her medical experiences, and a strong faith in God, she was a valuable asset to the evangelistic teams that traveled throughout the republic.

One of these trips exemplifies Natasha's persistent missionary spirit and faith in God. In 2000, a Ukrainian-based Christian organization sponsored a three-month, six-thousand-mile evangelistic trek across the tundra of Siberia in the dead of winter. The organization outfitted a large six-wheel-drive truck that functioned as home and vehicle for the volunteers. This trip was undertaken during the coldest time of the year because there was no road, and the terrain is traversable only when the ground is frozen. It was a monumental trip never before attempted. A truckful of believers made their way through the frozen tundra of Siberia visiting villages all along the way. In these villages they held evangelistic meetings, proclaiming the story of God's plan for the world and passing out Bibles and Christian literature.

It came as no surprise to anyone who knew Natasha that she volunteered to go on this evangelistic expedition, which would test the survival skills of any person. There was very little sunlight. There were no bathrooms. The participants cooked their meals on the way and slept in the back of the enclosed truck as temperatures hovered day and night at minus sixty degrees Celsius.

At one point in the middle of a vast wasteland of blowing snow, the truck broke down. It appeared the terrain had won. Two of the men decided to walk for help, a dangerous venture in those temperatures and conditions. But they had few choices. Dressing as warmly as they could, they headed off in search of help. Natasha stayed with several others to keep the oil fire burning for heat in their "home" on the bed of the truck. It made a surreal sight, a lone truck sitting in the middle of a huge white canvas of snow with a whisk of smoke curling out of the small black chimney protruding from the back of a black speck surrounded by white. Inside the small mobile hut, the occupants slept, sang, drank tea, and prayed, waiting to be rescued. The men eventually found help, but not without a price. Both suffered severe frostbite on their feet. Once again, Natasha cared for the injured.

But frostbitten feet and a stalled truck did not stop the expedition. The trip continued. Dozens of reindeer herders received the gospel. Hundreds of isolated villagers gathered in halls to hear what these traveling strangers had to say. Some were happy to hear the words and songs of these traveling evangelists and accepted the message of Jesus Christ. Others were skeptical, and some were hostile. The trip ended a success in the eyes of both the sponsors and the traveling volunteers. Many people in that vast, dark, frozen land heard a message they had never before known and some accepted Christ. Plans were made for a follow-up trip.

Now, over 500 believers are scattered among the 500,000 Yakutian people. The need and the challenges continue. Even though the years and the hardships have taken their toll on her body, Natasha presses on with the same tenacity, determination, and faith in God that saw her through medical college, the construction camp, and the trans-Siberian evangelistic trip.

MARTIN AND GRACIA BURNHAM

Martin (1960–2002) and Gracia Burnham (1959–), missionaries with New Tribes Mission (NTM) in the Philippines, were celebrating their eighteenth wedding anniversary on an island off the coast of Palawan, Philippines, at the Dos Palmas Resort. Life would change forever in the early dawn of May 27, 2001. The couple found themselves forced at gunpoint into a boat piloted by the ruthless Abbu Sayyaf ("father of the swordmans"), leader of a Muslim terrorist group. As the shivering, confused couple waited on the catwalk for the speedboat, Gracia whispered to Martin, "We are in big trouble" (Burnham with Merrill 2003, 7). For the next 375 difficult and depressing days, the Christian world prayed for their safety and release. But their collective prayers would not be completely answered. Martin would be killed, hit three times by gunfire, in a botched rescue attempt by the Philippine Rangers on June 7, 2002, on Basilan Island. Gracia sustained a bullet wound to the leg and returned to the United States in a wheelchair without her husband.

Gracia was born the fifth of six children to Norvin and Betty Jo Jones. Norvin was first a pastor and later a professor at Calvary Bible College in Kansas City, and he and Betty Jo provided a home that modeled Christ. When Gracia was seven or eight years old, a favorite Sunday school teacher led her to Christ. As she read about Amy Carmichael and the Scottish missionary Mary Slessor, the Holy Spirit began to plant seeds in her young heart. Impressed with the music program at Calvary Bible College, Gracia attended the college after graduating from high school. After earning her degree, Gracia took an administrative job at the college. It was here she met the missionary kid (MK) from the Philippines who would capture her heart.

Born in Rose Hill, Kansas, Martin grew up as an MK in the Philippines. His parents, Paul and Oreta Burnham, were NTM missionaries in the Philippines working at that time among the Ibaloi tribal people on the main island of Luzon. Flying in and out of the tribal area in the mission aircraft, Martin soon knew what he wanted to do with his life after high school—fly.

After graduating from Faith Academy (a school for MKs in Manila), Martin returned home to America to "buy a car, become a pilot, and make lots of money" (Burnham with Merrill 2003, 33). His father, however, had other ideas—one year of Bible school. Martin reluctantly gave in. He would eventually meet Gracia at Calvary Bible College, and they married soon afterward. Martin continued his career in aviation, advancing rapidly to the top. He then turned down a lucrative job because he believed God was leading them to the Philippines to replace a pilot he knew well, Rod Parks, who had been killed when his plane crashed on a remote landing strip in Luzon.

In 1985 the young couple went to the Philippines, where Martin served as a pilot and Gracia handled the daily activities to keep the aviation program going. This "take-charge, get-it-done missionary wife and mom" (Burnham with Merrill 2005, 4) also homeschooled her three children, Jeff, Mindy, and Zach—all born in the Philippines. As a pilot, Martin became the lifeline to many missionaries, bringing them not only mail and supplies but also human contact with the outside world. One of these assignments took the Burnhams to Palawan to supply the missionaries residing there. After a heavy schedule the couple looked forward to a relaxing overnight stay at the beautiful tropical island resort of Dos Palmas: "And then—in a moment of time—everything changed. I [Gracia] became a hostage who had lost all control of my life, my schedule, and my future. I could only sit on the ground and stare at the jungle, wondering what would come next. Did the unfinished items on that list back in the kitchen ever get done? I had no way to find out. In fact, to this day I still don't know. My world had forever shifted" (Burnham with Merrill 2005, 5).

> *I wasn't called to be a missionary. I wasn't called to the Philippines. I was just called to follow Christ and that's what I'm doing.*
>
> Martin Burnham
> (Gracia Burnham
> with Merrill 2003, 142)

Six hours after checking in at the resort they became hostages; their ordeal had begun. There would be no electricity, no hot baths, and no Bible for over a year. During their captivity the couple would experience malnutrition leading to open sores, physical exhaustion, malaria, diarrhea, emotional trauma, heat, cold, and seventeen running gun battles. A $330,000 ransom raised by the Burnhams' families was deemed insufficient by their captors around Easter. And then the last firefight began. The lives of Deborah Yap, a Filipina nurse, and Martin were snuffed out.

Finally far from her captors and safe with her family, Gracia faced a host of new questions. Where should she settle with her children? What about finances? Should she take all the speaking opportunities offered her? Would her leg ever heal? Would emotional healing ever take place? How did God want to use Martin's martyrdom to further his glory?

Gracia has since started the Martin & Gracia Burnham Foundation, which "seeks to extend the Good News of Jesus Christ through its support of missions around the world" (www.graciaburnham.org). In the Philippines, the Martin Burnham Mission Center, a five-story building, was constructed to facilitate missionary training. Martin's legacy so far has been instrumental in over seventy Filipinos joining New Tribes Mission in the Philippines to reach tribal people.

LESSONS IN THE LEARNING

It is a very different world since Paul and his teammates set out to reach Spain with the gospel. After two millennia of remarkably successful ministry, Christianity has gone global, including its missionary force. Philip Jenkins argues in *The Next Christendom* (2002) that Christianity is not only growing numerically—claiming approximately 33 percent of the world—but also shifting in a number of areas. Demographically, its center of balance has shifted from the West to the rest, from above the equator to below it. He calls it the "global south."

Theologically, Christians from the global south are more charismatic and open to all the gifts of the Spirit. Jenkins observes that by 2000, Pentecostals were increasing by some nineteen million each year (2002, 63). He projects that they should surpass the one billion mark before 2050. Economically, the global south is comprised predominantly of the poor and marginalized. These followers of Christ have less formal education than their Western counterparts. Nonbelievers perceive their teachings as dangerous and divisive, making them an inviting target for persecution. Relationally, Christians in the global south emphasize community rather than individuality. Behaviorally, they are more conservative. Institutionally, they rely less on building complexes.

In terms of expansion, Christianity no longer advances from the West to the rest. Rather, it is multidirectional, from all nations to all nations. Every nation is a receiver and a sender of missions-minded Christians. For example, while the United States sent out 118,200 missionaries in 2000, it received over 33,000—making it the largest receiving nation in the world (Barrett, Kurian, and Johnson 2001). Even so, the number of missionaries from the majority world continues to skyrocket. The Koreans serve as a prime example. Second only to the United States as a sending nation, South Korea has commissioned some 13,000 long-term cross-cultural missionaries (Moll 2006).

SUMMARY AND IMPLICATIONS FOR TWENTY-FIRST-CENTURY MISSIONARIES

Thomas Carlyle (1795–1881) argued that the history of the world is composed of the biographies of a few powerful and famous men. Just as the Internet and globalization has challenged his theory, so does the history of global missions. The history of missions is composed of, yes, a few famous and powerful men—but they are not the majority. The latter are best described as the weak, the obscure, the poor—and this includes women as well as men. And all of them are works in progress as they expand God's kingdom globally. That is the beauty of being co-laborers with the Creator—important and purposeful work is open to everyone who is willing.

What then are some implications for today's missionaries? Here are a few insights that can be gleaned from the heroes and heroines described in this chapter:

- Strong spirituality is required (Taylor, Martin and Gracia Burnham).
- God calls his choice co-laborers out of both secure (Zinzendorf) and insecure (Moravians) settings.
- We are to go no matter what the cost (Moon, Macomber, the Burnhams, seventy-nine CIM missionaries and their children).
- We should expect culture shock, stress, and loneliness (the Taylors, Macomber, Shetler).
- Persecution is inevitable—and can come at any time (Macomber, the Burnhams).
- Missionaries should stay on the field no matter how long it takes (Shetler, Natasha).
- Every missionary comes with strengths and weaknesses (all).
- Team conflict, as well as conflict within a mission agency or sending church(es), is a reality (Taylor and CIM, Moon).
- Teamwork is possible (the Serampore Trio, Shetler and Fetzer).
- Missionary snobbery exists between mission agencies and educational institutions (experienced by Taylor and CIM missionaries).
- Lifelong learning (nonformal, formal, combination of both) is necessary (Hudson, Maria Taylor).
- God uses the nonformally educated (Taylor) as well as the formally educated (Bush, Winter, Gava).
- Missionaries can serve in both strategic (Winter, Bush) and practitioners' roles (Macomber, Natasha).
- Ministry roles and models can and should vary considerably—from business (Zinzendorf) to teaching (Macomber) to Bible translating (Shetler) to evangelizing (Natasha) to training (Gava) and TEE (Winter), mobilizing (Bush), and aviation (Martin Burnham).
- The role of women in missions has a valiant past (Macomber to Burma [1830], Moon to China [1877]) and present (Shetler to the Philippines [1962], Natasha to Siberia [1990s]).

- Reaching people groups is a better strategy than splitting the task into geographical or economic domains (Winter, Bush).
- God's reign is expanded through the church that is elected for service (Indians, Burmese, Balangaos).
- Ministry should be holistic in nature, demonstrating that Christianity is not just a religion but a total way of life (Luke, Carey, Natasha).
- God rewards faith and faithfulness (Taylor, Gracia, Martin, Gava, Natasha).
- Missions is not just the West to the rest but multidirectional (Gava, Bush).
- People become followers of Christ and churches are born, mature, and multiply in spite of the shortcomings of missionaries and agencies (Carey's family suffered, Macomber was left on her own).

Understanding Key Ideas
and Terms

If you wish to converse with me, define your terms.

Voltaire (D. Anderson n.d.)

Every aspect of life is afloat with terms that provide precise meaning, making miniscule differentiations possible. Every occupation, from plumbing to psychology, from computer technology to teaching, from machine work to meteorology, has them. The same is true of every academic discipline. If you attend a seminar or class in an unfamiliar field of study you may soon begin to feel you are listening to a foreign language. What is true of occupations and academic disciplines is also evident in the field of missions.

Over time, academicians and practitioners in the field of missions have coined, borrowed, or adapted terms to help others better understand the multiple nuances of God's mission. They do this to identify key concepts of missions even though the term itself, for example, "missions," may not be found in the Bible, God's "sacred storybook."

In this chapter we identify some of our assumptions, provide definitions of key terms for the study of missions, and note helpful resources for examining these terms in greater detail. We also provide a quick reference list of terms used throughout the rest of the book as an orientation to the discussion that follows. We begin with some of our foundational assumptions.

ASSUMPTIONS AND DEFINITIONS

Behind this book lie the foundational assumptions and definitions of the authors. Before defining key terms related to missionary life and work, we highlight several of our prominent assumptions, defining them and noting their implications for other definitions that follow. We begin with the Bible and then consider terms related to God's mission.

The Bible

The Bible serves as the cross-cultural Christian worker's source of comfort, character, guidance, and sometimes strategies. It is far more than a self-help book, claiming to meet the emotional needs of people. It is far more than a theological textbook, designed to impress the mind and categorize doctrines. Rather, it is God's sacred storybook designed to integrate the mind, the imagination, and feeling. It is the "discourse about God in the setting of story" (Van Engen 1996, 49).

The Bible is the story of God's persistent and passionate pursuit to glorify himself through the institution of his rightful rule. He accomplishes this through grace and justice by restoring repentant people, defeating antagonistic spiritual powers, leading to the inevitable restoration of the material world. This results in Spirit-comforted communities of loyal, enthusiastic, willing worshipers/co-laborers who enjoy refreshing rest in a world that impatiently awaits final restoration. The thousand plus stories that highlight good and evil through over 2,900 characters center on one central character, Jesus Christ. The sacred storybook reveals the missional nature of the Triune God and God's goal for the world—global worship of the King of kings.

The Mission

MISSION

This section reviews the definitions found in *Introducing World Missions* (Moreau, Corwin, and McGee, 2004) and adds to the discussion. "Mission" refers to all that God wishes to accomplish in the world so that he is glorified and God's kingdom expands universally and comprehensively. Mission serves as God's overarching vision-value statement, which should influence all activities and resources (human and material),

31

SIDEBAR 2.1
A DEFEATED FOE

F. Douglas Pennoyer (used with permission)

SCORE:

LAMB OF GOD: 7

DEVOURING LION: 0

1. Thrown out of heaven (Luke 10, Rev. 12)
2. Rebuked at Jesus's temptation (Matt. 4)
3. Demons cast out by Jesus (Gospels)
4. Defeated at the cross and resurrection (Heb. 2:14)
5. Demons cast out by disciples (New Testament until now)
6. Bound for a thousand years (Rev. 20:1–3)
7. Cast into the lake of fire (Rev. 20:7–10)

REFLECTION AND DISCUSSION

1. What can you learn about the enemy of humanity from the battles noted above?
2. How can this "scorecard" serve to encourage twenty-first-century cross-cultural workers?

---

inside and outside the church, that take place in heaven and on earth. George Peters understands mission as "a comprehensive term including the upward, inward and outward ministries of the church. It is the church as 'sent' (a pilgrim, stranger, witness, prophet, servant, salt, light, etc.) in this world" (1972, 11). "'Mission' is . . . the dynamic relationship between God and the world: God sends himself, his Son, and his church" (Camps, Hoedemaker, and Spindler 1995, 4). Mission defines God's overall purpose and intent for people, the spiritual world, and the material world as unfolded and detailed from Genesis through Revelation.

Mission is based on God's rightful role to rule over all his creation. But this cannot happen without spiritual warfare in that a "credible conflict" must and does exist, led by a wily, capable antagonist, Satan. As ultimate Creator-King of all, God has the sole right to reign over all creation. The kingdom of God has and will defeat the kingdom of Satan (see sidebar 2.1). Cross-cultural Christian workers can take solace in the fact that they are on the winning side.

MISSIO DEI

Closely related to the term "mission" is the Latin term *missio Dei* (or *missio Trinitatis*). *Missio Dei* refers to the idea of God's nature and expression extended to and stamped upon the world. God the Father sends God the Son who sends God the Holy Spirit; all three send the church. Cross-cultural Christian workers partner with the Trinity in fulfilling *missio Dei*.

MISSIONS

Missions refers to everything involved in carrying out God's mission on a generational, gender, and global level (Acts 1:8). Missions activities, performed by a host of multigifted, spiritually qualified personnel in both mono- and cross-cultural contexts vary widely. They include, but are not limited to, such things as evangelism, starting new churches and helping them mature, Bible translation, education, discipleship, leadership development, aviation, and mass-media broadcasting. Missions addresses the multiple needs of people, following the New Testament example of Jesus, the Twelve, and the Pauline teams. It neither minimizes people's spiritual needs, addressed through the broad framework of discipleship (evangelism, follow-up, church multiplication), or their physical needs, addressed through the spiritual gifts of help and healing, community development, and other means. This multidimensional, need-oriented approach to missions opens the door for a variety of people to participate in ministry.

Missions takes place primarily in three arenas. The first focuses on unreached peoples found today primarily in the 10/40 window (North Africa, Middle East, Asia). These peoples are adherents of major religions of the world, such as Islam, Buddhism, and Hinduism, which are difficult to reach through traditional missions approaches and activities. The second arena is that of previously reached peoples. It includes work in several countries in Europe, many of which now have less than 2 percent of the population claiming to be evangelical Christians. Interestingly, people reached by cross-cultural Christian workers from Europe are now being used by God to bring renewal to the countries of those who first reached them. The third arena focuses on encouraging and facilitating existing national Christian movements around the world.

MISSIONAL

Missional refers to something's association with God's mission. Christopher Wright defines it as "simply an adjective denoting something that is related to or characterized by mission, or has the qualities, attributes or dynamics of mission" (2006, 24). It focuses attention on the relationship of the topic to *missio Dei*, whether one is talking about one's job, finances, assets, plans, theology, preaching, the nature of any of the sixty-six books of the Bible, their authors, or the focus of their writings—Jesus Christ.

The Personnel Involved in Missions

MISSIONARIES

When Joanne Shetler volunteered to be a missionary in her youth, she had no clue what one was or did. Even today there is confusion over the term, with a host of stereotypes—most of them negative. What, then, is a missionary? A missionary can be a male or a female believer from any generation or geographical area who is called, gifted, impassioned, and sent with authority by the Holy Spirit and local churches to accomplish some aspect of missions. Missionaries do this in two distinct cross-cultural venues: (1) where the church already exists (existing missions whether successful or failed), and (2) where no church exists (frontier missions). Domestic (or home-assignment) missionaries work in their own country, usually in cross-cultural settings, while foreign missionaries do the same abroad.

Long-term missionaries enter missions for extended periods of time, typically several years or more. Short-termers go out for a few weeks to several years. In the case of long-termers, researchers have documented the reasons for attrition (causes for early departure from the field of service), identifying unpreventable causes (marriage, death of relative, medical, retirement) and preventable causes (personal failure, lack of mentorship, insufficient training, financial irresponsibility).

Some missionaries raise their own support (faith missions) or are supported by a denomination, while others—bivocationalists, market-place missionaries, kingdom professionals—support themselves fully or partially through a variety of jobs. Nonresidential missionaries live in an open country while operating in closed ones. All types are necessary to complete God's mission.

Although the term "missionary" is well recognized within the Western church, this is not necessarily so in other areas of the world. For example, for many parts of the world where Christianity has a long history (and residents have long memories) with Christian missions, a missionary is associated with imperialism, colonialism, proselytism, and legalism (Christians cannot drink and can have only one wife). This is particularly true for peoples who experienced the wrath of the Crusaders long ago, as well as followers of the major world religions today, particularly in the 10/40 window where you cannot enter with a missionary visa.

We must remember that the term "missionary" is not found in God's sacred storybook. In fact, as Phil Elkins is fond of pointing out, the phrase "Jehovah's Witness" has more biblical support than the term "missionary." This raises several pertinent questions. Since the term "missionary" has negative connotations for a large segment of the world that the Christian church is trying to reach, and is not found in God's sacred storybook, should another term or phrase replace it? If so, what are some valid possibilities? Due to negative baggage associated with the term, some prefer to use more contextualized or secular terms, such as teacher, worker, student, tentmaker, kingdom professional, cross-cultural worker, and so on. Consequently, we use a number of terms throughout

---

SIDEBAR 2.2
APOSTLES

Apostle: One called, gifted, and sent by God with authority into predominately unreached areas of the world to plant, develop, renew, oversee, and coordinate territorial movements of healthy, holistic, harvesting communities of faith

Authority: From God

Duration: Twelve (limited); others (unlimited, Rom. 16:7)

Goal: Oversee global multiplication of healthy church movements (Acts 16:5)

Geographic priority: Go where gospel not taught (Rom. 15:20; 2 Cor. 10:16)

Location: Itinerant

Team composition: Multinational, multigenerational, multigifted personnel

Ministry activities:

- Perform signs and wonders
- Assist with offerings for poor (Acts 4:35; 24:17)
- Give financially (Acts 11:30)
- Preach gospel (Eph. 6:19): OT-based, story-driven foundation (1 Cor. 3:10)
- Teach whole counsel of God (Acts 20:27)
- Congregate believers

- Foster and network movements (Acts 16:5)
- Appoint deacons and elders (Acts 6; Titus 1:5)
- Train elders (Acts 20)
- Administer church discipline (Acts 5; 1 Cor. 5)
- Set things in order (1 Cor. 11:34)
- Resolve conflict, human (Phil. 4:2) and doctrinal (Acts 15)
- Identify false prophets (2 Cor. 11:13)
- Revisit churches to strengthen (Acts 15:36)
- Have a continual concern for churches (2 Cor. 11:28)

REFLECTION AND DISCUSSION

1. In what ways is a "church planter" like an apostle, and in what ways is a "church planter" different from an apostle?
2. In what ways is a "missionary" like an apostle, and in what ways is a "missionary" different from an apostle?
3. Since the term "missionary" now carries significant negative baggage in many parts of the world, what would be good substitutes?

---

this text to capture the term "missionary," which is now tainted in many parts of the world. Whatever the term used, these individuals carry out God's mission through the execution of missions (see sidebar 2.2).

MISSIOLOGISTS AND MISSIOLOGY

Missiologists practice, reflect, and evaluate global missions with the purpose of discovering ways to improve the worker and the work. Whether a professional or a practitioner, formally educated and/or self-taught, these individuals seek to glorify the King of kings through improved spirituality, improved theories, improved models, improved strategies, improved partnerships, improved networks, improved research, improved Bible translation, improved curricula, improved culture and language acquisition, improved teaching, improved relief and community development, improved evangelism, improved discipleship, improved leadership, improved followership, improved church-planting movements, improved contextualization, improved literacy, improved businesses, improved justice, improved evacuations of field personnel, and so forth. *Stewardship of resources demands that all cross-cultural Christian workers become astute missiologists,* whether formally or nonformally trained, where they practice, or in the type of ministries in which they engage. To better understand the foundational role of missiologists in global missions, we must investigate the discipline associated with it, missiology.

Missiology, claims Charles Taber, is the "critical reflection on the task of mission" (2000, 10). It "is the conscious, intentional, ongoing reflection on the doing of mission" (Neely 2000, 633). It takes history seriously because it is "the study of individuals being brought to God in history" (Tippett 1987, xiii). As people come to Christ over the generations, missiology seeks to understand "the ways in which Christian faith becomes attached to different contexts" (Camps, Hoedemaker, and Spindler 1995, 2).

Missiology, therefore, is "multidisciplinary in character and holistic in approach" (Luzbetak 1988, 14), integrating four key categories: (1) history, (2) theology, (3) the social sciences, and (4) mission strategy. Mission history explores the expansion of Christianity from an Eastern and a Western perspective. It considers mission and church relationships as well as in-depth area studies of specific situations, documenting the lives of influential figures in the missions enterprise.

The social sciences provide a comprehensive toolkit to explore the missions movement. Social science disciplines that missiologists must consider include anthropology, sociology, psychology, economics, political science, communication, management, linguistics, language, world religions, demography, and education. Theology turns its attention to the kingdom of God, the gospel, mission, salvation of the lost, the church, the character of professors of faith, hermeneutics, homiletics, contextualization, and past and present theologies. Strategy is the organizational aspect of missions, including areas of study such as evangelism, church growth, church multiplication, literacy, health and medicine, radio, community development, international law, and kingdom professionals (tentmaking). Sidebar 2.3 considers the implications of focusing on strategies in missions from a managerial orientation, which is a deep concern for some.

SIDEBAR 2.3
MANAGERIAL MISSIOLOGY: GOOD OR BAD?

Samuel Escobar (2000, 109–12), echoed by James Engel and William Dyrness (2000, 69), uses managerial missiology in a pejorative way. For Escobar, the pragmatic, quantitative-focused Church Growth movement, AD 2000 and Beyond, and Spiritual Warfare movement have attempted to "reduce Christian mission to a manageable enterprise. . . . Missionary action is reduced to a linear task that is translated into logical steps to be followed in a process of management by objectives, in which the evangelistic task is reduced to a process that can be carried on following marketing principles" (2000, 109).

However, it can be viewed from a more positive perspective (see, for example, DeCarvalho 2001). Managerial missiology incorporates the integrative nature of missiology, mines the management discipline (among others), tests it through Scripture, and implements it contextually. It is management by the Spirit (MBS in contrast to the outdated management by objectives [MBO]) that is interested in the church as organism and organization, quantity and quality, discipleship and development, methods and the assumptions that drive them, maps that identify gaps, formal and informal leadership, statistics and stories, analysis and artistry, planning and prayer, process and posture, and strategy, stewardship, and the spiritual gift of administration.

REFLECTION AND DISCUSSION

1. What are the cultural norms and values (Latino and North American) that fuel this debate?

2. What are the implications—positive and negative—of approaching missions through a model based on management principles?

As a discipline, missiology's interest lies in mission, missions, missionaries, and Christian movements within the wider context of global history. The same is true of missiologists. Both serve as a constant conscience and challenge to the church, reminding it of God's unfinished agenda to establish his universal reign critically, contextually, and without compromise. Both will help stem the amateurization of missions, that is, the sending forth of uninformed cross-cultural workers, whether for short-term or long-term service. Both will challenge today's cross-cultural Christian workers at home and abroad to be not just active ministry practitioners but rather well-versed students, formally and/or nonformally, of mission history, theology, the social sciences (particularly anthropology), and strategy, able to apply the mined insights to their personal lives and a constantly changing world. It challenges today's cross-cultural workers to know the past and the present so that they can become the best workers possible in character and talent in God's global field.

37

SIDEBAR 2.4
SOME HELPFUL RESOURCES

The number and quality of resources available to cross-cultural Christian workers today is unprecedented. Wise missions workers will take advantage of them and add to them for future generations. Here are five types of resources that are of particular help to the missionary.

1. *Journals:* Many good journals are available to help you. Field missionaries appreciate journals that help them think more clearly about practices, strategies, and methods, such as *Evangelical Missions Quarterly, International Journal of Frontier Missions,* and *Mission Frontiers.* Those who are more academically inclined benefit from journals such as *International Bulletin of Missionary Research, Missiology: An International Review, Indian Missiological Review, Missionalia* (South Africa), *South Pacific Journal of Mission Studies,* and *International Review of Mission.*

2. *General reference works:* There are far too many reference works to list them all here, but the following are especially helpful resources:

   • David Barrett, George Kurian, and Todd Johnson, eds., *World Christian Encyclopedia,* 2nd ed. (Oxford University Press, 2001)

   • Patrick Johnstone, *Operation World: The Day-to-Day Guide to Praying for the World,* 5th ed. (Zondervan, 1993)

   • Scott Moreau, ed., *Evangelical Dictionary of World Missions* (Baker Academic, 2000)

   • Linda Weber, ed., *Handbook of North American Protestant Missions 2007–2009* (Evangelism and Missions Information Service, 2007)

   • Dotsey Welliver and Minnette Smith, eds., *Directory of Schools and Professors of Mission and Evangelism 2002–2004* (Evangelism and Missions Information Service, 2002).

3. *Web sites:* The Internet is a treasure trove of information. Five very helpful sites are Ask-a-Missionary (www.thejourneydeepens.com/askamissionary.asp), Brigada (www.brigada.org), MisLinks (www.mislinks.org), Mission Resource Directory (www.mrd.org), and the Network for Strategic Missions (www.strategicnetwork.org). See the appendix for a list of additional sites.

4. *Missiological Societies:* Another way to make a contribution (and keep abreast of missions in a fast-changing world) is to join a missions society. Choices include Association of Professors of Missions (www.asmweb.org/apm), Evangelical Missiological Society (www.emsweb.org), the American Society of Missiology (www.asmweb.org), and the International Association for Mission Studies (www.missionstudies.org). For a more extensive list, see www.mislinks.org/research/societies.htm.

5. *Mission Research Centers:* For those who desire to do specific research on some aspect of missions, a number of research centers are available. These include the Billy Graham Center (bgc.gospelcom.net), Overseas Ministries Study Center (www.omsc.org), Oxford Centre for Mission Studies (www.ocms.ac.uk), and the U.S. Center for World Mission (www.uscwm.org).

OTHER IMPORTANT TERMS FOR MISSIONARY LIFE

Following, we offer brief definitions of some additional terms that are important in the life of a missionary. You will see these terms in the following chapters in this book; our purpose in defining them here is to give you a quick orientation to them as well as a handy reference that you can use in your reading.

10/40 window: An imaginary rectangular "window" between the tenth and fortieth latitudes, bordered around Africa, the Middle East, and Asia. This window contains most of the unreached peoples in the world and most of the non-Christian religions (Moreau, Corwin, and McGee 2004, 12).

Attrition: Premature departure from the field, whether from unpreventable (e.g., retirement, health issues) or preventable (e.g., moral failure, financial irresponsibility) reasons.

BAM: Business as missions; the use of businesses for missions purposes. This can include establishing a business framed in Christian ethics as a means of witness as well as making a profit in order to finance missions.

Bonding: The initial process of building strong relationships with people of the host culture.

Burnout (or **Brownout**): Diminished energy that leads to lethargy and a lack of ability to cope with daily life.

Call: An intense conviction that the sovereign God, through the Word, the Holy Spirit, and the community of faith, set apart a follower of Christ for participation in a specific ministry.

Candidacy: The period when a person is accepted as being in the process of joining a missions sending body but has not completed the process.

Classical mission agency: A nonprofit organization, started by one or more visionaries to meet some need related to a specific aspect of the Great Commission and/or the Great Commandment.

Church multiplication: The planting, developing, and multiplying of churches that results in a Christ-centered indigenous movement.

Community development: The process of building local communities into self-sustaining ones in ways that lead to their betterment in all areas of life (including economic, social, physical, and/or spiritual).

Congregational-direct missions: Missions programs developed by local churches without reference to other churches, denominations, or agencies.

Contextualization: The core idea is that of taking the gospel to a new context and finding appropriate ways to communicate it so that it is understandable to the people in that context. Contextualization refers to more than just theology; it also includes developing church life and ministry that are biblically faithful and culturally appropriate (Moreau, Corwin, and McGee 2004, 12).

Creative-access country: Formerly referred to as a "closed country," a creative-access country is a nation-state in which traditional missionary work is illegal or banned. Missionaries who want to work in such countries must use creative means to gain entry and establish residence (Moreau, Corwin, and McGee 2004, 12).

Culture shock: Psychological disorientation resulting from being in an unfamiliar culture.

Culture stress: The result of facing constant strangeness of the new culture over time, leaving one constantly on guard. It is the accumulation of stress over a significant period of time.

Culture: A unique, total way of life for a specific group of people.

Denominational agency: An agency formed at the denominational level that is typically the official sending agency for churches within that denomination.

Deputation: The process of visiting churches and other gatherings of Christians to present missionary ministries for the purpose of developing prayer and financial support (Easterling 2000, 271).

Ethnocentrism: The belief that one's culture or ethnic identity is better than other cultures or ethnic identities.

Ethnodoxology: "The theological and anthropological study, and practical application, of how every people group might use their culture's unique and diverse artistic expressions appropriately to worship the God of the Bible" (www.worldofworship.org/Ethnodoxology.htm).

Ethnomusicology: "Looking at music as a part of a culture and social life and looking at the music system itself. Once these basic parameters are made then musics can be compared and studied across cultures and across time and in other ways, such as how music affects cultures and the people involved and how culture affects music" (www.sil.org/anthro/ethnomusicology.htm).

Faith mission: Agencies that place great emphasis on the centrality of the Word of God and faith that he will supply all the needs of the agency and its missionaries.

Furlough (See "home assignment.")

Globalization: In relation to missions, the breakdown of distinctions between "sending" and "receiving" countries as missionaries go from all the world to all the world, and international partnerships are being created among sending agencies.

Glocalization: The ability to think and live creatively between local and global realities.

God's sacred storybook: Term used in this book for the Bible, which is the story of God and his relationship to people and the rest of the created order.

Great Commission Companies (GCC): "A socially responsible, income-producing business managed by kingdom professionals and created for the specific purpose of glorifying God and promoting the growth and multiplication of local churches in the least-evangelized and least-developed parts of the world" (Rundle and Steffen 2003, 41).

Hidden peoples: People groups that currently have no access to the gospel. They are hidden not in the sense that they are invisible but in

UNDERSTANDING KEY IDEAS AND TERMS

the sense that it is impossible, given current conditions, for them to hear the gospel in their own language in a way that makes sense to them (Moreau, Corwin, and McGee 2004, 12).

Holistic mission: Mission that takes into account the whole of human needs: spiritual, social, and personal. Holistic mission includes both evangelism and church planting as well as development and social transformation (Moreau, Corwin, and McGee 2004, 12).

Home assignment: Can refer either to time spent in the home culture on deputation or to reassignment to service in the home culture.

Indigenous church: A church that fits well into the local culture. Traditionally defined in terms of three "selfs": self-governing (not dependent on outside agencies to make decisions), self-financing (not needing outside funding to carry on its work), and self-propagating (able to evangelize within its own culture effectively). More recently "self-theologizing"—the ability to develop its own theological understandings from the Scripture—has been added to the criteria (Moreau, Corwin, and McGee 2004, 13).

Indigenous missionary: A missionary from what was once considered a receiving nation. This term tends to be broadly applied to both indigenous evangelists (who do not cross cultural boundaries) and indigenous missionaries (who may cross significant boundaries even though they stay within their country of residence) (Moreau, Corwin, and McGee 2004, 13).

Journey plan: A document, always under constant revision, that expresses what you believe God is leading you and your team (where applicable) to accomplish in cross-cultural service.

Kingdom professionals: Often used in place of "tentmaking"; kingdom professionals devote their professional lives to further God's kingdom through everything they do no matter what the cost.

Majority world: Multiple terms have been used to describe the non-Westernized world, including "developing world," "Africasia" (McGavran 1970, 9), "third world," "two-thirds world," "underdeveloped world," and "world A." The terminology is still in flux, with political agendas tied to most of the terms. In this book the term "majority world" is used to refer to this area (Moreau, Corwin, and McGee 2004, 13).

MCK: Multiple-culture kids; coined to reflect the reality that many MKs and TCKs grow up in more than three cultural settings.

Member care: Proactive and reactive holistic care offered to the missions community from pre-field to on-field to reentry to retirement. It is best provided by those familiar with cross-cultural ministries.

MK: Missionary kid; a child of missionaries.

Nongovernment organization (NGO): Often a charitable or social service organization that provides government-like support but is not government directed or controlled (e.g., the Red Cross, the Tear Fund, Habitat for Humanity, World Vision) (Pocock, Van Rheenen, and McConnell 2005, 16).

41

Nonresidential missionary: A missionary who, for whatever reason, is unable to permanently live in the country or among the people that is the main focus of his or her ministry. This tends to be the case more often for creative-access countries (Moreau, Corwin, and McGee 2004, 13).

Peoples, people groups: A people is usually defined by ethnic or linguistic terms. It is estimated that there are some 12,000 distinct languages and dialects and as many as 24,000 people groups in the world today (Moreau, Corwin, and McGee 2004, 13).

Pioneer missions: Cross-cultural missions in places where the gospel has little or no foundation and the people are yet to be evangelized.

Pluralism: The idea that there is more than one correct approach to truth or reality. In its most extreme form, pluralists advocate the blending of all sets of competing ideas, each representing a portion of the whole and each true in its own way. In religious terms, those who promote pluralism claim that no religion has an exclusive hold on religious truth and that all are legitimate within their own sphere of influence (Pocock, Van Rheenen, and McConnell 2006, 16).

Posttraumatic stress disorder (PTSD): Reaction to a trauma or series of traumas that results in particular types of coping behavior.

Pre-field preparation: Typically the process of preparing to depart once the missionary is officially accepted and finances are secured.

Reentry: The time when cross-cultural Christian workers return to their home country, whether for retirement, because of leaving the field, or due to home assignment.

Relief and development agency: Agency that focuses its efforts on providing for the immediate physical needs of a people (relief) and/or enabling long-term ability (development) to do so.

Service agency: Agency that provides ongoing support for other missions agencies, including such areas as aviation, information technology, Bible translation, mass-media development, and legal assistance.

Short-term missions: This term usually refers to trips with a mission focus ranging from one week to one or two years. They may be organized by churches, agencies, or even individuals for a variety of reasons (from English-language camps to church-building projects to evangelistic campaigns) (Moreau, Corwin, and McGee 2004, 13).

Spiritual formation: A radical and continuous transformation by Christ, the Word, and the Holy Spirit that involves the practice of spiritual disciplines in solitude, community, and ministry (Nouwen 1995, 81).

Spiritual warfare: Reflects the reality that Satan does not want unbelievers to come to Christ or believers to live fruitful, holy lives. The warfare we as Christians face involves Satan and his hosts constantly trying to maneuver Christians into spiritual lethargy or depression while they seek to live the abundant life Jesus promised (Moreau, Corwin, and McGee 2004, 13).

Syncretism: The replacement of core or important truths of the gospel with non-Christian elements.

TCK: Third culture kid; a child of any family living in a culture other than their home culture.

Tentmaking: The practice of using paid employment to gain entry into and maintain access to a cross-cultural setting. Tentmakers work as professionals and engage in ministry activities in addition to their wage-earning work (Moreau, Corwin, and McGee 2004, 13).

Traditional mission agency: Organization focused primarily on starting, developing, and multiplying new churches that result in an ongoing movement.

Transformation: Working to change society by transforming its unjust structures into more just ones. In the twentieth century, evangelicals did not typically think of transformation as appropriate missionary work. However, advocates of transformation rightly note that the historical fights against the slave trade, infanticide, widow burning, and foot binding are all examples of transformational mission (Pocock, Van Rheenen, and McConnell 2006, 15).

Worldview: Set of assumptions—typically below the surface—that define how people or cultures tend to live, including their beliefs and values.

SUMMARY

Terminology related to missions can help provide cross-cultural Christian workers with precision, depth, clarity, and credibility in regard to God's (and our) purpose and role in the global task of making disciples. Having established the guiding assumptions and definitions used in this book, we will now further develop the ideas presented in these opening chapters, providing helpful insights, tales, and tools for those who follow God's leading into cross-cultural service for the King of kings.

PART 2

Home-Front Preparations

3

Decision Making
and the Will of God

The Bible contains very little specific advice on the techniques of guidance, but very much on the proper way to maintain a love relationship with God.

Philip Yancey (1983, 27)

The Ifugaos of the Philippines discern the will of the spirits through observing certain phenomena. For example, should a redbird (*pit-pit*) cross their path as they head for a particular destination, they will return home immediately because they see the redbird as an omen of imminent danger. In order to gain health, wealth, or long life through the sacrificial system, shamans examine the liver of a chicken or a pig to divine direction. The Ifugaos also discern the future through dreams. Dreams project the future, providing guidance for daily living. For example, an Ifugao walked seven hours to ask us for a pancake. As I probed for the basis of this unusual request, I learned that his pregnant wife had dreamed about eating a pancake. Figuring the Americans would have pancakes, he made the arduous journey to our home. We made him a pancake, and he delightedly returned home with the required item.

Dreams unveil the future, providing the Ifugaos guidance for life. Wise Ifugaos take their dreams seriously.

How does God reveal his will today to twenty-first-century cross-cultural Christian workers? Is it different from Old Testament models? How do you know if you are "called" to missions? Who should be your mate? Where should you go to school? How will you know which people group God wants you to minister among? Should you serve at home or abroad? Should you focus on conventional ministries such as evangelism, church planting, or Bible translation, or move in the direction of community development or establishing a business? Should you teach English? Start a national school? Should you go out under a church? A mission agency? As an independent? How do you choose the right one? Should you go short-term? Long-term? How will your children be educated? At what socioeconomic level should you live in the host country? This chapter attempts to help answer these important questions. We begin by defining God's will, move to discerning God's will, and conclude with discussion about the "missionary call."

DEFINING GOD'S WILL

Garry Friesen's *Decision Making and the Will of God* challenged the status quo in relation to discerning God's will (Friesen with Maxson 1988, 80). In this groundbreaking text—which some Christian leaders found threatening—he differentiated between three understandings of God's will found among Christians: God's sovereign will, his moral will, and his individual will. God's sovereign will refers to "God's secret plan that determines everything that happens in the universe" (32). God's sovereign, perfect plan was formulated in eternity for all of history. There are no surprises for God because he is the one who authored the beginning, the middle, and the end of the sacred storybook, which gives validity to all other stories. God's moral will typically means "God's revealed commands in the Bible that teach how men ought to believe and live" (33). This aspect of God's will provides general principles that are universal in nature yet not applicable to every decision. In marriage, for example, followers of Christ are told not to marry an unbeliever but are not told which believer to marry. God's individual will refers to "God's ideal, detailed life-plan uniquely designed for each person" (35). The person who follows this is described as being in God's perfect will in every decision of life.

Of the three types of God's will—sovereign, moral, and individual—which are normative? For Friesen, there is no question about the first two: the sovereign and the moral are normative for all time. But he does not consider the individual will, that is, finding God's perfect will

48

for every decision, to be normative. Why not? Simply put, the idea of God's individual will is based on the theology of the Designer who appreciates order (1 Cor. 14:40) and is omniscient (Ps. 139:7–10). There is therefore one perfect answer to each specific decision because God is a God of order and knows his plan from beginning to end. This requires that each individual discern God's specific will for every decision made. Friesen contends that this level of discernment is impossible—indeed, it is not even necessary.

Friesen identifies two metaphors that capture this popular idea of God's individual will: the blueprint and the dot. A person who does not follow the exact blueprint or cannot find the single dot in the center of the circle will miss God's will. This creates unnecessary fear in sincere followers of Christ. Friesen challenges this perspective, arguing that there is no "ideal will of God" for an individual, and it therefore cannot be discovered. He prefers freedom of choice within revealed limits, believing this to be part of the Creator's design from the very beginning: "[I]n those areas where the Bible gives no command or principle (in non-moral decisions), the believer is free and responsible to choose his own course of action" (Friesen with Maxson 1988, 377).

One reason Friesen opposes the traditional view of "God's will" is its inconsistency in distinguishing important decisions (what vocation should I seek?) from ordinary decisions (should I brush my teeth?). A second reason is that the possibility of not finding the one and only correct response to options in life cre-

> *Nor do I really know myself, and the fact that I think I am following your will does not mean that I am actually doing so. But I believe that the desire to please you does in fact please you. And I hope I have that desire in all that I am doing. I hope that I will never do anything apart from that desire.*
>
> Thomas Merton (1958, 79)

ates anxiety in the believer; in contrast, those who recognize that they have a multitude of good options can be grateful rather than anxious. Friesen also argues that the traditional view tends to promote immature approaches to decision making. Who can challenge foolish behavior if God told the person to do it? Who can challenge someone's "call" to ministry even if maturity and ministry practice mitigate against it? Finally, Friesen notes, an element of subjectivity still enters the decision-making process for those looking for the "dot." Relying on circumstances for guidance, for example, still requires subjective interpretation. We would add that the static nature of the metaphors "blueprint" and "dot" fail to make multiple answers a possibility. Organic metaphors, such as a strawberry plant that spreads indiscriminately, that allow for choices in time seem more appropriate when describing individual decision making. The ultimate definitions of decision making are determined by the metaphors that define them.

Friesen is correct in that God's sovereign and moral will should guide the follower of Christ in all major areas of life. In the minor areas, however, God gives his followers choices and responsibility within boundaries. Jesus's command to love God *and* love others encompasses not only the Ten Commandments but all other laws as well (Matt. 22:37–40). This generalization provides his followers multiple choices for obedience, all of which can glorify their Creator. In light of this, then, how do we discern God's will?

DISCERNING GOD'S WILL

How do you discern God's will? To help answer this question, we begin with some foundational issues, after which we offer a brief survey of the guidance models presented in Scripture and then conclude with discussion of the "call" to missions.

Spiritual direction refers to fostering one's love relationship with God particularly through communicative prayer (Barry and Connolly 1982, 5–8). It is making God the center during the inevitable ups and downs of one's spiritual journey. This discipline does not promise "magical solutions," rather it calls for a growing personal relationship with the Creator. Just as the Twelve's understanding of Jesus Christ continued to develop and mature over time as they traveled with him, the same should be true of followers of Christ today. Consistent quality time spent with Jesus Christ provides opportunity for genuine spiritual transformation. The authors contend that "[i]f there is mutual communication and mutual acceptance of hopes, desires, ideals, fears, and frustrations, the relationship cannot be anything but close" (35). Relationship with God is the central issue in spiritual direction.

In *Celebration of Discipline*, Richard Foster argues that when the divine center is lost, security is found in the "insane attachment to things" (1988, 80). Greed for goods replaces God's graceful provisions given according to need (Matt. 6:33). This produces false security and at the same time increases anxiety. The garnered goods must now be guarded. To challenge this way of life, the spiritual discipline of simplicity must be restored. If simplicity is restored, followers of Christ will find freedom. This is because freedom is based on three inner attitudes: (1) everything we have is a gift, (2) God cares for everything we have, and (3) what we have is available to others. The absence of anxiety and the resulting freedom come when one seeks the kingdom of God first.

Another aspect of keeping Christ in the center, claims Foster (1988, 126–40), is the discipline of service. True service produces humility, the foundational attitude necessary for God-driven ministry. Jesus demonstrated humility in life and death, something that continues to draw people to him today. While maintaining the existence of positional power and authority, Jesus challenged their traditional understanding. He "redefined greatness" with a towel and a basin. The towel redefined position and title. The basin redefined community. This requires an attitudinal change on our part. Whether in offering hospitality, listening to others, guarding the reputations of others or the gospel, bearing the burdens of others, sharing the Word with others, or working to earn an income, humility must dominate. We must learn to serve.

But there is something more; we must also learn to be served by others. For many people, it is much easier to serve others (being in control) than to be served by others (being out of control). Both are necessary for true humility to prevail. When followers of Christ place him at the center, materialism falls by the wayside and humility influences daily behavior, clearing the way for godly spiritual direction.

Guidance Models from Genesis through Pentecost

The author of Hebrews writes, "In the past God spoke to our forefathers through the prophets at many times and in various ways" (Heb. 1:1). We will now look at some of the ways God chose to reveal his will from creation through Pentecost.

In *Finding the Will of God* (1995), Bruce Waltke identifies six ways in which God chose to reveal his will, all supernaturally, to those of faith. Absent among these six ways is anything that relates to magic, sorcery, spells, or contacting the dead (Deut. 13:1–5; 18:10).

In the Old Testament people went to prophets and prophetesses to receive God's answers to their questions. Whether finding lost donkeys (1 Sam. 9), determining Israel's role in war with the Canaanites (Judg. 4), ascertaining correct behavior, or going up the mountain to hear from God, the prophets were the go-to people for life's answers. The prophets served as God's mouthpiece. But there were other prophets, false prophets, whom the people of Israel were to avoid and reject. Truth was to be found only through God's spokespersons.

A second way Old Testament people discovered God's will was through the Urim and Thummim. Although much remains to be learned about this means of discovering God's will, we do know that it operated much like rolling the dice. If the thrown stone or sticks turned up white, the answer was yes. If black, the answer was no. The use of the Urim and Thummim seemed to fade during the early monarchy with only one scriptural reference to it after the Babylonian exile.

Another means to discover God's will was the use of the sacred lot. Proverbs puts it this way: "The lot is cast into the lap, but its every decision is from the LORD" (16:33). Sacred lots were cast before the Lord to determine land distribution for the twelve tribes (Josh. 18:6), distribute spoils of war (Nah. 3:10), determine priestly roles and duties (1 Chron. 24), identify the guilty (Josh. 7), and select a king (1 Sam. 10) or an apostle (Acts 1); the selection of Matthias is the last time Scripture mentions the use of casting lots.

A fourth way to discern God's will was through dreams. Mentioned over eighty times in Scripture, dreams were one of God's favorite ways to communicate his will to humans. Dreams were used to inform Joseph that his family would survive the famine (Gen. 37), encourage Gideon to lead Israel into war (Judg. 7), describe the end of the world (Dan. 7), and inform Joseph about the virgin birth (Matt. 1). Joel and Luke remind us that dreams will continue: "In the last days, God says, I will pour out my Spirit on all people. Your sons and daughters will prophesy, your young men will see visions, your old men will dream dreams" (Acts 2:17; cf. Joel 2:28).

Signs were also used to communicate God's will. God spoke to a timid Moses through a burning bush, calling him to lead the Israelites out of bondage (Exod. 3). God sent fire from heaven to consume Gideon's sacrifice. Still not entirely persuaded, Gideon placed wool on the ground as another test. The first time God made it wet and the ground dry as requested by Gideon. The second time God kept it dry and made the ground wet as requested. God did all this to prove to Gideon that he should rescue Israel by crushing the Midianites even if he came from the weakest tribe and was the least important member of his family (Judg. 6). Jesus performed numerous signs to convince people that he was God's promised Messiah (John 20:30).

The sixth way people discerned God's will was through hearing an audible voice. Sometimes he spoke directly to people, such as to Abraham, Moses, and Elijah ("the soft whisper of a voice" [1 Kings 19:12 GNT]). Sometimes he spoke through angels, such as to Gideon, Balaam, David, Ezekiel, and Zechariah (Luke 1). Waltke concludes, "After Pentecost there is no instance of the church seeking God's will through any of the forms of divination listed above. . . . God's method of revealing his mind with regard to specific choices in a perplexing situation before Pentecost is not normative for the church" (1995, 54–55).

We would add one more to this list—visions. God came to Abraham in a vision (Gen. 15:1), provided Isaiah a message for Judah and Jerusalem through a vision (Isa. 1:1), and interpreted the vision for Daniel concerning the end times (Dan. 2:19).

SIDEBAR 3.1
EIGHT WISDOM SIGNS TO DISCOVER GOD'S WILL

Steve Hoke (Hoke and Taylor 1999, 76--78)

Steve Hoke provides the following
list of signs to help you in the process
of discovering God's will. In light
of Friesen's arguments, discuss your
reactions to the list by responding to the
questions below.

1. Common sense
2. Spiritual counsel
3. Personal desire
4. Circumstances
5. Scripture

6. Prayer
7. Previous experience
8. Peace

REFLECTION AND DISCUSSION

1. Do you agree that each item deserves
   to be on the list?
2. How might you prioritize them (from
   most important to least important)?
3. Are there other signs that you would
   add to the list?

Guidance Models Post-Pentecost

Post-Pentecost guidance models differ slightly from the Genesis through Pentecost models. On the supernatural level, visions continue to reveal God's will, as Peter discovered in Acts 10. Peter had to learn a hard lesson: God treats everyone, including Gentiles, on an equal basis. To help Peter grasp this, God, using a vision, lowered three times to earth a large sheet that contained all kinds of animals, reptiles, and wild birds. He then asked Peter to kill and eat before taking the sheet back to heaven. The implications slowly but surely began to sink in. This new understanding of God's view of people made it possible for Peter to stay with an "unclean" Gentile, eat nonkosher food, and hear what God had to say through Cornelius. Acts 16:9–10; 18:9; 22:17–21 provide other examples.

Signs and wonders to convey God's will continued. The Spirit of the Lord took Philip from the baptism of the eunuch to minister in another area (Acts 8:39–40). Paul received a vision of a man of Macedonia begging him to come over and help them (Acts 16:8–10). Paul told the Corinthians that they had observed many signs and wonders confirming his apostleship, and therefore they should listen to his message from God (2 Cor. 12:12).

Hearing God's voice is evident in a number of passages. Philip was told to go to the eunuch's chariot (Acts 8:29). A voice asked Saul why he was persecuting him before being told to go to Damascus and wait for further direction (Acts 9:3–6). A discouraged Paul received encouragement after hearing the voice of God (Acts 18:9; 23:11).

53

Some different models are introduced in the post-Pentecost period. Implementing God's will is also found in the use of common sense, the counsel and efforts of friends, and the "convergence of circumstances," as observed in Acts 9:25–30. Saul used common sense and the convergence of circumstances to escape capture by having his friends lower him down the side of the city wall. Barnabas took Saul to meet the apostles while other friends escorted him first to Caesarea and then to Tarsus.

Another model is the open-door policy. Paul asked the Colossians to "pray for us, too, that God may open a door for our message" (4:3). Paul believed that prayer opened opportunities for the gospel message so that hearers could be transformed. One example of a door opened by God was when Paul went on his first missionary journey, to Ephesus and to Troas (Acts 14:27; 1 Cor. 16:9; 2 Cor. 2:12).

Another aspect of the open-door policy is that when God shuts one door, he opens another. Should Paul go east or west? Hindered by the Holy Spirit from entering the province of Bithynia, where should Paul and his party go? Paul had a vision of a Macedonian begging them to come and help (we may also note that several of the early church fathers relied on dreams for spiritual direction; see Kelsey 1975). In that the door to the east closed, Paul and his group headed west to Macedonia. We should note here that the "Macedonian call" had nothing to do with a missionary call. The Macedonian vision was given to veteran missionaries in search of guidance for where next to take the gospel of Jesus Christ (see Moreau, Corwin, and McGee 2004, 160–61). Paul's example may teach cross-cultural Christian workers to keep marching until God shuts the door and then to look for the next open one (Acts 16:8–10).

God also leads some through a "message of knowledge" (1 Cor. 12:8) given by the Holy Spirit for specific occasions. When a course of action requires direction, God sometimes works through believers to provide other followers of Christ direction, encouragement, or whatever advice is needed.

Although followers of Christ are not told to find God's will or provided a set of steps to discern it, Bible examples of heroes and heroines of the faith from both Testaments do provide insights for today's cross-cultural Christian workers. While all guidance models are supernatural to some degree as the Supernatural communicates with his created, some are more so, such as visions, signs, an audible voice, and dreams. This causes some to conclude that guidance through highly supernatural avenues is no longer normative for today. Noticing the absence of such supernatural guidance in their own lives and those of the same theological persuasion, they consider such supernatural means of guidance a first-century phenomenon necessary for the new Christian movement to take root.

We do not feel comfortable assigning supernatural guidance to the first century alone. Some cultures are much more open to supernatural activity than those influenced by the Enlightenment, particularly the West. Possibly more important is the need for supernatural guidance and activity when the gospel first enters an unreached people group. If first-century Christianity required supernatural guidance to aid a fledgling movement, the same may be true for certain pioneer efforts in the twenty-first century. Whichever side you take on this issue, you will likely agree that all guidance coming from God, no matter how it is given, requires personal and/or collective faith and obedience to revealed truth on the part of the recipient.

THE MISSIONARY CALL

The idea of the "missionary call" has stirred countless discussions down through the ages (see Moreau, Corwin, and McGee 2004, 159–71). Does God specifically call an individual to become a missionary? If so, how? Is not every follower of Christ called to be a missionary? How do I know if I have received a call? Can I be a missionary without such a call? Is the Great Commission all the call that one needs? Is there a difference between a call to missions and a call to a secular vocation? Does the call differ from guidance?

The call to ministry usually relates to the roles of pastors and missionaries. In an advertisement for The Southern Baptist Theological Seminary, President R. Albert Mohler Jr. noted that Charles Spurgeon referred to his call to ministry as "an intense, all-absorbing desire for the work." Martin Luther referenced it as "God's voice heard by faith." Whether for the pastorate or for missions, the call refers to an intense conviction that the sovereign God, through the Word, the Holy Spirit, and the community of faith, has set apart a follower of Christ for participation in a specific ministry. The time frame or geographic location may or may not be known immediately. Seldom do churches, however, refer to secular vocations, such as a teacher, businessperson, doctor, nurse, homemaker, lawyer, politician, or mechanic, in relation to a call. Although congregational rituals exist to recognize the call to the pastorate and global missions, the same cannot be said for secular roles. It would seem healthier if each church recognized and ritualized the validity of every call received by its congregants.

How were various Bible personalities called to ministry? A brief overview of these individuals can provide valuable insights for today. We begin with Moses.

Moses ("one who draws out") was tending sheep and goats in the desert when an angel of the Lord appeared as a flame in a burning bush

(Exod. 3). When Moses approached the bush, the Lord spoke to him. He related the plight of the Israelites and his plan to free them with the help of Moses. Moses balked. The Lord told Moses he would tell him what to say and promised that the Israelites and the Egyptians would listen to him. In fact, Egypt would provide Israel material help. Unconvinced, Moses queried: "But suppose. . . ." God responded with two acts of miraculous power, turning Moses's walking stick into a snake and making his hand leprous. Even so, Moses refused to take the leadership offer, adding that he was unable to speak. This resulted in a heated exchange between God and Moses, ending with a reluctant Moses willing to take the leadership role with Aaron's assistance. Aaron spoke to the Israelites, Moses performed miracles, and the people believed and worshiped the Lord.

In a time when very few messages or visions came from God, he spoke to Samuel ("name of God"). Serving the Lord under Eli as a young boy, Samuel heard God call to him several times during the night but thought it was Eli. Eli told him that the next time God spoke, he should say: "Here I am; you called me" (1 Sam. 3:8). Samuel followed his instructions and was given some sobering projections about Eli's family. When Samuel told Eli what God had said to him, Eli said: "Let him do what is good in his eyes" (3:18), providing an excellent model for the young boy now pronounced a prophet of the Lord.

When King Uzziah died, God called Isaiah ("the Lord saves") to be a prophet through supernatural events. Isaiah saw the Lord sitting on his throne surrounded by flaming creatures worshiping him. Their voices caused the temple to shake and later to be filled with smoke. Isaiah was humbled and acknowledged his sinfulness. Then the Lord said: "'Whom shall I send? And who will go for us?' And I said, 'Here am I. Send me!'" He said, "Go and tell this people" (6:8–9). A humbled prophet received God's message to communicate to the people.

The book of Ezekiel records how God searched for someone to be his spokesperson but could find no one. "I looked for a man among them who would build up the wall and stand before me in the gap . . . but I found none" (22:30). The result: "I will . . . consume them" (22:31).

Amos ("the Lord carries"), like Moses, was a shepherd with family members unconnected with prophets. But God changed that. He told Amos to go and prophecy to "my people." A herder and caretaker of sycamore-fig trees became God's prophet to announce God's destruction of the northern kingdom.

Another reluctant servant, Jonah ("dove"), headed out of town when he heard God's request. God told him to go to Nineveh and speak out against it. Jonah went in the opposite direction (1:1–2). It would take a number of miracles and a second "word of the Lord" for Jonah to head

---

SIDEBAR 3.2
FOUNDATIONS FOR RECEIVING A MISSIONARY CALL

Thomas Austin (2000, 645--46)

1. Belief in and commitment to the lordship of Jesus Christ such that it produces unconditional love for him and obedience to his will.
2. A commitment to obey the will of God in our walk with him.
3. Openness to the leading of the Holy Spirit.
4. Belief in the Word of God as authoritative and a commitment to obey the principles and guidance laid down in it.
5. An understanding that the Great Commission was given by Jesus to all Christians, and therefore each person should be involved in helping to fulfill this command.

REFLECTION AND DISCUSSION

1. How does this list differ from what you have considered foundations to a missionary call?
2. Is there anything that you think should be added to this list?
3. What might you say to a person who has diligently done all of these things but still has no sense of calling?

---

to Nineveh. Even so, Jonah experienced no joy when the people of Nineveh responded positively to God's compassion.

Jesus called those he wanted to serve with him, and twelve responded (Mark 3:13). Some were brothers, some were zealots, some were humble fishermen, one was a despised tax collector, three were considered pillars, one was a traitor. When called, they dropped what they were doing and followed Jesus to focus exclusively on full-time ministry, never to return to their prior occupations (Matt. 4:20, 22). He designated them as apostles and sent them out to preach, heal, serve, drive out demons, and so forth. The selection of the Twelve demonstrates that Jesus did not want to do the job alone; he preferred co-laborers.

One of the most unique calls to salvation and service is that of Saul, later called Paul (Acts 9). While Saul was en route to Damascus to arrest any followers of Christ he could find, a blinding light and a voice from heaven transformed him forever. The persecutor of people of the way became a preacher of the message of grace, interrupting full-time ministry occasionally to earn funds by making tents (Acts 18). After being helped by Ananias, he went straight to the synagogues and preached Christ for a year before beginning the missionary journeys (Acts 11:26; 2 Tim. 1:11).

In Acts 13, the community of faith was worshiping and fasting when the Holy Spirit told them: "Set apart for me Barnabas and Saul for the

57

SIDEBAR 3.3
GO WITHOUT A CALL?

When Garry Friesen wrote *Decision Making and the Will of God*, he identified one mission society (SIM) that was "willing to consider candidates who cannot pinpoint a decisive call to the mission field." He asked director emeritus Raymond Davis and the then general director Ian Hay: "How does SIM react to a person who expresses an interest in foreign service, but who can't honestly say he has had a missionary 'call'?" Here are the responses he received (Friesen with Maxson 1988, 328–29):

Ian Hay: "SIM reacts with understanding. We want those people who are first of all committed in their lives to the lordship of Christ, people who understand that their basic responsibility is to do the will of God as outlined in the Scriptures. The person who comes with this attitude is precisely the type of person we're looking for, whether he understands what a 'call' is or not. Actually, the use of that word bothers me. There's a lot of

misunderstanding regarding a 'call.' The word has assumed overtones that I think we can do without."

Raymond Davis: "The concept of a 'call' as a necessary introductory experience for serving God cannot be scripturally substantiated. Some, like Paul, did have such an experience, but many others didn't. We've built up the idea of a 'call' into something which simply was not known in the days of the early church."

REFLECTION AND DISCUSSION

1. How do you respond to these comments?
2. How does culture influence our understanding of the missionary call?
3. How might you advise a church missions committee that asks your thoughts on what they should look for in a call to someone who wants to go into missionary work from their church?

---

work to which I have called them" (v. 2). These highly visible, active church leaders were called by God and the church to take the gospel and start new churches in the then-known world. The local church called out the called. Their absence would provide others opportunity to test their gifts and skills in the Antioch church while opening the world to the message of grace through Barnabas and Paul.

In summary, a number of points can be observed from these biblical case studies that can help develop a "theology of the call":

- The call can refer both to salvation and to service.
- Some who were called had relatives already in ministry while others did not.
- Both adults and children were called by God to ministry.
- The supernatural played a vital role in the call.
- Some already involved in ministry were called to a new role.

SIDEBAR 3.4
IS THERE A DISTINCTION BETWEEN VOCATIONAL AND MINISTRY CALLS?

The following quote explains Friesen's stance on the call to ministry versus the call to a vocation. Carefully read his position and then reflect on the questions that follow.

> People speak only of "the call to the missionary," or "the call to the ministry" as though these are the only believers that God calls. Now God does call missionaries and pastors. But He also calls printers, nurses, mechanics, carpenters, and housewives to their life-work as well. One's vocation is just one part of God's overall blueprint. Such an important aspect of your life could

scarcely be omitted by the Master Designer. God's vocational call is for saints only—not for missionaries and pastors only. (Friesen with Maxson 1988, 47)

REFLECTION AND DISCUSSION

1. What distinctions do you make between a vocational call to a secular job and one to full-time Christian ministry?
2. Respond to the statement: "All vocations are sacred."
3. Should the church validate calls to secular fields as well as to ministry?

- Some were called to minister in their own cultures, some were called to minister cross-culturally, and some ministered to both.
- Some were active in "secular" occupations when called.
- Availability often counted for more than ability.
- Time spent with God helps produce humility, something vital to any call to ministry.
- There was sometimes heated dialogue between the called and the Caller.
- Sometimes others assisted in the call to ministry.
- Not all of the called accepted, creating severe consequences for the unserved.
- Not everyone called to ministry proved faithful.
- Some who accepted the call to ministry did so for selfish reasons.
- The call to ministry is both private and public.
- The call to service and suffering originates in the call to salvation.

In the past, too much emphasis was placed on the call to missionary service, resulting in much unnecessary stress. Since a "call" and a "vocation" are basically equivalent, more emphasis should be given to spiritual guidance and spiritual gifts (Acts 13:2) in relation to service and suffering. The call to service and suffering has its origin in the call to salvation (Rom. 1:7; 8:30; 1 Pet. 2:20–21). The call to service is an outgrowth of a call to salvation. The highest priority, therefore, should be continual obedience to truth (Col. 2:6). Faithful obedience to the known biblical principles will lead to and reveal the unknown specifics of your particular ministry: which people group? where? when? with whom? how long? at what cost? This raises a number of key questions that should be asked: Are you analyzing your spiritual gift set? Are you active in ministry? Most importantly, are you listening for that "gentle whisper" (1 Kings 19:12) and acting accordingly?

SUMMARY

Unlike the Ifugaos, followers of Christ look to the Creator for guidance rather than to the created. God's sovereign plan is in place, accompanied by moral laws that provide guidance for all major areas of life. Finding God's unique plan for an individual, however, is much more challenging. We appreciate Friesen's conclusion that in the minor areas of life, God gives his followers choices and responsibility within boundaries.

Spiritual direction is based on fostering one's relationship with the sovereign God. It is placing God at the center of all beliefs and behaviors. Rather than accumulating material goods, the sincere follower of Christ seeks first the kingdom of God, joyfully knowing that God will provide for his or her needs. The follower of Christ not only seeks to serve others but is humble enough to also be served by others. Such an attitude prepares the way for more detailed spiritual guidance.

The guidance models from Genesis through Pentecost differ slightly from those found post-Pentecost. One thing they have in common, however, is supernatural influence. Some people have thus concluded that such mystical infusions in daily life are no longer normative today. This conclusion may be more reflective of worldview than sound theology.

> Jonathan's [Saul's son] focus was not, What is God's will for my life? but How can I give my life to fulfill God's will?
>
> Erwin McManus (2002, 64)

It is interesting to note that most bibliographic resources referencing the missionary call are not recent. Has globalization taken the mystique out of missions in that many people interact with internationals at work, at church, and/or have traveled abroad? Cable networking is also a factor. News is 24/7 from anywhere in the world. News is also instant, making distant lands no longer seem so far away or foreigners seem so strange. It also appears that many people today have a more holistic view of life, making global engagement almost a given. Ministry is done wherever and whenever and is done collectively. Many people feel "called" conceptually to global ministry corporately (not just as an individual) even though they may not be familiar with the phrase.

A changing culture has influenced understanding of the extrabiblical phrase "missionary call." Positively, people want to participate in ministry corporately on a global perspective. Negatively, they tend to transport rather than transform familiar models into very different contexts. But a changing culture must never minimize faithful obedience to revealed truth. We are provided wise advice in Proverbs 3:5–6: "Trust in the LORD with all your heart and lean not on your own understanding; in all your ways acknowledge him, and he will make your paths straight." Giving your life to fulfilling God's will just may be more important than your attempts at discovering God's will.

4

Spiritual Formation

My God, I love Thee . . .
And in Thy praise will sing,
Solely because Thou art my God,
And my eternal King!

Francis Xavier (1506–52),
translated by Edward Caswall (1814–78)

A Google search for "definitions of spirituality" resulted in over twelve thousand hits! They covered a gamut of concerns ranging from "rational spirituality" to "spirituality in mental health care and counseling," "spirituality in cancer care," "spirituality in the workplace," "spirituality and ecology," "humanist perspectives on spirituality," "spirituality and self-realization," "postmetaphysical spirituality," and, yes, among them was "religion and spirituality." Christian definitions were overwhelmed and almost lost in the midst of this deluge.

These results should not be surprising to any of us. We have been talking about postmodernity for several decades now and know that one of its characteristics is the proliferation and privatization of spiritualities. They are considered subjective and relative. All spiritual experience is seen as equally valid. Claims of absolute truth seem archaic and irrelevant.

Our purpose in this chapter is to help you to find your way through this confusing maze of postmodern spiritualities and begin your journey toward Christ-centered spiritual formation. After a brief look at the spiritualities that are expressed through historical religions, traditional religions, folk religion, and the New Age movement, we focus on Christian spirituality. What does it look like? How does it differ from other spiritualities?

Since this textbook is written for prospective missionaries, we also take time to examine spiritual issues you are likely to encounter in the midst of complex relationships, cultural stressors, and the demands of ministry. Then we enter into an in-depth discussion of the radical transformation of our innermost being that we call spiritual formation. It begins with our times alone with God, focusing on Jesus, the Scriptures, and the practice of spiritual disciplines. Then it spills over into our lives in community with others, where we experience forgiveness, celebration, interdependence, and deep, caring relationships. Ultimately, as we live in community and are empowered by the Holy Spirit, we are sent into the world by Jesus Christ to engage in holistic ministry.

We conclude the chapter with a challenge to keep stretching and growing as you explore other streams of spirituality and experience the diversity of its expressions in other cultures.

RELIGIOUS SPIRITUALITIES

Expressions of religious spiritualities have been observed around the world and across the centuries. Ancient Israel lived in the midst of the gods of Egypt and the gods of the land they entered. Today we encounter historical world religions, traditional religions, and folk religion. We discuss these below and then give special attention to the New Age movement.

Historical World Religions

The oldest of the historical world religions is *Hinduism*. Key elements of Hinduism are traditional texts, a pantheon of gods, temple sacrifices, and meditative practices in a world driven by the dynamics of reincarnation, the caste system, and ethical progression (karma) (Lewis 2000, 434–37). *Buddhism* challenges the spiritual value of the caste system and the divine character of the Hindu pantheon and moves toward a more personally centered, interior-based set of practices (Muck 2000, 149–50). *Judaism* has influenced the formation of both Christianity and Islam and is characterized by its stress on monotheism, the Ten Commandments, the observance of the Sabbath, circumcision, food laws, and festivals, especially the Passover and the Day of Atonement (Harvey 2000, 519–21). *Islam* includes five pillars of faith—confession ("There is no god but God, and Mohammed is the apostle of God"), ritual prayer five times a day, almsgiving, fasting, and pilgrimages to Mecca (Woodberry 2000, 504–6).

Traditional Religions

The recent attention world events have directed toward historical religions can cause us to all but forget the indigenous, *traditional religions* that have been a major focus of the modern missions movement. These are spread throughout sub-Saharan Africa and around the globe. Since traditional religions usually have no sacred books or known founders, they must be studied locally through their oral narratives and rituals. Although caution is needed in making generalizations, some commonalities have been observed. Traditional religions usually affirm life—health, prosperity, honor, and progeny—as essentially good. Since evil forces try to destroy life, the purpose of religion is to prevent misfortune and maximize good fortune. The all-powerful Creator God is relatively uninvolved, leaving the responsibility for appeasing evil forces and regulating human lives to minor deities, ancestors, elders, and various religious functionaries (Tienou 2000, 46–48). While some believe there is discontinuity between African traditional religions and Christianity, others consider African traditional religions as *praeparatio evangelica*, a preparation for the gospel (Mbiti 1970, 2).

Folk Religion

Local, traditional religions, which attempt to give meaning to life, explain death, and deal with crises (spirit possession, droughts, famines, defeats in battle, injustices in the social order), are often intermingled with "high" religions. This ad hoc mixture is called *folk religion*. Folk religionists will go to the mosque or the temple for the answer to some questions and to the shaman for others. They will go to church on Sunday and to traditional healers, exorcists, and diviners during the week. The result is often syncretism and extreme cultural accommodation (P. G. Hiebert 2000a, 364–65). In Brazil, for example, Afro-Brazilian cults such as Candomblé and Umbanda celebrate the Catholic Church's calendar of saints' days with festivals that merge veneration of the saints with that of ancestral divinities.

The New Age Movement

Among the many contemporary expressions of religious spirituality, the New Age movement has perhaps gained the most attention. It is a countercultural magnet for a wide range of non-Christian worldviews (among them Hinduism, Buddhism, druidism, shamanism, and the

Western occult). It encourages people to draw from many sources in developing their individual spiritualities.

In spite of its extreme diversity, there are some common elements in the movement: looking to one's self for spiritual power; affirming the unity of humans with one another, the planet, the universe, or God; harnessing the power of our divinity through consciousness-transforming hypnosis, yoga, visualization, meditation, and (sometimes) drugs; having a pleasant view of death as involving experiences of peace and light, and the afterlife as a benign kind of reincarnation; rejecting the absolute claims of Christ (he is a guru who has taught us how we can obtain his status through Christ-consciousness); and creating our own reality and moral authority through our oneness with the divine (Groothuis 2000, 677–78).

Recognizing these elements in a New Age worldview sheds light on the proliferation of spiritualities that surround us. It also helps us to understand the confusion we sometimes feel when we attempt to separate conflicting views of spirituality from the truth claims of Christianity. "The effectiveness of Christian witness in our pluralistic world depends in part upon the Church's response" to matters of spirituality raised by so much diversity (Netland 2001, 157). We will try to sort out some of these issues in the section below.

CHRISTIAN SPIRITUALITY

What Makes Christian Spirituality Different from Other Spiritualities?

With so much confusion about spirituality surrounding us on every side, a good starting place in understanding Christian spirituality is to recognize what it is *not*.

CHRISTIAN SPIRITUALITY IS NOT JUST THE SUBJECTIVE FEELINGS PEOPLE HAVE.

All spiritualities can offer "feel-good" experiences. They can help people to transcend materialism; experience the beauty of nature, music, and the arts; and be more in tune with themselves and with others. Some have developed ways of worshiping, praying, and meditating that cause ecstasy or even "out of the body" experiences. Christian spirituality is expressed experientially, but it is far deeper and more profound than the way we feel.

SIGNS, WONDERS, CURES, AND EXPULSION OF DEMONS ARE NOT ALWAYS EXPRESSIONS OF CHRISTIAN SPIRITUALITY.

Although Satan and the spirit world are very real, and Christians are called to engage in spiritual warfare (Eph. 6:10–18), there is sometimes "a

65

tendency to overemphasize the role of spirits which produces a Christian syncretism with [spiritism]. People use the Bible as a good luck charm to protect one from evil spirits, prescribe certain words or expressions to be used in dealing with demons, or assume that knowing the name of a demon gives more power over it" (Warner 2000, 903).

SPIRITUALITY IS NOT BASED ON OUR EFFORTS TO BE MORAL AND ETHICAL.

It goes beyond being a "good" person who has quiet times, treats others kindly, goes to church, gives to the poor, and cares about the environment. It is not just abstaining from drugs, alcohol, smoking, and sex outside of marriage. All religions and even secular philosophies have ethical and moral values. Trusting in our good behavior can keep us away from God rather than draw us toward him. The Pharisees felt holy and righteous when they brought the adulterous woman to Jesus and asked if she should be stoned. Jesus turned guilt and grace around. He condemned the Pharisees, who thought they were forgiven, and forgave the woman, who acknowledged her guilt (John 8:2–11; Tournier 1962). Yes, "good" behaviors can be fueled by pride and self-righteousness. They can lead to what Dietrich Bonhoeffer called "cheap grace," which looks for forgiveness without repentance, church discipline, confession, discipleship, the cross, and the living and incarnate Christ (Bonhoeffer 1949, 47, 55, 57; cited in Piper 2004, 90–91).

CHRISTIAN SPIRITUALITY MUST NOT ALLOW THE ENEMY (WHETHER ONE'S SELF OR SATAN OR OTHER PEOPLE) TO RUB IN OUR GUILT.

It refuses to trivialize either the darkness of our sin or the light of God's forgiveness. John Piper calls this stance "gutsy guilt" (2004, 87–90). Along with Micah (7:8–9), we recognize that we are guilty of real sin. It cannot be hidden under a rug. The gloom of our failure is real, and God's displeasure is real. But even while he is disciplining us, we are "fighting for joy like justified sinners" (Piper 2004, 72), knowing that he will plead our cause, execute judgment for us, and vindicate us.

CHRISTIAN SPIRITUALITY GOES BEYOND OUR PRACTICE OF SPIRITUAL DISCIPLINES.

One can practice solitude, silence, private prayer, fasting, and meditation on the Word without being "spiritual." You probably remember the story of the tax collector and the Pharisee who went to the temple to pray. The Pharisee thanked God that he was not like other people, especially the tax collector who was nearby. He fasted twice a week and gave a tenth of all he received. In the meantime, the tax collector just stood there beating his chest and crying, "God, have mercy on me, a sinner!" Jesus said that it was the tax collector who went home justified, and not the self-righteous Pharisee (Luke 18:9–14).

SPIRITUALITY EVEN TRANSCENDS CHRISTIAN MINISTRY.

We can share the gospel, teach and preach, help churches grow, take short-term missions trips, get involved in social action, or be in a situation of hardship and suffering without being truly spiritual. Neither is being an exemplary friend, employer or employee, professor or student, father or son, mother or daughter, husband or wife always an expression of Christian spirituality. Why? Because these good activities and behaviors can grow out of wrong motives. They can reflect pride, self-righteousness, or a need for attention and recognition. They can be energized by our own strength, abilities, and resources.

By now you have probably anticipated the answer to the question we raised above: what makes Christian spirituality different from other spiritualities is its starting point. It is not turned inward on ourselves, or focused on esoteric experiences, or acting like we are spiritual so others can see us.

CHRISTIAN SPIRITUALITY BEGINS WITH THE TRIUNE GOD.

God the Father loved the world so much that he sent his Son Jesus Christ to redeem us from sin and become our Savior and Lord. The Father and the Son have sent the Holy Spirit to comfort us, lead us, and empower us. We respond to God's love by living out the "Jesus Creed" (McKnight 2004), loving him with our whole being (our heart, will, soul, mind, and strength) and loving our neighbors as ourselves (Matt. 22:34–40; Mark 12:28–34; Luke 10:25–28).

What Does Christian Spirituality Look Like?

Spirituality that grows out of our heart response to God's love has been described in a variety of ways (see sidebar 4.1). J. Robertson McQuilkin (2000, 213–14) focuses on *unconditional commitment to the Lordship of Jesus Christ,* which causes us to be fully at God's disposal and spills over into our vocation, possessions, relationships, talk, and play. It will make us into world Christians. We will be proactive, eagerly listening for God's call, searching for God's will concerning our involvement in world evangelization, whatever our location or specific vocation. Confidence in God's call will cause us to stick it out in hard times.

Responding to God's love allows him to transform our lives so that they will manifest more fully the fruit of his Holy Spirit. The foundational manifestation is love, the reflection of God's very essence. It will be seen in our lives through the priority we give to people and our love for the

67

SIDEBAR 4.1
WHAT IS SPIRITUALITY?

McKnight (2004, 5)

Below are expressions of some of the desires and longings of historical and contemporary spiritual masters. In what ways do they reflect the spiritual longings of your own heart?

complete union with God
Thomas à Kempis

a desire to converse with God constantly
Brother Lawrence

striving to do what is right in every situation
John Woolman

being fired by holy zeal for God
J. I. Packer

grace for inner spiritual transformation through the spiritual disciplines
Richard Foster

a hunger, in this physical existence of ours, to be like Christ
Dallas Willard

pining to morph into the image of Christ
John Ortberg

thirsting for a life driven by God's purposes
Rick Warren

marginalized and the unlovely. Joy is the Spirit's manifestation in our lives as we worship him both privately and with other believers. Peace quells anxieties and calms the storms of our life as we cry to our Master (Luke 8:22–25). Patience (long-suffering) helps us to trust and wait on God in the midst of difficult situations. Kindness is reflected in words or acts that minister to others. Goodness is moral excellence. Faithfulness includes loyalty, commitment, and steadfastness. Gentleness is curbing our tendency to ride roughshod over others. Self-control allows our passions to be controlled by the Spirit (Dollar 2000, 377–78).

Dallas Willard (n.d.) reminds us that New Testament passages that outline progression in spiritual growth (Rom. 5:3–5; Col. 3:12–14; 2 Pet. 1:4–7) always conclude with love (in Greek, *agape*). All other moral virtues grow out of love.

Paul's description of the armor of God provides other insights into what Christian spirituality looks like (Eph. 6:10–20). We are in a battle, a life-and-death struggle against the powers of this world and against spiritual forces of evil in heavenly realms. If we are going to take our stand against the devil's schemes, we need to put on God's whole armor: truth (the belt buckled around our waist); righteousness (our breastplate); the gospel of peace (our boots); faith (our shield from Satan's arrows); salvation (our helmet); and the Word of God (the sword of the Spirit). To make sure we recognize that our battle and our weapons are spiritual, Paul ends with a

---

SIDEBAR 4.2
"MAY THE MIND OF CHRIST MY SAVIOR"
KATE B. WILKINSON (1859–1928)

Brown and Norton (1995)

Kate B. Wilkinson's hymn "May the Mind of Christ My Savior" provides a beautiful and all-encompassing description of the dimensions of Christian spirituality. You may want to memorize it and sing it as your prayer throughout the day.

May the mind of Christ, my Savior,
Live in me from day to day,
By His love and pow'r controlling
All I do and say.

May the word of God dwell richly
In my heart from hour to hour,
So that all may see I triumph
Only through His pow'r.

May the peace of God my Father
Rule my life in ev'rything,
That I may be calm to comfort
Sick and sorrowing.

May the love of Jesus fill me
As the waters fill the sea;
Him exalting, self [transforming]
This is victory.

May I run the race before me,
Strong and brave to face the foe,
Looking only unto Jesus
As I onward go.

May His beauty rest upon me
As I seek the lost to win,
And may they forget the channel,
Seeing only Him.

---

plea for prayer for all kinds of requests for all believers, and for himself, that he will be courageous and fearless while he is in prison (vv. 18–19).

WHY IS SPIRITUALITY ESPECIALLY IMPORTANT IN INTERCULTURAL CONTEXTS?

It is not by accident that Paul's plea for believers to be clothed with the armor of God is made in the context of persecution and suffering. Those who are in the heat of the battle in a culture that is strange to them have special spiritual needs. This is certainly true of today's missionaries. Many of them live in high-stress situations in which they face complex relationships, difficult cultural adaptations, demanding ministry contexts, and sometimes crises, conflicts, and suffering.

Relationships

The relational networks that are a part of missionary life can be extremely complex. Back in the home country, family ties and friendships must be maintained. Sending churches and individual supporters expect regular communication. Mission agencies require regular reports and accountability.

At the same time, missionaries are trying to build relationships in their host country. They are surrounded by colleagues, church leaders, local groups of believers, and people-related ministries—including evangelism, church planting, discipling, leadership development, theological education, literature, and social outreach efforts. And that is not all. They want to connect with the neighbors, shopkeepers, and institutions around them.

If you ask missionaries what makes their ministries most satisfying, most of them will answer, "It is relationships with people." But if you ask these same missionaries what makes their ministries most stressful and painful (and may even have made them think about going home prematurely), they will still answer, "It is relationships with people."

Developing and maintaining healthy relationships requires conflict management and relational skills. Even though these are important, and we will keep coming back to them as we progress through this textbook, by themselves these skills are not enough. Truly Christlike relationships grow from the inside out as they are permeated with the fruit of the Spirit (Gal. 5:22–23). An extra portion of these virtues is needed when we are living in stressful intercultural situations.

Adaptation

Adaptation to another culture also makes demands on a missionary's spiritual resources. Before you leave home, there is the stress of getting ready to go and then the good-byes. Later, after a few hours on the airplane, you find yourself in the middle of a new culture, being bombarded by unfamiliar sights, sounds, and smells. Everything seems so exotic and adventurous!

But before many weeks have passed, the honeymoon is over. You may feel confused and disoriented. So much is going on around you. It is hard to interpret what is happening, especially when you can't understand what people are saying, let alone communicate with them. To make matters worse, you can't even handle the logistics of everyday living. Trying to take care of your home, clothes, driving, shopping, going to the bank, and even setting up your computer to e-mail become major hurdles you must get over. Even your physical surroundings are hard to handle. You had been told that the climate would be hot and humid, but you weren't prepared for unscreened windows, sleeping under a mosquito net, or killing cockroaches (perhaps even rats!).

These cultural adaptation issues are dealt with in depth in chapter 11. The point being made at this stage in the discussion is that in the midst of all these stresses of cultural adaptation God has not left you alone. He has provided the spiritual resources you need. He is right there to help you. He will not let you slip or fall. He will keep you from harm. He will watch over your comings and goings, right now, during the rest of your life, and forever more (Ps. 121).

Ministry

As you start getting involved in ministry and become more immersed in the culture, you become increasingly aware of other kinds of pressures and tensions. You may feel overwhelmed by the economic, educational, and social needs around you. Your nationality, ethnic origin, or religion may create barriers. If you are an American, you may discover that your country is not loved and sometimes even hated. Since you are a Christian, you may find people suspicious of you and even distancing themselves from you. Compounding these issues are cultural differences in ministry strategies (ways of evangelizing, teaching, preaching, and so on). You may wonder if you will ever be able to share the gospel with these people you have come to reach.

In the midst of these kinds of experiences, remember that we are surrounded by "a great cloud of witnesses" (Heb. 12:1) to encourage us and inspire us. The author of Hebrews has just provided a long list of these people in chapter 11. Now he challenges us to follow their example of faith and obedience, throwing off everything that hinders us and the sin that so easily entangles us, so that we can run with perseverance the race marked out for us. Let us fix our eyes on Jesus! (Heb. 12:1–2).

SPIRITUAL FORMATION

Spiritual formation begins with an act of worship through which we offer ourselves to God, allowing his Spirit to continue transforming us into his glorious likeness (Rom. 12:1–2; 2 Cor. 3:18). When God spoke from the burning bush, Moses took off his sandals and hid his face (Exod. 3:1–5). When Isaiah saw the Lord exalted on the throne surrounded by seraphs who were praising his holiness and glory, he despaired because of his own uncleanness (Isa. 6:1–5). When a light from heaven flashed around Saul on the Damascus road, Jesus revealed himself as the one Saul had been persecuting (Acts 9:1–6).

All three of these instances involved radical spiritual transformation that spilled over into ministry. Moses was called to lead the people of God out of Egypt into a good and spacious land (Exod. 3:7–10). When Isaiah said, "Here am I. Send me!" God told him to warn callous-hearted and dull-eared people of the destruction, desolation, and captivity of their land that lay ahead (Isa. 6:8–13). When a light from heaven flashed around him on the Damascus road, Saul was left blind, fasting, and praying until the Lord sent Ananias to him. As Ananias placed his hands on Saul, his sight was restored, he was filled with the Spirit, and he journeyed toward his God-given calling to ministry among the Gentiles (Acts 9:10–19).

Radical and continuous spiritual transformation involves the practice of spiritual disciplines. Henri Nouwen reminds us that discipleship and discipline come from the same root word. In our spiritual lives, discipline means much more than mastering a body of knowledge or controlling an unruly child's behavior. "It is the effort to create some space in which God can act. [It] means to prevent everything in your life from being filled up" (1995, 81). This space for God is created by moving progressively through disciplines of solitude, community, and ministry. Nouwen sees these movements illustrated in Luke 6:12–19 as a beautiful story that "moves from night to morning to afternoon. Jesus spent the night in solitude with God. In the morning, he gathered his apostles around him and formed community. In the afternoon, with his apostles, he went out and preached the Word and healed the sick" (ibid.).

We will look more carefully at this progression in the discussion that follows.

Solitude as a Discipline

Time alone with God is essential to spiritual formation. Through the discipline of solitude, we can experience God's love and listen to his voice as we focus on Jesus, the Scriptures, and spiritual disciplines (Foster 2003).

FOCUSING ON JESUS

Earlier in this chapter, we reminded ourselves that Christian spirituality grows out of the "Jesus Creed": loving God the Father and his Son Jesus Christ with all of our heart, soul, mind, and strength, and loving our neighbor as ourselves. Loving Jesus means believing in him, abiding in him, surrendering to him, being restored by him, forgiving others in him, and reaching out with the good news about him (McKnight 2004, 181).

> Jesus went out to a mountainside to pray, and spent the night praying to God.
>
> Luke 6:12

Nothing is more important in Christian spiritual formation than our need to remain ever focused on Jesus. This is not formation in general but rather formation in Christlikeness. Everything hangs on this. Everything. Jesus gives skeleton and sinew and muscle to our formation. In Jesus we find definition and shape and form for our formation. Jesus is our Savior to redeem us, our Bishop to shepherd us, our Teacher to instruct us, our Lord to rule us, our Friend to come alongside us. He is alive. He teaches, rules, guides, instructs, rebukes, comforts. Stay close to him in all things and in all ways (Foster 2003, 1).

Focusing on the Scriptures

Careful inductive and exegetical study is essential to our understanding of Scripture. It helps us to understand what a passage says, what it meant to the original hearers, and what it means for us today. But, as important as these background and analytical studies may be, they may fall short of the goals and purposes of spiritual formation if they are imprisoned in linear logic and rigidly structured thought patterns that leave no room for global thinking, intuition, and creativity. If spiritual formation is to occur through the Word, the Word itself must be our focus, and our focus must be holistic. Choices of the personal over the propositional and relationship over revelation are unnecessary. David L. Larsen uses marriage to illustrate this point: "We do not choose love in marriage over legality in marriage—we choose both. In fact a marriage without legal sanction places love in jeopardy, because the long-term rights and interests of both parties would not be safeguarded" (2001, 14).

Likewise in theology, relationship without revelation is like a love affair with an unknown and unknowable God. We sing, "Beyond the sacred page, I seek thee, Lord." But apart from what the New Testament tells us of who he is, what he has done, and what he will do, how can we know that the Lord is in fact the Lord Jesus Christ? What do we know that the New Testament does not tell us? Scripture as the Word of God not only sustains the inner life by which we live (Matt. 4:4), but it reveals propositionally the parameters of spiritual truth (Larsen 2001, 14).

In a similar way, Richard J. Foster reminds us that "[s]ometimes we study the Bible for information alone in order to prove that we are right and others are wrong in particular doctrines or beliefs or practices. At other times we study the Bible to find some formula to solve the pressing need of the moment. But both approaches to the Bible leave the soul untouched. . . . [W]e need to study the Bible with the view to the transformation of our whole person and of our whole life into Christlikeness. . . . We must read humbly and in a constant attitude of repentance" (2003, 2).

Focusing on Spiritual Disciplines

You may have noticed that we talk about spiritual disciplines without a definite article. There is no master list of *the* spiritual disciplines. When we use the term, we are referring to the many and varied means God has given us to intentionally train ourselves in godliness (1 Tim. 4:7; Foster 2003, 3). The most common disciplines that we practice in solitude are silence, fasting, meditation, and prayer. But remember that

---

SIDEBAR 4.3
THE SPIRITUAL RICHES OF GOD'S WORD
"SPIRITUAL FORMATION: A PASTORAL LETTER"

Foster (2003, 2--3)

This sidebar is worth copying and carrying in your Bible. Its insights can help you gain a more thorough grasp of the spiritual riches God has made available through his written Word.

- We can begin with the *Gospels* looking at the "with-God" life that is fully portrayed in Jesus.

  And we seek this life abundant that comes in and through Jesus alone.

- We study the *Epistles* to see the life of God being poured through his people, the Church.

  And we seek that life for ourselves and for our families and for our churches and for our times.

- We study the *Psalms* and see the people of God at prayer.

  And we too enter a living experience of prayer, working in co-operation with God to see his kingdom come and his will be done here on earth.

- We study the *Pentateuch* to understand the Mosaic Law in the light of grace.

  And we seek to conform our lives to the heart and spirit of the Law.

- We study the *Historical books* to understand how God works through the historical particularities of a people.

  And we ask for God's life and God's work in the specifics of our histories.

- We study the *Prophets* and see their bias in favor of the downtrodden.

  And we seek the power to live continually with a sensitized social conscience.

- We study the *Wisdom books* and discover God's interest in the practical details of everyday life.

  And we pray for wisdom in the minutes of our little life.

- We study the *Eschatological books* and discover that "He's got the whole world in his hands."

  And we place our little destiny in God's hands too.

these and other disciplines are means and not ends in themselves. Our "end" (purpose, goal) is to allow God to transform our lives as we listen to him and are quiet before him, enjoying him and learning to know him better, love him more, and serve him more faithfully.

The surest way to stifle spiritual formation is to try to discover formulae or stuff the process into a box. Remember that when we are in Christ we are God's new creation (2 Cor. 5:17). We "are being transformed into his likeness with ever-increasing glory" (2 Cor. 3:18). Intentionality that degenerates into rigidity will only get in the way. We must let go of our own efforts and let God take control.

Solitude. To begin, we will need a place where we can be alone. It is true that we can sometimes experience aloneness with God in a noisy coffee shop, in the midst of a crowd, or during free times in our schedule at work or school. These moments can be important, but they are not enough. We need regular times when we get away from noises and crowds to hear God's voice. With this in mind, let us look more closely at the disciplines we mentioned above.

Silence. Our practice of personal spiritual disciplines will not get very far until we set aside a quiet place where we can intentionally practice *silence.* We are so in the habit of being surrounded by sound that we may initially feel uncomfortable with our TVs, computers, sound systems, iPods, and cell phones turned off. But once we have gotten rid of the distracting noises, we will find ourselves relaxing and enjoying sounds we may not have listened to for a while. We will hear birds singing, wind blowing in the trees, and thunder in the distance as we find our hearts stilled and silenced before God.

Fasting. Fasting can be an important discipline during this time of solitude. Whether you are alone with God an hour, a morning, a full day, or a weekend, try to avoid trips to the refrigerator, keeping snacks beside you, or thinking of your next meal. Putting your physical appetites aside will help you to humbly and quietly focus your attention on God. It will intensify the earnestness of your prayer by helping you to say with both your body and your heart that you long to be satisfied in God alone (Piper 2004, 171).

Meditation. The centerpiece of your time with God is listening to him while your mind, heart, and will are focused on his Word. You may find John Piper's "IOUS" acronym helpful as you spend time in the Scriptures (2004, 151–52):

- *I—(Incline!)* The first thing my soul needs is *an inclination toward* God and his Word . . .
- *O—(Open!)* Next I need to have *the eyes of my heart opened* so that when my inclination leads me to the Word I see what is really there, and not just my own ideas . . .
- *U—(Unite!)* Then I am concerned that *my heart is badly fragmented.* Parts of it are inclined, and parts of it are not. What I long for is a joyful heart where all the parts say a joyful *Yes!* to what God reveals in his Word . . .
- *S—(Satisfy!)* What I really want from all this engagement with the Word of God and the work of his Spirit in answer to my prayers is for *my heart to be satisfied with God,* and not with the world.

Prayer. Prayer is also an essential component of our times of solitude. Some have used another acronym (ACTS—adoration, confession, thanksgiving, and supplication) as a guide for prayer. It is helpful in reminding us that worship is first and central, confession needs to be linked to thanksgiving, and our supplications extend beyond our own needs to include our families, friends, acquaintances, and the world.

Many people find keeping a spiritual journal useful in releasing pent-up emotions and staying centered and focused in the midst of the diffused thoughts, feelings, and activities that make up their day. They sometimes also discover that the process of writing things down helps them to gain insight into God's purposes in their lives when things around them seem meaningless and to recognize his presence in the midst of difficult experiences. A spiritual journal includes these psychological and personal elements, but it does not stop here. Its primary focus is on listening to God and expressing your love for him.

As we focus on the inward disciplines and keep learning to love God more and more, his love spills over into our relationships and ministries. We look at some of the ways in which personal spirituality overflows into the rest of our lives in the discussion below.

Community as a Discipline

Living in community is another discipline that creates space for God to act and speak. It involves forgiveness and celebration, interdependence, one-on-one relationships, and relationships within small groups and extended networks.

FORGIVENESS AND CELEBRATION

True community grows out of the disciplines of forgiveness and celebration. Forgiveness means loving those who hurt us or can only give us a little love in return. It allows us to come together in nonmanipulative and nondemanding ways. When we forgive, we are able to celebrate one another's gifts and celebrate one another's humanity (Nouwen 1995, 83). Creating this kind of community within missions contexts is not always easy. Missionaries may find themselves feeling hurt, anxious, irritated, or put down by the words and actions of hard-to-get-along-with colleagues. And to complicate matters, their coworkers may be having the same kinds of struggles in relating to them! This is where forgiveness and celebration come

> *When morning came,*
> *he called his disciples to him.*
>
> Luke 6:13

in. As we allow God to fill our hearts with his love, we learn to forgive those who hurt us and celebrate the gifts God has given them, even as we ask our Father in heaven and those whom we have hurt to forgive us as well (Matt. 6:14–15).

INTERDEPENDENCE

Community begins to happen as we acknowledge our need for one another, our *interdependence*. Missionaries in the 1940s and 1950s were caught up in the individualistic modern-mission paradigm. They were told that on the mission field they would have to be their own pastor and be able to care for their own spiritual needs. Other missionaries would be too busy to take care of them; national Christians would expect missionaries to be their caregivers. There were strong expectations of self-sufficiency and being able to "go it alone."

Today, in stark contrast, some young people look toward missionary service with exaggerated expectations of dependence and spiritual support. They want lots of mentoring and spiritual direction and find it hard to survive when they are left on their own. Either extreme can be unhealthy. What is needed is an interdependence in which individual spirituality is fostered through the practice of personal disciplines (such as silence, fasting, meditation, and prayer) within the context of caring, loving, nurturing communities (McKinney Douglas 2006, 282–85).

ONE-ON-ONE RELATIONSHIPS

We have many kinds of relationships. We interact with our families, friends, members of our church, classmates and professors, colleagues at work, interest groups, and people we encounter in our extended communities. In a broad sense, everyone we relate to and interact with in some meaningful way can contribute to our spiritual formation. But when we look at *intentional* spiritual formation our list is much smaller; it probably includes only a handful of people.

A one-on-one relationship with a mentor (or spiritual director, discipler, counselor, coach, pastor) can provide encouragement and accountability. Beware of working with someone who acts like an all-knowing physician, gives you a "prescription," and checks at the next meeting to see how you are doing. You need a mature and discerning mentor who will be an encouraging friend, offer you resources, and help you to talk about what God is doing in your life (Smallbones 1995, 37–44). Make sure that your mentor takes spiritual formation seriously and keeps focused on Jesus, the Scriptures, and spiritual disciplines. (These concerns have been discussed earlier in this chapter. See pages 72–76.)

RELATIONSHIPS WITHIN SMALL GROUPS

Small groups are found in a variety of settings (churches, theological schools, university campuses, and the workplace, to name just a few). They take on many different forms and shapes and have many differing purposes. Some groups are focused on Bible study and personal

77

SIDEBAR 4.4
WORKSHOP: LOVED BY THE FATHER

A group session from a course on Christian spirituality in São Paulo, Brazil, with monthly meetings during the year 2000. Led by Osmar Ludovico da Silva; translated by Lois McKinney Douglas (used with permission).

PERSONAL MEDITATION ON KEY BIBLE TEXTS

1. Read and meditate on John 1:12–13; Romans 8:14–17; Galatians 4:6–7; 1 John 1:3. Write a short paragraph about your personal relationship to God the Father.
2. Recall negative memories you may have of your relationship with your earthly father. How may these have tarnished or distorted your relationship with God? Write a prayer asking for freedom and release from these memories.
3. Read Jeremiah 31:20. Copy this verse, substituting your own name for the name of "Ephraim." Meditate on the verse, allowing it to speak to your heart. Write two or three sentences about your experience.
4. Meditate on Hosea 11:3–4. Visualize the shelter and comfort of your heavenly Father: a tender, loving Father who covers you with his pardoning grace, a Father who nurtures you, shapes you, and helps you. Allow yourself to experience the presence of God's love in your life.
5. Write a paragraph about your love for God the Father. Express your feelings, not just your thoughts.
6. Write a prayer of thanksgiving for this experience.
7. Group reflection based on the personal meditation (above).

8. Read Henri Nouwen's *Return of the Prodigal Son: A Story of Homecoming* (1999). Then write your own poem, prayer, or story based on the story of the return of the prodigal, as Lois McKinney Douglas has done here:

The Prodigal Daughter

I stood in awe before the painting.
It was the portrait of a father
When his wandering son had come home.
How deep the father's emotions were!

I felt his compassion, his tiredness, his gentleness,
His love, his tender memories, and his forgiveness.
He had closed the distance that separated them,
And was hovering over his returning son
As if he were a mother eagle covering her nest.
He wasn't worried about his own immaculate garments
Being soiled by the filthy rags of the prodigal.
Nothing else mattered. The son he loved was back home!

But then, as I came closer, the scene changed.
The father's arms and cape were still providing a covering;
His strong and tender hands were still offering protection.
But the young man in dirty clothes was no longer there.
Instead, I saw a small woman with gray hair—
And I rejoiced in the embrace of my Father!

9. Share your prayer, poem, or story with your group.

growth; others are evangelistic groups that encourage seekers to explore the Christian faith. Some are training groups that prepare leaders for a variety of Christian organizations and ministries; others are caring and sharing groups, designed to give warmth, closeness, encouragement, and restoration to the members. These groups that focus on study, evangelism, training, caring, and sharing are important. We need their emphases in our personal lives; the churches and schools in which we study, worship, pray, and serve need them as well. In a variety of ways, these groups all include elements of spiritual formation.

What is it, then, that makes spiritual formation groups different from the other groups we have mentioned? It is their intentionality and singleness of purpose. Spiritual formation is not just an element within another activity. The Word, prayer, meditation, and creative reflection are all directed toward a single goal. The only focus is on knowing and loving God. A session from a spiritual formation group in action in Brazil will help us to see how these purposes and goals can be implemented in a concrete setting (see sidebar 4.4).

RELATIONSHIPS ACROSS EXTENDED NETWORKS

The forgiveness and celebration Nouwen (1995) emphasizes must not be limited to face-to-face and small group encounters. It should be experienced in churches, theological schools, and other local outreach ministries. Then these efforts in our neighborhoods and cities need to overflow into denominations, associations of theological schools, and other regional, national, and global networks. Without unity rooted in forgiveness and worship that grows out of celebration, extended communities and networks can become fragmented, self-absorbed, and virtually indistinguishable from the secular organizations that surround them. But when these communities and networks practice forgiveness and celebration, they become united and able to reach out in ministry.

Ministry as a Discipline

Jesus's day began the night before while he was praying alone on a mountain. It continued the next morning in community with his disciples. Then it culminated in loving and caring ministry to the multitudes that followed him (Nouwen 1995). Not only did Jesus model ministry, he also commissioned his first disciples and generations of faithful followers since then to follow his example. His call to obedience

> *[A] great number of people from all over [were there] . . . who had come to hear him and to be healed of their diseases.*
>
> Luke 6:17–18

and service continues today. We have been sent into the world by Jesus Christ, empowered and guided by the Holy Spirit, to embrace a global vision and engage in holistic ministry.

WE HAVE BEEN SENT INTO THE WORLD BY JESUS CHRIST.

The risen Lord announced this during his first encounter with his disciples after his resurrection: "As the Father has sent me, I am sending you" (John 20:21). The disciples' commission is amplified in Matthew's Gospel. They (and we!) are being sent by Christ. He is the exalted King, the Lamb sitting on the throne (Rev. 7:9–17), with total authority in heaven and earth (Matt. 28:18). He will always be with us, to the very end of the age (Matt. 28:20). His commission is to "go into all the world and preach the good news to all creation" (Mark 16:15), making "disciples of all nations, baptizing them in the name of the Father and of the Son and of the Holy Spirit, and teaching them to obey everything I have commanded you" (Matt. 28:19).

WE ARE EMPOWERED AND GUIDED BY THE HOLY SPIRIT.

On one occasion, after his resurrection and just before his ascension, while Jesus and his apostles were eating together, he instructed them not to leave Jerusalem, but to wait a few days until they were baptized with the Holy Spirit. He told them that they would receive power when the Holy Spirit came on them and would be his "witnesses in Jerusalem, and in all Judea and Samaria, and to the ends of the earth" (Acts 1:4–8). The coming of the Holy Spirit happened on the day of Pentecost: "[The disciples, women who were following him, Jesus's mother and brothers] were all together in one place. Suddenly a sound like the blowing of a violent wind came from heaven and filled the whole house where they were sitting. They saw what seemed to be tongues of fire that separated and came to rest on each of them. All of them were filled with the Holy Spirit and began to speak with other tongues as the Spirit enabled them" (Acts 2:1–4).

Other direct interventions of the Holy Spirit have been recorded in the book of Acts, especially at points of transition or when special guidance was needed. Among these are Philip's encounter with the Ethiopian eunuch (Acts 8:26–40), the Holy Spirit's coming on those who heard Peter's message in Cornelius's home (Acts 10), his direction in the selection and sending of Barnabas and Paul on their missionary journey (Acts 13:1–4), and his intervention in Paul's plans to preach in Asia, redirecting him and his followers to Macedonia instead (Acts 16:6–10). The Holy Spirit continues to be actively involved in our decision-making processes, offering guidance, direction, and peace as we seek God's will.

We are called to embrace a global vision.

God loves the whole world (John 3:16). We are called to disciple all nations (Matt. 28:19), go into all the world and preach the gospel to all creation (Mark 16:15), and be witnesses in Jerusalem, Judea, and Samaria, and to the ends of the earth (Acts 1:8). Today these concentric circles of outreach have multiplied and become globalized. The gospel is being spread from all nations to all nations. Sending and receiving countries are becoming increasingly harder to distinguish from each other. But there are still frontiers where people have not yet heard the gospel. Where churches exist, needs for discipling and renewal are all around us. And in a world plagued by poverty, epidemics, natural disasters, political upheavals, terrorism, and wars, our social responsibility becomes overwhelming.

We are committed to engage in holistic ministry.

Nouwen (1995, 85–87) sees ministry as growing out of solitude and community and being expressed through the disciplines of gratitude and compassion. Through ministry, we learn to be grateful to God in the midst of pain and suffering, and to be filled with compassion for the poor and the oppressed when surrounded by a world in need. Without this spiritual core our efforts to fulfill the Great Commission will turn into empty activism. Ministry must grow out of our love for God and our love for our neighbor.

This kind of commitment allows the Great Commandment to become the foundation for the Great Commission. Combining a love for God with all our heart, soul, mind, and strength with a love for our neighbor as ourselves will lead us toward holistic ministry. We will proclaim Christ through our preaching and teaching and practice his presence through love and compassion. The Great Commission and the Great Commandment, Christian proclamation and Christian presence, and evangelism and social responsibility will go hand in hand (McKnight 2004).

The Consultation on the Relationship between Evangelism and Social Responsibility in Grand Rapids, Michigan, in June 1982 recognized this holistic integration clearly, identifying three kinds of relationships between evangelism and social responsibility: social responsibility can create a bridge to evangelism, be a partner to evangelism, or be a result or consequence of evangelism. The delegates concluded that "[s]eldom if ever should we have to choose between satisfying physical hunger and spiritual hunger, or between healing bodies or saving souls, since authentic love for our neighbor will lead us to serve him or her as a whole person" (Grand Rapids Report 1982, 14).

Stretching and Growing

Spiritual disciplines transform our lives as we worship God, get to know him better, and learn to love him more. We must keep stretching and growing for this to occur. Many things can get in the way. We can let busyness or poor time management crowd out our time for solitude. Conflicts, disappointments, anxieties about major decisions, or feelings of guilt can also make us less eager for times alone with God. When we are going through experiences like these, we need to remember that our loving Father is eager to welcome us home, put his arms around us, and talk to us.

Something else that can get in the way of our practice of spiritual disciplines is routine. It is easy to let our times of solitude, or even our practice of community and ministry, degenerate into a pattern that we follow in exactly the same way day after day. When this happens, the practice of spiritual disciplines is no longer something we look forward to. It can become a duty or even feel like drudgery at times.

God wants our times of solitude, our lives in community, and our ministries in the world to be creative, joyful experiences of knowing him better and loving him more. Some people have found that exploring other traditions of spirituality and extending beyond our own cultural boundaries have brought new vitality to their spiritual life.

Exploring Other Streams of Spirituality

No single approach to spirituality can incorporate all that God is doing and wants to do in the lives of believers and in the life of his church. Our spiritual lives will become more mature and balanced as we incorporate practices from other streams of faith. Even while we remain faithful to our own spiritual roots, we must not allow spiritual formation within our lives and communities to be stifled and stilted by trying to put God in a box. Our knowledge of God and our love for him will be deepened as we explore other practices of spirituality.

Reading Richard J. Foster's *Streams of Living Water* (1998) is a good place to begin this journey. He introduces six "streams" of faith and practice that define Christian tradition and comprise our foundation of belief. The contemplative stream focuses on the prayer-filled life within a context of solitude, quietness, and meditation. The holiness stream emphasizes the virtuous life as we allow Christ to keep cleansing, transforming, and sanctifying us. There is also the charismatic stream, which encourages a Spirit-empowered life characterized by ecstatic worship and the exercise of spiritual gifts in our witness and service. The social justice stream flows out of personal compassion and integrity, which thrusts us into social, institutional, and cultural action. The evangelical

---

SIDEBAR 4.5
TWO IMPORTANT WEB SITES

If you want to explore issues involved in spiritual formation more deeply and broadly than we have been able to in this chapter, log on to these sites. They offer complementary perspectives and a wealth of resources to help you keep stretching and growing.

Renovaré (www.renovare.org) is committed to working for the renewal of the church of Jesus Christ through a balanced vision of the spiritual life growing out of all its multifaceted expressions. It is international in scope and ecumenical in breadth.

The Spiritual Formation Forum (www .spiritualformationforum.org) sponsors discussion forums, articulates models of spiritual formation, provides training opportunities for ministry leaders, and encourages them to implement appropriate models in their spheres of ministry.

---

stream has a Word-centered focus on the study and proclamation of the Scriptures, which calls hearers to personal conversion and commitment. Finally, there is the incarnational stream, which celebrates the sacramental relationship between the spiritual and the material in both corporate worship and our everyday lives. Your love for Christ, others around you, and a world that needs him will be deepened and broadened as you allow these streams of faith and practice to enter your life.

EXTENDING BEYOND CULTURAL BOUNDARIES

When you live and work in other cultural contexts, you will certainly encounter different concerns and approaches to spirituality that will enrich your love for God and your walk with him. As you share your own spiritual experiences within the global family of Christ, the lives of those in other cultures will be enriched by your experiences as well.

Some specific things can be learned from the global family of Christ (Taylor 2001). From Asia we can learn spiritual depth, discipline, and respect for our elders and ancestors. From Latin America and much of the Caribbean, we can learn enthusiasm, passion, and creativity. From Africa we can learn people-centered, warm, and dramatic worship; deeply expressive music; spontaneity and exuberance; and cultural adaptability. From the Middle East, we can learn to understand what it means to be a steadfast and faithful witness in the midst of war, hatred, and violence. From Russia and Eastern Europe, we can learn to appreciate historical continuity and a theology of martyrdom. All around our turbulent globe, we can learn what it means to be faithful witnesses in the midst of crises and suffering. This theme will be developed in chapter 15.

SUMMARY

Spiritual formation begins with individuals and culminates in a global celebration before the throne of God. It is easy to miss the full impact of this global celebration if we focus only on the multitude and fail to see the individual persons who are there. They are wearing robes washed white in the blood of the Lamb and waving palm branches. Their voices are celebrating God's salvation. They are serving him day and night in his temple. They are sheltered in his tent. Their hunger, thirst, and tears are gone. Their earthly anguish and suffering in the midst of tribulation was God's instrument of salvation and sanctification that has prepared them to worship and glorify him forever (Rev. 7:9–17).

This is what spiritual formation is all about. It grows out of *missio Dei*, what God is doing in the world through his church and through the lives of individuals as he prepares each of us to love and serve him forever before his throne (McKinney Douglas 2006, 276).

5

Personal Readiness

Women most suited for work in Calabar are "consecrated, affectionate women who are not afraid of work or of filth of any kind, moral or material. Women who can nurse a baby or teach a child to wash and comb, as well as to read and write; women who can tactfully smooth over a roughness and for Christ's sake bear a snub, and take any place which may be open. Women who can take everything to Jesus and there get strength to smile and persevere, and pull on under any circumstances. If they can play Beethoven and paint and draw and speak French and German, so much the better, but we can want all these latter accomplishments if they have only a loving heart, willing hands, and common sense. Surely such women are not out of our reach."

Mary Slessor (1848–1915) (Livingstone 1916, 135)

The moment has finally arrived. You may have been dreaming of becoming a missionary for a long time, perhaps even since you were a child. You have already shipped several boxes of books and personal items ahead of you to your overseas destination and are packing suitcases to take on your flight.

As you look at the piles of clothes, toiletries, keepsakes, documents, books, and papers stacked all over the room, you may be tempted to throw them out the window. Or, less drastically, you may wish you could bypass the sorting process by scooping up armloads of your belongings, cramming them into suitcases, and sitting on them to make them close. But you know it is not that easy. Important decisions must be made. So you start by sorting out the things you will need on the flight, making sure that necessary documents and valuable items will be taken on board. Once your carry-ons are ready, you begin filling the suitcases that will accompany you. It does not take long before you realize that you are trying to take far too many bags along and that they weigh far too much. You will need to get rid of the excess baggage.

Packing bags provides a good metaphor as we look at issues related to personal readiness for missions. Throughout your life, God has been helping you to develop attitudes, values, traits, and skills that can become important intercultural competencies. These are valuable; you will want to take them with you in your "carry-ons." But you may also be weighted down with "excess baggage" that will make it difficult for you to adapt to another culture, develop healthy relationships, and engage in effective ministry with people who are different from yourself. You will need to lighten the load before you travel.

Our purpose in this chapter is to help you to keep cultivating the intercultural competencies God has given you as you get ready for the missions assignment that lies ahead. It will also encourage you to recognize and deal with issues that may become excess baggage on your overseas journey.

THE "CARRY-ON" LIST: WHAT DO YOU WANT TO TAKE WITH YOU?

"Of the making of books there is no end." This well-known quote from Ecclesiastes 12:12 could be applied to descriptions of intercultural competencies as well. Hundreds of lists and scores of scales have been developed by international businesses, government agencies, and nongovernment organizations. The global missions movement has also been concerned with intercultural competencies. Sending churches, mission agencies, and host churches often prepare lists of the qualifications they are seeking in missionaries. Even the apostle Paul filled his letters with descriptions of traits, attitudes, knowledge, and skills that the Lord's servants need.

Many academic textbooks and reference works provide descriptions, lists, and scales to aid in the assessment of intercultural competencies. Three helpful examples of these efforts are Carley H. Dodd's textbook, *Dynamics of Intercultural Communication* (1998), L. Robert Kohls's *Survival Kit for Overseas Living* (2001), and Sherwood Lingenfelter and Marvin Mayers's *Ministering Cross-Culturally* (2003). Dodd includes scales

---

SIDEBAR 5.1
TIMOTHY, MY SON . . .

The apostle Paul's two letters to Timothy are packed with instructions about preaching the Word (2 Tim. 4:2), confronting false doctrine (1 Tim. 1:3–4), and handling a broad range of church issues including worship (1 Tim. 2), the roles of overseers and deacons (1 Tim. 3), and advice related to widows, elders, and slaves (1 Tim. 5:1–6:2).

But Paul's concerns do not end with Timothy's ministry. As the following texts illustrate, they extend to a special interest in him as a person.

- "Timothy, my son, I give you this instruction in keeping with the prophecies once made about you, so that by following them you may fight the good fight, holding on to faith and a good conscience" (1 Tim. 1:18–19).

- "Don't let anyone look down on you because you are young, but set an example for the believers in speech, in life, in love, in faith and in purity" (1 Tim. 4:12).

- "But you, man of God, flee from all this [false doctrine, quarreling,

and a love for money] and pursue righteousness, godliness, faith, love, endurance and gentleness" (1 Tim. 6:11–12).

- "You then, my son, be strong in the grace that is in Christ Jesus. . . . Endure hardship with us like a good soldier of Jesus Christ" (2 Tim. 2:1–3).

- "Flee the evil desires of youth, and pursue righteousness, faith, love and peace, along with those who call on the Lord out of a pure heart" (2 Tim. 2:22).

REFLECTION AND DISCUSSION

1. What traits, attitudes, values, and skills is Paul asking Timothy to take with him?

2. What does he want him to leave behind?

3. Which of these do you especially want to take with you on your mission assignment?

4. What "excess baggage" do you want to leave behind?

---

for assessing personal communication worldview (103–4), perceived homophily (216), monochronic-polychronic time orientation, ethnocentrism, interpersonal comfort, self-confidence, dogmatism, and rigidity (264–72). Kohls lists sixteen skills he considers important (tolerance for ambiguity, low goal/task orientation, open-mindedness, nonjudgmentalness, empathy, communicativeness, adaptability, curiosity, sense of humor, warmth in human relationships, motivation, self-reliance, strong sense of self, tolerance for differences, perceptiveness, and ability to fail) (110). Of these, he believes *the* most important are a sense of humor, low goal/task orientation, and an ability to fail. Lingenfelter and Mayers focus on conflicting values that create tensions in relation to values, time, judgment, handling crises, goals, self-worth, and vulnerability. They include a basic values questionnaire (29–35).

87

PREDICTORS OF INTERCULTURAL EFFECTIVENESS

Muriel I. Elmer (1986) analyzed research related to intercultural effectiveness. Several predictive indicators were uncovered. These became the foundation for the development of the Intercultural Competency Scale, which assesses twelve competency factors through a forty-item instrument (M. I. Elmer 1988). The predictive indicators that Elmer identified through her literature review provide an outline for this section of our chapter.

Accepting People Who Are Different (Tolerance)

Shortly after a couple arrived in a European country, cleared customs, and received warm greetings from their expatriate missionary colleagues, one of the men on the team suggested going out for dinner. His wife protested, "You are not going to make them eat in a local restaurant their first night here!"

A missionary who grew up in a bilingual, bicultural community on the Mexican border still remembers the day she came home late from school. Her grandmother asked where she had been. She said she had been playing in a Mexican friend's home. Her grandmother panicked, pulled her into the bathroom, checked her hair for lice while she ran bathwater into the tub, and scolded, "Don't you ever go inside a Mexican home again!"

Incidents like these are not the rule, but unfortunately they are not the exception either. Missionaries are not exempt from stereotyping, prejudice, ethnocentrism, and judgmental attitudes. Sometimes they may have been raised in homes where they experienced harsh punishment, love was dependent on "good" behavior, and there was rigid moral education, status-based relationships, negative stereotyping of out-groups, and a hierarchy of authority in the family. These factors can combine to create an adult who demonstrates what some have called an "authoritarian personality" (Adorno et al. 1982). These people are unquestioningly submissive to authority, legalistic and rigid in their behavior, closed and tight in their belief system, and prone to reject out-groups. Attitudes like these must be transformed into tolerance, openness, and freedom from prejudice if the missionary is to be effective (Brislin 1981, 55–56).

Responding to People and Their Needs (Sensitivity)

Sensitive people are empathetic. They are able to perceive people's feelings and understand situations from other people's points of view. They treat others in ways that make them feel valued and important. They pay attention to what others are saying and understand what is

SIDEBAR 5.2
INTERCULTURAL COMPETENCY

Below we present predictive indicators and descriptions of factors related to intercultural competency. Read these carefully and then rate yourself (using a scale of 1 to 5; 5 is high) on each item.

PREDICTORS OF INTERCULTURAL COMPETENCY

Adapted with permission from Muriel Elmer (1988)

An analysis of the literature reviews in Elmer (1988) revealed that several predictive indicators of intercultural effectiveness have been identified in precedent research studies.

- *Tolerance:* The inclination to be accepting of people who are different and situations that are ambiguous.
- *Sensitivity:* The tendency to be responsive to people and their needs.
- *Security:* A self-confidence that is expressed in various behaviors that strengthen relationships with others.
- *Flexible Perspective:* Cognitive skills that expand understanding and develop insight into experience.
- *Enterprise:* The disposition to attempt the difficult or untried venture.

THE INTERCULTURAL COMPETENCY SCALE: A DESCRIPTION OF THE FACTORS (FORM E)

M. I. Elmer 1988 (used with permission)

- *Approachable:* Establishes contact with others easily.
- *Intercultural Receptivity:* Interested in people, especially people from other cultures.

- *Positive Orientation:* Expects that one can be a success living and working in another culture.
- *Forthrightness:* Acts and speaks out readily.
- *Social Openness:* Inclined to interact with people regardless of their differences.
- *Enterprise:* Tends to approach tasks and activities in new and creative ways.
- *Shows Respect:* Treats others in ways that make them feel valued.
- *Perseverance:* Tends to remain in a situation and feel positive about it even in the face of some difficulties.
- *Flexibility:* Open to cultural learning.
- *Cultural Perspectivism:* Able to imaginatively enter into another cultural viewpoint.
- *Venturesome:* Inclined toward that which is novel or different.
- *Social Confidence:* Tends to be self-assured.

REFLECTION AND DISCUSSION

When you have finished your self-rating, take some time for thoughtful and prayerful reflection:

1. What have I learned from this self-assessment about my personal strengths?
2. What have I learned about my personal weaknesses?
3. What can I do now to keep these weaknesses from becoming "excess baggage" when I cross cultures?
4. What can I do to keep growing in strong areas, so that they can become even more useful "carry-on" items?

89

being said. They enjoy learning about groups of people who differ from themselves in their beliefs, values, and customs. They like being with others and make friends easily (M. I. Elmer 1986, 159–60).

These relational skills are important in interpersonal and intercultural communication. Some of us tend to be self-centered. We enjoy doing all the talking and may be so wrapped up in ourselves that we are clueless about what others are thinking and feeling. At the other extreme, we may tend to be shy and withdrawn, finding it hard to bridge culture gaps and feeling awkward in relating to people who are different from us. Communication patterns like these are learned early in childhood and can be difficult to change. But with awareness, prayerfulness, help from friends and counselors, and a desire to keep growing, these self-centered or shy traits may be transformed into gifts that God can use as we cross cultures.

Expressing Self-Confidence (Security)

Self-confidence grows out of a strong sense of who we are. It helps us to accept challenges, handle crises, be courageous and frank, and accept ourselves as worthwhile, capable human beings. We will take the initiative in starting discussions, tackling problems, and making contact with others. We can express what we are really thinking and feeling and face opposition to our ideas and actions without exploding in anger. As we look forward to an overseas experience, we expect that, even in the middle of difficult adjustments, it will be enjoyable (M. I. Elmer 1986, 161–62).

Once again, childhood experiences can make a difference. A retired missionary still remembers her father with gratitude. While she was growing up, girls still faced quite limited career options. They were expected to become secretaries, nurses, or elementary schoolteachers. But her father had higher aspirations. Over and over, he told her, "You've got what it takes. You can do anything. You can even be a doctor or a lawyer." He often reinforced his affirmation by telling stories like the one about a mountain climber who got caught in a storm, ran out of food, and could hardly keep from sliding back down the steep, rocky slope. But—in spite of all the obstacles—he kept on going and made it to the peak. His daughter didn't become a lawyer, but she did become a missionary!

Even if your earthly father was not this affirming, your heavenly Father is. He wants you to run life's race well. You do not need to be weighted down and held back by a negative self-image. He will often bring friends, family, small groups, professors, pastors, or counselors into your life to help you to keep growing and changing as you look toward intercultural ministry (Heb. 12:1–2).

90

Expanding Understanding and Developing Insight (Flexible Perspective)

To live cross-culturally is to live in the midst of intellectual challenges. You are sure to be confronted with different ideas and beliefs. You may have studied world religions and feel that you can dialogue with a Muslim, a Hindu, or a Chinese person, and still not be ready to handle the challenges of day-after-day encounters with people whose beliefs are different from yours. You may not know how to respond when a Muslim taxi driver angrily talks about Christians and Jews killing his people while he is driving you home. After you have shared Jesus's promise of eternal life with a Hindu, you may be taken aback by his reaction to what you have just said: "Eternal life! That's the last thing I want. I'm sick and tired of being reincarnated over and over again." Or, after you have shared the many changes Christ has brought in your life with a Chinese friend, you may be frustrated by his culturally attuned response: "If Jesus brings good luck to your life, maybe I can worship him and he will bring me good luck and prosperity too."

A flexible perspective allows us to view the expressed beliefs of others as valid even when they differ from our own. We enjoy working out alternative answers to new questions. We can see similarities in divergent pieces of data. We are curious about what is going on around us. We tend to notice things that are not obvious and other people often overlook (M. I. Elmer 1986, 162–64).

Some missionaries have experienced upbringings in which ideas are either right or wrong and categories are narrow. Flexible perspectives will often be difficult for them to acquire. But if they are concerned about intercultural effectiveness, they will need to develop problem-solving, inquiry, and observational skills that will embark them on a lifetime journey toward ever-expanding understandings and insights. Intellectually rigid missionaries can make both themselves and the nationals and missionaries they interact with miserable. Developing flexible perspectives can be challenging, transforming, and stimulating, not only for us but also for the communities in which we are involved.

Attempting the Difficult or the Untried (Enterprise)

The history of modern missions has been punctuated by the stories of venturesome, enterprising missionaries. Among these are William Carey, J. Hudson Taylor, and Charlotte "Lottie" Diggs Moon, who have already been introduced in chapter 1. William Carey challenged the church at the end of the eighteenth century to a radical reassessment of its role in world evangelization, discarding the idea that missions stopped with the apostles and affirming a continuing role for the church on a global

91

scale and in every generation. The Bible translation, evangelism, church planting, education, and medical and relief strategies that he developed during his forty-one years as a missionary in India became a basic model for missions around the world and across two centuries.

Half a century later, J. Hudson Taylor shattered traditional Protestant missionary precedents by adopting a cross-cultural lifestyle to the point of wearing Chinese clothes, shaving his head, and dying his sandy pigtail black. He founded the China Inland Mission (now Overseas Missionary Fellowship), which departed radically from the practices of other missions. All the missionaries were to live "by faith," with no solicitation of funds. Missionaries with blue-collar backgrounds and without formal education were welcomed.

Still later, as the nineteenth century bridged into the twentieth, Charlotte "Lottie" Diggs Moon was a Southern Baptist missionary in China. Her mother's model of independence and a strong will rubbed off on her and was evident throughout her ministry. She quickly tired of her initial assignment (teaching children) and found herself embroiled in issues related to equality in policy making and ministry opportunities for women. She used the power of the pen to challenge mission tradition, recruit new workers, and solicit funds.

Even though our own stories are unlikely to become a part of missions folklore, our disposition to attempt something difficult or get involved in an untried venture is still part of an effective missionary's profile. It is important that we persist in undertakings, even when there is difficulty and opposition. We will need to be able to switch leader/follower and teacher/learner roles easily, change the ways we speak and act as the situation around us requires it, and enjoy doing things differently in order to keep learning and growing. We will intentionally build relationships with people who are different from ourselves, both in their values and their lifestyles (M. I. Elmer 1986, 164–65).

Some people are persevering, adaptable, experimental, and enterprising by nature. Others are more cautious. We may tend to give up easily, hesitate to challenge the status quo, or be afraid to risk relationships with those who are very different from ourselves. Even when we feel weak and afraid, we can claim God's promise that

> Those who hope in the LORD
> will renew their strength.
> They will soar on wings like eagles;
> they will run and not grow weary,
> they will walk and not be faint.

> Isaiah 40:31

SIDEBAR 5.3
AN EAGLET NAMED VICTOR

Lois McKinney Douglas

A newly hatched eaglet was snuggling in his nest in the cleft of a rock, high in a rocky mountain range. His mother and father had dreamed of a son who would become strong and courageous and learn to soar majestically in the sky. So they named their newborn "Victor."

At first, Victor was brave and adventurous. Every day he flew a little higher. But, little by little, he started becoming afraid of heights and feeling tired when he spent long periods of time in the air. Things kept getting worse until, finally, he refused to leave his nest. His mother and father did all they could to help their son, but to no avail. Victor had been overcome by fear.

There were frequent earthquakes in the region. One day, while the rest of the family was soaring high in the sky and Victor was alone in his nest, a strong shock made the mountains tremble. A landslide rolled into the cleft where Victor was perched and buried him under rocks, dirt, and debris. Alone and terrified, he began to cry out to his father with a muffled eagle call.

His father, who loved Victor, was already close by. He heard his son's cry and flew quickly to the rubble where he was buried. With strong talons, he dug through the rocks and dirt until he reached his son and gently lifted him out of the nest. Then he covered Victor with his wings and flew him to safety on the mountains' highest peak. It was not long until the little eaglet's soul was restored, and he began to fly again—this time "Victor-iously" with the strength, courage, faith, and hope that came through that salvific encounter and the continued presence of his Father.

- I carried you on eagles' wings and brought you to myself (Exod. 19:4).
- Hide me in the shadow of your wings (Ps. 17:8).
- He will cover you with his feathers, and under his wings you will find refuge (Ps. 91:4).
- Those who hope in the LORD will renew their strength. They will soar on wings like eagles; they will run and not be weary, they will walk and not be faint (Isa. 40:31).

EXCESS BAGGAGE: WHAT DO YOU WANT TO LEAVE BEHIND?

The taxi Lois was expecting did not arrive. By the time she was able to arrange for another one and the driver had fought his way through heavy traffic to Chicago's busy O'Hare Airport, she had only two hours left before her flight back to Brazil. She was loaded down with three large suitcases and a carry-on crammed full of things she wanted to take back with her. Her frustration mounted as she nudged her way through crowds of people both inside and outside the terminal to find a luggage cart. None was to be found. Nor were baggage attendants anywhere to be seen. Rumors were flying that things were stalled because security was on high alert. And there was Lois in the midst of it all with four bags and only two arms to pull them. The moral of this story is clear: When you are going on a long trip, try to avoid excess baggage.

By the time you reach this point in the chapter, and especially as you analyze the case studies below, you probably recognize some of your own attitudes, values, and traits that could become excess baggage when you cross cultures. You may even feel discouraged and wonder if you have what it takes to become a missionary. There is good news for you. Your load can be lightened, and even transformed, through self-evaluation, help from others, and help from God.

CASE STUDIES: EXCESS BAGGAGE

Lois McKinney Douglas

The case studies below tell true stories of missionaries who took "excess baggage" to the field with them. As you read each case, try to answer the following questions:

1. What kinds of attitudes, values, traits, and skills did these missionaries take along with them that got in the way?
2. What kinds of experiences in their backgrounds might have created this kind of unwanted baggage?
3. What could they have done before they crossed cultures to help prevent these sad experiences from happening?

CASE 1. "BUT, PROFESSOR . . ."

After years of preparation and eager anticipation, a missionary from North America arrived in his host country. He spent a short time in language school and then began teaching Christian education in a seminary. He held a doctorate in religious education from a prestigious theological school and was eager to pass on his knowledge to the students.

The experience quickly turned into a disaster. His language acquisition was so poor that students struggled to understand him. Even worse, his only goal seemed to be to import religious education models from the United States. Almost from the first class, the students began to challenge him: "But, Professor, what you are teaching will not work in our churches. Here we do things differently." The missionary became hostile and defensive. He had spent ten intensive years developing competence in his field. And these students, most of whom were taking their very first education course, were

Self-Evaluation

There are a variety of tools for self-evaluation. Three we suggest are assessing your strengths and weaknesses, becoming aware of your basic values, and keeping a journal.

ASSESSING YOUR STRENGTHS AND WEAKNESSES

The Predictors of Intercultural Competency and the factors in the Intercultural Competency Scale (see sidebar 5.2), together with other similar lists and instruments, can help you assess your strengths and weaknesses and develop strategies for personal growth.

BECOMING AWARE OF YOUR BASIC VALUES

Many of the stresses and conflicts in cross-cultural living grow out of the tensions created by differences in basic values. Lingenfelter and Mayers (2003) describe several of these. Remember that these values

---

confronting him in class! The situation went from bad to worse, and at the end of the term the host-culture director of the seminary dismissed him from his teaching role.

CASE 2. REAL WINE

When a couple arrived in France for language study on their way to a French-speaking African country, they looked forward to attending their first worship service with French believers. They visited the church on communion Sunday. How beautiful it would be to celebrate the Lord's Supper with believers from another culture. But the shock came when they received the cup. It held real wine! They had both made firm commitments never to touch alcoholic beverages. Taking even a sip of wine in a communion service violated their convictions. They solved their problem by staying away from church services on communion Sundays for the remainder of their time in France.

CASE 3. HERESY

A missionary couple arrived on the field eager to begin planting churches in their adopted culture. They developed language fluency extremely quickly and were soon in the midst of their ministry. All went well until they discovered that virtually all the national pastors and leaders in the denomination they were working with embraced amillennialism. To the couple, this was gross heresy. The same denomination in their home country was premillennial, and they personally held a strong premillennial position. It wasn't long until they had resigned from their sending mission and decided to stay in the country to combat heresy through their own church planting movement. Needless to say, this created confusion, misunderstanding, and division within the national churches that were affected.

represent composite cultural norms. We must be careful not to apply them stereotypically to everyone we relate to within a culture. Even as we are looking for predictable patterns, we must recognize and respect individual differences.

Some cultures are time oriented. Time is a commodity to be spent wisely through punctuality, tight schedules, and goal-directed activities. Other cultures are event oriented. The emphasis is on enjoying the present experience, regardless of the time involved (Lingenfelter and Mayers 2003, 41).

There are also tensions related to judgment. Some cultures tend toward dichotomistic thinking, in which judgments are black or white, right or wrong, and there are clear and systematic categories for organizing society, information, and experience. In other cultures, judgments are open-ended and thinking is holistic. There is security in multiple interactions with the whole of society, rather than within confined roles and categories (Lingenfelter and Mayers 2003, 54).

Ways of managing crises can also create tension. Cultures with a crisis orientation anticipate crises, emphasize planning, and seek quick resolutions to problems. Noncrisis cultures downplay the possibility of crises and avoid taking action ahead of time (Lingenfelter and Mayers 2003, 71).

Collisions between task orientation and person orientation can also create tension. Task-oriented cultures focus on tasks and principles and find satisfaction in achieving goals. Person-oriented cultures focus on relationships and social interaction (Lingenfelter and Mayers 2003, 80).

Status and achievement focuses can affect cross-cultural encounters. In status-focused cultures, personal identity is ascribed by formal credentials of birth and rank. In achievement-focused cultures, the amount of respect one receives varies with personal performance (Lingenfelter and Mayers 2003, 95).

Finally, cultural tensions may be felt in regard to vulnerability. Some cultures encourage the concealment of vulnerability, protecting one's self-image at all costs and avoiding error or failure. Other cultures are willing to expose vulnerability. People are open to criticism and willing to talk freely about their personal lives (Lingenfelter and Mayers 2003, 104).

Here is an exercise that can help you identify possible tensions and conflicts in your own intercultural relationships. First, describe your own values in relation to each of the six dimensions of tension described above. Then, in each of these areas, describe how you respond (or believe you would respond) when you encounter people whose values are different from your own. Strong negative feelings and reactions are "excess baggage" that can get in the way when you try to cross cultures.

SIDEBAR 5.4
THINGS TO INCLUDE IN A JOURNAL

If you choose to keep a journal as part of the process of self-evaluation, here is a helpful list of things to reflect on in your journal entries.

- *What happened?* Describe the social situation, the people involved, the activities, and the conversation as fully as you can.

- *What did you feel?* Try to recognize and identify your feelings.

- *What made you feel the way you did?* Focus on the emotional content of the situation.

- *How did you respond?* An angry outburst? Crying? Withdrawing? In some other way?

- Can you think of other recent occasions when you responded in a similar way?

- Can you recall childhood experiences that followed the same pattern?

- *How did the other person(s) who were involved respond to the incident?* Why do you think they responded as they did? (If possible, check your perceptions with the other person(s). You may be surprised by how differently they interpreted what was happening.)

- In what ways do you want to change and grow?

- What can you do to change and grow?

If you would like to study cultural values in greater depth, take time to read Lingenfelter and Mayers (2003). Beyond the wealth of information this book offers, it also provides a basic values questionnaire that will help you identify and analyze your own values and develop your personal values profile (29–35).

KEEPING A JOURNAL

It can be helpful to keep a journal of relational incidents and conflicts that cause you to feel angry, hurt, inadequate, helpless, alone, misunderstood, or ashamed. Try to analyze them and learn from them. See sidebar 5.4 for things to include in the journal.

Help from Others

While you are assessing your strengths and weaknesses, becoming more aware of your basic values, and beginning to keep a journal, you may find yourself wanting to share what is happening with others. Good! It is not healthy to try to process such deep issues by yourself. God has created us to live in community. He wants us to seek out others when we need help and to reciprocate by helping others when they need us.

97

SIDEBAR 5.5
"HE MUST WIN THE BATTLE"

Martin Luther (1483--1546)

If you have not already memorized these words from Martin Luther's great hymn, take time to do so now. Then keep singing them in your heart in the midst of your spiritual battles, especially when you feel weak and afraid.

Did we in our own strength confide,
Our striving would be losing,

Were not the right man on our side,
The man of God's own choosing.
Dost ask who that may be?
Christ Jesus, it is He—
Lord Sabaoth His name,
From age to age the same,
And He must win the battle.

This help can come from trusted friends, family members, support groups, professors, school counselors, pastors, or other people who are part of your relational network. If the issues you are working on are deep and persistent, you may want to enlist professional help. People within your relational network may be able to assist you in finding the right person. Mission agencies you are in touch with may be helpful. The American Association of Christian Counselors (www.aacc.net) can provide access to counselors in your geographical area through their Christian Care Network. Before you commit yourself to counseling sessions, make sure the person you choose is a licensed clinical professional counselor (LCPC), a licensed clinical social worker (LCSW), or has other similar credentials. It is also important that he or she has experience in working with cross-cultural issues.

Help from God

Recognizing our weaknesses and working on areas in which we need to grow can be tiring and discouraging at times. This is not surprising. We are in the middle of a spiritual battle. It cannot be won through our own energy and strength. But as Martin Luther reminded us in his great Reformation hymn, we are not alone. The right Man, the Lord "Sabaoth" (the Lord who is ruler over all!), is on our side. He must (and will!) win the battle (see sidebar 5.5).

As we allow the Lord to rule our lives, the attitudes, values, traits, and skills he has given us for our cross-cultural journey will become even more bountiful. And something else will happen. There—hidden among the personal strengths we have recognized for a long time—we will discover weaknesses that God has been transforming into new strengths.

They have become added treasures of his love and grace to take with us on our sojourn.

THE CHECKPOINTS: HOW ARE MISSIONARIES SELECTED?

Once again, our travel metaphor provides legitimate comparisons. The steps in the missionary selection process can sometimes seem every bit as complicated (and even annoying) as the airport checkpoints where suitcases are x-rayed, documents examined, and security screening takes place. But like most metaphors, this one soon breaks down. The impersonal agents at the airport are interested only in security screening. Those involved in the missionary selection process care about you as a person. They want what is best for you, for the churches and agencies that will be sending you, and for the churches and teams you will be working with on your overseas assignment.

What are some of these checkpoints? The first checkpoint is initiated by you. It involves your own information gathering, decision making, prayer, and care in your selection of the organization or mission agency with which you would like to serve.

When your personal decision has been made, and you have contacted the agency of your choice, the next checkpoint has been reached. It is the mission's turn to select you. This process usually involves checking references, administering psychological tests, conducting personal interviews, and perhaps arranging for extended opportunities for interaction with you through activities such as candidate schools, orientation seminars, or short-term assignments.

The selection process is still not over. At least two more checkpoints lie ahead. First, you will want and need the affirmation of churches and individuals who will be praying for you and supporting your ministry. Second, you will probably be exchanging e-mails with the expatriate team and national ministry leaders with whom you will be working and may even visit them on the field. These contacts with those who will be sending you on your way and those who will be receiving you when you begin your new assignment can help affirm God's leading in your life.

Even after explanations and reassurances, the process of going through so many checkpoints may still seem unnecessarily long and complex. It *is* complicated, but it is also extremely important. The red lights, caution lights, and green lights that flash as checkpoints are passed are important indicators of decisions that must be made.

Red Lights

It would be unfair to prospective missionaries, and others who have a stake in their selection, to allow them to pass through checkpoints while red lights are flashing and loud alarms are going off. Their appointment could have disastrous results for both them and the institutions and ministries that are involved. Mission agencies will help these people to redirect their interests and goals. As painful and disappointing as this process may be at the time, many potential missionaries who saw red lights flashing ahead of them are later able to see God's providence in the decisions that were made. They learn to thank him for his love and protection in taking them on a different journey.

Yellow Lights

Passing through checkpoints may also turn on yellow lights. When this happens, prospective missionaries are usually told that their long-term prospects for effective intercultural ministry are good. The mission continues to be interested in exploring a future relationship with them. However, the decision to accept them has been postponed to allow them more opportunities to grow and mature in their spiritual, personal, and ministry readiness. If you find yourself in this situation, do not allow it to fuel resentment. Even delays and setbacks can be used for God's glory.

Green Lights

We have saved the best news for last. Most of the time your years of preparation and anticipation of a missions career are affirmed by bright green lights. Acceptance by the sending agency becomes a moment of fulfillment, and a long-awaited cross-cultural ministry begins. Another milestone in your life has been passed. To paraphrase the well-known hymn: God's amazing grace has brought you to this significant moment in your journey with him. He will continue to lead you and guide you throughout the rest of your life and then will lead you home.

SUMMARY

In this chapter we have taken you on a long journey toward your missionary appointment. We began with carry-on lists—the attitudes, values, traits, and skills you want to take with you, especially focusing on Muriel Elmer's (1988) predictors of intercultural competency. Then we gave some examples of the excess baggage you will want to leave behind and encouraged you to recognize some of your own excess baggage by assessing your strengths and weaknesses, becoming aware of your basic values, and keeping a journal. We encouraged you to get help from others while you are processing these deep issues and to open your heart to help from God.

In the last section, we continued our travel metaphor as we guided you through the complex steps of the missionary selection process and on toward the fulfilling moment when you are appointed by a missions agency and your missions journey gets underway. Your travels are just beginning! You will be packing and unpacking your bags many times during your missionary career and repeatedly making decisions about what to take with you and what to leave behind. Your personal and spiritual journey will also continue, as you keep on learning, growing, and maturing. Our prayer is that when your travels end, you will be able to echo the words Paul wrote to Timothy: "I have fought the good fight, I have finished the race, I have kept the faith" (2 Tim. 4:7) and share in his joyous expectation that "there is in store for me the crown of righteousness, which the Lord, the righteous Judge, will award me on that day" (2 Tim. 4:8).

6

Ministry Readiness

Experience is the hardest teacher because she gives the test first; the lesson after.

Author unknown ("Instant Wisdom" n.d.)

The greatest of all faults is to be conscious of none. Recognizing our limitations and imperfections is the first requisite of progress. Those who believe they have arrived believe they have nowhere to go.

Dale E. Turner ("Instant Wisdom" n.d.)

What do cross-cultural Christian workers need to know, do, and be so that effective, realistic, sustainable cross-cultural ministry can take place? It seems that everyone involved in providing cross-cultural training has his or her ideas about what constitutes quality preparation, what roles certain institutions should take in the process, and the time required to complete the training. Some consider two weeks sufficient, others require two years of Bible study, while still others will accept nothing less than a master of divinity (MDiv). Some believe that the local church(es) should provide all necessary training. A number rely on mission agencies or academic training institutions. Some focus on the acquisition of cognitive knowledge, while others prefer extensive hands-on experience to test commitment and character. Some focus entirely on pre-field training while others include on-field training. A growing number have added post-field training (during home assignment). This chapter will identify key areas that require preparation and suggest possible means to obtain them.

SETTING THE CONTEXT

The Edinburgh (1910) missions conference called for significant improvement in four areas of missionary preparation: the spiritual, the moral, the intellectual, and the physical. Agencies and institutions have attempted to address this concern primarily through training and educating. Those involved in training cross-cultural Christian workers for home or abroad tend to focus on specific contexts and to be more practical in nature. Those involved in educating tend to be more global in focus and more theory based.

Curricula used in training and educating vary from global to task specific. Some curriculum developers look around, see what others are teaching, and pick and paste together a curriculum that they feel best prepares people in a general way. Others believe that the tasks required of graduates should determine every curricular decision. They identify all the major tasks of the ministry in relation to what students should know, do, and be. From these tasks they identify the competencies, character, and commitment levels necessary to accomplish them. Once this is done, they create a profile of the type of person who can accomplish the tasks. From the profile they project backward to identify the curriculum necessary for specific ministry effectiveness (see Ferris 2000).

What is true for training and educating is also true for the selection of personnel (see Graham 1987). Some churches send anyone who believes that God has called him or her into cross-cultural ministry. Some mission agencies take every warm body that comes their way. Other churches and mission agencies are more selective about the type of personnel they desire. They take seriously their role in the stewardship of God's human and financial resources. Following the process noted above, they select and send those who match the profiles created for specific cross-cultural ministries at home and abroad. Within this approach, sidebar 6.1 provides a general profile for a cross-cultural church planter.

Whether for selection, training, or education, ministry-specific profiles bathed in prayer and supported by Scripture can aid everyone involved in the missionary preparation process—from selectors and those selected to trainers and trainees to educators and those educated.

103

SIDEBAR 6.1
CROSS-CULTURAL CHURCH PLANTER PROFILE

Hoke and Taylor (1999, 26--27)

Below is one profile of a cross-cultural church planter. As you consider the specific qualities, skills, and goals involved, brainstorm in a small group about the types of things that you would include in a curriculum that has the purpose of developing candidates into competent cross-cultural church planters.

CHARACTER QUALITIES	MINISTRY SKILLS	KNOWLEDGE GOALS
Spiritual maturity	Language learning	Foundational Bible
Family wholeness	Cultural adaptation/ contextualization	Ministry and missions
Single wholeness		Leadership and servanthood
Servant's heart	Evangelism and discipleship	
Adaptability	Church planting and development	
Cultural sensitivity	Leadership development	
Church and stewardship	Leadership/"followership" skills	
	Interpersonal relationships	
	Professional bivocational skills	

Not only will this approach help keep expectations realistic for all parties, but it will also be helpful in matching the right person to the right ministry.

Daniel's position in Babylon is instructive. Selection, education, and physical qualifications preceded Daniel's appointment (Dan. 1). All this took place over a three-year period before Daniel was qualified to enter the king's service. The selection requirements stipulated that these individuals had to come from a royal family, be young and male, have no physical defects, be handsome, have an aptitude to learn every discipline quickly, and be well informed. The educational requirements called for learning the Babylonian language and literature. The physical requirements assigned them food and drink that came from the king's table. At Edinburgh (1910), as noted above, participants sought to improve missionary preparation in spiritual, moral, intellectual, and physical areas. What, then, are some specific areas that will better prepare Christian workers for cross-cultural ministries at home and abroad? We begin with memorable moments.

MEMORABLE MOMENTS

Some life-changing situation has stopped you dead in your tracks. You realize that your life is about to change forever. Whether it was a trip to Urbana (www.urbana.org), a missions speaker at a church, a walk along the ocean or in the mountains, reading a magazine or a book, a short-term mission trip, talking to a friend, or attending a retreat or a missions conference, it just won't leave you. You now know that God wants you involved in cross-cultural missions. Costly obedience stands before you. Even though you have challenged the memorable moment from every level and angle, you recognize God's hand on your life. Like Abraham, you decide to move ahead, uncertain of the final destination. Your journey of faith continues, but from a new starting point. Following the leading of God, you are headed for cross-cultural ministry somewhere.

GAIN SPIRITUAL MATURITY

Fundamental to any short- or long-term ministry is a personal and collective experiential knowledge of the God behind the Great Commission and the Great Commandment. This knowledge comes from God's sacred storybook. One writer in this book calls it the beginning of wisdom. This wisdom provides a weighty anchor that will bring stability to the midst of the inevitable cross-currents associated with triumphs and tragedies. It also results in animated rejoicing, deep reverence, and responsible actions (Ps. 95). Only through constant interaction with the Author of the book can Christian workers experience true worship and begin to grasp and experience his staying power.

Those heading for cross-cultural ministry must feel comfortable with their grasp of God's sacred storybook. Their comfort zone should extend beyond the pages of the New Testament (25 percent) to include its foundation, the Old Testament (75 percent). They recognize that the New Testament is not just an addition to the Old, but rather an extension of, and dependent on, its

> *In the book of Acts and in the history of the church, some of the most brilliant people gave themselves to minister to the unreached. One thinks of Paul, Henry Martyn, and Stephen Neill. Is this same thing happening today? Some of the most brilliant minds in the church should be working among AIDS patients, the desperately poor, the extremely rich, Muslims, New Agers, and in nations where the percentage of Christians is negligible. There is so much in our ministerial structures that prevents this from happening.*
>
> Ajith Fernando (2002, 78)

105

foundation. They respect the literary nature of the book, recognizing the multiple genres, with narrative being predominant (65–75 percent), and noting that the sacred story has a beginning, a middle, and an end, as well as a storyline (Jesus Christ) that connects the beginning to the end (Steffen 2005).

They also understand the need to know more than systematic theology. Wise cross-cultural Christian workers develop a deep appreciation for the themes, characters, and events that tie the sacred storybook together and give systematic theology its foundation. They give equal attention to biblical and narrative theologies, recognizing that no one theology will provide a full picture of the Triune God. They strive to develop character theology using some of the more than 2,900 Bible characters to define more abstract qualities and concepts, just as Paul did when he used Abraham and David (concrete characters) to define justification by faith (abstract proposition; Rom. 4:1–25).

> [T]he ambassador uses every form of courtesy among the people to whom his appointment takes him, speaking their language, and adapting himself to their culture and manner of life, yet without yielding one inch on any point where the interests of his King are involved. He is the King's representative, and loyalty to his Royal Master is his first consideration.
>
> Mildred Cable and
> Francesca French (1946, 55)

Cross-cultural Christian workers should evidence an unwavering confidence in a sovereign God who is active in their lives and in the world. They know God personally before the first home assignment, have identified their human weaknesses, and know where to find specific spiritual help. A world in need of Christ requires strong, committed workers who have a dynamic relationship with the living God.

Cross-cultural Christian workers depend on the Holy Spirit throughout their lives and ministries for direction, comfort, and challenge. They trust the Holy Spirit to open and close doors to ministry opportunities (Acts 16:6–7). They recognize that the Holy Spirit has prepared people for the gospel long before their arrival. Once there, they will seek out those individuals that God has already prepared for their arrival. In his first volume, Luke calls these individuals people of peace (10:5). As they pass the baton to nationals and depart, they are assured that the Holy Sprit will continue to work in the lives of the people. They know that it is not up to them; it is up to the Holy Spirit, and they rejoice.

Prayer demonstrates dependence on God. Wise Christian workers pray continually, individually and collectively. They understand that a close relationship with the God of the universe requires constant communication

---

SIDEBAR 6.2
PRAYER RESOURCES FOR PEOPLE GROUPS

Is there a particular people or language group that God has impressed on your mind? When God brings a people group to your attention, begin to pray for these people consistently and see what happens. You may find the following resources helpful in exploring this area:

1. Patrick Johnstone's *Operation World* (www.gmi.org/ow), which offers a country-by-country profile including the state of evangelization in each country.

2. Joshua Project's (www.joshuaproject .net) People Group Profiles, which offer extensive information on thousands of people groups around the world.

3. The Mislinks People Groups page (www.mislinks.org/practical/peoples .htm), which has an extensive listing of people group resource links available on the Web.

---

between the created and the Creator. They pray for direction fervently. As part of that effort, they look for resources that will help them pray with knowledge and insight (sidebar 6.2, for example, offers help in praying for particular people groups).

Spirituality, or the lack thereof, is contagious. Wise cross-cultural Christian workers, therefore, take time to keep themselves spiritually fit. They have a "to-be" list as well as a "to-do" list because nothing speaks louder than authenticity. Nor do they ever graduate from God's school. If "disciple" means "learner," then spirituality must be defined as a lifelong process. To bring spiritual life to others demands that you continue to grow spiritually yourself.

CONNECT WITH GOD'S PEOPLE

The theme of community runs from Genesis to Revelation. Amos (5:25) talks about the household of Israel; Paul talks about the household of God (Eph. 2:18–19). The author of Hebrews warns his readers that followers of Christ should not neglect assembling together for worship. Metaphorically, Paul calls all New Testament believers "the body of Christ," indicating oneness and the need for one another. Almost sixty times Paul uses the expression "one another," emphasizing the communal nature of the body of Christ. Both the Old and the New Testament emphasize the need to gather together, worship, and learn from one another.

Paul and Barnabas did not bypass the local church before beginning their first missionary journey. Rather they were active in the church over a period of time, recognized by the leadership for their character,

107

commitment, competencies, and calling, and sent out with the church's blessing (Acts 13). Their actions in the first-century church provide a model for today's cross-cultural Christian workers.

KNOW THE STORYLINE EXPERIENTIALLY

The storyline of the sacred storybook is the story of Jesus Christ that runs from Genesis to Revelation. This story has the power to restore people's relationship with God and transform lives (see Moreau, Corwin, and McGee 2004, 27–70). Having experienced this transformation, cross-cultural Christian workers are driven to tell this story to others no matter where they may reside.

The storyline informs people of the wisdom of God, demanding in return respect and repentance. This message has a core of components that distinguishes it from all other religious messages in the world. The components include at least the following: God's creation of people to worship him in a pure environment; the conflict between God and Satan; the reality of personal and collective sin; separation and judgment from God (both human and cosmic); a grace-based solution; Jesus Christ's substitution for our sins and restoration of the cosmos; the requirement of an allegiance change; and action-oriented faith as the basis of reconciliation.

No matter what type of ministry cross-cultural Christian workers assume, they should be able to articulate the life-changing message comfortably, clearly, concisely, and contextually. Telling one's faith story (testimony) contextually just may be the most powerful evangelistic tool that exists. And in so doing, they will make every effort possible not to compromise the victorious message won through Jesus's agonizing death and triumphal resurrection.

CONTEXTUALIZE THE STORYLINE WITHOUT COMPROMISE

When Paul addressed a Jewish population, he wrapped the storyline in a cultural package recognizable by the hearers. He did this by reviewing key Old Testament characters (such as Abraham, Moses, David), symbols (such as the tabernacle and the temple), and themes (such as law and grace). Paul did the same thing when addressing Gentiles. For this audience Paul emphasized the God behind creation, the coming judgment, and the accompanying accountability. While the storyline remained unchanged, the package it was delivered in varied according to the audience. The context determined the wrappings of the once-for-all delivered gospel of Jesus Christ.

Wise cross-cultural Christian workers will follow Paul's model when communicating the storyline. To avoid legalism, nominalism, syncretism, and other undesirable "isms," they will contextualize the good news without compromising it (1 Tim. 6:20). To accomplish this they need to have not only an intimate knowledge of the components that comprise the storyline but also an intimate knowledge of the host culture and their own culture.

TAKE VISION TRIPS

Pre-field training can begin with a local church's short-term vision trips at home and abroad. Established benchmarks in commitment, competency, and character provide participants opportunity to gauge advancements. But unlike most short-term trips, emphasis is placed on taking a "learner" role, rather than a "helper" role. This can begin with Web searches for information about the people and the city to be visited, joining Internet chat groups, scanning local newspapers, watching local TV, and learning some of the culture and language. All these undertakings will raise awareness of the complexity of cross-cultural ministry. Once you are there, the challenges faced by national believers will provide new insights into culturally biased interpretations of Scripture, communication styles, preferences in teaching methods, and decision-making patterns. Team activities will underscore the need for unity and clarity of the stated vision. Vision trips provide an excellent opportunity to reshape cross-cultural ministry expectations. What will make these trips successful? Several things need to be kept in mind. Go as a learner. Go as a guest and respect your national hosts. Go as a guest and enjoy your national hosts. Like Paul, trainers can say to those taking vision trips, "We did warn you what to expect" (1 Thess. 3:4; Phillips 1996). And do not forget to thank the expatriates who spent significant time and energy with you in spite of their busy schedules.

GAIN CROSS-CULTURAL EXPERIENCE

Have you ever noticed the types of people God used in significant ways during Bible times? Many of these were bi- or tricultural (Noah, Abraham and Sarah, Moses, Joseph, Isaac, Jacob, Rahab, Samson, David, Daniel, Paul, Timothy). People without a cosmopolitan background found it difficult to minister cross-culturally. For example, when Peter tried to reach the Gentiles after God's promptings, he still found stepping into their world very difficult to do (Acts 10; Gal. 2).

Even minimal pre-field cross-cultural exposure and experience at home or abroad go a long way to prepare you for cross-cultural ministry. Ask your church leaders to assist you in becoming a multicultural person. They probably have some procedure for assisting candidates in this area as they move toward ministry. If your school offers a study semester or a study year abroad, take it. This experience will expose you to the geopolitical, economic, and religious realities of the country. It will also provide continuous movement toward degree completion while at the same time allowing you to gain more crucial cross-cultural experience.

For those heading overseas or across town, cross-cultural ministry experience does not have to begin upon arrival in the country or culture. Whenever possible it should begin before you take the trip. In many cities in North America, you will find members of the people group you wish to reach living in concentrated areas (China Town, Little Saigon, Little Tokyo); university campuses also offer many opportunities for interacting with members of other people groups. Whether across town, across campus, or down the hall, learning and ministry opportunities with the host culture are present for the taking. Avail yourself of them. If this is too difficult or inconvenient to do now, it's time for a reality check regarding your commitment level.

After locating members of the host culture, don't worry about communicating the gospel to them immediately. Rather, befriend them. Become a learner. Learn their stories. Learn what is in a family name. Learn something about their culture. Learn some of their language. Go out to eat their food with them. Run errands together. Attend community events together. Become a friend. Learn to laugh at your mistakes. This more time-consuming approach does not open the door for ministry; it is ministry! In genuine ministry, living the gospel often precedes telling the gospel.

Eventually your new friends will ask about your story. Having an initial grasp of their worldview, you can now attempt to communicate your faith story, that is, how you came to Christ. Do not be disappointed if it does not cross the cultural boundary smoothly. As in all areas of life, cross-cultural ministry requires practice. Keep practicing.

You may also want to tell Bible stories that you think will resonate culturally. No matter which approach you take, your message will be heard by friends, not strangers. You have earned the right to be heard in that a transfer of trust has taken place.

There is nothing like cross-cultural experience to highlight areas of weakness. Modeling and articulating the gospel message bring to light cultural and linguistic areas in need of further research. The questions raised by your friends will no doubt identify areas of the gospel message that they did not grasp. These areas may not be understood because of foundational gaps or cultural issues such as decision-making patterns, learning styles, time orientation, and so forth. Whatever the reason, it underscores the need for cross-cultural Christian workers to be lifelong learners: of themselves, of the sending organization, of the host culture, of Bible cultures, and of God. Hudson Taylor sought recruits who were not only willing but also skillful. Pre-field experience can help potential missionaries fit this description.

ACQUIRE APPROPRIATE EDUCATION AND TRAINING

Your vision trip(s) and cross-cultural ministry experience may have made you aware of the need for further education and training. This may not sound too enticing for those who still have a degree to complete, who may feel that it is just more work, more delay, more uncertainty, and more debt. The solution may be to think of education and training as lifelong rather than just front-end. What must be done now? What can be undertaken later? Marshall Goldsmith, Beverly Kaye, and Ken Shelton correctly observe that "[t]ruly effective people learn from all of life and learn all their lives" (2000).

Extra time taken to acquire pre-field learning at home provides numerous opportunities for you to gain valuable cross-cultural ministry experience, learn about the culture and language, learn about your own culture, learn to distinguish the Bible cultures, learn the Bible better, participate in a local church, get job experience, pay off school debts, learn to live with ambiguity, and select an appropriate avenue to reach your destination.

Lifelong learning for the cross-cultural Christian worker falls into three categories: pre-field, on-field, and post-field (home assignment). It also can occur on three levels: informal (daily activities), nonformal (seminars), and formal (academic institutions). The delivery systems for the latter two, which can be secular or Christian, range from distance learning to residency and classroom attendance, or perhaps some combination of both.

Whatever type of learning you choose, this question demands an answer: What must you know (competencies), do (competencies), and be (character and commitment) to accomplish the task God has assigned you? Take the time to talk to mission pastors, missionaries and mission representatives, missions professors, and specialists in your discipline about this. Read extensively to grow in your awareness of the answers to this question. Jot down what you learn and ask God to show you how to prepare for cross-cultural ministry. These and many more ideas have been discussed in greater depth in chapter 5.

On the pre-field level, numerous programs exist that can prepare you for effective cross-cultural ministry. Offerings will differ as to length, content level, accreditation, and requirements for participation. Some focus heavily on knowledge transfer. Some use practical approaches such

111

as case studies, simulation exercises, and testing to assess a Christian worker's potential for cross-cultural ministry. Others require intensive exposure and participation with the host culture, followed by in-depth reflection of the experience.

For those interested in further training in the United States and Canada on a nonformal level, several training opportunities are worth exploring.

First is the widely taught "Perspectives on the World Christian Movement" course (www.perspectives.org). This course is taught over twelve to fifteen weeks by experts, providing an overview of global missions and identifying ways to participate in reaching the unreached. More than sixty thousand students have taken the course since 1974.

> *Suffering is our preparation for ministry in a world of suffering. . . . This is not a world for shallow people with soft character. It needs tested, toughened disciples who are prepared, like their Lord, to descend into hell to redeem the lost.*
>
> Mark Galli (2004, 42)

Mission Training International (www.mti.org), located in Colorado Springs, Colorado, provides training for hundreds of churches and missions agencies, having trained over fifteen thousand missionaries in the past fifty years. Its mission is to "see cross-cultural messengers of God's grace and their families experience effectiveness, longevity and a deep sense of satisfaction in their calling." Some of its offerings include SPLICE (Spiritual, Personal, Lifestyle, Interpersonal, Cultural, Endure/Enjoy), CHIPS (Children's Intercultural Program), PILAT (Program in Language Acquisition Techniques), and DAR (Debriefing and Renewal).

The Center for Intercultural Studies (www.cit.online.org) located in Urban Mills, North Carolina, takes seriously the whole missionary. CIT's goal is not just to help the missionary get to a cross-cultural setting, but to enable them to remain there in effective ministry for the long term.

The Institute for Cross-Cultural Training (www.wheaton.edu/bgc/ICCT), operating through the Billy Graham Center at Wheaton College, offers an on-campus summer-school program, special workshops, publications, and consulting. These resources focus on three key areas: skills for learning a new language, preparation for teaching English to speakers of other languages (TESOL), and practical help for those who work with on-field language and culture learners.

Worldview Resource Group (www.wrg3.org) is another group located in Colorado Springs. Its members travel the world to equip, train, and consult cross-cultural workers in worldview analysis, storytelling, animism, church multiplication, and chronological Bible teaching. Their mission is to "provide training in cross-cultural church planting methodologies with a particular focus on a worldview approach."

The U.S. Center for World Mission offers an intensive study program, INSIGHT (www.uscwm.org/insight), that integrates global history and theology from creation to the present. Transferable credit is available for this thirty-two-semester-unit program from some institutions on the BA and MA levels.

For those interested in further Christian education at the formal undergraduate or graduate levels, whether at a Bible college, a liberal arts college, a university, or a seminary, investigate the missions programs available through www.mislinks.org/research/progs.htm, which provides access to every bachelor's, master's, and doctoral program in missions and evangelism in North America, as well as links to the institutions that offer these programs.

As you peruse their programs on the Web, here are several important questions to ask yourself:

- Are the courses offered in missions minimal in number in relation to the total courses required for the degree?
- Do those who teach the courses have field experience?
- Are courses taught from a multidisciplinary perspective? For example, Biola offers a course on spiritual warfare taught by a theologian, an anthropologist, and a psychologist.
- Are courses offered online?
- Are the institute's programs also offered in foreign countries taught by professors from the United States or Canada?
- Are courses open to auditors?

Do your homework and take advantage of these fine educational opportunities. Remember that while formal education is for some, lifelong education is for all.

A growing number of cross-cultural Christian workers are graduates of secular colleges and universities. With a degree in hand in medicine, business, political science, community development, teaching English as a second language, math, engineering, history, and so forth, they look forward to participating in ministries somewhat differently than do those who focus primarily on evangelism and church multiplication. Some have been able to run their disciplines through the biblical grid, identifying strengths and weaknesses. Others are still in the process. Some lack sufficient understanding of the Bible and missiology and need to add depth in these areas. Nevertheless, this significant workforce anticipates participation in cross-cultural ministry at home and abroad, using the disciplines they have studied.

Almost everywhere you go, formal education is not cheap, especially at private institutions. More and more students amass huge debt while completing their degrees. According to the National Student Loan Survey conducted in 2002, over half of the graduates of private institutions owe almost nineteen thousand dollars, while graduates of public institutions owe over sixteen thousand dollars (see www.finaid.com/calculators for information on how much your student debt will really cost).

For those entering ministries that require raising support, delays seem inevitable. The graduate must seek a job to pay down the debt, if not pay it off entirely. Although it involves a delay, this may be a good move. Debt responsibility is far too often overlooked. The Great Commission Community (assemblies, agencies, academics) is also taking action to help reduce and pay for school debt. Recognizing that this is a challenge for all stakeholders of the Great Commission, they are partnering together to address school debt. On the debt reduction side, Ben Sells, in *Mission Frontiers* (2004), calls for taking college credit courses while completing high school, attending a local community college before transferring to a four-year program, and asking for more grants. On the school debt payment side, much remains to be done. More institutions like Project MedSend, which assumes the loan payments for medical personnel—including psychologists, psychiatrists, doctors, nurses—involved in missions, are necessary for those entering other types of ministries. For example, through one generous donor a sizable annual endowed scholarship is now available at Wheaton College for undergraduates who complete their studies with large educational debts. Those who qualify have their loans paid off over the course of four years of overseas service. For all students, even those who have access to such programs, it is always wise to keep your debt as low as possible, find ways to reduce it, and—as early as possible—learn about debt policy in the agency or institution under which you wish to serve.

Part of lifelong learning means keeping abreast of the missions journals, and those within other relevant disciplines. Subscribe to the key journals, either hard copy or online, so that you can keep up with your specialty and be refreshed spiritually. Depending on your budget, these should include *Evangelical Missions Quarterly*, *International Journal of Frontier Missions*, *Missiology: An International Review*, *International Bulletin of Missionary Research*, and *Strategies for Today's Leaders: Global Church Growth* (see www.mislinks.org/research/periodicals.html for a more complete list as well as access to the online versions). Also collect several books in each of the following categories: your ministry focus, cultural anthropology, intercultural communication, and spiritual formation. Sidebar 6.3 suggests texts in a variety of areas that are important for successful missionary work.

SIDEBAR 6.3
SUGGESTED READING ON IMPORTANT TOPICS

SPIRITUAL FORMATION

Bruce Demarest, *Satisfy Your Soul: Restoring the Heart of Christianity* (NavPress, 1999).

Richard Foster, *Celebration of Discipline: The Path to Spiritual Growth* (Harper, 1988).

Dallas Willard, *Renovation of the Heart: Putting on the Character of Christ* (NavPress, 2002).

CULTURAL ANTHROPOLOGY

James Peoples and Garrick Bailey, *Humanity: Introduction to Cultural Anthropology* (Wadsworth, 2005).

Paul Hiebert, *Cultural Anthropology* (Lippincott, 1976).

Charles Kraft, *Anthropology for Christian Witness* (Orbis, 1996).

INTERCULTURAL COMMUNICATION

Carley Dodd, *Dynamics of Intercultural Communication* (McGraw-Hill, 1998).

William B. Gudykunst, Stella Ting-Toomey, and Tsukasa Nishida, *Communication in Personal Relationships across Cultures* (Sage, 1996).

R. Daniel Shaw and Charles Van Engen, *Communicating God's Word in a Complex World: God's Truth or Hocus Pocus?* (Rowman & Littlefield, 2003).

BUSINESS AND MISSIONS

Ken Eldred, *God Is at Work: Transforming People and Nations through Business* (Regal, 2005).

Patrick Lai, *Tentmaking: Business as Missions* (Authentic, 2005).

Steven L. Rundle and Tom A. Steffen, *Great Commission Companies: The Emerging Role of Business in Missions* (InterVarsity, 2003).

CHURCH MULTIPLICATION

David Garrison, *Church Planting Movements* (Witgake, 2003).

George Patterson and Richard Scoggins, *Church Multiplication Guide: Helping Churches to Reproduce Locally and Abroad* (William Carey Library, 2001).

Tom A. Steffen, *Passing the Baton: Church Planting That Empowers* (Center for Organizational and Ministry Development, 1997).

TESOL

Douglas Biber, Susan Conrad, and Geoffrey Leech, *Longman Student Grammar of Spoken and Written English* (Pearson ESL, 2002).

Donald B. Snow, *English Teaching as Christian Mission: An Applied Theology* (Herald, 2001).

Donald B. Snow, *More Than a Native Speaker: An Introduction for Volunteers Teaching English Abroad* (Teachers of English to Speakers of Other Languages, 2006).

Continued

Sidebar 6.3—Continued

NARRATIVE DISCIPLESHIP	COMMUNITY DEVELOPMENT
Thomas E. Boomershine, *Story Journey: An Invitation to the Gospel as Storytelling* (Abingdon, 1988).	Jeffrey Cohen, *Economic Development: An Anthropological Approach* (Rowman & Littlefield, 2002).
Trevor McIlwain, *Building on Firm Foundations*, 9 vols. (New Tribes Mission, 1965–1992).	Bryant Myers, *Walking with the Poor: Principles and Practices of Transformational Development* (Orbis, 1999).
Tom Steffen, *Reconnecting God's Story to Ministry: Cross-Cultural Storytelling at Home and Abroad* (Waynesboro, GA: Authentic Media, 2005).	Bryant Myers, *Working with the Poor: New Insights and Learnings from Development Practitioners* (World Vision, 1999).

JOIN TOGETHER WITH OTHER MISSIONARIES OR MISSIOLOGISTS

It will be worth your while to join one of the many available missiological societies. You can keep up with recent thinking and research as well as network with people who can help you with your questions and the issues you face. The relationships you form through joining one or more societies can become lifelong friendships that will make a significant difference in your own life and ministry. If you want to explore more than those we describe here, browse to www.mislinks.org/research/societies.htm, where you will find links to numerous additional US and international organizations.

The Evangelical Missiological Society (EMS; www.emsweb.org) began in 1990 under the able leadership of David Hesselgrave through a reorganization of the Association of Evangelical Professors of Mission (AEPM). EMS offers regional and annual meetings, an annual book that includes the major papers presented at the national conference, and a dissertation series in partnership with William Carey Library. Membership includes evangelical professors, mission agency executives, and missions pastors who take seriously the authority of Scripture and the priority of evangelism and church planting.

The Association of Professors of Mission (APM; www.asmweb.org/apm) was founded in 1952 by R. Pierce Beaver for American professors teaching missions. This organization schedules its annual June meeting just before the American Society of Missiology (ASM) meeting.

ASM (www.asmweb.org) was founded in 1972 by Gerald Anderson, R. Pierce Beaver, and Ralph Winter. It meets annually and publishes *Missiology: An International Review* as well as a book and a disserta-

---

SIDEBAR 6.4
HOW TO CHOOSE A SENDING CHURCH OR AGENCY

Jennifer Stadelmann (personal communication, 2006; adapted and used with permission)

You should ask the following questions when you are in the process of choosing an organization (whether church or agency) to join. Personalize the list for your own circumstances.

- Whom do I report to regionally? Nationally? Internationally? Who is close to me in the field?
- What kind of team will I have? Will they be in the same city? Region?
- Do you have field-based counselors for your missionaries?
- What are your policies for raising support? Does the agency receive a percentage? Is it pooled?
- Do benefits include health care at home and abroad? Retirement? Workers' compensation? Disability?
- What schooling options are available for children? Missionary school? International school? Homeschooling? National school?
- How often do teammates meet together? Have retreats? Have conferences?

- How often will a married missionary need to travel apart from a spouse? With a spouse? How often will the family be separated?
- What do you think about vacation time?
- Who determines our ministry schedule? How much structure/ flexibility is built into our goals and daily schedules?
- Is the missionary alone considered the full-time employee? Is the spouse required to work a certain number of hours each week?
- How often do we take home assignment? For how long?
- What happens if we have a shortfall in our monthly support?
- How often do you contact the sending churches? How do you contact them?
- What if there is a medical emergency? Is there evacuation insurance?
- Is there a field evacuation plan should something catastrophic happen in the country?

Continued

tion series. Membership includes evangelicals, Roman Catholics, and conciliar Protestants.

The International Society for Frontier Missiology (ISFM; www.isfm. org) was founded in 1986 by Ralph Winter. This intergenerational and international society comprised of professors, executives, and students focuses on the remaining task that requires "pioneer" work even where the national church exists. It publishes the *International Journal of Frontier Missions*, which focuses on the theme of the unreached where frontier missions is necessary.

The Gospel and Our Culture Network (GOCN; www.gocn.org) was formed in the early 1980s in the United Kingdom and moved to North America in the late 1980s. Influenced by Lesslie Newbigin, this US and

Sidebar 6.4—Continued

- What kind of relationship do you have with the national church?
- What kind of opportunities exist for ongoing education? Study leave?
- What type of reports does our supervisor require? How often?
- Where does culture/language acquisition take place? For how long? Can ministry be conducted while learning the culture and language?
- What is the personality of your organization? What makes it unique from others? Is leadership centralized? Decentralized?
- In what type of ministries does your agency participate? Do the different ministries interact? How often will we be involved in headquarters activities?
- How often do we attend conferences? Retreats? In-house training on the field? Off the field?
- Whom do we talk to when we have problems (e.g., conflict with coworkers or teams, spiritual warfare, problems with local authorities)?
- Do you work with other mission agencies on the field? If so, in what capacity? If not, why not?
- What is your security policy in closed or sensitive countries (e.g., China, Muslim countries)? How do your employees enter the country (with what kind of visa)?
- For singles, what are your dating policies? Whom can they date? Marry?
- Can couples adopt?
- Can divorced people apply to your agency?
- What pre-field orientation is required? How long is it? Are both spouses required to attend?
- Are your personnel required to use a particular method or materials for evangelism and discipleship?

Canadian network advocates social and cultural analysis, biblical and theological reflection, and vision for the church and its mission. The network's goal is to integrate theology and missiology to encounter Western culture with the gospel. To help accomplish this, it offers a quarterly newsletter, an annual consultation, and a book series.

INVESTIGATE AVENUES OF SERVICE

Who will you go out under? A local church? A mission agency? A partnership of both? Some other means? Approach this challenge as you would looking for a lifelong spouse. Do not be afraid to ask lots of questions (sidebar 6.4 offers some examples) and start the courtship process early.

FIND A MENTOR

Every cross-cultural worker will benefit from finding a mentor who will push you and not be content to simply let you sit still. The memorable moment received at a missions conference such as Urbana or

118

elsewhere will slowly subside under the daily pressures of life. Those once-reached or unreached people groups living in distant lands or your backyard become even more distant in your mind. God's call seems harder to hear and less clear. To help offset the inevitable, find a good

CASE STUDIES: COMPLEXITY AND INSTITUTIONAL PARTNERSHIPS

TOM STEFFEN

The following cases, all true, are not intended to demean those who participated in them, or the churches, agencies, or academic training institutions they represent. Rather, we include them to demonstrate the complexity of cross-cultural ministry and the need for ministry-long training through institutional partnerships. Reflect on each and discuss the following questions:

1. How valid were the team members' expectations?
2. Were they realistic?
3. How could the team members have been better prepared for the ministries assigned them?

CASE 1. TO THE CIS WITH LOVE

A coalition of churches set a goal to plant churches in the Commonwealth of Independent States (CIS). To accomplish this goal, they planned to send initial teams to plant churches, followed by other teams to provide follow-up. Before leaving for ministry, team members received several months of American evangelism and follow-up training, along with tips for living in a different cultural milieu.

When the initial team arrived in the CIS, they went where they felt there was a need that God was calling them to meet. They procured translators to convey their message. Through the translators, team members immediately conducted street drama and preaching. They invited willing seekers to be their personal guests at the nightly services. Two weeks after the first team's arrival, they returned home, having planted a church.

To train pastors and provide follow-up in the newly formed churches, the sending churches depended on several strategies. They commissioned "nurturing teams" to go to the CIS for "a few weeks to a year or more" to provide grounding in the Word. American pastors also flew over to provide short-term, one-on-one training. Uncontextualized taped Bible studies and videos from the United States served as the training curricula. Certain nationals were selected and sponsored to attend Bible college in the States and eventually return to the CIS to take up ministry positions. Less than two years after pronouncing the initial goal, the sending churches reported that their teams had planted nine additional churches. They did not feel it necessary to transform their brand of Christianity to the CIS context— transferring it was considered sufficient.

Continued

mentor who will continually remind you of the great multitude in heaven from every nation, tribe, people, and language (Rev. 7:9–10) and not allow the vision that God has given you to participate in this plan to die. Take his or her advice wisely. Accept his or her encouragement. Take his or her challenges seriously. Godly mentors can make the difference between making it to the field or becoming another casualty lost along the way.

Complexity and Institutional Partnerships—Continued

CASE 2. TO RUSSIA WITH LOVE

The frontier missionary team spent five weeks in a city in the former Soviet Union. During the five-week stay, they acquired all the information they could on the host people and the city because the agency provided them no background information. At the same time, team members were to share the gospel and disciple new believers.

One team member commented, "We went in with our guns firing but with little awareness of their lifestyles or even follow-up for the crucial months ahead." Although the short-term trip changed the seminarian's life forever, he sadly discovered later that most of those who had made "decisions for Christ" lost interest in their "summer decision." The chance to tell family and friends that they had associated with Americans seemed to influence the decision-making process more than Jesus Christ.

CASE 3. TO EUROPE WITH LOVE

The missionary team formed abroad ad hoc; had no previous church planting experience; gave little attention to team development, demographics, culture and language acquisition, or the time required to see churches born and equipped; and did not consider what the new church should look like or agree on a coordinated vision statement. They began with a door-to-door survey that produced a strong response, but like a tender green shoot under the noon rays of a desert sun, interest soon wilted. After several months, the team began a second follow-up. Five came to know the Lord, including one tourist. Follow-up became virtually impossible as no one would give out addresses; the church plant folded.

But the team did not give up. They began a prayer time and initiated another church plant among a specific people group rather than with anyone who would listen. Friendship evangelism produced few results, open-air evangelism produced even fewer. No one wanted to attend anything "Christian."

In time, a small group of believers emerged. Again, the team elected to use the cell group model. Home assignments took certain church planters in and out of the picture. As team members prepared the growing group for division into smaller cell groups, it became evident some preferred a more traditional church model. They found it very difficult to get attendees involved in any aspect of service or leadership. Some of the families moved, leaving two weak cell groups. Within fourteen months another church plant ground to an abrupt halt.

SUMMARY

The three cases at the end of this chapter signal the need for tighter, co-ordinated pre-field, on-field, and post-field learning. They also underscore the need for institutional partnerships at home and abroad. Although we applaud the vision, passion, fervor, commitment, and entrepreneurship of team members, we worry about a common cross-cultural ministry pattern failing to take seriously the complexity of cross-cultural ministry. In *Scripture and Strategy*, David Hesselgrave captures our concern and hope in the following comment made after hearing Paul Fleming, founder of New Tribes Mission, speak in chapel in 1942: "He was indeed a man of vision and passion, but he greatly oversimplified the task of world evangelization, leaving the strong impression that the message of John 3:16 is sufficient for its completion and that anyone, with or without special gifts, abilities and training, can communicate John 3:16. It did not require an extended time on the mission field to realize that that simply is not the case. It is especially significant that now after fifty years, New Tribes Mission supplies a much needed corrective [the Chronological Teaching approach]" (1994, 119).

Cross-cultural Christian workers must not rely solely on passion, entrepreneurialism, or spontaneity, but like the airplane pilot boarding a plane full of passengers, must also know the answers to the when, what, where, how, and why questions of the trade. In the next chapter we consider some of the major avenues to cross-cultural ministries.

7

Avenues to Cross-Cultural Ministries

Ask about your neighbors, then buy the house.

Jewish Proverb

Not only does the missions force require people with the necessary spiritual and psychological development, skills, education, training, and ministry experience; it also demands specific avenues to get them to all parts of the world. In this chapter we consider the various avenues available to Christian workers to participate in cross-cultural ministry. In chapter 8 we look at more specific roles from a field-operational perspective.

There are three primary avenues available for entry into viable cross-cultural ministry. The first avenue is to go out as an independent, free to operate as you discern the Holy Spirit leading. The second avenue is to be sent out by local churches. The third avenue is to join a parachurch (alongside the church) organization (typically, but not always, a mission agency) that matches your spiritual gifts and ministry philosophy. In addition to these, there are many alternative avenues that do not fit neatly into a single category but should be briefly discussed. What are the major differences among the avenues? What are the pros and cons of each? Before answering these questions some background issues should be addressed.

PRIMARY AVENUES

Each of the major avenues that exist to enable Christian workers to move into cross-cultural service—independency, the church, parachurch organizations—overlap the others in a number of areas. Short-termers and long-termers can be found in all of them. Workers going out through each may work openly or clandestinely in a given context. Multiple ministries can be engaged through each: evangelism, education, relief and development, media, curriculum development, church multiplication, Bible translation, TESOL, athletics, business, medical, aircraft, technology, research. All generations may be present in each, although the more anti-establishment boomers may prefer the independent avenue while those GenXers who prefer teamwork, partnerships, and networks may join a parachurch organization as a team. Churches and denominations may allow only one avenue that reflects their theology and philosophy of ministry. Megachurches, able to adapt without denominational oversight, may attempt to do it all.

Independents

A certain segment of the cross-cultural Christian workforce prefers to go it alone. These Christians find working under any organization, whether a church, a mission agency, or some kind of conglomeration, too confining, too limiting, too restrictive, or too time-consuming. Their pioneering entrepreneurial spirit allows them no time to participate in long debates to decide schedules, direction, budgets, policy, methodology, or the color of paint for the walls. "Why waste time trying to convince others of a great idea when you can just implement it immediately?" they ask.

Typically churches, denominational and parachurch agencies, partnerships, and networks have their own ways of doing things, leaving little if any opportunity for new ideas. Independents do not want to be slaves to any leader or the philosophies and methodologies they may espouse. The Holy Spirit is too spontaneous for canned methods and techniques no matter how effective they may have been in the past. Independents prefer the spontaneous freedom found in the Holy Spirit; they prefer to be accountable to him rather than to others or the structures they represent. In table 7.1 we list several pros and cons for those who choose to go the independent route to cross-cultural service. Brainstorm further ideas to add to both sides of the list.

TABLE 7.1
PROS AND CONS FOR INDEPENDENTS

Pros	Cons
• Can quickly respond to current needs. • Can focus intensively on specific ministries. • Provides more time for ministry rather than administrative responsibilities, meetings, or maintaining team relationships.	• Little if any accountability, at least on the field. • Fails to take the body principle, the Jesus model, or the Pauline team model seriously. • Must handle transfer of currency and government legal work to remain in a country.

Local Churches

What role has and should the church play in sending cross-cultural workers? Some see the church as the only biblical way to send missionaries, while others understand it as one avenue among several. Whatever the theological conclusion, from a pragmatic perspective, it is the latter view that is reflected in US missions. We will begin with a brief overview of the role of the church in missions before identifying some of the key issues that have arisen over time. For an excellent overview of this topic, see Bruce Camp (2003, 203–47).

Luke opens Acts with 120 dejected, despondent disciples cowering in a room in Jerusalem, contemplating the next move after their leader's unanticipated departure. He ends the book with a healthy movement in place that has reached Rome. All this happens in a little over three decades. How was this accomplished? By independents? By parachurch organizations? By partnerships or networks? Roland Allen concludes: "In the beginning the Church was a missionary society: it added to its numbers mainly by the life and speech of its members attracting to it those who were outside" (1962, 117).

Allen indicates that this was the situation "in the beginning" because over the course of history something happened that changed the role of the church in missions. In AD 313, the locus of missions shifted from Christians and the church to the government when Christianity became a state religion under Emperor Constantine's Edict of Milan. The empire's desire for unity in all areas of life was now complete. A unified religion was now added to a single citizenship and a single law. A totally unified empire now existed under one emperor.

One result of this change was the understanding that the pagans requiring missionary effort were outside the empire. The church redefined missions as a geographical issue; missions was conducted over there, not here. This created a major problem because the church was without

Sidebar 7.1
Elements for a Top-Notch Local Church Missions Program

Tom Telford (1998, 158–60) has identified the following elements for excellence in a local church missions program.

- An outward focus and strategy
- 30 percent or more of the budget to missions
- An ongoing training program for missionary candidates
- Missions education integrated throughout the church's programs
- The church sends its own people
- The church must be concerned about and pray for the lost

- A pastor who leads in vision and outreach
- The church helps other churches in missions
- A strong local evangelism program

Reflection and Discussion

1. As you reflect on the church you know best, which elements would you say characterize that church?
2. In what ways might you help your church missions program grow toward excellence?

a structure to conduct missions at a distance. To address this issue the monastic movement developed, most notably among the Celts. While not initially intended to be missional, monasteries were established among unreached populations, and a missionary orientation developed. Regulations for monastic life and witness evolved, culminating, after several centuries, with the emergence of formal orders such as the Franciscans (1210), the Augustinians (1215), the Dominicans (1216), and the Jesuits (1540).

The Protestant movement, begun in the early 1500s, was initially reluctant to consider that God had a global plan beyond their countries' borders. Kenneth Scott Latourette (1971) identifies several reasons for the Reformers not reaching those outside western Europe. First, the effort necessary to address issues with the Catholics took most of their focus and energy. Second, theological issues distracted them from global missions. The Lord's return was so imminent, claimed Luther and Melanchthon, that there was no time to conduct missions. Calvin maintained that it was God's, not people's, duty to reach the lost (election). Zwingli believed those "called of God" should be sent out by the church. Third, they were preoccupied with wars between Protestants and Catholics. Fourth, the newly formed Protestant governments were not really interested in reaching pagans. Fifth, Protestants lacked a monastic structure (rejected by Luther) that could make missions happen, and no alternatives (such as modern mission agencies) had been developed.

125

Sixth, and finally, Protestants had little contact with non-Christians, since they arose out of Catholic contexts.

God used Philip Spener (1635–1705), the "father of Pietism," to challenge the dead Protestant state churches. An emphasis on an individual relationship with God that was constantly nurtured and rejuvenated through the living Word of God resulting in active witness and help for the needy did little to endear the Pietists to the state church. The pietistic movement was instrumental in making the individual and local churches, rather than the state, central in the propagation of missions. A number of significant mission efforts and organizations resulted from the movement, including the Danish-Halle Mission and the Moravians. A possible unintentional outcome of Pietism was that missions became seen as something advocated by special-interest groups, rather than as the duty of all followers of Christ (Neill 1975).

William Carey (1761–1834), through writings and example, established the need for mission agencies to fulfill the role of global missions that the church refused to take. His inspiring effort, among others, would ultimately result in the modern proliferation of all types of mission agencies found around the world.

It was not until the early 1900s that the evangelical churches began to reassume their rightful role as institutions responsible for world missions. The World Missionary Conference (1910), the Berlin Congress (1966), the Wheaton Congress (1966), and the Lausanne Congress on World Evangelization (1974) aided in reaffirming the central role of the church in world evangelization. A quote from the Lausanne Covenant captures the participants' perception of the church's duty: "World evangelization requires the whole church to take the whole Gospel to the whole world. The church is at the very center of God's cosmic purpose and is the appointed means of spreading the Gospel." A solid theology of the church (ecclesiology) definitely permeated Lausanne 1974.

By the 1970s, evangelical and large independent churches were demanding more hands-on participation in global missions. They no longer were content to simply supply mission agencies with their finest and the finances to support them. Churches began to ask for accountability and more "bang for their buck." Recognizing the tensions, the Green Lake Conference in 1971 addressed church-mission relationships. Items discussed included recruitment (improving an impersonal relationship between church and agency); mission structures (improving communication and involvement between leaders who represent two very different leadership structures); finances and publications (clarifying the role of the church and agencies in relation to funding recruitment, selection, administrative expenses, and supporting nationals who replace expatriates); and mission personnel (clarifying local church responsibilities in relation to accountability, stewardship, member care, missionary participation during furlough, post–high school care of missionary children remaining in the United States).

John Stott, commenting on the Lausanne Covenant (1974), questioned if parachurch agencies would survive for long. The Consultation on World Evangelism at Pattaya, Thailand, (1980) declared that the local church is the "principal agency for evangelism, whose total membership must therefore be mobilized and trained" (Stott 1975). Out of that conference came the first major publication addressing church-mission tensions, titled *Co-operating in World Evangelization: A Handbook on Church/Parachurch Relationships* (Lausanne Committee for World Evangelization 1983). Dogmatism, rivalry, and suspicion between church and mission were challenged. In the preamble, Stott maintained the primacy of the church in missions, challenging mission agencies to take into account that "independence of the church is bad, co-operation with the church is better, service as an arm of the church is best."

RESPONSES BY LOCAL CHURCHES

Over the years local churches (excluding megachurches, which are covered below) have responded positively and negatively to their role in missions. In the quest for more control, some churches have demanded that missionaries who receive their financial support must minister among unreached people groups living within the boundaries of the 10/40 window. Once a missionary is accepted for support, they require that multiple reports and forms, demonstrating continual successful ministry, be filled out and returned promptly. In these reports, social issues tend not to receive the attention that spiritual issues do. Some also request that at least four months be spent in the area of the supporting church during furlough. The following example is not uncommon.

> We do not understand. As we read your yearly reports, we notice that the number of Thais becoming converts under your ministry is very low. Your report shows that in three years you have seen only twenty-four Thais become Christian. This does not make sense to us when we just heard from a short-term missions team that they were instrumental in seeing 125 people become Christians in a span of two weeks. Unless you become more productive, we may have to stop supporting you financially and shift our funds to more productive missionaries. (Lo 2004, 363)

Other local churches are much more realistic in their approaches. Recognizing different spiritual gifts and skills, they prefer that missionaries go to places where these qualities can be utilized. They understand that the world requires workers not only for unreached people groups but also for nurturing existing national churches and renewal of those that have lost their way. They also recognize that limited finances make it impossible for one church to support several missionary singles and/or families. Most likely, missionaries will need to travel extensively to gain the needed support and therefore must spend time with a number of churches pre-field and during home assignments. They recognize that some religions in a country are much more difficult to reach with the gospel than others. They also are alert to the fact that some responses to the gospel are made for the benefit of maintaining a relationship with the missionary for multiple purposes, the least of which may be following Christ.

Responses by Large Churches

The larger the church, the more opportunities for greater participation within missions. Possessing abundant finances and personnel, some large churches, especially the megachurches, have decided to go it alone. From mobilization to recruitment, selection, pre-field training, funding, member care, on-field training, and home assignment, megachurches can handle it all. Often theology, Western in flavor, dominates their training and philosophy of ministry. The type of music, order of service, even recorded sermons used in their church services, as well as the books written by their pastors, are exported for use in cross-cultural contexts. They assume that proven models and strategies used at home will work cross-culturally anywhere if kept simple and pragmatic. All too often missiology has yet to enter the theology, philosophy, or curricula of these well-intentioned servants of Christ. Large churches expect results from missions leadership and those they send to minister around the world, as demonstrated in this example:

> A large church in the U.S. was helping support a missionary couple being sent to work in a certain country. Without conferring with the couple, the church's mission committee set goals for their pioneer work. In the first year the missionary couple was to plant three congregations; by the third year, ten churches; and by the fourth year, fifteen churches. The couple questioned the plan's feasibility; "Why, we don't even know the language. We are hoping to spend the first term learning how to communicate." However, when they approached the chairperson of the mission committee, they were told, "Either produce or lose our support." (Lo 2004, 363–64)

They also expect control over everyone sent out, even those assigned to mission agencies. For example, a missions elder from a megachurch told Sam Metcalf of Church Resource Ministries in Pasadena, California, why his church had decided to discontinue the ministry of a missionary:

"We didn't approve of what the missionary was doing, so we told him that he and his family had to return to the States," the elder said. "After all, he's supported by us 100 percent. He's our missionary."

"But doesn't he work for an agency?" Metcalf asked. "Aren't they his employer and supervisor?"

"Yes," the elder replied, "but we pay the bill; the agency doesn't." (Metcalf 1993, 142)

Two large churches doing a superb job in cross-cultural training and ministry are Wasilla Bible Church (eight hundred attendance) in Alaska and the Willingdon Church in British Columbia (three thousand attendance). Wasilla offers high school students short-term trips from their freshman through senior years. All participants must go as a team. The freshman trip involves no cross-cultural element. During their sophomore year participants go to Mexico with YUGO (Youth Unlimited Gospel Outreach). Outward Bound is offered in their junior year, while the senior year trip is to a sister church in Siberia.

Willingdon starts short-term trips in junior high school, continuing through high school and college, and like Wasilla, all participants must go as a team. Junior high students stay in British Columbia, learning and practicing ministry skills in the mornings, and participate in organized fun activities in the afternoons. All participants must qualify (which includes ministry experience) to go on this trip and any succeeding ones. Not all applicants are accepted. None of the trips include building projects. One of these two-week trips is to Mexico, led by team members from the church who know Spanish. During their college years, students are encouraged to take eight to ten months to go to a field of choice for cross-cultural ministry. The church provides 50 percent of their support. Willingdon uses this trip to recruit for full-time ministry.

Both churches prepare participants for long-term, quality cross-cultural ministry through teams. The smaller church accomplishes this through partnerships with other institutions; the larger church does so with its own international personnel. In both cases the church intimately knows the gifts and skills of those it chooses to send forth and support, whether short-term or long-term. These two large churches take seriously the learner role of the cross-cultural Christian worker, the need to move personnel from short-term to long-term engagement, the need for missiology to influence all areas of ministry (including theology), and the value of partnering with mission agencies that can offer specific knowledge and expertise in various countries gained over years of service. In table 7.2 we list several pros and cons for those who choose the local church route to cross-cultural service. Brainstorm further ideas to add to both sides of the list.

TABLE 7.2
PROS AND CONS FOR LOCAL CHURCHES

Pros	Cons
• Biblical support for the central role of the local church to make disciples globally is evident to many.	• Going it alone can demonstrate a lack of understanding of the body principle.
• The desire for a more hands-on involvement in missions by the church is a move forward.	• The Great Commission (spiritual issues) found in Matt. 28:18–20 often excludes the Great Commandment (social issues) in missions practice for many churches.
• Human and financial resources are more abundant in megachurches than in smaller churches.	• Local churches, including megachurches, often lack missiological training; therefore they tend to transfer Western culture rather than to transform the host cultures.
	• Missiologically influenced ministry is often missing.

Parachurch Organizations (Mission Agencies)

The third avenue to conduct global missions is through parachurch organizations, most of which are known as mission agencies. We will present a brief history of their existence, examine the tensions between the role of the church and the role of agencies, and identify three major players as they emerged sequentially over time: (1) classical mission agencies, (2) denominational agencies, and (3) faith missions. In table 7.3 we list several pros and cons for those who choose to go through parachurch organizations. Brainstorm further ideas to add to both sides of the list.

CLASSICAL MISSION AGENCIES

In this book we use the term "classical" mission agencies to refer to nonprofit organizations started by visionaries that are not under the authority of local churches to meet specific unmet needs in relation to the Great Commission, the Great Commandment, and renewal. They

TABLE 7.3
PROS AND CONS FOR MISSION AGENCIES

Pros	Cons
• Allows for those of the same theological persuasion to advance their cause.	• Can view the local church as simply a means to fulfill its objectives through funds and personnel.
• Can provide new and veteran personnel with specialized, specific training gained through years of practice in a particular culture.	• The organization seldom dies even if the purpose statement is completed.
• Allows visionaries the opportunity to address unmet needs.	• Accountability can be an issue.

SIDEBAR 7.2
TRENDS IN THE US MISSION MOVEMENT

The following list is compiled from a study of seven hundred US Protestant mission agencies based on statistical analysis of trends over the previous ten years (Moreau 2004 and 2007). As you read through the list, brainstorm on the positive and/or negative implications for each trend.

- From 2001 to 2005, a decrease in both long-term missionaries (more than four years) and "middle-term" missionaries (one to four years).

- From 1996 to 2001, significant growth among short-termers (two weeks to a year), but a leveling off of them from 2001 to 2005.

- Income for overseas missions grew consistently from 1992 to 2005, but from 2001 to 2005 almost all the income growth was reported by agencies that identify their primary activities in the areas of relief and development.

- Denominational missions are experiencing decreases in personnel and finances.

- Deployment of full-time residential missionaries after 2001 shifted away from Latin America and Africa and toward Asia and Europe.

---

usually find their support through Christians and churches. Although they may require workers to be active in local churches and typically have workers from various denominations on their rosters, they are independent from the control of local churches and denominations.

Some trace the origin of mission agencies back to London's Society for the Propagation of Christian Knowledge in 1699 and the first Anglican Society for the Propagation of the Gospel in Foreign Parts (SPG) in 1701. William Carey, among others, gave this approach a theological justification, advocating the rightful role for voluntary societies (not just clergy and churches).

These societies took shape around a variety of foci such as geography (China Inland Mission), methodology (Society for the Propagation of the Gospel), or denomination (Church Mission Society). By the close of the eighteenth century, the true parallel to today's parachurch organizations existed.

Throughout the 1900s mission agencies proliferated in the United States. In fact, until the 1990s, more mission agencies were founded in every decade than in the prior decade (Moreau 2000b, 36). J. Alan Youngren (1981) believes that the frontier spirit helped create a mind-set that played a major role in the increase. This mind-set included little respect for tradition, belief in the autonomy of one's community, self-reliance, an independent spirit, and an infatuation with anything

> **SIDEBAR 7.3**
> **SHIFTS AND TRENDS IN THE CANADIAN MISSION MOVEMENT**
>
> The following list is compiled from a study of 120 Canadian Protestant mission agencies based on statistical analysis of trends over the previous ten years (Moreau 2004 and 2007). As you look through the list, brainstorm on the positive and/or negative implications for each trend.
>
> - The long-term (four years or more) full-time missionary force declined by 33 percent between 1992 and 2005.
> - The full-time missionary (one year or more) force declined 21 percent between 1992 and 2005.
>
> - As with US agencies, income for overseas missions grew consistently from 1992 to 2005, but from 2001 to 2005 almost all the income in growth was reported by agencies that identify their primary activities in the areas of relief and development.
> - From 2001 to 2005 the deployment of Canadian personnel shifted from Europe to Africa, Central America, and the Caribbean.

new. Sidebar 7.2 lists several of the most recent statistical shifts and trends seen among some seven hundred US Protestant mission agencies. Sidebar 7.3 offers a similar list for Canadian Protestant mission agencies.

Others are not willing to give such a late date to the existence of mission agencies. They believe that mission agencies (the form, not the term) existed in first-century Christianity. This group maintains that Pauline teams worked with local churches but reported to no one specific church; they considered themselves separate from but united with the local church; they were outside the local church, but worked alongside the local church. Ralph Winter uses the terms "modality" (stationary local churches) and "sodality" (mobile mission agencies) to distinguish the two structures. Although without exact one-to-one equivalency, the terms do help differentiate the two roles. In *Announcing the Kingdom: The Story of God's Mission in the Bible*, Arthur Glasser and his colleagues contend that today's mission agency is in reality an "apostolic team" (2003, 300–304). Advocates of the first-century view believe that the roles of the local church and mission agencies in discipling the world for Christ are distinct, separate but equal. One cannot exist without the other.

DENOMINATIONAL AGENCIES

The end of the eighteenth century saw the expansion of a multitude of mission agencies. The chief ones, which were interdenominational, included the London Missionary Society (1795), the British and Foreign Bible Society (1804), American Board of Commissioners for Foreign Missions (1810), and the American Bible Society (1826). Denominations, including the Anglicans, the Wesleyans, the Methodists, the Baptists, the Presbyterians, and the American Congregationalists, established agencies during the early years of the nineteenth century. By 1925, around 75 percent of all American missionaries were associated with denominational agencies. Newer denominational agencies include WorldVenture (formerly CBInternational) of the Conservative Baptists and Mission to the World of the Presbyterian Church in America. The numbers involved in mainline denominational agencies dropped over the course of the century as liberalism and the social gospel eroded the centrality of the Word and the command to "make disciples" of all peoples. Those denominations that have kept Scripture central have not experienced the same drastic decline in membership and monies as have many of the mainline denominations. In table 7.4 we list several pros and cons for utilizing a denominational mission agency as your route to missions engagement. Brainstorm further ideas to add to both sides of the list.

TABLE 7.4
PROS AND CONS FOR DENOMINATIONAL MISSION AGENCIES

Pros	Cons
• Size allows for adequately funding the personnel and goals of denominational agencies.	• Decision making requires time to run the gauntlet of multiple layers of bureaucracy.
• Size allows for recruiting the best-trained personnel for multiple ministry needs.	• Activists often push agendas that do not necessarily represent the membership majority.
• Denominational agencies offer a broad perspective of Scripture.	• Size decreases the need for outside partners or those who can challenge group think.

FAITH MISSIONS

By the latter part of the nineteenth century, faith missions, many founded and led by women, made their debut. As a reaction to the perception that denominational agencies were not reaching unreached parts of the world, that they were becoming theologically liberal, and that they operated only on the basis of budgets they had set, faith missions were founded. These missions were independent of denominations rather than interdenominational, they were theologically conservative, and they depended on God to supply the means to support the missionaries who joined them (see Covell 2000a). The first American faith mission came into existence in 1860 with the birth of the Woman's Union Missionary

Society. The first British agency was the China Inland Mission (1865). Others soon followed, including the Christian and Missionary Alliance (1887; a blend of denominational and faith missions), The Evangelical Alliance Mission (1890), the Sudan Interior Mission (1893), and the African Inland Mission (1895).

What brought about the reaction to the mainline denominations that made it necessary to forge a new type of mission agency? Those belonging to faith missions sensed a lack of respect for the Word among the denominations. They found the liberal views expressed in many denominations theologically unpalatable.

Those representing faith missions also recognized the lack of desire to evangelize unreached peoples. Evangelism was slowly but surely being replaced with the social gospel. Advocates of faith missions wanted to make sure that the Great Commission drove missions. Once this happened, faith missions could focus their attention where the unreached resided, the interior parts of countries. A number of agencies, therefore, included "interior" in their name, letting their brand define their intention. The success of their effort is evident in the international faith missions around the world that continue the vision begun in London and the United States.

Faith missions advocated total trust in God to fund all endeavors. It was God's work; he would therefore supply all needs. Some of the early faith missions forbade members to ask potential supporters for financial assistance. They were told to cast God's vision for reaching the unreached among the churches, and God's people would respond and support it.

The growing movement of faith missions required training institutions that would not compromise the Bible. Bible institutes were established to meet this need, including Missionary Training Institute (now Nyack College and Alliance Theological Seminary) founded in 1882, Training School of the Chicago Evangelization Society (now Moody Bible Institute) in 1886, Boston Missionary Training School (now Gordon College) in 1889, Johnson Bible Institute (now Johnson Bible College) in 1893, Toronto Bible Institute (now Ontario Bible College) in 1894, Providence Bible Institute (later Barrington College) in 1900, Bible Institute of Los Angeles (now Biola University) in 1908, and Columbia Bible School (now Columbia International University) in 1923 (see Mulholland 1996, 43–53). Over the course of the twentieth century, many of these schools changed names and became accredited degree-granting colleges and universities. Faith missions continue to draw heavily on these schools for well-educated and spiritually qualified personnel. In table 7.5 we list several pros and cons for choosing the avenue of a faith mission agency as your route to missions engagement. Brainstorm further ideas to add to both sides of the list.

TABLE 7.5

PROS AND CONS FOR FAITH MISSION AGENCIES

Pros	Cons
• Keeps the Word central in vision and practice.	• A knee-jerk reaction to the social efforts of the modernists in the early 1900s resulted in a low view of social ministries for many fundamentalists.
• Opens the door for lay personnel in contrast to educated professionals.	
• Stresses the need to trust God for all one's needs.	• Easy to become isolationists.
	• Training institutions have not been as strong exegeting the cultural context as they have in exegeting Scripture. Nor have they tended to include other disciplines such as business, community development, economics, or TESOL.

PARACHURCH AGENCIES IN PARTNERSHIP

To assist mission agencies and churches (whether denominational, interdenominational, or independent), nonsending associations have been formed to increase ministry effectiveness at home and abroad through collaborative efforts. We look briefly at two: the Interdenominational Foreign Mission Association of North America (IFMA) and the Evangelical Fellowship of Mission Agencies (EFMA). In table 7.6 we list several pros and cons for participating in a fellowship of agencies to help you better understand some of the major issues involved. Brainstorm further ideas to add to both sides of the list.

The Interdenominational Foreign Mission Association of North America (IFMA)

Recognizing the need for mission agencies to gather together for prayer, strengthening effectiveness, reaching the unreached, and exchanging ideas on mission topics, Paul Groef, a Wall Street broker, called the heads of faith missions together in 1917. Out of this meeting emerged the Interdenominational Foreign Mission Association of North America (IFMA). Charter members included the South Africa General Mission, the China Inland Mission, the Central American Mission, the Africa Inland Mission, the Sudan Interior Mission, the Inland South America Missionary Union, and the Woman's Union Missionary Society of America.

The growth of IFMA began slowly. Today the theologically conservative IFMA has over one hundred member agencies representing more than ten thousand missionaries sent from North America plus five thousand from other countries affiliated with IFMA (www.ifmamissions.org). It provides members with know-how for recruitment, selection, and professional development. The IFMA assists mission business and financial personnel with seminars in management, taxes, and accounting. It also

TABLE 7.6
PROS AND CONS FOR FELLOWSHIPS OF AGENCIES

Pros	Cons
• Allows for those of the same theological persuasion to advance their cause with integrity.	• Can create group think.
	• Requires more meetings for busy personnel to attend.
• Can provide new and veteran personnel with specialized, contemporary training.	• Difficult to connect with new streams of missions such as missional churches, Great Commission companies, finishers, and other short-term volunteer organizations.
• Collaborating with other groups multiplies the ministry of all.	
• Provides the Christian community an accrediting agency for member organizations.	

offers mission executives assistance to enhance leadership and management skills as well as forums to keep abreast of the latest theological and missiological trends. Every three years the IFMA meets jointly with the Evangelical Fellowship of Mission Agencies (EFMA) and the Evangelical Missiological Society (EMS).

In 1964, the IFMA/EFMA formed the Evangelical Missions Information Service (EMIS) and launched the *Evangelical Missions Quarterly* (and later *World Pulse*). This cosponsorship continued until 1997, when EMIS was transferred to the Billy Graham Center located at Wheaton College. John Percy served as the first general secretary of IFMA in 1956, with Edwin Frizen Jr. succeeding him in 1963. John Orme led the IFMA from 1991 through 2006. Marvin Newell, professor of missions at Moody graduate school, took over the reins on January 1, 2007. The IFMA (now CrossGlobal LINK) is headquartered in Wheaton, Illinois.

The Evangelical Fellowship of Mission Agencies (EFMA)

Nothing remains static in the mission world. With the growth of liberal theology, many evangelical agencies felt their collective voice was no longer being heard. The actions of the Federal Council of Churches, which later would become the National Council of Churches, and its mission arm, the Division of Foreign Mission, which later became the Division of Overseas Ministries, led to a parallel development of the National Association of Evangelicals (NAE) in 1943. Harold Ockenga and Clyde Taylor led the NAE.

In 1945, Taylor called for evangelical mission agencies to gather to discuss missions-related issues. Out of this meeting the Evangelical Fellowship of Mission Agencies (EFMA) was born with fourteen mission agencies becoming charter members. Their mission was to provide a forum in which evangelical leaders, whether denominational or interdenominational, could exchange information, work together, and increase effectiveness on all levels. Today, the EFMA has over one hundred member agencies representing some twenty thousand missionaries worldwide (www.community.gospelcom.net).

The formation of EFMA did not go unnoticed by the IFMA. Why another voluntary, nonprofit association? Tensions existed between the two organizations until the 1960s, when collaborative efforts began. These efforts continue today, for example, in the joint triennial conferences.

The EFMA seeks the broadest collaboration possible without doctrinal compromise and so is broader theologically than the IFMA. It has provided an open door for agencies representing diverse theological streams such as the Pentecostal/Charismatic, Reformed, Wesleyan, Mennonite, Brethren, and Lutheran traditions.

The EFMA offers multiple services to agencies. Located in Atlanta, it serves as a clearinghouse for international security information and briefings. It stands before the Christian community as an accrediting agency, requiring all members to undergo an annual audit, thus assuring theological, financial, and organizational integrity. Through collaborative efforts the EFMA (now The Exchange) also serves as a "think tank" for mission leaders to plan and strategize for the future.

Clyde Taylor became the first executive director until 1975. The baton was then passed to Wade Coggins, who served from 1975 to 1990; Paul McKaughan served as the president and executive director from 1990 to 2006, when Steve Moore began his tenure.

ALTERNATIVE AVENUES

Going out as an independent, through a local church (small, medium, or large), through a mission agency, through a denomination, or through a faith mission are valid possibilities and opportunities for the Christian worker. But there are other alternative avenues as well. Whether influenced by theology, culture, globalization, or a combination of all, partnerships in missions is in vogue. Luis Bush and Lorry Lutz define partnerships as "an association of two or more Christian autonomous bodies who have formed a trusting relationship and fulfill agreed upon expectations by sharing complementary strengths and resources to reach their mutual goal" (1990, 7).

If partnerships pertain to more long-term associations and strong ties, networks tend to refer to shorter commitments, looser ties, strong relationships, and little concern for geographical location. While recognizing the need to work together, some prefer to work through more loosely associated networks. They like to get in, complete the task, and get out. Whether through partnerships or networks, mission leadership today has recognized the need for interdependence.

Fewer individuals, churches (including megachurches), and agencies are going it alone. Recognizing the complexity of today's world and the missionary task, the body principle, and the need for the stewardship of limited resources, twenty-first-century Christian workers, relying on the power of prayer and the Holy Spirit, also rely on one another and the synergy created through partnerships. The same is true of partnerships that include US churches, national churches, mission agencies, academic institutions, denominations, and businesses. The type of partnerships that can exist today is limited only by your imagination and view of Scripture.

> *I don't feel we have the time*
> *or expertise to do what a*
> *well-run agency can do.*
>
> Tom Steller, missions pastor
> (Guthrie 2000, 5)

Here is some of that imagination. The Antioch Network is an organization brought into being by local churches for local churches that desire to plant reproducing churches among unreached peoples. The Summer Institute of Linguistics (SIL) and New Tribes Mission (NTM) not only work together on various fields in Bible translation, literacy, and church multiplication but have also jointly produced Field Works to assist the Christian worker in language-culture acquisition. Epic Partners International is a global partnership involving Campus Crusade for Christ International (CCCI); the International Mission Board, Southern Baptist Convention (IMB); Wycliffe Bible Translators (WBT); and Youth With A Mission (YWAM) as they engage in chronological Bible storying among unreached people groups. A growing number of businesspeople have integrated for-profit businesses and church multiplication to reach unreached peoples. They call these Great Commission companies (Rundle and Steffen 2003). Many of these business entrepreneurs are associated with supporting churches and mission agencies.

SUMMARY

Finding one's way to the field can be an interesting and sometimes anxious experience. Wise Christian workers reflect on their theology, identify their spiritual gifts and skills, and become familiar with the specifics of each possible avenue before taking the leap of faith. Although each avenue comes with pros and cons, let your theology drive your decision. We now consider more specific avenues of ministry.

8

Finding Your Niche

Remember, if you're headed in the wrong direction, God allows U-turns!

Allison Gappa Bottke (Guillemets n.d.)

Changes within missions agencies and service organizations, as well as new players entering the missions arena, have opened the door to unprecedented opportunities for different types of missions ministries. New—and innovative combinations of—cross-cultural ministries abound. Time frames for service are much more flexible, ranging from short-term to long-term. Age is no longer considered a disqualifier once a particular year is reached. Medical challenges are no longer an automatic disqualifier. Training for cross-cultural ministries no longer must come solely through formal education. Nonformal training is now widely available. However, those educated in formal settings, secular or Christian, are sought for their expertise in a particular field. All careers are possibilities for missions in that they can be strategically integrated in a cross-cultural setting. In this chapter we look at some of the ministry possibilities open today.

CLASSICAL MISSIONS AND SERVICE AGENCIES

Figure 8.1 (adapted from Winter 1997) roughly identifies some of the diversity within various mission agencies attempting to expand God's kingdom globally. In this model, Ralph Winter focuses on field operations rather than the different sending mechanisms of denominational or nondenominational agencies. Sphere 1 refers to the classical mission agencies that go wherever necessary and do whatever is needed no matter what the financial or physical cost. They tend to focus on evangelism and church multiplication. Some of the agencies may also integrate social ministries. Examples of such agencies—both denominational and nondenominational—include the Assemblies of God, Frontiers, InterAct Ministries, Mission: Moving Mountains, Mission to the World, New Tribes Mission, Pioneers, the Southern Baptist Convention International Mission Board, The Evangelical Alliance Mission (TEAM), and World Team.

A second sphere addresses service and support for the classical mission agencies. Arriving on the scene post–World War II, these "service agencies" provide the necessary service support to make classical agencies successful. Mission Aviation Fellowship (MAF), for example, formerly supplied only air transportation as a service to missionaries and agencies. As the need for this service decreased and the need for e-mail and Internet access increased, it shifted significantly into information technology, for example, providing e-mail service to every corner of the globe. Bible translation was also necessary for evangelists and church multipliers. Add to the mix the American Bible Society and Wycliffe Bible Translators to provide Scriptures in the local dialect. To help broadcast the message through radio, Far East Broadcasting Company (FEBC), HCJB World Radio, and Trans World Radio (TWR), among others, were birthed.

Sphere 3 references the post–World War II agencies that focus on meeting the physical needs of people, with or without relationships to the classical agencies. Agencies that exemplify this slant include Food for the Hungry, Samaritans Purse, World Concern, and World Vision. "Development" would be added later as a major emphasis along with relief services. Some agencies are moving to include church multiplication as a vital part of their ministries, integrating the "social gospel" with the "soul gospel." In 1978, the Association of Evangelical Relief and Development Organizations (AERDO) was formed to "promote excellence in professional practice; to foster networking, collaboration, and information exchange; and to enable its membership to effectively support the church in serving the poor and needy" (www.aerdo.net/about.php).

The fourth sphere emphasizes financial support of "national believers." Why send high-priced foreigners who have a difficult time adapting to

FIGURE 8.1
SIX SPHERES OF MISSION OVERSEAS
(ADAPTED FROM WINTER 1997, 5)

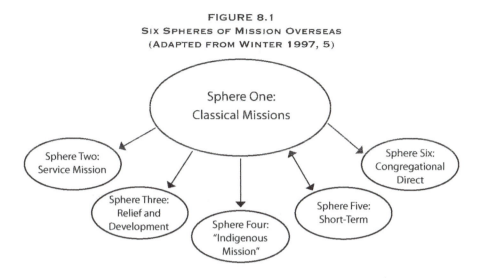

the local culture, do not know the local language, love to be in control, think they always know the best way to do something, and often find it difficult to adjust to the local food and climate, when you can support nationals who know the culture and language, do not have to adjust to the food or climate, will be there indefinitely in contrast to a four-year term or two, and only require a few dollars a month to support? Some examples of these types of agencies are Christian Aid Mission, Gospel for Asia, and Partners International. Early on they strongly opposed the participation of American missionaries (Yohanan 1986), but recently that position has been moderated as they have come to recognize that "both/and" may be superior to "either/or."

Short-term-focused organizations comprise the fifth sphere. Separate for the most part from classical agencies, this entity often focuses on youth and evangelism. Operation Mobilization (OM), Short-Term Evangelical Missions (STEM International), Venture Teams International, and Youth With A Mission (YWAM) provide young people short-term opportunities to minister in foreign contexts (see www.mislinks.org/practical/shterm.htm for an extensive list of such organizations). Participating young people tend to receive minimal training before embarking on cross-cultural ministry. While maintaining the short-term emphasis, a growing number of agencies now provide long-term opportunities for church multiplication with added training.

Sphere 6 refers to congregation-directed missions. Tired of providing classical agencies with their top personnel and endless financial support, while having little voice in major decisions, some churches have decided to go it alone. Many "charismatic" churches, including those connected with the Association of International Missions/Services (AIMS), along with megachurches large enough to finance their own ministries, have moved in this direction. Smaller churches have often formed an association to generate a pool of personnel and funds. Training provided to the in-house personnel typically consists of Western theology. Typically, little missions history or missiology is included, resulting all too often in the unfortunate and naive perpetuation of paternalism and dependency.

One thing is evident in the six spheres: all continue to adapt to current changes. Representative associations continue to be formed to provide broader scope for specific agendas. Agencies continue to move to more integrative ministries that give equal weight to word and deed. Local churches continue to take the lead in missions, giving higher priority to short-termers. Classical agencies continue to work hard to partner with local churches and one another. Besides more interchurch-agency partnerships, strong evidence indicates a growing number of partnerships with national churches. All spheres continue to change to keep pace with new theological insights and a shrinking world impacted by globalization.

With these and other changes constantly occurring in the missions world, an ever-increasing variety of opportunities abound for those wishing to participate as cross-cultural co-laborers. We now highlight some of these changes.

MINISTRY TIME FRAMES SHORTENED

Boat travel to foreign fields in the early twentieth century could take four to eight weeks, sometimes more. With the advent of the jet age that time was reduced to a day or two. Many missionaries who went to foreign fields in the late 1800s and early 1900s often stayed for life, which often meant an early death. Some packed their goods in coffins. As transportation improved, four years was considered a normal term of service, followed by a one-year furlough before beginning a second term. Today a term may be three years or less, with a summer off for furlough. One thing is certain; as time passes and transportation improves, terms shorten. Even the terminology has changed; what used to be called "furlough" is now called "home assignment."

Short trips have provided opportunity for literally millions of individuals to visit different parts of the world for a variety of ministries: prayer marches around cities, researching a specific population, evangelism, teaching a course, assisting in construction work, distributing literature, performing music or other artistic performances, providing technical assistance, helping plant a church, showing *The Jesus Film*. Rick Warren

142

encourages those who attend Saddleback and the more than 66,000 purpose-driven churches to use their vacations and free time to help fulfill the Global PEACE Plan: Plant churches, Equip leaders, Assist the poor, Care for the sick, and Educate the next generation. The church planting phase is done using Saddleback's "Church in a Box," a term used to describe equipping people to plant churches through small groups with a set of tools such as *The Jesus Film*, discipleship materials, sermon series, music, and so on.

Does this shift mean that long-term ministries are out for westerners? We cannot miss the significance of this question: one prominent US church in Georgia concluded that it will now only commission shorttermers in that God seems to be calling people only for short time frames. We are left with several questions. Will brief forays into cross-cultural contexts provide adequate understanding of the gospel and sufficient assistance for new national followers of Christ? What is the impact of short ministry stints into countries where relationships reign? How do nationals view these here-today-gone-tomorrow spiritual warriors? These questions, particularly those that relate to relationships, demand reflection by those living in the West who attempt to minister in the majority world.

We applaud the opportunities that short-term trips provide numerous followers of Christ. These should continue. But their continuance does not diminish the need for long-term ministries. Both are important and required in ongoing global missions. We must never forget that the "body" principle remains as valid today in global missions as it was in first-century Christianity. As Murray Decker (professor at Biola's School of Intercultural Studies) teaches, the short-term team's vision statement (v) should be connected to the long-term team's vision statement (V), as the long-term people are already present and capable of carrying the vision on long after the departure of the short-termers. See sidebar 8.1 for a global code of best practice in short-term missions.

Long-term ministries provide the opportunity for long-term relationships, something vital for quality ministry in any part of the world. Such relationships often begin with deeds rather than words: "In long-term cross-cultural ministry, living the gospel often precedes telling the gospel" (Steffen 1999, 83). True incarnation takes time but pays great dividends. If good missiology requires good listening, recipients of long-term Christian workers will not have to be shortchanged.

AGE NO LONGER AN AUTOMATIC DISQUALIFIER

One large shift in North American culture is that older people are no longer acting "old" anymore. Organizations such as Disney work hard to

---

SIDEBAR 8.1
CODE OF BEST PRACTICE IN SHORT-TERM MISSIONS

Adapted from www.globalconnections.co.uk/findresources/standardsinmissionpractice/CBP/

Recognize that short-term mission activity needs to fit into the long-term aims of the project and so affirm the long-term objectives and activities of the hosts.

Aims and objective: To encourage

- a biblically based, long-term vision for all partners,
- a purposeful project that has measurable goals.

Publicity, selection, and orientation: To ensure

- clear communication of aims and expectations,
- appropriate matching of people with projects,
- adequate briefing and equipping of all partners.

Field management and pastoral care: To ensure

- the aims and objectives are met for all partners,
- the care and development of the participant are provided for.

Reentry support, evaluation, and program development: To ensure

- the participant is supported postassignment,
- all partners are able to give feedback, leading to improvement of future programs.

REFLECTION AND DISCUSSION

1. How does your short-term experience measure up to this code?
2. If you were to repeat one of your short-term experiences, how might the objectives listed in this code help you improve it?

---

take advantage of this trend through advertising that their theme parks are not just for the young. This has a parallel in the missions world: older people want to participate on the missionary front lines and are taking steps to do so. Recognizing this growing interest, churches and agencies have provided missions opportunities for the life-experienced. Most organizations no longer have an age limit among their entrance requirements. This allows the agency's ministry teams to have mature personnel to serve as mother and father to younger personnel, many of whom have grown up without such role models. With years of secular and ministry experience, not to mention financial stability, they bring a wealth of know-how and funding to the missions world. No longer willing just to give money for missions, they want to personally participate. Teachers want to continue teaching; business entrepreneurs want to start new businesses. Lawyers want to seek justice or help people understand their legal obligations and rights better. Health professionals want to provide health care; construction workers want to build. All want to use their God-given gifts, skills, funds, and life experiences to glorify God in a global way.

One organization formed to aid those with life experience is the Finishers Project (www.finishers.org). Their mission statement reads: "To challenge North American adults, especially at mid-life, to make an informed decision about opportunities in local and global ministries by providing information, coaching and pathways through partner agencies and churches." The organization's vision statement is more specific: "To significantly increase the number of global kingdom workers, especially those at mid-life." Nelson Malwitz founded Finishers after leaving full-time employment in corporate America in 2000. Finding no phone number to call to get into missions as a second career yet discovering numerous unnecessary barriers, Malwitz formed Finishers to smooth the path to a second career in missions for the fifty and older age group.

MissionFinder (www.missionfinder.org/retirees) provides listings for global ministry opportunities for retirees. Categories include orphanages, medical-dental, med students, educators, teach English, Native Americans, missions training, and tradesmen-professionals. Some groups require fluency in another language and a specific time commitment, while others are more flexible. They run the range from requiring the missionary to raise no support to requiring her or him to raise full support—and everything in between.

Mission Nanny, for example, serves missionaries around the world. Founded by Betty Sullins in 1990, this agency sends mature Christian women to serve missionary families in their need. Activities may include cooking, teaching, tutoring, shopping, babysitting, providing music, and other domestic chores. Mission Nanny helps connect mature Christian women over fifty who have raised a family with missionary families or singles in need of extra domestic help. The women's short-term contributions enable the missionaries more freedom for productive ministry among the nationals. Financial support is the responsibility of the nanny.

In the twenty-first century, age no longer limits participation in global missions. The Western church has discovered that reaching a certain chronological point in life does not disqualify someone from personal participation in cross-cultural ministry. In fact, we have discovered that age can actually enhance the ministry contribution, particularly among the numerous cultures that respect age.

145

MEDICAL CONDITIONS NO LONGER AN AUTOMATIC DISQUALIFIER

It used to be believed—and in some cases put into policy—that people confined to a wheelchair, the blind, the deaf, and the otherwise medically impaired need not apply for global missions. The living circumstances in places where the church needs to be planted, developed, and multiplied were considered far too difficult for such people. Because medical facilities were not up to Western standards, it was believed that these individuals should stay home and focus on facilitating the cross-cultural ministries of the healthy.

However, people today are challenging the policies restricting participation of those with medical conditions. Granted that life may be much more difficult in some contexts. Granted that it may take longer to do things. Granted that the medical facilities may not be up to the same standard as that enjoyed at home. But, it is being asked, who can identify with the medically challenged better than the medically challenged? Who can reach the medically challenged better than the medically challenged? Churches and agencies are starting to recognize that medically challenged people who wish to participate in global missions do indeed have a place in expanding God's kingdom, not just monoculturally, but cross-culturally as well.

FORMAL PREPARATION OPTIONAL

Since World War II, most mission agencies have required some formal Bible education of those who wish to join them. The amount could vary from thirty semester hours to a completed degree. Some required not only an undergraduate degree but also an MDiv, even though most of the courses in these programs were directed toward the pastorate in the home country.

Today, as more and more churches take up the cause of missions individually or as an association, requirements are undergoing change. Convinced that Bible knowledge, ministry experience, and character evaluation are necessary for prospective cross-cultural Christian workers, they are bringing schooling home. They no longer see the need for extended periods of time taken off for formal education, the heavy focus on imparting information rather than on developing character or ministry skills. They recognize the realities of the high cost of formal education and its accompanying debt. These churches—especially the megachurches—believe they can provide all the training necessary in-house. This allows them to mentor those they send out while providing the necessary training at a minimum cost, all the while seeing them learn in ministry through participation rather than through formal education.

146

The cyclical pattern of education in the missions world tends to move from nonformal to formal and then back to nonformal. Denominational or nondenominational Bible institutes soon feel the need to provide accredited degrees so they become Bible colleges. After a few years Bible colleges sense the need to provide students a broader education so they obtain university status. Over time a reaction to formal education results, and the missions world moves back again to nonformal schooling. Nonformal, unaccredited training, narrower in scope, replaces formal, accredited education with its broader emphasis, but only for a season. Where the potential cross-cultural worker begins and ends his or her studies may have significant bearing on future job opportunities. Lifelong goals should determine the type of training and/or education you pursue.

ALL CAREERS UTILIZED

Building on Donald McGavran's mosaic perception of society, Ralph Winter dropped a bomb at the first Lausanne conference in 1974. He proposed that missions should no longer be perceived and strategized from a geographical perspective, but rather from a sociological one. Winter asked the question: "Can nationals do the job completely by themselves?" His conclusion: "No!" An army of trained cross-cultural church multipliers will be necessary to complete the job because not every people group can reach all other people groups. To help clarify his conclusion, Winter proposed a model based on three types of evangelism, which he labeled E1 to E3. E1 is evangelism of people of the same culture, E2 the evangelizing of societies that are close culturally, and E3 the evangelizing of cultures that are distant. Within the same context, a second question emerged from the discussion that has influenced missions dramatically: How many "hidden people" exist? A "hidden" people is a people group that has no access to the gospel and is unknown to mission groups. At a conference in Edinburgh in 1980, the number proposed was 16,500. As definitions tightened, the number dropped to 12,500. The Joshua Project estimates that if the number is based on ethnic (cultural-ethno-linguistic) peoples without reference to countries, there are around 10,000 (www .Joshuaproject.net/numbers.php).

The emerging church movement of today, like Winter, is helping followers of Christ to rethink Christianity and ministry. Participants in the movement are much more open to the mysticism of Eastern religions than were former generations. Not everything in the Bible, they conclude, can be understood and compartmentalized into nice tidy packages. Meaning for this group is more illusive, less black-and-white, more gray. Mystery and awe remain at the heart of Christianity. As a result they place art at the front and center of worship. They also believe that ministry should focus outwardly, rather than inwardly: "What can Christianity do for me?" (the affirming church). For Rob Bell, teaching pastor at Mars Hill Bible Church in Grand Rapids, Michigan, "Weak is the new strong" (Crouch 2004, 37).

Winter and the emerging church represent a broad spectrum of servant-based, cross-cultural ministry opportunities available today. These range from classical pioneer and/or facilitative evangelism and church multiplication to the arts. David Bosch captures its essence this way: "Mission is multifaceted ministry, in respect of witness, service, justice, healing, reconciliation, liberation, peace, evangelism, fellowship, church planting, contextualization, and much more" (Bosch 1991, 512).

Before highlighting some of the significant careers opening up to missions, let's consider another factor that influences ministry possibilities today. In 1987, through the book titled *The Urban Christian*, Ray Bakke popularized the need to reach the urban centers of the world. This added a geographical factor to the sociological definitions presented by McGavran and Winter. Geographically, the missions world moved from the coastlands (William Carey) to the inlands (Hudson Taylor) to urban centers (Ray Bakke). Serving in the cities of the world calls for a wide variety of ministries to meet the spiritual, psychological, and social needs of urbanites. Interestingly, few have noticed, much less strategized, the interconnection between these (Steffen 1993).

> *By calling every true Christian a missionary, the idea is to involve every believer in sharing his faith as a way of life. The intent is good, but confusion reigns because the earnest seeker for God's will is led to believe that there are no distinctions among Christians, that every Christian vocation, if not every vocation, is of equal value. In this view of the cause of world evangelism, role distinction is blurred and all roles appear of equal significance. . . . No, not everyone is a missionary and not all roles are of equal value in fulfilling God's purpose of world evangelization.*
>
> Robertson McQuilkin (1984, 75, 77)

Medical Missionaries

From doctors to dentists to nurses to psychologists, medical missionaries continue to be needed around the world. Whether short-term or long-term, in rural or urban settings, their skills bring not only physical and emotional healing to the needy but also opportunity for spiritual healing. With some 40 million people infected with the HIV/AIDS virus today, of whom 70 million are projected to die by 2020, vast numbers of medical personnel are needed. With half of the world's people having no access to primary health care, this is truly a necessary ministry of grace.

But medical education does not come cheap. One of the major deterrents for new medical graduates to go abroad as missionaries is the large debt incurred during their studies. To address this need, David Topazian and Daniel Fountain founded Project MedSend (www.medsend.org) in 1994 to provide grants to all types of medical personnel serving under the authority of mission agencies. As long as the graduates remain on the field, many of which are in restricted-access countries, Project MedSend will pay the missionaries' monthly student loans.

Teaching English to Speakers of Other Languages (TESOL)

TESOL made a major impact on global missions at home (among refugees, immigrants, international students, and the deaf) and in countries that are both open and closed to the gospel. Increasing numbers of students worldwide desire to learn English so that they can communicate with the broader world, secure jobs, conduct research, do business, and so forth. To meet this growing demand, secular as well as Christian organizations, such as the English Language Institute/China, the Southern Baptist Convention's International Mission Board, and Educational Services International, provide specialized training and avenues to all parts of the globe to teach English. Christian educational institutions, such as Azusa Pacific, Biola, Columbia (South Carolina), Oral Roberts, Regent (Virginia), and Wheaton, provide graduate-level training for teachers in TESOL and/or ESL (English as a second language).

The TESOL organization serves as a professional umbrella organization for American teachers to organize and promote their cause. Within this organization are a number of caucuses, an important one being the Christian Educators in TESOL Caucus (CETC). The CETC Web site, newsletter, and associated conferences provide opportunities for practitioners and researchers to share insights (www.cetesol.org).

But TESOL has not always enjoyed the popularity that it does today. A survey discussed at the 1910 World Missionary Conference in Edinburgh challenged the growing use of TESOL. The major concerns were that the English language would associate Christianity with the Anglo-Saxon culture and that graduates of programs would find themselves distanced from people of their mother tongue. J. Christy Wilson's tentmaking (using a secular occupation to disciple the nations) model of teaching English in Afghanistan in the early 1950s helped challenge these perceptions. As many countries of the world began to close their doors to traditional

---

SIDEBAR 8.2
EFFECTIVELY COMBINING MISSIONS AND TESOL

Kitty Purgason (personal communication, 2004)

The following suggestions will help TESOL professionals provide top-quality English language instruction while integrating their ability to minister cross-culturally appropriately with their professional roles. Read through them and see if you can think of additional suggestions.

- Work as a team. Don't try to do everything yourself. Partner with people from the local church (when there is one) or others who share your goals. For example, the teacher meets and invites people to a Bible study hosted by a teammate with the gift of evangelism; the study group then grows into a cell group nurtured by another teammate trained in church planting.
- Be a good teacher. Get the right training for the kind of teaching you will be doing. Training ranges from a one-month entry-level certificate, to a one-year certificate or diploma, to a master's degree. You will need less training if you are a conversation partner, more if you are a teacher, and even more if you are deciding on curriculum, setting up programs, and so on.
- Don't use your role as an English teacher as an excuse to avoid learning the local language.
- Be transparent about your identity as a Christian. Programs that use explicitly Christian materials should be open about their curriculum before students enroll. Respect students, their families, local cultural mores, and local institutions.
- Don't preach to a captive audience. Be wise about content in the classroom. Make use of out-of-class opportunities. Build in time for extracurricular activities with students.

---

missionaries, teachers of English flooded in to meet a perceived need of the residents rather than to promote an ideological agenda. Even so, the criticism of "linguistic imperialism" is a recurring theme.

Kitty Purgason (personal communication, 2004) has identified three approaches that Christian TESOL teachers have tended to take in cross-cultural settings. In the first type, the teachers know that TESOL and missions go together but are unaware of training and professional resources so they just rely on their skills as native speakers and fall short in terms of teaching students well. In the second type, the teachers know that TESOL and missions go together but are unaware of good mission principles so they go into the field simply as teachers and fail to maximize their impact as Christian witnesses. In the third, the teachers understand that TESOL and missions go together and get the training they need to do a good job in both. Sidebar 8.2 provides helpful insights for the third approach.

Business as Mission

One of the newer trends in missions today is the convergence of business and missions. Business as mission (BAM) consists of a growing number of lay businesspeople who no longer want to just sit on the sidelines and write checks to fund missions. Rather, they desire to participate in missions through business opportunities without changing careers (becoming professional missionaries). Sometimes called tentmakers, based on Paul's experience of making tents part-time while residing with Priscilla and Aquila (Acts 18), this growing group seeks to start micro- and macro-enterprises that glorify God through more than Christian values, pictures with Bible verses, and Bible studies at lunchtime or after business hours. They believe that Christianity should be modeled and communicated whenever possible during every hour the doors are open. These "businaries," or "holistic entrepreneurs," or "kingdom professionals," wish to overcome the sacred-secular dichotomy that is all too common in many Christian businesses. They believe that Christianity is a way of life and therefore should be lived in the workplace just as it is lived anywhere else. These businesses are missional by their very nature in that they integrate the business plan with the Great Commission plan (see 1 Thess. 4:11–12).

> *Faith exercises a power over a man's life of a remarkable kind because it leads him to serve God in his daily calling. . . . This makes drudgery sublime, and links the poorest menial with the brightest angel. Seraphs serve God in heaven, and you and I may serve him in the pulpit or in the kitchen, and be as accepted as they are.*
>
> C. H. Spurgeon (n.d.)

On the micro-enterprise level, individuals or small companies start cottage industries in an attempt to improve the local economic situations. Joseph Kilpatrick summarizes possible businesses: training people to use sewing machines and subsequently sell clothing; and establishing animal farms (fish, cow, chicken, goat, pig, water buffalo), vegetable farms, import and export businesses, Internet cafés, bakeries, beauty salons, wood and metalworking shops, upholstery shops, beanbag manufacturing operations, secretarial and photocopy services, and book sales. The business opportunities are limited only by one's creativity.

On the macro-enterprise level, larger businesses locally and globally provide long-term employment for larger companies. Steve Rundle and Tom Steffen define such Great Commission companies (GCCs) as "socially responsible, income producing business[es] managed by kingdom professionals and created for the specific purpose of glorifying God and promoting the growth and multiplication of local churches in the least-evangelized and least-developed parts of the world" (2003, 41). GCCs are about job creation that improves the lives of individuals and the country as a whole through taxes. This requires that GCCs make a profit, an ability given by God (Deut. 8:18). Jobs that pay a living wage make for healthy families. Healthy families make for healthy communities and healthy countries. Healthy communities and countries provide the seedbed for healthy communities of faith capable of beginning movements at home and possibly abroad.

GCCs attempt to fulfill the Great Commission through pioneer work, that is, by starting new businesses that make money and multiply churches. GCCs also facilitate the expansion of God's kingdom through funding and networking. These companies are intentional about participating in missions and seek means of accountability so that ministry balance continues. For these CEOs, no side of the triangle—money, missions, or social assistance—should wag the tail of a GCC. Rather there should be balanced integration.

In *Loving the Church . . . Blessing the Nations: Pursuing the Role of Local Churches in Global Mission*, George Miley writes: "[T]he concept of the missionary businessman is foreign to us. It is not part of our tradition" (2003, 180). Speaking at a conference in Atlanta in April 2004, Ted Yamamori noted that "the least-utilized of Christians are business people" (Yamamori and Warton, 2004). Both of these statements are no longer true. One major reason for this is the Kingdom Business Forum (KBF), instituted at the Consultation of Holistic Entrepreneurs in 2002. Established as a professional society, the KBF pronounces in its mission statement: "The Kingdom Business Forum shall contribute to the fulfillment of the Great Commission by providing a global forum for companies, organizations, and individuals who are seeking to achieve Biblical ministry through business and entrepreneurial ventures." KBF hosts an annual conference that results in an edited book of the papers presented. Other texts on this subject continue to roll off the press. Schools are beginning to add courses and programs to address the growing demand. Business-specific Christian journals include the *Business Reform* and the *Journal of Biblical Integration*. Righteous riches through business endeavors have an appropriate place in missions. See http://businessasmission.blogspot.com/ for an excellent blog.

Music and Mission

Another area of missions that continues to see steady growth is the discipline of ethnomusicology. "Ethnomusicology," a term coined by Jaap

---

SIDEBAR 8.3
WHY COMMERCE IS GOOD

Banister (2004, 87--88)

Doug Banister notes that "[c]ommerce is good because it is a wonderful place to share your spiritual story and help people fall in love with Jesus Christ" (87) and provides the following reasons why commerce is good. In a small group, critique these reasons and see if you can add to the list.

- God created commerce.
- Commerce creates community.
- Commerce creates economic viability.
- Commerce serves the poor.
- Commerce provides a natural way for the gospel to spread.
- Commerce is fun.

Kunst in 1958, refers to the historical and scientific study of the music of the peoples of the world. Interdisciplinary in nature, ethnomusicology draws from anthropology, communications, linguistics, and musicology.

Initially, missionaries paid little attention to indigenous music or ethnomusicology as a discipline. Traditional Western hymns were translated into the dialect using existing Western tunes, the secular origins of which usually received little attention. Transfer of music took preference over the transformation of music. As a result, Christianity often sounded foreign to the locals. Worship suffered.

Over time, ethnomusicology has impacted more and more crosscultural Christian workers. Taking the necessary time to study indigenous music, these researchers have discovered not only legitimate variations of music but also how the local culture is defined. The study of indigenous music has led them beyond song to an understanding of the people group's worldview and of indigenous ways to communicate the gospel, disciple followers of Christ, train leadership and followership, and most importantly, worship their Creator. Global research over time has led them to conclude that there is no such thing as Christian music, only lyrics, and that these lyrics can be communicated through multiple ways and means. When this happens, worship thrives because it is naturally supernatural, both at communal events and as a lifestyle.

According to Roberta King of Fuller Theological Seminary,

> It is an exciting time to be a musician and artist in the Church today. There is a growing wave of interest and available artists, especially musicians, in both ethnomusicology and what has come to be termed as "ethnodoxology." This can be seen with the inclusion of ethnomusicology in mission training at seminaries (i.e., Fuller, Bethel, South Western) and also new positions for serving with missions. The first-ever Global Consultation on Music and

153

Mission took place in 2003 at South Western Seminary with more than 300 people in attendance. During this event, the International Council of EthnoDoxologists was launched. EthnoDoxology serves as the council's official journal while worldofworship.org is the official website. Ethnomusicology cum EthnoDoxology is a burgeoning discipline with tremendous opportunity to communicate the Gospel at depths rarely known in today's global world. (King, personal communication, 2004)

> *God's concern about his worship must lead evangelicals to much more careful evaluation of their practice in worship. First, evangelicals must reconsider the new elements introduced into worship. Are visual elements such as drama, dance, and film acceptable to God? They do not seem consistent with a thoughtful application of the Second Commandment. Rather, they seem more like strange fruit offered to the Lord (Lev. 10:1). God in Scripture never approved of creativity or innovation in worship. How can evangelicals so blithely assume God approves of their new activities?*
>
> Robert Godfrey (1996, 167)

David Hall's hope is that cross-cultural Christian workers will eventually focus their attention on "ethnodoxology" rather than "ethnomusicology." Hall believes that if this happens the scope of research will expand beyond music to also include such topics as dance, drama, mime, offerings, preaching, architecture, and visual arts. This leads us to our next consideration, the visual arts.

Visual Arts

Visual arts, another trend in missions, refer to those creative expressions that are seen, such as paintings, sculpture, photography, and computer art. The fish, the plough, the star, and the cross were early Christian symbols. Sculptures of people with hands raised in prayer could be found in the catacombs of Rome. The visual arts played a prevalent and pertinent role in early Christianity. That would change as the visual arts became associated with idolatry, particularly during the Reformation, when the verbal replaced the visual.

The shift from visual to verbal had profound effects (Eire 1986). The centrality of verbal modalities altered worship first and then the fabric of society. Eire writes, "[L]anguage replaced the plastic arts as a medium of imagination" (1986, 41). It was taught that worship was the core of the believer's experience, but it was primarily verbal; the focus was the reading and preaching of the Word. Even the sight line of worship was altered, with all worshipers focused on one point and their involvement being that of listening. Spirituality and piety were turned inward. A "visual anorexia" (Finney 1999, 31) set in and defined Western

154

SIDEBAR 8.4

TEN REASONS WHY EVERY CHURCH PLANTING TEAM NEEDS A WORSHIP-ARTS LEADER

Hall (2000, 50–53)

10. Every church should be a worshiping church.

9. Worshiping churches worship in the heart language of the people.

8. Worshiping in a people's heart language requires worship leadership.

7. Worship leadership increases the effectiveness of both the church plant and the church leader.

6. We are worshipers first, missionaries second.

5. Missionaries who are fired up about God will be more effective witnesses for His glory.

4. Culturally relevant musical and artistic worship is a powerful evangelistic tool inside and outside the church.

3. The performing arts provide unique opportunities for evangelism.

2. The performing arts provide unique opportunities for creative access.

1. The battle against the enemy is won in worship.

REFLECTION AND DISCUSSION

1. Do you believe that worship should play such a preeminent role in a church planting team's makeup? Why or why not?

2. What would add or subtract from the list? Why?

---

evangelical culture until the late twentieth century. Calvin taught that the "spontaneous and uncontrolled" piety of the layman was a danger, so all external expressions of worship were controlled. The senses of seeing, tasting, and smelling were not to be engaged (Dillenberger 1999). The shift from valuing the experiential, sensual, or spatial to a logical, systematic, and scientific approach culminated in the modern era (Collard 2004, 81).

Even in postmodern times, Protestant visual artists find few platforms in local churches and agencies for expressing their creative gifts. There are some fundamental reasons for this, one of which pits those who advocate creative expression against those who attempt to maintain equilibrium. But this is slowly changing as both groups realize the need for multisensory worship and spiritual development in the postmodern world, which tends to appreciate the visible over the verbal. This change will continue to open the door for ethno-artists in cross-cultural ministries.

> Arts: "The imaginative rearrangement of human metaphors, symbols and signal systems in ways that connect us to the transcendent realities of life and of God."
>
> Byron Spradlin (2005, 130)

155

Member Care

Who will provide the overall care for all the cross-cultural Christian workers, no matter what their specialty? Beginning in the 1980s, three international conferences on Missionary Kids (ICMKs) helped set in motion the modern movement of member care in missions. Member care is now international in representation and available on Trans World Radio in a program called MemCare. The purpose of MemCare is to cultivate "spiritual intimacy, encourage, educate, and embolden the Christian community" (Trans World Radio n.d.) through a daily radio program. The fifteen-minute program (www.membercareradio.com) is directed toward Christian workers, NGO staff, and business personnel who are ministering among the least evangelized in restricted areas. Today, the New Testament "one another" injunctions are applied to families and singles serving on the front line. Professional and lay counselors work to provide comprehensive care that addresses the whole person: the physical, the emotional, and the spiritual.

Member care has moved to the forefront of many sending churches and agencies. Recognizing that they are responsible for the total well-being of their personnel, and that healthy personnel are more effective in ministry, a systemic view of the life cycle of the cross-cultural worker is necessary. This has led them to take seriously recruitment, selection, funding, pre-field training, geographical placement, selection of team-mates, and training provided on-field, while on home assignment (including reentry), and during retirement. All of this has created the need for a variety of care specialists at home and abroad. These individuals can help reduce preventable attrition caused by stress, burnout, personal issues, church issues, agency issues, family issues, financial issues, and so forth. When successful in caregiving, Christ's co-laborers can continue to extend God's glory to the spiritually needy (see www.linkcare.org and www.mti.org/mhm.htm).

Partnerships

Another exciting trend today is the unprecedented collaboration and integration of cross-cultural ministries. Churches collaborate with other churches. Agencies collaborate with other agencies. Churches and agencies collaborate with each other. And all of this is being done short-term and long-term not only on the monocultural level but also on the transcultural level. Books such as Luis Bush and Lorry Lutz's *Partnering in Ministry* (1990), William Taylor's *Kingdom Partnerships for Synergy in Mission* (1994), and Daniel Rickett's *Making Your Partnership Work* (2002) have been instrumental in promoting kingdom collaboration and integration. Organizations such as InterDev, led by Phill Butler for eighteen years, helped pioneer the

---

SIDEBAR 8.5
E-CARE: USING E-MAIL AS A TOOL FOR EFFECTIVE MEMBER CARE

Edward Scheuerman (personal communication, 2006)

Missionary member care begins with the missionary. But field leadership soon becomes an integral part of that care. The field leader has many tools available, one of which is e-mail. For e-mail to be an effective member-care tool, the field leader should know the following:

- The field leader and the missionary must enjoy a level of trust that can sustain the occasional (and unavoidable?) misunderstanding that is inherent in e-mail communication.
- E-mail is one of many tools. Other tools include the telephone, personal visits, and postal mail. E-mail's primary advantages include:
  - It is convenient and accessible (for most of the world).
  - Messages can be transmitted and received quickly.
  - It is asynchronous—replies are written when desired, unlike having to answer the telephone when it rings
  - It is written—by freezing the communication in writing, it can be referenced.

- Factors that impact how effective e-mail can be include the following:
  - Age—generally, younger missionaries prefer faster response times and a higher frequency of e-mail contact.
  - Gender—men tend to be less descriptive in their writing than women.
  - Personality and worldview—it may be possible to develop e-mail "profiles" based on personality preferences.
  - Sensitivity and grace—both are required for the field leader and the missionaries under his or her care.

REFLECTION AND DISCUSSION

1. What do you see as the pros and cons of e-care?
2. How do you think different generations will respond to this type of pastoral care?
3. How effective do you think e-care can be?

"partnership movement" to reach unreached people groups. The organization eventually dissolved and ceded all rights to Interdev Partnership Associates (www.interdev.org), whose goal is to promote and develop strategic mission partnerships through collaboration with churches, agencies, and nationals. It now serves over 450 agencies around the world.

Some people, particularly GenXers, may prefer to operate collaboratively on a smaller scale that provides opportunity for quicker responses. By operating through smaller networks, they feel it is easier to maintain one's identity while allowing for more autonomy. Phill Butler's new organization, VisionSynergy (www.visionsynergy.net), represents such thinking. Its vision is to "[a]ccelerate evangelization among the world's neediest and most unreached by empowering working Kingdom networks at points of extraordinary impact." Whether through partnerships or through networks, most people would probably agree that inclusion and interdependence are a definite improvement over isolation and independence. Collaborative missions efforts represent this type of thinking, opening the door for people of all ages, availabilities, educational attainments, medical statuses, career backgrounds, and ethnicities to participate in global missions.

SUMMARY

All legal occupations can and should be used in a professional manner to make the gospel known visibly and verbally. This opens the door for many more participants in global missions. Whether short- or long-term, young or old, medically challenged or healthy, formally or nonformally trained, experienced in secular or in Christian contexts, from rural or urban settings, serving through churches or agencies, each should, "Live wisely among those who are not believers, and make the most of every opportunity. Let your conversation be gracious and attractive so that you will have the right response for everyone" (Col. 4:5–6 NLT). Making "the most of every opportunity" requires Bible centeredness, Holy Spirit dependence, genuine friendships, and missiological astuteness so that familiar ministry models, curricula, and theology are transformed rather than transferred. It is now time to get going.

9

Getting Going

Courage is fear that has said its prayers.

Karle Wilson Baker (Baker n.d.)

W hile perhaps you at times have doubts about the whole idea of cross-cultural missions, you know that you want to become more than a visitor in a foreign culture; you want to be part of a team that sets out to accomplish a specific task no matter what the cost or how long it takes. It is now time to get going. In this chapter we investigate some of the earliest phases of that process, including selecting a field of service, writing a game plan, working the game plan, and leaving home.

SELECTING A FIELD OF SERVICE

Selecting a field of service, whether at home or abroad, is a challenging endeavor. Where does God want you to serve? Here are some questions and considerations that can help you make that difficult decision. Is there a particular people group that God has placed in your mind? Your travels at home and/or abroad may have exposed you to a particular people group that continues to remain on your mind and in your prayers. Once this group is identified, in what country (or countries) does it reside? In what part of the country? Rural areas? Urban areas? Suburban areas? When answering these questions, do not forget to include a new reality. Glocalization reminds us that ruralites, those who formerly lived in the country, reside in urban cities that center around electronic communication (global-postindustrial association), and urbanites reside in cities organized around religious buildings (rural-preindustrial community) or economic institutions (urban-industrial society) (Phillips 1996, 130–31). Are they sedentary or nomadic? What are the climatic conditions? Can your health handle such a climate? If you are married, what about your family members?

Another consideration is your ministry preference. What spiritual gifts and skill sets has the Holy Spirit given you? How needed are they among the people group of choice? Does the ministry require a pioneer role or a facilitative role? Good stewardship demands that there be a strong correlation between the future ministry and the Holy Spirit–supplied abilities to accomplish it.

What about the children's education? Will they be homeschooled? Taught by an expatriate teacher from outside the family? Sent to a national school? An international school? The age of the children and the ability of parents not just to teach others but to teach their own children will influence such decisions, possibly calling for different choices over time.

What is the stability of the country? With the present polarization of the world's major religions along with global terrorism, twenty-first-century cross-cultural Christian workers will face multiple short- and long-term psychological challenges. For example, some parts of the world, particularly the unreached areas within the 10/40 window, are centers of ideological, theological, and cultural challenge for Western Christian workers. Questions that demand reflection should include: How well can you cope with such uncertainties? What about your family?

Institutional preferences may also influence the selection of a people group. Some churches have adopted a specific people group. All human and financial resources, therefore, are funneled to reach them with the gospel. Some mission agencies focus on particular types of people residing in numerous countries. For example, New Tribes Mission focuses on all tribal peoples residing outside North America, while Frontiers has a similar focus centered on Muslims. Pioneers, on the other hand, pour their energy into reaching the tribal, Chinese, Muslim, Hindu, and Buddhist worlds. Some institutions participate in specific ministries such as church multiplication (spiritual needs) or relief and development (physical needs). Others prefer to combine them (holistic ministries). Following Romans 15:20, some institutions focus on pioneer ministries, while others prefer to take a facilitator role among majority world Christians. Other institutions combine both roles.

By considering these questions and conditions, we do not wish to imply that everything must be perfect or safe before you select a specific people group. Rather, we wish to raise some of the realities that should be considered when making such decisions. Whatever your decision, we are convinced that God does not close any door without opening a new one, whether we understand his reasoning or not.

WRITING THE GAME PLAN

Discussing your future missions plans with family and friends is one thing. Putting that discussion into precise prose is quite another. This takes work. Hard work. But it is rewarding work that we highly recommend. Not only will such a document provide you clarity and conviction of purpose but it also will do the same for those who will partner with you in the transformation of that part of the world in which God has assigned you.

Journey Planning

Journey planning is a faith adventure that attempts to envision the future already designed by a sovereign God before it arrives. It is an effort to march in concert with the King of kings as co-laborers. While journaling reflects on past events, journey planning reflects on future events.

Journey planning calls for persistent prayer, precise thinking, delicate dialogue, and a humble spirit. Adds the writer of Proverbs 24:3–4, "Any enterprise is built by wise planning, becomes strong through common sense, and profits wonderfully by keeping abreast of the facts" (TLB). When Sanballat opposed the rebuilding of the wall, the Israelites prayed, strategized, and acted: "But we prayed to our God and posted a guard day and night to meet this threat" (Neh. 4:9). Journey planning is genuine ministry.

Journey planning should result in realistic expectations. Plans that call for planting two churches in two weeks while on vacation in China, using English in a non-English context, should be challenged. How long does it usually take to accomplish this goal in the host country? What other types of ministries do you want to include? Do your homework so that realistic plans can result. If the Holy Spirit surprises the team, and things speed ahead of schedule, great! Your role as a journey planner, however, is to be a realistic futurist walking hand in hand with the Creator.

The journey planner should seek God's approval before the document is written and implemented, not afterward. All too often, planners draw

161

SIDEBAR 9.1
PLANNING

How do the following verses challenge cross-cultural ministry teams?

- "Plans fail for lack of counsel, but with many advisers they succeed" (Prov. 15:22).
- "In his heart a man plans his course, but the LORD determines his steps" (Prov. 16:9).
- "The heart of the discerning acquires knowledge; the ears of the wise seek it out" (Prov. 18:15).

- "Suppose one of you wants to build a tower. Will he not first sit down and estimate the cost to see if he has enough money to complete it? For if he lays the foundation and is not able to finish it, everyone who sees it will ridicule him, saying, 'This fellow began to build and was not able to finish'" (Luke 14:28–30).

---

up the plans and then ask God to bless them. Usurping God's role in planning or in any other endeavor is always a losing proposition. Wise journey planners seek the will of the greatest Strategist of all times before, during, and after planning.

Be process oriented. A journey plan should be seen as a living document in process rather than as a finished product. It is a document that is always under revision. Why? Because the world in which it will be implemented is in continual flux in ways unprecedented in history. Also, over time and through experience, you and your teammates gain valuable insights that demand continual updates of the journey plans. Dwight D. Eisenhower cogently observed, "Plans are nothing; planning is everything" ("Brainy Quote" n.d.).

The journey plan should begin with an executive summary, that is, one to two pages that provide a sweeping overview of the intended ministry (see case study box for examples). The executive summary is driven by a vision statement. A vision statement answers the following questions for a specific context: What does the team plan to do? What spiritual and social transformation does it hope to initiate through the dual power of the Holy Spirit and the Word of God? How long will it take? What will it cost? The answers to these questions should be stated in one pithy sentence. For example, the vision statement for the Antipolo/Amduntug Ifugao ministry read: "Plant three reproducing churches, one in the south, one in the center, and one in the north, in eight years at a cost of $185,000." Specific details for each aspect of the vision statement are then laid out—evangelism, social work, Bible translation, curriculum development, and so forth. Sidebar 9.2 provides an example of a detailed

SIDEBAR 9.2
STRATEGIC AND 2006 TACTICAL PLAN

Team Chiayi (used with permission)

Following is a section of the strategic plan for a missions team in Taiwan.

Mission: To glorify God by working in teams to establish a culturally relevant, indigenous, biblical church planting movement among the working class of Taiwan.

Long-Term Vision: A house church within reach of and reaching out to *every* working-class person in Chiayi, Taiwan and beyond.

5-Year Vision: By 2010, in partnership with local Taiwanese, establish at least 10 reproducing churches that are led by men among the Taiwanese working class in Chiayi, Taiwan.

KEY RESULT AREAS FOR 2006
EVANGELISM

2006 Objective: Work with TWC believers to develop and implement strategies for warm and cold evangelism among the TWC.

GOALS

1. Warm evangelism
2. Using decision continuum, develop and evaluate contact list to determine whom to focus on
3. Develop targeted warm evangelism
4. Cold evangelism
5. Continue to develop existing cold evangelism resources
6. Create one new mass cold evangelism with short-termers
7. Evangelism training
8. Develop methods to encourage and train believers to evangelize

2006 ACTION STEPS

GOAL A	GOAL B	GOAL C
1. Mini conference for people to develop and evaluate personal goals for their contact list using the decision continuum 2. Orchid Street Evangelism: Develop an outreach plan 3. Betel Nut Ladies: Develop an outreach plan 4. In cooperation with Chiayi South church develop plan to follow up on ladies from foreign brides' Mandarin class	1. Report on puppet project progress or completion 2. Develop and evaluate one new mass cold evangelism with short-termers and TWC believers 3. Organize for annual Christmas parade	1. Train new believers to help with short-term team mass cold evangelism 2. Find evangelistic/ service opportunities to involve TWC and do it (i.e., orphanage)

Continued

Sidebar 9.2—Continued

REPRODUCING CHURCHES

Strategic Objective: By 2010, in partnership with local Taiwanese, establish at least 10 reproducing churches that are led by men among the Taiwanese working class in Chiayi, Taiwan.

2006 Objective: Establish and maintain at least one house church with significant leadership by Taiwanese working-class men being mentored by team members

and begin at least one more men's evangelistic/seeding group.

GOALS

1. Start and maintain one house church
2. Start at least one more evangelistic/seed group
3. Maintain current women's group
4. Do at least two combined "celebration" meetings
5. Continue youth group planning

2006 ACTION STEPS

GOAL A	GOAL B	GOAL C
1. Have first meeting 2. Have monthly meeting 3. Use tea night to encourage them to lead the HC 4. Discipleship with HC new believers 5. Encourage them to invite friends/neighbors	1. Start a new men's group (tea night) with new contacts from foreign brides outreach/classes that Chiayi South church does 2. Have additional activity for all possible contacts from Easter meeting with a goal to start a new group with them 3. Start a new group with current contacts	1. Maintain women's group report
GOAL D	**GOAL E**	
1. Easter combined celebration meeting; invite all contacts possible 2. Christmas combined celebration meeting; invite all contacts possible	1. Continue thinking and developing plan for youth work among TWC	

In the original plan, there are parallel outlines for the additional areas of resources for evangelism, team development, mobilization, and training.

REFLECTION AND DISCUSSION

1. What are some things you can see in this plan to help you develop your own journey plan?

2. In the original plan, the name of the person responsible and the month in which the goal was to be accomplished was listed for each goal. Why might this be done, and what would be the benefits?

breakdown of a vision statement from World Team members working in Taiwan.

Other foundational questions that the journey plan should include are:

- What classes of people reside in the host culture?
- What is the context in which this missions endeavor will be done?
- Is the ground spiritually hard? Stony? Soft and fertile?
- What are the major religious beliefs in the area? What impact do they have on society?
- What history does the host culture have with Christianity?
- How can you partner with a team to make this objective become a reality?
- Who can provide this information for you before arriving in the host country?

Answering these questions will help determine strategic prayer points, produce a realistic timeline, and establish a realistic cost estimate. This document should be long enough to provide precise details, presented in doable bites. It should also include a one-page executive summary at the beginning of the document. The journey plan will be useful not only for you and your teammates but also for potential supporters and potential ministry personnel.

The timeline should be based on accomplished benchmarks rather than projected time frames. Short-term timelines are much easier to achieve than long-term ones. Either way, time projections are ultimately determined by event fulfillment. The projected completion date should also be included in the one-sentence vision statement.

The budget will be determined by the longevity of the assignment and bivocational possibilities. Through on-site self-employment, some team members are able to supplement their support. The bud-

> *There is no more powerful engine driving an organization toward excellence and long-range success than an attractive, worthwhile and achievable vision of the future, widely shared.*
>
> Burt Nanus (1992, 3)

get can be divided into three parts: (1) start-up costs, (2) living expenses, and (3) ministry expenses. Start-up costs include transportation to and from the assignment and purchase of the immediate items necessary to accomplish the assignment. Long-term living expenses include what

165

is required not only for day-to-day living but also for medical coverage, insurance, schooling for the children, and retirement. Ministry expenses include all costs involved in fulfilling the vision statement, such as travel, materials, and so forth. As with the timeline, this projection should be added to the vision statement.

Remember, not to plan is a plan. Good stewardship demands a well prayed-through, thought-out journey plan that is revised constantly and implemented with precision and courageous faith. Now it is time to have the journey plan heard and seen, but not just by anyone. The journey plan must be heard by the right people and communicated through appropriate media.

WORKING THE JOURNEY PLAN

With the journey plan now in written form, it is time to share it with family, friends, and other interested parties, raise the necessary funds, and prepare for departure to the cross-cultural site of ministry.

Be Heard by the Right People

Every community and organization has those within it who serve as gatekeepers. Gatekeepers have the power to allow others to enter the community legitimately. Bypass these individuals and you can expect to forfeit their influence and possibly taste their anger. The opposite is also true. Respect their position and you may enjoy legitimate entry into the community. Begin with the gatekeepers.

Friendships are built on trust; they take time to develop and time to maintain. Paul Johnson's answer to the following question is right on target: "Why does anyone invest in someone else? One reason: we invest because we *trust*" (2006, 76). Johnson goes on to say, "Get accustomed to asking for help. You won't get to the mission field without it" (105). We would add, nor will you remain on field without continuing the practice. Start at home with the gatekeepers and continue the practice abroad. Putting oneself in relationships that require someone else's assistance is an excellent way to challenge egocentrism and ethnocentrism. Humility will help you be heard by the right people at home and abroad.

Raise Friends and Finances

Bob and Betty (not real), good friends at a Christian college, met in the student lounge to relax between classes. Their discussion centered on support raising. Both were adamant: they were looking for an organization that did not require them to raise financial support. Who wants to be humiliated begging for money? Besides, neither felt they had contact

CASE STUDIES:
EXECUTIVE SUMMARIES OF MINISTRIES

CASE 1. EXECUTIVE SUMMARY, WORLD TEAM KYRGYZ, PROJECT–PHASE II (USED WITH PERMISSION)

Consider a people without hope; a people without the light of Christ in their lives. They have often been labeled "indestructible"—a name they have lived up to through years of war and oppression. These are the Kyrgyz.

A significant challenge facing the poor of southern Kyrgyzstan is that key leaders and the few existing believers leave to go to the big cities or Russia for jobs to feed their families. Since the fall of communism, the distribution of wealth has been less consistent. Outside the capital city of Bishkek, the common people find themselves in a much more difficult condition.

The recent "Tulip Revolution," which took place Easter week of 2005, demonstrates the fact that there is a problem with distribution of government wealth. It was the poorer southern regions that rose up and took over government facilities in protest to what they deemed corruption of the country's President. They protested the outpouring of funds to the urban area in the north and the lack of attention given to the southern regions. Their growing protest swept the country in just a few days and caused the President to flee. Now the Kyrgyz people wait to see if things will be better.

No matter what happens with the new government, the poorer regions outside the urban capital city will wait a long time before reforms take place and impact their world. Thus there is a great need to be a catalyst of hope in these regions. The country is ripe for a "cup of cold water" given in the name of Hope. Now is the time to:

- Help meet the many needs of the Kyrgyz people who are in despair
- Help this very underdeveloped area of the world with developmental services that will build dignity into a hurting people and help them stand on their feet
- Help key society leaders and the few believers outside the major urban settings to remain in their communities, have credibility, help their people live a life of dignity, provide for their families and let the light of God spread through a parched land

With the completion of Phase I, the goal of the Kyrgyz Project–Phase II is to see 15 workers plant reproducing, nationally led churches with a focus on church multiplication movements among the people of the Fergana Valley (southern Kyrgyzstan) by 2009. This vision has at its roots a holistic Gospel that not only meets the spiritual need of the Kyrgyz people, but their physical need as well.

The desire is to see church planting through businesses established with key leaders in the community who will in turn infuse the local economy with outside money as well as create hope and stability.

Continued

167

This will allow an increase in the standard of living so that these leaders can remain in their communities and become spiritual leaders.

For this to happen, it will take a team effort. There is an urgent need for additional workers to put roots down in these communities, so that their light can shine. These workers are key to the growth of the business, as well as the growth of the spiritual condition of those responding to the light. Workers need many partners behind them to care for them and fund them in this effort. The overall project need is $139,650 by 2009 to develop opportunities that will increase the economic and spiritual climate in several villages.

How much sacrifice is a soul worth? Ask the One who paid the ultimate price. How much time, energy, money and prayer will be given by those who have much, so that those who have little can receive hope in this life and the greater hope of eternity? The Kyrgyz Project–Phase II seeks to provide an opportunity not only for workers who are willing to go and live without many of the luxuries of life, but a way for churches, businesses and individuals to give out of their abundance to those in darkness and without hope.

CASE 2. EXECUTIVE SUMMARY, WORLD TEAM FRANCE (USED WITH PERMISSION)

In a country that gave rise to the Protestant Reformation, France has been perceived over the past number of years as a "resistant" field, as a country that has rejected the gospel. Renewed efforts to plant evangelical churches in France after World War II gave rise to internal fighting and a proliferation of denominations, as well as a significant number of independent churches who have no relationship to any other group or association. The evangelical landscape in France has been dotted with national churches, missions and other associations working in total isolation from each other. In recent years, the French evangelical community has experienced God's grace in drawing together the various strains of evangelicalism towards a concerted effort to seeing a church multiplication movement spawned in this country. Evangelical leaders (national and expatriate) have committed themselves to seeing one church established for every 10,000 inhabitants, where the present average, in the best case scenario, is one church for every 33,000 inhabitants.

PURPOSE

France VIE (World Team France) desires to partner with this movement of God to commit ourselves to seeing 50 churches started over the next 20 years. During the next four years, our goal is, through direct church planting and in the encouraging of others to plant daughter churches, to begin four new French pioneer works by 2008.

STRATEGY

Three main avenues will be pursued in order to achieve this goal. First, we will work to *establish* new churches through multi-cultural teams. Second, we will work to *encourage/assist* churches with which we have a working relationship to achieve the goal of planting daughter churches. And, third, we will commit ourselves to *train* ten French national church planters in pioneer church planting.

This strategy marks a significant change or development in the way we have pursued ministry in this country. Emphasis will be placed on the communication of the vision of multiplication to both the expatriate missionary force and church leaders; the development of networks with other missions, national church groups and associations in order to facilitate church planting; the growth of our missionary force to include a larger percentage of national workers; the training of our missionary force and church leaders in church planting with a view to multiplication; and the development of an administrative structure which will permit this growth and allow us to pursue our goal of seeing 50 churches started in the next 20 years.

REFLECTION AND DISCUSSION

Carefully read and compare these two executive summaries.

1. Which do you find the most helpful? Why?
2. What other types of information do you wish the authors would have included?

with many potential donors outside their respective churches. Even if they had numerous contacts, Bob knew he was not a "platform person" nor a "salesman." "I'm not a fund-raiser," he said, "I'm a TESOL teacher." Each would need to have a lot of contacts because Betty's home church would provide no more than 25 percent of her total support while Bob's ceiling at his home church was 50 percent. And both of their churches required that potential support recipients participate in weekly ministries at the churches, demonstrating commitment and ministry giftedness. Betty lamented, "How in the world are we to raise the rest of the support if we have to be present every week at church? How many of these churches will say that our funds are already maxed out? How long do you think it will take to raise our total support?" Discouraged, as Bob and Betty left the lounge they discussed looking online to see if they could find organizations that provided full financial support so that they would not have to live on the poverty level.

Bob and Betty represent the feelings of many who must personally raise financial support if they want to be sent out. They sometimes feel embarrassed, out of their element, wasting their spiritual gifts and skills, more like beggars than missionaries. All these sentiments raise valid questions: Is the present support-raising model valid for the twenty-first-century church? Is it a universal model that can work in the majority world? Has it passed its time? How many people does it discourage from entering long-term cross-cultural ministry?

At the same time, there certainly are merits to a self-support model. One church identified these: (1) it will provide a budgeted, acceptable

169

living allowance; (2) faith is expended and spiritual growth occurs; (3) it enriches prayer life; and (4) it personalizes involvement of Christians. It also noted two misconceptions: (1) begging for a living is considered a trick of the mind to overcome; and (2) some pastors feel the church's income will drop if money is given individually to missionaries. All these seem to ring true, except for the statement on begging. So true, in fact, one wonders why they are not applied to all ministry appointments? Would not church pastors and staff benefit by experiencing such merits over several years as they raise support for their positions? If so, why does one model provide salaried positions while the other requires fund-raising? Paul's question is apropos: "Who serves as a soldier at his own expense?" (1 Cor. 9:7). There seems to be a deep discrepancy between the two models.

It now takes around two years to raise one's support in the United States. Several important reasons may be noted. On the national level, Robert Putnam and Lewis Feldstein argue that beginning in the late 1960s, Americans en masse began to "join less, trust less, give less, vote less, and schmooze less" (2003, 4). The reasons are broad: "A variety of technological and economic and social changes—television, two-career families, urban sprawl, and so on—has rendered obsolete a good share of America's stock of social capital" (4). Robert Reich notes that Americans work longer hours and harder than ever (2001), leaving them little free time: they average 350 more work hours a year than the typical European and even more hours than the industrious Japanese.

Another factor that helps explain why it takes several years to raise support is the explosion of personal debt of Americans who hold one credit card (many hold three or more). According to CardWeb.com (2006), the average American household holding at least one credit card (excluding mortgage debt) owed $10,371 in February 2004. By February 2006 the figure rose to $11,669. During that same time frame, late payments increased almost 20 percent. During 2002, only 40 percent of cardholders paid off the monthly balance. Half of the remaining 60 percent, or one in four cardholders, make the minimum payment (CardWeb.com, 2002). Depending on the interest rate, many cardholders pay over $80 a month on interest alone.

What about the evangelical subcommunity that presently comprises approximately 9 percent of the US population? Citing the Barna Report, Ted Olsen (2005a) notes that mainline Protestants gave $1,304 to their churches in 2004, while evangelicals gave $3,250. According to the Barna Group (2005), the average donor gave a church $895 in 2004, which is about 2 percent less than given in 1999. As for tithing, just 6 percent now give 10 percent of their income to churches and parachurch

SIDEBAR 9.3
DISCERNING GOD'S WAY OF SUPPORT RAISING: TWO VIEWS

Tom Steffen

Discerning how God wants you to raise financial support can be confusing. Below are the principles of two stalwarts of the faith, who differed in their approaches.

George Muller	D. L. Moody
Prayer	Prayer
Secretive faith	Shared faith
No information	Full information
No solicitation	Full solicitation
No debt	Debt
Full disclosure	Full disclosure

REFLECTION AND DISCUSSION

1. Which man's approach to support raising are you most drawn to, George Muller's or D. L. Moody's? Why?
2. Did God meet the financial needs of both Muller and Moody? How does the answer to this question confirm or challenge your answer to the first question?

organizations. Olsen (2005a) sadly notes that in an Empty Tomb survey of twenty-eight Protestant denominations, only two cents of every dollar donated was spent on overseas missions.

Another challenge facing current support raisers is that younger donors prefer supporting single-donation projects or short-term missionaries over long-term projects and missionaries. As an aging donor generation moves toward a fixed income, securing long-term monthly support for long-term ministry may prove more difficult.

Church leadership and donors certainly have responsibilities and privileges in funding global missions in spite of the relentless pressures and changes noted above. When they fail, the church fails. But cross-cultural Christian workers also have a role to play, even in the midst of the present realities noted above. As they seek to raise support, they must be disciplined, bold, persistent, precise, and clear. Whom they approach has varied over time. Traditionally, the first institutional stop to solicit prayer and financial support was the local church. But as parachurch organizations proliferated a change took place. Rather than approaching just the missions committee, parachurch personnel also purposely sought out individual attendees to solicit their support. This resulted in a drop in the funds that normally would have passed through the church coffers to fund such programs because the money now went straight to the parachurch organizations. Add to this the more recent phenomenon of short-term missions and the net result is tapped-out budgets and fatigued donors on the individual and the local church levels.

We realize that this news can be discouraging. However, before you decide to drop out of missions, read on and be encouraged. Dedicated followers of Christ concerned about global missions have made some serious adjustments to make it easier for cross-cultural Christian workers to raise and maintain prayer and financial support. A number of the models have managed to keep the church central in the process. We begin with an established model before considering some of the more recent ones.

People connected to denominations will often find well-structured steps that lead to cross-cultural ministry. Candidates do not have to worry as much about having multiple contacts to solicit funds because these already exist. In some cases, platform performance is not necessary, while in other cases it is. Those qualified will receive guaranteed funding, making it possible to enter cross-cultural ministry in a very short period of time. The denominational model takes seriously the issue of stewardship of the candidate's spiritual gifts and skills. While some denominations have experienced a drop in funding, this has not stopped those without prior denominational ties from adding their names to the rosters, thereby circumventing the challenge to raise funds on their own.

One of the more recent and popular models calls for a number of churches in a geographical area to form a coalition responsible for selecting, training, and funding cross-cultural Christian workers (see sidebar 9.4). The coalition establishes unified qualification requirements, assessment standards, amount of funds that can be received, training, continuing education, communication with the coalition, member care, furlough, retirement, and so forth. This model minimizes travel for the candidate, allows for ministry participation in one church, provides ample funding without making one feel like a beggar holding out a tin cup, uses the candidate's spiritual gifts and skills immediately, and enables him or her to arrive at the ministry site faster. Those soliciting funding will find a friendly environment to enter with few surprises. The coalition model addresses a number of the concerns raised by Bob and Betty, though it can raise new questions for the churches if one decides to pull out of the coalition.

Not all candidates will belong to a denominational church or desire to join one. Not all will be able to locate a missional church coalition. What are some other possibilities? One is raising funds the old-fashioned way, locating interested parties. But this lone-ranger model can be improved upon. Those going out under mission agencies should request assistance that goes beyond a form letter from the director or how to write a prayer letter that gets read. See sidebar 9.5 for examples without addresses or pictures. Can they set up small group and church meetings for you? Can they have one of their gifted speakers join you? The candidate should not have to go it alone.

SIDEBAR 9.4
CHURCHES PARTNER TO PROVIDE FINANCES, AND MORE

Geoff Williams (personal communication, 2007)

When Beth and I were appointed by the Association of Baptists for World Evangelism (ABWE) as church planters in Colombia, we had the privilege of visiting churches to communicate our ministry opportunities and to gain new friends for support. On one occasion I was invited to the Treasure Valley of Idaho to a missions conference that included ten churches in a twenty-five-mile radius.

Each year these ten churches hold their missions conference simultaneously. It lasts for two weeks, extending over three Sundays. I was invited to speak at a different church morning and evening on Sundays, and at both on Wednesdays. In addition there is an all-church youth activity one evening and an all-church missions banquet held at the Nampa Conference Center. There were also other occasions such as a potluck.

As a result of this missions conference, six of the ten churches began supporting us. In addition to that, several individuals from the area have included us in their monthly giving. Twenty-five percent of our total support was provided by the ten churches. One of the pastors contacted another church in Salem, Oregon, on our behalf. That pastor committed his church to supporting us before we ever visited the church to present our work.

It has been our observation over the years that while there is no contract between the churches, there is an understanding. If a missionary is supported by one of the churches, it makes good sense for the other churches to assist as well. As a fellowship of independent churches, it is understood that their strength for missions is synergistic.

I might add that on our furlough we were able to move to the Treasure Valley for two months and spend that time being involved in these churches for an extended period of time, rather than visiting for a Sunday only. We participated in a VBS at one church and even joined the softball league and played on the team of one of our supporting churches.

On a personal note I would mention that the friendships established on the first trip to Idaho have lasted throughout our ministry. A couple of the pastors traveled to Colombia to minister and visit with us. One work team from the combined churches traveled to help build "our" camp. Several individuals on other occasions came to visit and serve on short-term assignments. The relationship developed through casting our God-given passionate vision for Colombians is far deeper than financial support; it is numerous prayer partners, some of whom will participate in "our" ministry through short-term efforts.

REFLECTION AND DISCUSSION

1. Discuss the pros and cons of raising financial support through a consortium of missions-minded churches.
2. Do you know of other similar models? If so, what have you heard from those who have participated? How do those you know differ from Geoff and Beth's model?

> **SIDEBAR 9.5**
> **SAMPLE PRAYER LETTER**

The following prayer letter is intended to suggest things to discuss and how to present them. It is used by permission of the author. While pictures, addresses, and some locations from the original were removed, we have kept as much of the letter intact as possible so that you can read it as the original readers saw it.

E-NOTES FROM THE HORN OF AFRICA (PLEASE DO NOT POST THIS SAMPLE ON THE WEB, BUT FEEL FREE TO SHARE IT WITH YOUR CHURCH OR FRIENDS.)

Today is Timket according to the Ethiopian Orthodox calendar. Timket is a celebration of the baptism of Jesus. It has a long, historic symbolism for the Orthodox of Ethiopia.

It is high time for an update. Last time all you knew was that we had arrived back in Ethiopia and that we were having trouble getting enough water at our house. Then we were silent! The reason is because shortly after that we began having trouble sending e-mails through our previous account.

FAMILY NEWS

The boys are back at school and are both doing very well in their studies. They are happy to be back with their friends as well, although both boys return having seen a couple of their closest friends return to their countries while we were away. Megan has settled in nicely. She loves meeting people and even trying out the few Amharic words she knows.

CAROLE'S NEW ROLE

Carole has taken a position at the International Evangelical Church. She is the new children's ministry coordinator for English ministries. She is very excited about this as it will enhance her abilities to direct children's ministries in a very strategic setting, and she is excited that the church would like for her to introduce and implement the Children Desiring God Sunday school curriculum.

Carole would like to still be available to the Ethiopian church with regard to their getting the Amharic CDG materials translated and published, but for now

Another possible model is going as a bivocational, a tentmaker, or what some have called a kingdom professional. This model assumes that the Christian worker has some professional means to earn partial or full support in a cross-cultural setting. Some accomplish this as teachers, businesspeople, consultants, researchers, diplomats, relief workers, community developers, linguists, doctors, or nurses. No matter which profession you go under, or whether the job earns full or partial support, you will want to remain connected to local churches for prayer support, and in some cases, partial financial support.

Proponents of all models find theological support to provide validity. The bivocational model relies on Paul's tentmaking activities found in a this opportunity gives her a good place to make an impact that will likely influence the Amharic and English translations, and even one day other languages.

DANIEL'S UPDATE

We return with much more latitude toward the ministries God has envisioned us with. Our number one concern is for the unreached peoples of the Horn of Africa. But the task of mission evangelization among them is not one that can be done alone, or simply by "western" missions. It must involve the local churches of Ethiopia (and other places around the world) working together. With this in mind I am still in the process of implementing the World Christian Foundations study program, which seeks to be a catalyst for those interested in cross-cultural ministry. This is merely one step, but an important one.

Carole and I are also very much involved in building relationships with our Muslim friends. It is important for us to understand them and for them to know where we are coming from. We are open and honest with them about who we are and show them a genuine interest in their specific people group and religion. Doors are opening. Pray for significant relationships to form and that discussion will lead to the importance of Isa (Jesus) as the only one through whom salvation comes.

I also will be teaching for the next two months at Berhane Wongel Theological College.

PIONEERS

Things are going well as we establish Pioneers here. Please pray for our relationship with those who have already expressed interest in partnering together for the Great Commission. We need wisdom as we proceed. There are numerous possibilities!

PRAYER

Prayer is the most important role any of us can play. Instead of making a list here, let me just ask you to reread this update and pray over the issues we've mentioned.

May the Lord bless you as you participate with us in this great cause,

Daniel and Carole Harris
Blake, Brett, and Megan

REFLECTION AND DISCUSSION

1. What are the strengths of the prayer letter?
2. If you were a financial supporter of the family, what additional information would you have liked to receive?
3. What are suggestions you would make to improve the letter (bearing in mind that pictures and addresses from the originals were removed, as were some locations)?

number of passages (Acts 18:3; 20:33–35; 1 Cor. 4:12; 1 Thess. 2:9; 2 Thess. 3:7–8) as well as Priscilla and Aquila's business, which resulted in three house churches planted in three different cities: Corinth, Ephesus, and Rome (Acts 18:26; Rom. 16:5; 1 Cor. 16:19). The traditional individual support-raising model relies on the New Testament, which shows the different churches financially supporting Paul and his teams (2 Cor. 11:7–9; Phil. 4:15–16). Parachurch organizations find their fund-raising support model validated by the same verses used by the traditional individual support-raising model. It is interesting to note, however, that Paul never used one of his breaks to go from church to church to raise funds.

Whether for short-term ministry, long-term ministry, or something in between, raising prayer and financial support begins with raising friends. Central to the human success of any ministry, which has impact on eternal spiritual success, are the people who back it. Betty Barnett, addressing the individual support-raising model, cogently captures this concept in her book *Friend Raising: Building a Missionary Support Team That Lasts* (1991). Some practical beginning steps could include: (1) listing all family members and friends that come to mind, (2) prioritizing them as to level of interest in your present relationship and missions, (3) beginning to pray for them and an opportunity to meet with them, (4) contacting them to set up a meeting time, (5) visiting them and listening to their story, (5) telling them your story, (6) following up on the visit in an appropriate manner—e-mail, card, phone call, and so forth, (7) continuing to pray for a strong connection to emerge between you and the people you've contacted.

Every cross-cultural Christian worker must have a large contingency that can be counted on during the highs and lows of ministry, no matter what the duration, short or long. Having a point person at home in charge of various aspects of your ministry, for example, prayer, finances, correspondence, will help keep your busy prayer and/or financial supporters abreast of your current situation. Why? Because "it is not distance that separates us but silence" (P. Johnson 2006, 163). Missions is a partnership, as William Carey so cogently pointed out to his Baptist supporters in England when he said, "I will venture to go down (into the pit), but remember that you—you who remain at home—must hold the ropes" (E. M. Harrison 1954). Continual communication will help span the distance, creating the possibility for genuine partnerships.

Leaving Home

The foundations are now in place. During the process of getting ready to go, you may have had thoughts about quitting. But the Bible, the Holy Spirit, your family, friends, and mentors—whether through encouragement or challenge—have helped you keep your eyes focused on the vision Christ has given you. You have made it. It is now time to leave home.

Be forewarned: for those leaving the country, completing stacks of government paperwork becomes a necessary evil. And paperwork there is. Start early and keep at it. The visa will eventually arrive. Today, almost all mission agencies have people who are experienced in this part of the process and who can help you through it. If you are going on your own or as part of a local church, however, you will need to learn those ropes as you go along.

Determine what you will send ahead or take with you. In today's global world most necessities can be purchased in the host country. No longer is it necessary to ship multiple crates and barrels of personal and household effects. Rather, it is advantageous to purchase the goods in the host country. This not only helps the local economy but it also provides opportunities to establish friendships with nationals. If your organization has people already working in your country of service, they will be able to help you decide what to bring and what to purchase once you are on-site. If you are on your own, it will help to contact expatriates living in the host country to help you determine what should be brought to the host country and what can be bought locally.

> *Modern Christians are characteristically much afraid of being caught out doing too little for God, let alone nothing. But there are moments, far more frequent than we suppose, when doing nothing is precisely the gospel thing to do . . . biblical not-doing is neither sloth nor stoicism; it's a strategy.*
>
> Eugene Peterson (1997, 164)

One of the most important things that can be done during this time is to implement a communication system with supporters. Communication, both postal and e-mail, should be frequent yet brief for the general populace, while insiders can receive more detailed accounts. Good communication should include human stories coming from the host culture, personal stories of the ups and downs of ministry, pictures, and so forth. E-mail provides a great avenue to accomplish this, but messages must be coded for those working in restricted countries. Recipients of those e-mails must also know how to respond appropriately. To protect those ministering in delicate countries, terms such as "Jesus," "church planting," and "missionary" should not be used. You may also want to create a personal Web page where pertinent information and pictures can be regularly posted.

Something of significance for both senders and the sent is a public commissioning ceremony that celebrates God's call on the missionary. Such a ceremony reinforces the biblical basis for ongoing missions, alerts everyone present about ministry opportunities to expand God's kingdom, reminds the senders and the sent of their respective responsibilities, and provides encouragement for those being sent. Luke's recounting of the send-off for Barnabas and Saul (Acts 13) provides an excellent example for present-day churches to follow. Couples may also want to consider something significant for their marriage, such as renewing their vows, as part of the ceremony.

Finally, do not forget to ensure that any on-site personnel know the date and time of your arrival. Not every new arrival has been met by a welcome party!

SUMMARY

Part of getting going is selecting a field of service. Just as God opened and closed doors for the Pauline teams, so he will do the same for you. Another part of getting going is to prepare a journey plan. This ongoing exercise will help you become more precise in what you believe God wants you to do while providing supporters with concrete information. Now it is time to work the plan by approaching the right people so that friends will partner with you in the ministry vision that God has revealed. Then it will be time to leave home. All along the journey, never forget "the Father of compassion and the God of all comfort" (2 Cor. 1:3). Whether for a short term or a long term, partially supported or fully supported, be ready to be surprised by God. And do not be afraid to take some do-nothing-time to discern God's direction for your journey.

We will now move from home-front preparation to on-field preparation by considering various aspects of culture: What is culture (chapter 10)? How do you become at home in a different culture (chapter 11)? How do you learn culture and language (chapter 12)?

On-Field Preparations

10

What Is Culture?

> This is how humans are: we question all our beliefs, except for the ones
> we *really* believe, and those we never think to question.
>
>   Orson Scott Card (Guillemets n.d.)

nderstanding someone's culture is a difficult but certainly do-
able task. In fact, it can be an exciting journey that results in
lifelong friends, not to mention a clearer perspective of one's
own culture. When you examine the culture of another, you are also
examining your own culture. We begin with Tom's story of growing up
as an Apostolic Christian. From there we identify several key aspects
that help define culture and apply them to Tom's story. We conclude
with responses to culture.

GROWING UP APOSTOLIC CHRISTIAN

When I (Tom) was a young boy, each Sunday was a long but anticipated day that found me along with my older sister and younger brother
in church with my grandparents, various aunts and uncles, and friends.
There was a sense of security and well-being found in being part of a
group that lived out traditions and beliefs brought to America by German

and Swiss Anabaptist immigrants a hundred years before, the Apostolic Christian Church (ACC).

Sunday Mornings

On Sunday morning the children and young people would meet together in the church basement while the adults met upstairs. Like us, the adults began with group singing. While they proceeded to have a regular church service, we would go to our individual classes. Our dedicated, enthusiastic teachers told us riveting stories about Bible characters that were made even more exciting through flannel graph (high tech for those days!), as well as songs, often accompanied with hand motions. Each Easter Sunday we would all line up and the teachers would pass along a nail that one of the ministers had brought back from the Holy Land. We were told it was just like the ones that were used to nail Christ to the cross, causing each of us to fearfully consider the price that was paid for our salvation.

While Sunday school was always a fun time, the best was yet to come: the lunch hour. After class we would all enter the large communal dining room to enjoy milk and donuts. As the adults drank coffee and continued to visit, we would play outside with our friends until the afternoon service began. Then we reluctantly marched back upstairs to sit dutifully with our parents for more singing and a long sermon.

During the sermon I learned to draw, interpret the German hymnal, or just space out. When the service began, it was fun to see which minister would give the sermon because that would determine how long we would sit there. Before the sermon began, four or five ministers would file up to the pulpit area and sit down. After singing and a prayer, they looked back and forth at each other until one finally decided that he was appointed by the Holy Spirit to give the sermon. No premeditated messages were allowed, only that which the Holy Spirit had just revealed. The ministers were called "brothers" and considered as equal to the other brothers, except that they had the gift of teaching and leadership. Each church generally had an elder brother, who had more power than the ministers. The elder could hear confessions, counsel people through problems, serve communion, and baptize.

Before the sermon began, we children would bet among ourselves as to who would speak. After the sermon another minister, led by the Holy Spirit, would summarize the sermon and add his own thoughts. Then a lay brother would offer a song and another would pray. After church it was not uncommon for the adults to take another hour to visit. Most Sundays after church we would go to the home of mutual church members, or they to ours, for a big, tasty German dinner. The

182

summer often found us heading to the lake for swimming and a picnic with the same friends.

Learning Theology and Traditions

As I grew up, I paid more attention to what I heard and saw. While I had hours to play, the adults were always talking with us and treating us as part of the group. They were sure of their faith and their traditions and never hesitated to share the reasons for both. As we grew older, the adults went out of their way to teach and include us in the discussions. I felt they did this out of true love and expectation that we, in time, would teach the same to our children.

One example is the European tradition that women sat on one side of church while men sat on the other. This was true not only during church service but also at lunch. "Friends of the truth" (nonmembers) often sat together in the back pews, usually on the female side. Everyone knew that they were not members but visitors.

The women who were members were required to have long hair and roll it up. They also wore handmade black lace veils purchased from Switzerland. Younger female members wore a circle veil. Since the Bible says a woman should not decorate herself in an unseemly manner, only brooches and watches were allowed. Married couples did not wear wedding rings. No beards or mustaches were allowed for male members.

When I "converted" to Christ at fourteen, a process began that would eventually lead to church membership. My father and I visited the head elder to make our intentions known. He asked me to "repent," that is, confess my sins to him, and then take the time necessary to confess to any others I had sinned against. During the following Sunday service, an announcement was made that I was "repenting." Once confessions were completed, we had a second meeting with the head elder. If no one in the church objected, a date for water baptism was set.

Baptisms were a festive event for the church. Friends of my parents and relatives from churches in various states came to my baptism. A dinner followed in the church dining room. All the women in the church cooked ahead and brought covered dishes. The parents of those being baptized helped pay for certain expenses, and women members did the serving and cleaning up afterward, allowing for several hours of fellowship after the meal.

At my baptism I was not only received as a member into the only "true" church; I also was to have received the Holy Spirit. At that point, I was no longer permitted to participate in high school sports because Timothy said that "bodily exercise profiteth little." However, I exercised a little rebellion of faith and eventually won my varsity letter jacket.

SIDEBAR 10.1
DEFINING CULTURE

Doug Hayward, School of Intercultural Studies, Biola University

Most anthropologists agree that anthropology is the systematic and comparative study of humankind. What is not so widely shared by anthropologists is how to define the term "culture" in that particular branch of anthropology known as cultural or social anthropology. In 1952 Alfred Kroeber and Clyde Kluckhohn gathered 164 definitions of culture, but if a similar survey were conducted today, some fifty-plus years later, the varieties of definitions would undoubtedly be found to have grown exponentially. Despite the varieties of definitions used to identify what it is that constitutes the field of inquiry associated with the term "culture," the vast majority of these definitions will fall into three distinct theoretical camps.

INCLUSIVIST DEFINITIONS OF CULTURE

Inclusivist definitions of culture generally subsume under the term everything that humankind does or thinks as part of a learned tradition. The very first definition of culture was an inclusivist definition proposed by E. B. Tylor in 1871, when he declared that "culture, or civilization . . . is that complex whole which includes knowledge, belief, art, law, morals, custom, and any other capabilities and habits acquired by man as a member of society" (Kroeber and Kluckhohn 1952, 81). The inclusivist tradition continues today in a number of theoretical traditions including that of Marvin Harris, Daniel Bates, and other authors of textbooks currently in circulation on college campuses. One of the significant outcomes of this definition of culture is that it has promoted a holistic approach to the study of humankind committed to examining both the ideas and the shared behaviors of a particular society as a complex system that includes economics, social organization, and ideology.

BEHAVIORALIST DEFINITIONS OF CULTURE

Behavioralists have reacted to the inclusivist definition of culture and have proposed that culture is best understood in terms of observable patterns of behavior that members of a society learn from one another. One definition illustrative of this approach states, "Culture is the learned and shared kinds of behavior that make up the major instrument of human adaptation" (Nanda 1994, 467). While behavioralists do not totally ignore the role of ideas, they tend to minimize their explanatory function in understanding

Questioning Theology and Traditions

A custom I found despicable but obliged to participate in was what took place when members met each other at church or church functions. Both males and females greeted each other with a "holy kiss"—males with males, females with females. I often carefully maneuvered to make sure I avoided "greeting" those I disliked.

humankind. For behavioralists, culture, by its very nature, constitutes a power that causes behavior; therefore, if we want to understand humankind we must engage in the comparative study of social systems as adaptive strategies. The role of ideology, then, is to come alongside the social systems to support and justify social institutions and patterns of behavior. This understanding of culture is currently represented by those anthropologists who embrace social structuralist theory, such as George P. Murdock and Mary Douglas, or a culture and power approach to society, such as Richard Adams and Aaron Wildavsky.

IDEALIST OR COGNITIVE DEFINITIONS OF CULTURE

Idealists argue that inclusivist definitions hold no power for explaining culture because culture is defined as everything humankind does or thinks; thus, the reason humankind does what it does is because it is culture—obviously a non sequitur. Behavioralist definitions are also inadequate because they assert that too much power is ascribed to culture, leading to cultural determinism as the causative force for explaining human behavior. As a representative of the idealist or cognitive approach to culture, Ward Goodenough has described culture as what people within a society need to know or believe in order to behave in a manner acceptable to its members (1957, 167). Another writer, Clifford Geertz, taking a semiotic approach, declares that culture is constituted by a web of significances that humans spin using the symbols, motivations, moods, and thoughts of their particular society. From this perspective, then, culture is an idea, a perception about the nature of reality, and in response to this perception social

patterns of behavior begin to emerge as creative responses to these perceptions. As a consequence, from an idealist perspective, worldview assumptions, epistemological understandings, beliefs, and values lie at the heart of all cultures and constitute causal forces in explaining human behaviors.

APPLICATION

These theoretical differences in understanding culture have an impact on missionaries as they seek to act as agents of transformation in introducing change to traditional beliefs and practices. If culture is understood to be everything that people believe and do, then the gospel must be presented as a totally new way of doing and believing. If culture is understood to be the product of learned behaviors, then the gospel must be presented in terms of transformed lives, living examples, and social activism that promotes justice, human dignity, and well-being that will in turn lead to ideological reform and a new belief system. If culture is driven by ideology, then the gospel must be preached as a knowledge system. Changes in behavior will follow as a logical consequence of a new understanding regarding reality.

REFLECTION AND DISCUSSION

1. Why do you think so many views of culture have been proposed?
2. Though you may not have formally studied anthropology, which of the approaches seems best to fit your understanding of culture?
3. How might this influence the way you would communicate the gospel?
4. What would you say are the strengths and weaknesses of your approach?

185

All worship conducted in the sanctuary was without a piano or an organ, as musical instruments were forbidden. However, we could use a guitar or a piano at church gatherings in our homes. One positive outcome of this practice was that we learned to read music and sing a cappella. Large singing gatherings held with visiting churches were the vehicle for most young members to meet prospective spouses, for we had to marry within the church to retain our membership.

The ACC considered itself God's only true church. As for missions, the church focused primarily on social work, such as the Heifer Project. The church did support one couple to go to Japan in the early 1950s. This couple dutifully transferred the all-important church building architecture, the number and order of services, lunch between services, and the egalitarian leadership structure to their church planting project in Japan, making it hard to distinguish the resulting church there from any ACC in the United States. I often wondered what the Japanese substituted for donuts at Sunday lunch!

In the early 1960s, a revival broke out in the ACC, with many hundreds of young people joining the church, including my sister. Because the missionaries to Japan were from our home church, some of the young people began to question why that couple could be accepted as missionaries but not others. My sister and some friends challenged the head elder. Eventually, she left the church for formal missions training, which was considered a willful break from the church. I vividly remember listening as a visiting head elder publicly read the letter of her excommunication. Shortly after that, I left the church to pursue my own studies in missions.

Growing up in the ACC laid the foundation for a life-long missiological journey. The many contradictions alerted me to the fact that culture influences theology, that truth differs from Truth, that reality differs from Reality. It taught me to look critically at how I perceive Christianity, and how I was expected to pass faith on to people of a different culture. For that I am eternally grateful.

UNDERSTANDING CULTURE

What is culture? Why should culture be studied? There are foundational reasons for every person working cross-culturally to invest some time in the study of culture. The academic disciplines of cultural and applied anthropology examine the integrative patterns of societal life. Most cross-cultural Christian workers must have a good understanding of the host culture so that they can successfully adjust to the new environment, build solid relationships with key members of the society, and be effective in contextual ministry. In this chapter we help you understand the concept of culture as found in societies around the world. It is our hope that this introduction will help you understand culture better and make you more effective at learning how to live in the new culture where you serve.

Though we use it freely in everyday conversation, "culture" is a difficult term to define. In 1952, two well-known anthropologists cited 164 definitions that had been published (Kroeber and Kluckhohn 1952). Many more could be added to that list today. In sidebar 10.1 we present the various approaches to culture used by anthropologists and summarized by Doug Hayward of Biola University.

Possibly more important than the definition of culture, however, are the analogies and theory-driven assumptions that lay behind them. Most simply put, culture is a unique, total way of life for a specific group of people.

Several key components that comprise the definition of culture can be seen in the many ways culture is like stories (Steffen 1998). For example, stories are dynamic in nature and global in perspective, just as cultures are dynamic in nature and operate within a global context. Each of the sections that follow further reflects how culture is like stories and discusses applications from Tom's story.

Culture, like Stories, Proceeds from Environment

Dominant environmental realities—such as snow, drought, floods, rain, fire, tornados, typhoons—deeply influence culture. Those living on islands see the world differently than do those living on land-locked territories, as do lowlanders as opposed to highlanders and sedentary peoples as opposed to nomads. Human-engineered environments also matter—urbanites perceive the world very differently than do people who grow up in rural areas. The environment and the impact it has on daily life play a major role in how the world is understood by people living within that environment.

Application: From listening to German hymns, hearing German being spoken by my grandparents and sometimes at church, and participating in numerous social gatherings associated with the ACC, my German-Swiss background began to be formed—the need for community, a strong work ethic, and generous sharing were some of the values I learned that had been shaped by my environment.

Culture, like Stories, Is Communicated through Symbols

Humans around the world have become very adept at creating symbols and sets of symbols from the individual to the global levels and assigning respective meaning(s) to them. Through visible and invisible symbols (forms), culture receives its meaning, providing social participants daily direction. Some of these symbols are more foundational to a society than others, helping to define worldview. These symbols—such as the red, white, and blue American flag; hot dogs; and fireworks—tend to find their way into communal ritual during celebrations, for instance, the Fourth of July. A society finds meaning in symbolic forms in that these forms provide commonly understood implications and help people navigate relationships and life.

Application: Numerous symbols defined life for me. Women wore veils, signifying that they were members in good standing. Brooches signified wealth for some, even though the absence of a wedding ring for married couples in the community demonstrated commitment to a simple lifestyle. The five or six chairs that surrounded the pulpit portrayed egalitarian pastoral leadership. The absence of facial hair on men signified membership in the ACC. Terms such as "brother" and "sister" denoted inclusion in the "true" church, as did a "holy kiss."

Culture, like Stories, Is Communicated through Rituals

Every society uses ritual to reinforce its central cultural stories and symbols. They exist on the individual, family, community, and national levels. They are performed in times of transition as well as in times of stability or crisis. Rituals may follow the life cycle or the annual calendar or be dictated by emergencies. Communion, for example, serves as a communal ritual performed by Christian churches to remind its followers of Jesus's death. Stories associated with communion go back to the Passover, then jump to the Passover meal of Jesus and the disciples. Symbols include the wine (Jesus's blood) and the bread (Jesus's body). Some churches follow a calendar cycle to determine when to serve communion, while others do it "as the Lord leads." The purpose of this ritual is to maintain cultural identity by reinforcing its deepest stories and symbols.

Application: My baptism served as a major transition ritual to reinforce the beliefs and values of the ACC. People gathered from churches in state and out of state. When I gave my testimony (or faith story), I reinforced the ACC culture for everyone who heard, including myself. The elder who performed the baptism reinforced his status and role. The water served as a symbol of new life coming out of death. The feast that followed served as a means to confirm community.

Cultures, like Stories, Have Official Versions and Street Versions

For every "official" (formal) version of how things should be said, thought, done, or made, there exists a parallel "street" (informal) version. Often they are very different from each other. The Bible challenges followers of Jesus Christ to live like him. Striving for perfection is very different from actually reaching perfection. There is the official, or ideal, view of reality, and then there is the real version. The first sets the standard for society; the latter deals with human reality. Both are always present.

Application: The ACC idea that participating in high school sports had little value did not fit my—or my friends'—worldview. We had many theological discussions on the topic only to conclude that the ACC had no clue what it was talking about. High school sports taught me self-discipline, teamwork, how to win and lose (very often) graciously, how to work through pain, how to develop healthy self-confidence, and that I could excel in something. These are all lessons that continue to influence me today.

Culture, like Stories, Is Expressed through a Host of Venues

Culture comes in verbal, written, visual, and acted venues, to name a few. Culture is communicated verbally through intentional and unintentional speech and songs. "Johnny, eat your vegetables!" "Jane, raise your hand before you talk." "Did you hear that new song by . . . ? Great lyrics!" Such statements not only communicate culture to Johnny and Jane but also instruct and reinforce it to everyone within hearing. Culture can also be found in written forms from sacred texts, such as the Qur'an or the Bible, to a personal letter. It is also conveyed visually through material artifacts and monuments, such as baskets and the presidents carved on Mount Rushmore. Dramas, movies, and television also communicate culture through the plot-driven actions of the actors.

> *When we travel to a new country, we feel an almost irresistible impulse to smooth over the strangeness, the distinct particularity of the people we meet. We slip seamlessly into supposing that they are just like ourselves, and we almost forget to marvel at the differences. It's not until we have dwelt in the new country long enough to be shocked, repeatedly, at the wrongness of our assumptions that we begin to notice the crucial things we have missed.*
>
> Sherry Anderson and Paul Ray
> (2001, 41)

Application: My sister's excommunication took place from the pulpit, as did mine, even though I was not there to hear it. Times around the dinner table with relatives in state and out of state also provided times to communicate shared values. Rituals such as baptisms and other social gatherings centered around food reinforced trusted values.

189

Culture, like Stories, Constantly Changes

Walter Goldschmidt's proposal that "people are more alike than cultures" (1966, 134) certainly rings true. A number of researchers have tried to identify the universal categories found in all cultures. George Peter Murdock, for example, compiled an exhaustive list of over seventy categories in his Human Relations Area Files (HRAF). Robert Redfield preferred a reduced inventory of sixteen universals. New Tribes Mission uses eight universals: (1) material, (2) art and play, (3) economic organization, (4) social organization, (5) political organization, (6) social control, (7) enculturation, and (8) worldview.

More recently, Donald Brown (1991) warns us that some universal traits and complexes do not always stand the test of time. Some are new in that certain peoples will add them to their culture, while others are discarded and are now seen as "former universals."

Whatever the number of universals one settles on, how they are believed and the behavior that results tend to differ from one culture to another and even from one subculture to another. What is true of symbols as mentioned earlier is also true of universals. Culture is extremely complex, wonderfully depicting its Creator!

Application: As some members of the church explored outside the ACC, their vision for God changed and expanded. They wanted more missionary activity from the ACC. When the elders debunked their efforts, they went underground to do what they believed to be right. Large sums of money were donated to missions agencies outside the ACC. This action would eventually lead to a church split. Some, including my parents, began a church that gave 51 percent of the offerings to missions. The ACC, on the other hand, began to prioritize more effort toward social ministries.

Culture, like Stories, Is Integrative

Although universals can be discussed separately, culture demands that each universal be seen in relation to all other universals. No universal can be understood adequately without perceiving its interconnection to other universals, particularly since not all carry the same weight in a given society. The same is true of behavior that is visible but always has invisible assumptions that drive it. People's observable behavior is intrinsically tied to an invisible belief system. Culture perceives life as an integrative, total package with each element assigned a particular price tag.

Application: The ACC, the religion universal, dominated all aspects of the lives of its members. The only true church told its members how to use its finances, how to dress, and what sports they could participate in, and identified the political roles and status of church leaders and the laity. It encouraged a strong work ethic as well as play within the community. Before anyone acted in any area of life, the beliefs of the ACC were considered because its cultural values ran deep through every area of that person's life.

Culture, like Stories, Expresses Value-Driven Behavior

The speech and the action or inaction of an individual or a group of people convey values that involve reason, imagination, and emotion. Most cultural participants unconsciously weigh their words and actions in relation to good and evil, right and wrong, fairness and unfairness, legality and illegality, honesty and dishonesty, humility and arrogance, and the multiple shades of permissibility between such bookends. Expressions such as "Everybody oughta know" assume that culture communicates values, even for the blurry gray zones. No valueless culture exists.

Application: Community drove much of the life for members of the ACC. They came to church early to chat, continued the discussions over lunch, and then again after the second service. We belonged to a group of roughly five extended families that did everything together, from going to the lake for a picnic after church to going on annual vacations together. They were wonderful times, and their values became my values.

Culture, like Stories, Centers on Characters

Culture is dependent on the characters of the society in which the culture is found, including the people (as individuals and as groups), spiritual entities, and animals. On the human side, some anthropologists give most attention to the individual while others focus on groups. In Acts, Luke includes conversion stories about individuals, such as Paul and the Ethiopian eunuch, as well as groups, such as Cornelius and his relatives and friends, Lydia and her household, and the jailer and his household. Other human groups that play a role in Acts include the Pharisees, the Sadducees, the apostles, the Israelites, and the Gentiles.

Concerning spiritual entities, some cultures pay careful attention to beliefs about the spirit world, while others dismiss its existence (and therefore dismiss its importance). In Acts, the dominant spiritual character is the Holy Spirit, with Satan mentioned only twice (individual entities). Also noted are angels and evil spirits (spiritual groups).

Concerning animals, anthropologists note that they play a teaching and/or entertainment role in some societies. While animals do not play a significant role in Acts, they do in other parts of Scripture (e.g., the plagues in Egypt and some of the judgments in Revelation).

Application: Characters that helped mold my understanding of culture were many. From extended family members whom we visited annually in a different state to friends from church whom I spent hours with every week and on vacations, people taught me what I should know about the world. My high school coach questioned why I would give up sports. I knew my answer (at that time) made no sense to him or to me. My junior high Sunday school teachers taught periodically about the indwelling of the Holy Spirit that would take place during baptism. I never questioned their wisdom. I remember being taught very little about Satan or demons; they did not play a formative role in the ACC worldview. My grandfather, a farmer, taught me what is required to take care of animals—patience, toughness, love, responsibility, and dependability no matter what the weather or how you felt. All these lessons helped shape me into the person I am today.

Culture, like Stories, Defines Social Relationships

Every culture operates through a power system of social relationships that define status and role. Status refers to the relative position of people in a society based on their perceived social power. General and private, judge and jury, missionary and national, teacher and student— all have different status levels. Role, however, relates to the appropriate behavior associated with a specific status. In some societies status is typically granted through an ascribed means, for example, the family you are born into, reaching a certain age, or being male or female. Other societies allow members to gain status through achieved means, for example, earning an academic degree, being given a prize or a reward for a service rendered, being elected to a particular office. Whether the focus is on ascribed status or achieved status, all societies accomplish the necessary tasks they face through leaders and followers of varying status and roles.

Application: In the ACC, the head elder was the first among equals. He (never she) held the most power and had the role of serving communion, baptizing, and hearing confessions. The other elders were considered equal in relation to preaching and decision making. Members of the church were to dutifully follow what God told the elders to say. Cautionary tales were often told from the pulpit to keep members in line. Men and women had separate seating in the sanctuary and the lunchroom. The distinction between members and nonmembers ("friends of the truth") was precisely defined through dress, terminology, and actions.

Culture, like Stories, Is Driven by Opposing Themes

Themes refer to those concepts that organize reality and relationships. In many cases, a central cultural theme has an opposing theme, resulting in healthy tension that keeps a society balanced. While living among the

Ifugaos, I (Tom) discovered a number of themes that defined the Ifugao worldview (children, unity, land, rice, rice wine, animals, reciprocity, family, education, Catholicism; Steffen 1997, 260). I also found that there were unifying and opposing themes. For example, while unity is a major theme found in Ifugao stories, counter or opposing stories focus on cursing people and animals so that no one gets too far ahead of others economically. Ifugao culture, like all cultures, is filled with tension as opposing themes vie for supremacy.

Application: One theme and opposing theme that vied for supremacy in my ACC community was greeting with a holy kiss. My friends and I despised the so-called biblical greeting. What did the neighbors think when they passed the church as men were kissing men and women were kissing women on the front porch? What was wrong with a strong handshake? It was good enough for us, and we set up spotters around the church to make sure we could avoid every possible encounter with those who favored what the ACC taught as the biblical model of greeting.

Culture, like Stories, Defines "Reality"

"Reality" refers to the assumptions and beliefs that define worldview, providing personal and collective identity. This identity is accomplished over time, often intuitively. Says Pierre Bourdieu, "[W]hat is essential goes without saying because it comes without saying" (1977, 167). In creating and affirming "reality," culture validates, criticizes, organizes, comforts, instructs, integrates, stabilizes, entertains, offers hope, mobilizes, and continually transforms those living under its presence. These realities distinguish "us" from "them" and provide the "why" behind "what" different people groups say and do.

Application: The ACC defined reality for my family for many years. Without much outside exposure to a broader Christianity (after all, there was none), few considered the possibility of alternatives. Life centered around the church, which integrated work and play, the spiritual and the social, friends, family, and a potential mate. What more of a reality could one ask for?

Culture, like Stories, Is Learned Imperfectly

No one is born with social absolutes. Rather, over the course of time, shared symbols, stories, and rituals become authoritative symbols, stories, and rituals that in turn finally become canonized symbols, stories, and rituals. People are socialized to accept a specific life script formally (institutional education), nonformally (seminars), and most often, informally (daily activities), through symbol-based stories retold and reinforced through rituals.

193

Social control, often through gossip, helps keep society members marching in the same direction. However, culture is never adopted completely from one generation to the next. It only serves as a "potential guide" and "tends to be shared." Just as stories are open to multiple interpretations (not unlike propositions), so is culture. There is therefore always, as Chuck Kraft is fond of saying, "room to wiggle" in the lifelong enculturation process.

Application: My dear parents no doubt often wondered what type of children they were raising. We were certainly learning the ACC culture imperfectly. When my sister headed off to train for missions before serving eight years in Central America, my father almost disowned her. That eventually changed even as Dad and Mom attended sporting events in which I participated. There is nothing like seeing your parents in the crowd. Maybe we helped them to learn the ACC culture imperfectly as well. They too would eventually serve abroad, eight years in the Philippines.

Culture, like Stories, Has Rival Stories

The controlling myths of a community that provide a library of scripts are never without rival stories that challenge the status quo. Societies, therefore, undergo constant change as people revise the standard scripts to meet new challenges. Worldview and identity constantly change because rival stories coming from within and without the society offer new answers to (often new) personal and societal questions. If a way of life can be learned through touchstone stories, symbols, and rituals, it can also be unlearned through the same means. The gospel provides such a rival story, offering a totally new way of life through an allegiance transfer. Rival stories demand reflection and resolution, creating cultures that are constantly reconstructed. They create conflict that demands choices resulting in personal and group consequences.

Figure 10.1 illustrates the interacting components of culture and shows that they can be used either for reinforcement or challenge. Every major aspect of culture will be found in the interrelationship of story, symbol, and ritual. Reflection on that interrelationship, which is continually at work, will either reinforce the existing understanding of a specific aspect of culture or present a rival story that will challenge it, calling for its abolishment or modification.

Building on the ritual section above, communion has Old and New Testament stories that provide background and instruction. It also has symbols, the wine and the bread, that are administered periodically (ritual) by those sanctioned within a given church. Stories abound among people who understand the symbol of bread to be the literal body of

FIGURE 10.1

STORIES, SYMBOLS, AND RITUALS DEFINE CULTURE AND IDENTITY

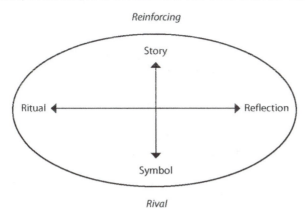

Christ. Rival stories that understand the symbol of bread to be representative of the body of Christ also abound. The same is true with regard to
who can serve communion, laity or clergy. Each story serves as a rival or
a reinforcing story of one's culture and identity, demanding reflection.

Application: We learned the ACC culture imperfectly because we heard
rival stories. Many missionaries stayed in our home over the years, telling
us about what God was doing in remote parts of the world. We eagerly
listened to them around the dinner table and late into the night. They
often left little gifts from the countries they represented. These became
symbols that helped keep their stories alive. Their stories and symbols
challenged the stories we were hearing. After much reflection, their
stories—fanned by the symbols given us—would eventually prevail over
the stories we continued to hear that reinforced the ACC perspective.

Culture, like Stories, Has Reinforcing Stories

To offset rival stories, challenged people revert to those stories that
provide validation for their identity. Sometimes these are cautionary tales,
such as the story found in Acts 5 about Ananias and Sapphira. Listeners
hear the consequences of placing self over God. Hero stories (David and
Goliath), comfort stories (Ruth and Boaz), and hope stories (Hannah
and Samuel) serve the same purpose. Every culture has a repertoire of
reinforcing stories to combat rival stories.

Application: When under attack, any good organization tries to reinforce its culture through stories. The same was true of the ACC. Many
of the cautionary tales of shipwrecked members given by the ACC pastors were meant to reinforce the status quo of the church. They actually

195

had the opposite effect, causing us to delve deeper into Scripture in an attempt to separate culture from theology.

Summary Application

Growing up in the Midwestern United States in the German-Swiss Apostolic Christian Church played a major role in defining my worldview and forming my identity. The church building (symbol of sacred space) provided the central place to meet family and friends every week (ritual). It was here I heard (socialization through theme-driven stories) who really understood God's Word and the ideal way Christianity should be expressed and lived. The same was true of the homes, where adults included children in discussions, teaching them traditions, challenging them to convert to Christ, even before "sowing their wild oats." I saw the reality.

The discrepancy between the ideal and the real raised a host of questions, but few answers. Life seemed very complex. Why were some songs sung in German? I certainly did not understand them! Why no musical instruments in the sanctuary—and yet David often talked about them in the Psalms? Even if bodily exercise profited little, was there not some profit in school team sports? If this church was God's only true church, why was so little emphasis given to missions? Why such isolationism if total truth resided in the ACC? Why should the beloved "friends of the truth" (outsiders) come to the ACC rather than the ACC go to them? When did one really receive the Holy Spirit?

As a result of these questions, I focused more on rival stories. The Apostolic way of life was totally integrated, controlling its followers from birth to death. The status of elders and lay members showed clear demarcations, providing church leadership with the final word from God. The leadership structure was egalitarian with a first among equals. Leaders knew their roles as did the member brothers and sisters. As years went by and my exposure to the larger world increased, I was confronted with a number of rival symbols, stories, and rituals. I knew these demanded an allegiance change, and I took the necessary steps in spite of the comments (social control through gossip and cautionary tales) of family members and friends.

It should also be noted that the Apostolic Christian Church is an organizational culture. The denomination influenced my worldview and identity because, like humans, the church has a culture. Edgar Schein, who pioneered in this area, defines organizational culture as "a pattern of basic assumptions—invented, discovered, or developed by a given group as it learns to cope with its problems of external adaptation and internal integration—that has worked well enough to be considered valid and,

196

therefore, to be taught to new members as the correct way to perceive, think, and feel in relation to those problems" (1985, 9).

This is important for Christian workers to know for a number of reasons. Too rarely are they aware of the intricacies of their own cultures, or those of the organizations that influence(d) them. Such organizations could include churches (theology, traditions, symbols, rituals), educational institutions (Western thinking, pedagogy), businesses (economics), and mission agencies (structure). Each organization operates as a culture, making certain demands on those who participate within it. Christian workers should exegete organizational cultures with the same passion that they exegete the host culture. Such studies should result in better understanding, better adjustment, better communication, better critical contextualization, and most importantly, better relationships.

RESPONSES TO CULTURE

The socialization process, in spite of rival symbols, stories, and rituals, is usually quite successful. If you do not believe so, just try changing some aspect of culture. Offer the left hand when shaking hands. Drive in the left lane rather than the right. Serve your guests raw hamburgers on buns. Cut in front of the line at the grocery store. Cancel Christmas. People learn culture so well that they tend to "judge other cultures by the values and assumptions of their own culture[;] of course by one's own culture's criteria, all other cultures appear inferior" (P. G. Hiebert 1976, 334). This attitude is what missiologists call ethnocentrism.

Ethnocentrism, like egocentrism, is found in every person; it is universal. Overall, people tend to believe that their way of life is superior to all others. This tends to lead to stereotypes: religious versus secularist, liberal versus conservative, rich versus poor, civilized versus uncivilized, literate versus illiterate, developed versus undeveloped. Sometimes these stereotypes are driven by an attitude of superiority, not just differences. For example, first-century Jews were disdained by Gentiles not just because of their imageless worship, perceived laziness as evidenced by the Sabbath rest, or their avoidance

> *The first step to overcoming ethnocentrism is the recognition that my own values are not necessarily the same as God's. All Christians hold many values derived from their culture. A second step is to understand that our own interpretation of Scripture comes from a particular cultural context. A third step is to see that God's values may be enfleshed differently in another culture from how they are in my own.*
> Bernard Adeney (1995, 15)

197

of pork, but because of the Jews' cold contempt for all other religions (Barclay 1975). The Jews' perceived position of privilege resulted in the name of God being brought into disrepute, shutting the heart's door of many Gentiles (Rom. 2:17–29).

Christian workers must move beyond stereotypes and cold contempt to empathy. By empathy we mean genuine respect for the people of a different culture. Empathy demands that the Christian worker understand the world as the host culture understands it, feel about things as the host culture feels about things. This does not mean, however, that the Christian worker must compromise his or her moral values. Empathy calls for understanding the host culture's beliefs and behaviors, not necessarily accepting them. For empathy to become genuine, participation with members of the host culture will become necessary.

> *Your attitude should be the same as that of Christ Jesus: Who being in very nature God, did not consider equality with God something to be grasped, but made himself nothing, taking the very nature of a servant, being made in human likeness.*
>
> Phil. 2:5–8

Christian workers must move beyond stereotypes and cold contempt to identification. Identification advances beyond empathy, requiring that the Christian worker participate within the host culture. A major part of this participation would be the ministry of learning the culture and language so that the "whys" behind beliefs and behaviors become evident. It is impossible to learn the host culture without participation within it. Identification requires that the Christian worker take a learner role while becoming involved with members of the society.

Identification can be outward and inward. Hudson Taylor dressed and wore his hair as Chinese men did. Many would agree that he had an effective ministry overall. For men serving among Muslims today, beards will no doubt prove helpful. Dress, housing, standard of living, and so forth definitely affect one's ability to identify with the host culture. But identification must surpass outward expressions; it must also be inward.

Inward identification is more difficult to obtain and superior to outward identification. David Hesselgrave (1978) is correct when he states that the hardest distance the Christian worker must traverse is not the geographical distance from home to host country, but the last eighteen inches to the heart. Inward

> *Though I am free and belong to no man, I make myself a slave to everyone, to win as many as possible.*
>
> 1 Cor. 9:19

identification is representative of the kind of attitude that brought Jesus Christ to earth to complete an unselfish mission. People want to be with and learn from this type of person. Jesus's incarnational model sets the standard for all Christian workers, yesterday, today, and forever.

Incarnational ministry, driven by inward identification, helps create meaningful relationships, increasing ministry potential because it addresses what Marvin Mayers (1987) identified as the "prior question of trust" (PQT). That is, nothing really substantial can happen until the trust bond is established, and Mayers exhorts all cross-cultural workers to keep this question in mind for everything that they do: "Is what I am doing, thinking or saying building or undermining trust?" Wise cross-cultural work-

> Incarnation: *"When God in Christ became man, Divinity was translated into humanity, as though humanity were a receptor language."*
>
> Andrew Walls (1996, 27)

ers will not only ask this question continually but also learn how to answer it in light of the values of the culture in which they serve rather than just according to their own values.

An epitaph inscribed on a British tombstone in Pakistan reads: "Here lieth the man who tried to run the East by the West." In one brief sentence the reader vividly perceives the inner feelings of those who dealt with the deceased. This raises a fundamental question: What epitaph would the nationals who knew us best write on our tombstone should we die on their soil? "The one who never allowed her children to play with ours"? "The one who liked only those who joined his religion"? "The one who wore our clothes but not our hearts"? "The one who had time to teach us, but not to visit us"? "The one who lived not just among us but with us"? "The one who led us to God's path"? Christian workers who take seriously the need for genuine empathy and identification will go a long way toward receiving a positive epitaph, figuratively or literally. When deep relationships result through empathy and identification, ministry potential increases.

SUMMARY

Christianity is a total way of life. For this to become a reality in a cross-cultural setting, Christian workers must understand the total way of life of the host culture. This means knowing their culture as defined through their central stories, symbols, and rituals. Christian workers must understand equally well their own culture (including their own organization) and the cultures of the Bible. Our analogies and assumptions of culture, however, will determine how we define and understand the society in which we serve. Using the analogy of stories that takes seriously the living, dynamic nature of culture within a global context, we have identified fifteen dynamic elements to help define culture.

Cutting through the confusion of another culture will require that the Christian worker become as a little child, for whom everything is new and strange. He or she must become a learner, demonstrating empathy and identification (inward as well as outward) without compromising integrity so that valid ministry can occur. How does the Christian worker adapt to a new culture and bond with its citizens? How does he or she begin to feel at home in a different culture? To that topic we next turn.

200

11

At Home in the Culture

An early church father once wrote the following concerning Christians from diverse cultures:

> Yet while living in Greek and barbarian cities, according as each obtained his lot, and following the local customs, both in clothing and food and in the rest of life, they show forth the wonderful and confessedly strange character of the constitution of their own citizenship.
>
> They dwell in their own fatherlands, but as if sojourners in them; they share all things as citizens, and suffer all things as strangers. Every foreign country is their fatherland, and every fatherland is a foreign country. (Lake 1913, 2:359–61)

Come on in, and make yourself at home. If there is anything you need, just let me know." When close friends or relatives welcome you with this invitation, you will usually know how to respond. Do you want a cup of coffee? Did they forget to put a towel out for you? No problem. Just ask them politely or look around a bit on your own and your needs will be met. But suppose you are the guest of people you do not know well. You are hesitant to ask for things, and you do not feel free to snoop around their house. You are outside your comfort zone.

In a more radical way, this is what happens when you cross cultures. Your new missionary colleagues and host-national friends may be giving you warm welcomes and wanting you to "feel at home." But you are not at home. You are surrounded by strange people, sights, and sounds. Even taking care of your basic needs seems overwhelming. In this chapter, we try to help you take a journey from cultural entry, past the initial discomforts and stresses most new arrivals experience, and on toward cultural adjustment and adaptation.

ABRAHAM'S JOURNEY

Abraham's story provides a graphic example of what it means to be at home with God when the world around us keeps shifting and changing.

The Past: Leaving a City

Abraham lived in a city, Ur of the Chaldeans (Gen. 10:31). The most likely site of Ur was in what is now southern Iraq. Ruins of buildings, a temple, and hundreds of inscribed tablets have been found there. Ur appears to have been an important religious, cultural, and economic center.

God told Abraham to leave all this affluence and culture and head toward an unknown destination. Abraham didn't know where he was going, but he believed God's promises. So he left the security of his home (Heb. 11:8).

The Present: Wandering in a Strange Land

God led Abraham to the land he had promised him. Abraham became a nomad there. He exchanged the stability and security of a city for the life of a shepherd and a herdsman, living in tents and wandering among the inhabitants of the land like a stranger in a foreign country. He chose this life by faith. When God told him that this land would belong to him and his descendants, he believed God's promises and obeyed him (Heb. 11:8).

The Future: Looking toward the Heavenly City

Abraham never went home again. Instead of looking back on the city he had left, he looked forward to another city. It was not his tent city that was constantly being moved. It was a city with strong foundations that God himself had planned and built—the heavenly city (Heb. 11:10).

Like Abraham, Christians today are being called by Jesus Christ to leave their homes, lands, countries, and families for his sake (Matt. 19:29; Mark 10:29–30; Luke 18:29–30). They embark on a pilgrimage without knowing where they are going. Acting out of faith and obedience to the

God who has called them, they pull up the stakes of their tents when he says to move on. When he tells them to stay, they willingly pound them down again. They are not looking back at the city they left behind. Off in the distance, they catch a glimpse of the city God has prepared for them. Jesus's promise to his disciples keeps echoing in their ears: "I am going there to prepare a place for you" (John 14:2); "I am with you always" (Matt. 28:20).

This chapter was written in the midst of media reports and images of the devastation that tsunamis, hurricanes, earthquakes, and floods had left in their wake. On a microcosmic scale, the dynamics involved in saying good-bye to our home culture and entering a new one can be very much the same. There are multiple separations and losses. Every area of our lives needs to be rebuilt. We need to get settled in our new home and learn how to shop, go to the bank, pay bills, mail a letter, ask for directions, and acquire many other basic skills that were second nature to us in our first culture. Very early in our cross-cultural encounters, we will want to start building relationships. Then, as we begin to immerse ourselves more deeply in the culture, we find ourselves making decisions about norms and lifestyles and interacting with the culture's beliefs, values, and worldview. The dynamic of these interactions will be explored throughout the remainder of this chapter.

CULTURE SHOCK

Definitions and Descriptions

Culture shock is "the term used to describe the pronounced reactions to psychological disorientation most people experience when they move for an extended period of time into a culture markedly different from their own" (Kohls 2001, 91). Other less frightening descriptors, such as culture stress, adaptation, transition, adjustment, and socialization have also been used to describe this phenomenon (Dodd 1998, 158).

These reactions occur when our cultural maps and guidelines no longer work (P. G. Hiebert 1985, 66). We have been cut off from the cues and patterns that help us to function, express our feelings, and interpret the new situations that surround us. We brought our culture-based values along with us. Now we find many of them being challenged in our new setting, and we may even find ourselves questioning them. And in the midst of all these upheavals, we are expected to function well. How can we when we do not even know the rules (Kohls 2001, 93–94)?

Kalvero Oberg (1960), who has been credited with creating the term "culture shock," gives examples of a few of the all-pervasive situations in which we lose the clues that help us to function: "These signs and clues include the thousand and one ways in which we orient ourselves to the situations of daily life: when to shake hands and what to say when we meet people, when and how to give tips, how to give orders to servants, how to make purchases, when to accept and when to refuse invitations, when to [pick up a restaurant bill] and when not" (Oberg 1960, cited in Kohls 2001, 94).

And the list goes on and on. So many losses: not only the loss of familiar cultural cues but also the loss of our cultural identity, roles, and sense of community. No wonder we experience culture shock! It can be painful, stressful, and even physically and emotionally debilitating. But, fortunately, we do not have to be "stuck" here. For most of us, it is a relatively brief transition period on our journey toward cultural adaptation and at-homeness.

Stages

Several stages have been identified along the journey toward cultural adaptation. Even though various authors have named and organized them differently, their sequencing and descriptions are quite similar (Dodd 1998, 159–62; P. G. Hiebert 1985, 74–78; Kraft 2000, 256–57; Kohls 2001, 94–99).

FIRST STAGE: EVERYTHING IS BEAUTIFUL. "THIS IS JUST LIKE HOME!"

When you arrive in your new culture, you may feel as if you are on a honeymoon. You take pictures and act like a tourist. Everything is beautiful. The food is great, the people are friendly, and there are all kinds of interesting things to see and do. Life does not seem all that different from what it was in the culture you left behind. When you send a glowing report to your friends and supporters back home, it does not ring true. They know things cannot be that perfect!

SECOND STAGE: DISENCHANTMENT. "I WANT TO PACK MY BAGS AND GO HOME!"

This is the stage when the symptoms of cultural shock begin to kick in. You may find yourself feeling anxious, impatient, restless, disappointed, irritable, and critical. Communication and getting around are next to impossible. The smells are nauseating and the sounds are irritating. You are concerned about the water and the food and may fear being robbed or cheated. When the inevitable frustrations arise, you may lose control and blow up or feel helpless and depressed.

Not everyone experiences these symptoms with the same degree of intensity. For some, cultural adaptation stresses may be so mild that they hardly get in the way. For others, they are difficult but tolerable.

204

But new missionaries occasionally find themselves in situations that seem so unbearable that they decide to pack their bags and go home. Returning too soon is always sad. It has implications not only for the individuals and families who are directly involved but also for the churches and agencies who sent them and the national churches who received them. When things seem so bad that you want to leave, it is far better to talk to a friend or a local counselor, wait and see how you feel after a few weeks, and make a slow decision about what to do (Foyle 2001, 81).

Marjory F. Foyle (2001, 80–81) extends her "go slowly" suggestion to other expressions of culture shock as well. If you are experiencing fatigue, loss of energy, frustration, and anger, be kind to yourself. When you need to, withdraw briefly by staying home, playing music you enjoy, or reading a familiar book. Then, while you are being careful to keep your cultural exposure below your anxiety level, reexpose yourself to the local areas, beginning with the pleasant places and gradually moving beyond these until you are back to normal. Concentrate on finding the good things in the new country, and do anything you can to reduce tensions and an overload of responsibilities.

THIRD STAGE: ADJUSTMENT. "I AM FINALLY BEGINNING TO FEEL AT HOME."

This is the "turn-around" stage. You have hit "rock bottom" and are on your way up. Life has become more comfortable, you feel less isolated, and your sense of humor has returned. You are beginning to understand what is happening around you. Little by little, important decisions are being made, you are developing culture and language skills, and the shattered pieces of your life are beginning to come back together. You are well on your way toward feeling at home.

This can be both good news and bad news. The good news is that you are recovering from culture shock. The bad news is that, now that the anxieties have subsided and the stresses have lessened, you may start believing you have "arrived." If you allow yourself to plateau at this point you may be settling for mediocrity in your culture learning and ministry and falling short of the long-term happiness and fulfillment that ever-deeper immersion in your new culture can bring.

RESOURCES

While you are on this long journey from cultural shock toward cultural adaptation, it is good to remember that you are not alone. God has given you spiritual and personal resources and has surrounded you with people.

SIDEBAR 11.1
DEALING WITH NEGATIVE FEELINGS

Here is a good exercise to help you overcome this tendency to internalize negative feelings about yourself:

First, recall your life story and perhaps share it with a friend. Tell about your home, parents, siblings, childhood experiences, education, vocation, avocational interests, ministry, and (if you are married) your husband or wife, children, and family life. Focus on what has been going on inside you—your intellectual, psychological, and spiritual journey.

Next, make as long a list as you can of the things God has given to you and wants you to share with others. Include your knowledge, personality traits, life experiences, abilities, skills, and especially the ways in which God has been teaching you and helping you to grow throughout your life.

As you are making your list, keep thanking God for these precious gifts and give them back to him to use as he pleases in your new cultural context. Ask him to integrate the difficult experiences you are going through now into his broader plans and purposes for your life.

Spiritual Resources

Asking you to tap into your spiritual resources may be a tall order while you are in the throes of culture shock. You may be feeling alone, angry, discouraged, afraid, confused, and overwhelmed. God may seem far away. You may even be projecting these negative feelings onto him, asking why he has abandoned you in your struggles and is not hearing your cries for help.

You are not the first missionary who has had these kinds of feelings in the midst of cultural stress. Talk to God about what you are experiencing. That is what David did over and over in the Psalms. Are you feeling alone? The righteous will never be forsaken (Ps. 37:5). Do you feel as if you are in the midst of a storm? Be still before God (Ps. 46:10). Are you afraid of the darkness? The Lord is your light and salvation (Ps. 27:1). Do you feel weak and helpless? He is your strength and shield (Ps. 28:7). Do you feel tired and hopeless? Your rest and hope are in God alone (Ps. 62:5). He is with you and hears your cries for help.

Personal Resources

When you are experiencing negative feelings, it is easy to attach your identity to them. It is just one small step from saying, "This is what I am feeling and experiencing" (I'm feeling afraid), to saying, "This is who I am" (I am a fearful person). The exercise in sidebar 11.1 (above) can help you to break this pattern as you tap into the personal resources God has given you.

People to Help You

You do not need to go through cultural stresses and face the issues involved in culture adaptation by yourself. If you look around you, you will soon discover that even in the midst of your loneliness there are people who want to be with you and help you. If you are married, there is your spouse. Cultural stress sometimes tears couples apart. It does not have to. As you pray, share, cry, and rejoice together in the midst of your cross-cultural experiences, they can enrich and strengthen your marriage. Then there will be mission colleagues, housemates, new host-culture friends, teachers and students at your language school, members of your church, neighbors you wave to, and shopkeepers you meet. As opportunities develop, let others into your life.

More and more frequently, professional help is becoming available in contexts where missionaries are serving. Mission agencies, language schools, and local church leaders may be able to put you in touch with a qualified person. There are many instances in which counseling on the field has helped the new missionary who is facing serious adaptation problems to survive and succeed. It is a sign of strength rather than weakness to seek help when you need it.

CULTURAL ADAPTATION

Cultural adaptation is not a sequence of steps to be taken or tasks to complete. The processes described below are happening all at once. Even while you are learning to understand the worldview, values, and norms of your new culture, you will be making lifestyle decisions and developing coping skills. Some aspects of these processes will be discussed in this section of the chapter.

Understanding What Is Happening

WORLDVIEW

Basic understandings of your new culture's worldview can go a long way toward alleviating anxieties and setting you firmly on the path toward culture adaptation (P. G. Hiebert 1985, 45–49). When you arrive in your new culture, you will likely be bringing your basic worldview assumptions with you. You will have *cognitive assumptions* about time, space, logic, and authority. These assumptions affect the way you develop categories, decide what exists and what does not, and perceive and store information. You will also bring along your *affective assumptions*, your feelings about people and life, together with your aesthetic notions about music, art, and dress. *Evaluative assumptions* will also be a part of your worldview package. These include your highest values and primary allegiances and encompass all you love or hate, find beautiful or ugly, or consider to be right or wrong.

Until you entered a new culture, these basic assumptions were largely implicit. You believed, felt, and valued them deeply and may have reacted strongly when they were challenged or attacked, but you did not spend much time reflecting on them. If you have been immersed in North American culture, you may have learned to value technology, material goods, business, and wealth. You will probably be surprised to discover that for many Indians, purity, the priestly caste, religious themes, and temples are more important. You have also brought moral values with you and are not prepared when you discover that, in your host culture, losing one's temper may be as serious as violating sexual mores (P. G. Hiebert 1985, 45–49).

VALUES

Our cognitive, affective, and evaluative assumptions about reality are reflected in cultural values associated with interpersonal relationships and societal expectations (Dodd 1998, 102–12; Lingenfelter and Mayers 2003).

In some cultures, interpersonal relationships are hierarchical and based on status; in others, the equality of people and personal achievement are emphasized. Humanitarianism in some cultural contexts involves obligations to a family, tribe, and friends. In other situations, that concern extends to outsiders and may even become global in scope. Honesty is defined differently as we cross cultures. What is considered dishonest in some contexts may be interpreted as slyness or cleverness in bargaining with others, and what we may call a bribe may be seen by others as a payment for a favor. Harmony and saving face are all-pervasive values in some cultures; directness and confrontation are avoided. In-group loyalties and memberships, along with the exclusion and rejection of out-groups, are common when people of different ethnicities, races, religions, social statuses, or reference groups are in close contact with one another.

Expectations and values extend to societies as a whole. In North America, morality and ethics are usually highly personal issues; among many peoples, group perceptions and decisions are more important. Rugged individualism and personal achievement are often valued by Americans; among the Japanese and other Asian populations, loyalty to the group is paramount. Innovation is valued in some cultures; tradition in others. Americans tend to be time and task oriented; many Latin Americans blend work and play and see time as an event to be enjoyed. Europeans and Asians often consider North Americans too emotional

208

Sidebar 11.2
When Norms Collide: Some Examples

Collected by Lois McKinney Douglas

An international student from an upper-class family was earning good money by washing dishes in a Michigan State University cafeteria. "My parents would be shocked if they knew what I was doing!" he confided.

A missionary's housekeeper insisted on opening the driveway gate with a flourish and carrying the packages, briefcases, and bags from the car to the house when she returned home. When the missionary grew tired of this and told her it was not expected, her helper was shocked. "What will the neighbors think if I let you carry your own things in?" she objected.

When a young student returned to his home country after several years of seminary in the United States, he scandalized the church that had invited him to preach by not beginning with an apology for his immaturity and an acknowledgment of the older and more experienced ministers who were in attendance.

A Western missionary in Indonesia stood out when he wore a Hawaiian-style shirt, shorts, and thongs in a seminar. The Indonesian men were all dressed in embroidered white dress shirts, long black slacks, and closed black shoes.

And the examples go on and on. Try to create and share some of your own.

---

and vulnerable about their feelings. Latin Americans, on the other hand, may see us as distant and cold. With these and many other conflicting values bombarding them, it is no surprise that many new missionaries find themselves struggling to relate to their new contexts.

Norms

Cultural worldviews and values are manifested through the behaviors and products used by a group of people to organize and regulate what they think and feel and do (P. G. Hiebert 1985, 30). These ways of thinking and acting are normative. In some situations, they are governed by explicit sets of rules and sanctions. In other contexts, they may be implicit expectations that members of the culture accept and conform to without being able to articulate them or explain their social function.

People take these rules and norms very seriously. Depending on the issues at stake, small deviations from these expectations are usually tolerated. But straying too far from cultural norms can result in rejection and sanctions. A part of cultural learning involves growing in your understanding of rules and norms in order to act in more appropriate ways. Sidebar 11.2 provides some concrete examples of ways in which cultural norms can collide.

SIDEBAR 11.3
PERMANENT OR TEMPORARY?

Ralph Covell and Marshall Shelley (1982)

Understanding and practicing cultural norms becomes more complex in situations in which a cultural practice seems to be in conflict with biblical teaching. It is important to learn to sort out what is "permanent" (the gospel) from what is "temporary" (cultural). Ralph Covell and Marshall Shelley (1982, 8–9) have provided an exercise that will help you to get a handle on this problem. Work through it alone—or better still, with a friend or in a group.

Which of these specific practices and commands that appear in the New Testament are meant to be permanent and to apply at all times in all places? Which are merely temporary, needed at one particular time in one particular place, but not necessarily applicable at other times and in other places? Read each item thoughtfully, and circle the P if you consider the practice or command to be permanent, or the T if you believe it is temporary. After you have finished, make a list of principles you used in making your decisions. If possible, discuss these with a friend or in a group.

1. "Greet one another with a holy kiss" (Rom. 16:16).   P   T
2. Abstain from meat that has been sacrificed to idols (Acts 15:29).   P   T
3. Be baptized (Acts 2:38).   P   T
4. A woman ought to have a veil on her head (1 Cor. 11:10).   P   T
5. Wash one another's feet (John 13:14).   P   T
6. Extend the right hand (left hand?) of fellowship (Gal. 2:9).   P   T
7. Ordain by the "laying on of hands" (Acts 13:3).   P   T
8. "It is disgraceful for a woman to speak in the church" (1 Cor. 14:35).   P   T
9. Have fixed hours of prayer (Acts 3:1).   P   T
10. Sing songs, hymns, and spiritual songs (Col. 3:16).   P   T
11. Abstain from eating blood (Acts 15:29).   P   T
12. "Slaves, obey your earthly masters" (Eph. 6:5).   P   T
13. Observe the Lord's Supper (1 Cor. 11:24).   P   T
14. Do not make any oaths (James 5:12).   P   T
15. Anoint the sick with oil (James 5:14).   P   T
16. Permit no women to teach men (1 Tim. 2:12).   P   T
17. Preach two by two (Mark 6:7).   P   T
18. Go into Jewish synagogues to preach (Acts 14:1).   P   T

Making Lifestyle Decisions

You will not be learning about worldviews, values, and norms in a vacuum. You will be developing these understandings and insights in the context of cultural interaction and lifestyle decision making. The discussion below grows out of Carley Dodd's (1998, 163) adaptation of

19. Eat what is set before you asking no questions of conscience (1 Cor. 10:27).	P	T
20. Prohibit women from wearing braided hair, gold, or pearls (1 Tim. 2:9).	P	T
21. Abstain from fornication (Acts 15:29).	P	T
22. Do not seek marriage (1 Cor. 7:27).	P	T
23. Be circumcised (Acts 15:5).	P	T
24. Women should pray with their heads covered (1 Cor. 11:5).	P	T
25. Drink communion from a single cup (Mark 14:23).	P	T
26. Take formal religious vows (Acts 18:18).	P	T
27. Avoid praying in public (Matt. 6:5–6).	P	T
28. Speak in tongues and prophesy (1 Cor. 14:5).	P	T
29. Meet in homes for church (Col. 4:15).	P	T
30. Work with your hands (1 Thess. 4:11).	P	T
31. Lift your hands when praying (1 Tim. 2:8).	P	T
32. Give to those who beg from you (Matt. 5:42).	P	T
33. Pray before meals (Luke 24:30).	P	T
34. Support no widow under sixty years old (1 Tim. 5:9).	P	T
35. Say "Amen" at the end of prayers (1 Cor. 14:16).	P	T
36. Fast in connection with ordination (Acts 13:3).	P	T
37. "Wear sandals but not an extra tunic" (Mark 6:9).	P	T
38. "Wives, submit to your husbands" (Col. 3:18).	P	T
39. Show no favoritism to the rich (James 2:1–7).	P	T
40. Use unleavened bread for communion (Luke 22:13, 19).	P	T
41. Cast lots for church officers (Acts 1:26).	P	T
42. Owe no man anything (Rom. 13:8).	P	T
43. Have seven deacons in the church (Acts 6:3).	P	T
44. Don't eat meat from animals killed by strangulation (Acts 15:29).	P	T
45. If anyone will not work, don't let him eat (2 Thess. 3:10).	P	T
46. Worship on Saturday (Acts 13:14, 42–44).	P	T
47. Give up personal property (Acts 2:44–45).	P	T
48. Have self-employed clergy (2 Thess. 3:7–8).	P	T
49. Take collections in the church for the poor (1 Cor. 16:1).	P	T
50. Long hair on a man is a disgrace (1 Cor. 11:14).	P	T

Abraham Maslow's (1999) hierarchy of human needs. Survival skills must be developed first. Then, as these physiological needs are increasingly being cared for, a person will begin to focus on the belonging needs that are met through bonded relationships and adequate role definitions.

Survival Needs

When you first arrive in your new culture, you will likely find your time and attention almost totally absorbed in survival. You need to learn

211

SIDEBAR 11.4
MISSIONARY LIFESTYLE DECISIONS

Collected by Lois McKinney Douglas

The following scenarios illustrate some of the situations you may confront. Try to interact with each, explaining how you would respond and what you would do.

Situation 1: You want to live in the same middle-class urban neighborhood where you are working in church planting. The field conference wants you to live an hour away in mission-owned property. Living in the church neighborhood will cost extra rent money. Housing funds are pooled. What should you do?

Situation 2: You and your missionary colleagues own cars. National workers ride motorized bicycles or use public transportation. A pastor who has just acquired a driver's license wants to borrow your car to take a group of young people on an evangelistic trip. What should you say?

Situation 3: You are working in an area where the heat is oppressive most of the year. Your missionary colleagues all have air-conditioning. None of the national leaders do. Should you have air-conditioning?

Situation 4: The accepted cultural pattern in the country where you are working is for middle- and upper-class people to have household servants. You want to identify with the poor. Should you have household help?

Situation 5: You are supervising a group of young people from the United States who are preparing to visit a rural village where the water supply is contaminated. As a precaution you take along plenty of pure drinking water, only to discover when you arrive at your destination that your village hosts have made lemonade for your group. Lemons and sugar are expensive, but they know Americans like drinks made with them, and they wanted to please you. Should you accept the likely-to-be-contaminated lemonade?

Situation 6: Missionaries from Mission X are instructed to exchange money at the official government rate. Mission Y missionaries exchange their funds on the "parallel" market, where they receive at least three times the official rate of exchange. The parallel market is illegal, but even government agencies use it. You do not belong to either of these missions. What exchange policies would you recommend for your team?

---

how to shop for and prepare your food, take care of your clothing, and find housing and transportation. Your children's schooling needs urgent attention. You will also likely need to attend to health care, financial, and legal issues.

Such activities can be time consuming, but thanks to help from other missionaries and your new national colleagues, they are usually resolved rather quickly. What is harder to come to grips with in many contexts are lifestyle issues. In your home culture, you are a missionary living on a modest income provided by your supporters. In many parts of the world, without changes in either your income or your lifestyle, you are suddenly considered wealthy. You will want to be a good steward of your resources, address the lifestyle issues that surround you, and live in culturally appropriate ways.

BELONGING NEEDS

Our most basic needs for belonging are met through God's love, which extends across the millennia, around the globe, and from eternity to eternity.

He sent his Son, Jesus Christ, to a specific place in a moment of history to incarnate his love here on earth. Jesus expressed his Father's love through deep, caring friendships with Mary, Martha, Lazarus, and others. He also poured out his love through disciple making. The Gospels provide a detailed story of the three years Jesus spent preparing his disciples, with incredible patience and understanding, to carry on his ministry.

Jesus's love was not limited to this inner circle. He had deep compassion for the multitudes that surrounded him, ministering holistically as he fed the hungry, cured the sick, caused the lame to walk, gave sight to the blind—all of this in the midst of meeting their spiritual needs. He shared himself as their living Water and Bread from heaven and culminated his earthly ministry with his ultimate gift of love, the offering of himself for the sins of the world.

These ways in which Jesus expressed his love provide a model for us as we cross cultures. We will want to make friends, prepare disciples, and reach out to people who are in spiritual and physical need. These roles are distinct from one another, and yet they become intermingled as we develop bonded relationships and role identities in our new culture.

BONDED RELATIONSHIPS

What happens when relationships deepen is sometimes called *bonding* (Brewster 2000a, 138). Bonding involves close interpersonal relationships that extend beyond the missionary community and allow people from other cultures to enter our lives in significant ways. Our social needs are largely met within the culture. We let ourselves love and be loved. There is mutuality and commitment as we celebrate our commonalities and learn from our differences. The relationships that emerge are characterized by empathetic listening, sharing, and openness. We help one another to grow and try to be there when others need us. Sidebar 11.5 reminds us that these kinds of relationships do not just happen. There are some challenging realities that must be faced as we develop them.

You may find that there are limitations to bonding. It can be stressful. Families will sometimes find it more difficult to bond in the culture than

213

SIDEBAR 11.5
SEVEN REALITIES OF CROSS-CULTURAL FRIENDSHIPS

Hill (1993)

1. They must be intentional.
2. They require proximity.
3. They must appreciate differences and similarities.
4. They cross economic classes.
5. They involve vulnerability.
6. They must be selective.
7. They must be flexible.

REFLECTION AND DISCUSSION

1. Think of any cross-cultural acquaintances or friendships you may have. Which of the seven realities would you say best characterize these relationships?
2. Which of the seven realities would you say least characterizes these relationships?
3. What steps can you take to build on your strengths and improve your weaknesses?

---

single missionaries do. Bonding will usually be easier when cultures are similar. And of course there must be reciprocity; it will be hard to bond with others unless they want to bond with you. Remember that all is not lost if you "blow" the first weeks or months or even years. Bonding can happen later, and it can happen gradually. Whatever the obstacles, and however belatedly it may occur, it is worth the effort. You need close, meaningful relationships within the culture, and your cross-cultural friends and colleagues need you. Some examples and challenges related to bonding are provided in sidebars 11.6, 11.7, and 11.8.

Bonding develops friendships and enables effective ministry. It also creates a lifetime of rich memories. I (Lois) had arrived at a congress on world evangelization in Thailand. I was at the registration desk when I heard my name in Portuguese. Manuel Alexandre Jr., the director of a seminary in Portugal, was there. He had been my student in Portugal years before. Later, when he came to the United States to study, I had helped him and his family to get settled. We were happily catching up on news when my name was called a second time. Jonathan Ferreira dos Santos, director of a thriving mission agency in Brazil, had arrived. I had directed his master's thesis while I was in Brazil. Jonathan had consoled me and ministered to me when my father died. What I found so special about this occasion was being able to introduce a friend from Brazil to a friend from Portugal at a congress in Thailand while I was living in the United States. To me, it was a foretaste of what heaven will be like!

SIDEBAR 11.6
LET PEOPLE INTO YOUR LIFE SPACE

Lois McKinney Douglas

A husband and wife who were prominent leaders in the evangelical movement in Brazil were invited to speak at a gathering of expatriate missionaries. Their topic: "Missionary-Brazilian Relationships." When the wife's turn came, she caught everyone's attention immediately, as she shared her observations and concerns. Here is the essence of her address:

First, I want to thank you all for inviting us to be with you during your conference. My husband and I have thoroughly enjoyed getting to know you better as we have participated with you in conversations, meetings, laughter, and informal activities.

But I am going to be very honest with you now. I don't like you nearly as well when I see you in our Brazilian churches. You come across as aloof, distant, cold, reserved, and unapproachable. You make it hard for us to get to know you.

The other day I happened to see a copy of a letter an American missionary had sent to her supporters in the States. Her husband travels constantly in his ministry, and while he was away on a trip, she received word that a parent had died. After she had written in her letter about the loneliness and grief she was experiencing, her concluding cry was: "Can you imagine what it was like to be all alone in a foreign country, without anyone to talk to, and to have to go through this experience all by myself?"

The room grew very quiet after the speaker's wrap-up statement:

And there, only a few blocks away, was a church full of brothers and sisters in Christ who knew her, and who would have loved to put their arms around her and comfort her in her time of grief.

Please let us into your life space.

DEFINED ROLES

In your first culture, you probably thought very little about the roles you played. You faced some important role changes when you became a student at a university, an employee in a new job, a member of a new church, or a participant on a sports team. If you are married, you became a husband or a wife, and perhaps a mother or a father. Although these transitions involved upheavals, you understood the cultural expectations of your new roles, and the discomfort and stress were probably short-lived.

When we cross cultures we can expect role confusion. In some situations, there is no role for a "missionary," and even if there is one, it can generate negative stereotypes or even hostility. Missionaries are sometimes seen as emissaries of their sending country and responsible for its perceived aggression and exploitation of the local peoples. Even when missionaries

215

SIDEBAR 11.7
A BRAZILIAN LOVE STORY

Lois McKinney Douglas (names have been changed)

How can we show people from another culture that we love and respect them? Use the story of Marcos and Julia to start your discussion.

Marcos was a seminary student and a youth pastor in a large church. He was blond, handsome, and of Italian descent. Julia was a seminar leader and conference speaker for a Sunday school publishing house. She was talented and outgoing. Her ethnic origin was Japanese.

Marcos and Julia met and fell in love. Her parents opposed their relationship. Regardless of how fine a person Marcos was, they felt that Julia should be developing friendships only with Japanese men.

But neither Julia nor Marcos was interested in seeing anyone else, so Marcos launched a campaign to win over the family. Gradually, he learned to speak Japanese and practice Japanese cultural customs. He continued to be kind to Julia's parents, even when they rebuffed him.

Five years passed. It was Christmastime, and Marcos and Julia were in her parents' home. Julia's father noticed Marcos sitting correctly at a low table, eating with chopsticks, and speaking Japanese. He realized that Marcos was doing all of this because he loved Julia! He called him aside and told him he could marry their daughter.

---

are warmly received, their new roles can be hard to adjust to. They may have had visions of initiating and directing programs that national church leaders would accept and follow. Instead, they may find themselves functioning outside their areas of specialization and expertise and frustrated by the limited impact they are having on the ministries around them.

There are likely to be other role tensions. Mission administrators and sending churches in their homeland may be bombarding their field missionaries with requests for reports and even attempting to direct field activities from afar. Members of field teams sometimes find it hard to define their roles clearly. There may be added stresses on marriages, especially when wives' roles are not clearly defined. Parenting roles can become confused and hard to balance with other expectations. Single women who are missionaries struggle with role identification in situations where there is little room for them in church leadership, or they are perhaps even perceived as second wives or mistresses (P. G. Hiebert 1985, 255–83).

One of your challenges as a new missionary is to find yourself in the midst of this maze of expectations. It will involve time, patience, and dialogue with your mission agency, field team, and the national church. But this effort will be more than worthwhile when you find yourself experiencing an enhanced self-image, fulfillment in ministry, and joy in your service to Christ.

Developing Coping Skills

While you are learning to understand what is happening around you and are making lifestyle decisions, you will also be developing strategies for handling the demands and stresses around you. We are all different; no two people have identical coping styles. What follows here are suggestions that many people who live in a second culture have found helpful.

REALIZE THAT STRESS IS INEVITABLE

Missionaries tend to go off the top of the scales psychologists use to measure stress. As if learning to live in a new culture and handling cross-cultural relationships and conflicts were not enough, missionaries in many parts of the world are serving in the midst of violence, persecution, natural disasters, hunger, HIV/AIDs epidemics, displacement of refugees, and scores of other crises. Learning to cope in these kinds of situations will be the focus of chapter 15.

DON'T ALLOW SURVIVAL NEEDS TO FILL YOUR LIFE

When you are living in a cross-cultural setting, it is easy to let home and vehicle maintenance, cooking and cleaning, shopping and doctors' appointments, and trips to the consulate or embassy fill your life. One of the more challenging aspects of cross-cultural living is to manage your time well, so that your primary focus is on bonded relationships and role fulfillment in ministry rather than on survival. Making this happen will take flexibility and planning. Observe how your national counterparts and missionary colleagues handle these issues. In situations where it is appropriate and expected, be sure to enlist help with home and yard care, maintenance and repairs, and so on. Your time is too valuable to be spent in perpetual struggles with survival needs.

LET NATIONALS BE YOUR PRIMARY MENTORS

When you enter a new culture, you are likely to be surrounded by missionary colleagues who will deluge you with information about what the culture is like and the ways you should think, feel, and act as you relate to it. Thank them graciously and accept what you can learn from the wisdom they may have gained through their cross-cultural experience. But do not let missionaries be your primary mentors, and do not depend on information and suggestions that may be filtered and secondhand. Your best source of help in culture and language acquisition will be a qualified national. We will emphasize this point again in later chapters.

Be Sure to Enjoy the Good Things

A missionary in northeastern Brazil faced quite profound culture shock when she found herself surrounded by extreme heat, many kinds of flying and crawling creatures, and abject poverty. But then, as she started recuperating, she began to appreciate the good things around her. It was not hard to enjoy the early-morning aroma of freshly baked rolls that came from the bakery down the street, or the luxury of having two of them delivered to her door every morning in time for breakfast. Neither was it difficult to appreciate the four-part harmony of the frog chorus she heard each evening as the sun went down, or nights when the moon was shining so brightly that she could see the hands on her watch. Later, as fulfilling relationships and satisfying ministries began to multiply, she became so at home in the culture that it was hard to say good-bye.

Become Part of a National Church

Even if your primary involvement is in a theological school, hospital, literacy ministry, community development program, business venture, or a "tentmaking" ministry, it is extremely important to become part of a national church. Even when you are in contexts where believers must meet secretly, you will want to share with them as completely as the situation allows. Remember that *missio Dei* (God's mission) in the world is expressed in and through his church. The other ministries in which we are involved are extensions of and services to local congregations and to the global church.

Take Time for Hobbies

A missionary in South America became an expert on caterpillars. He studied them scientifically and even took photographs and wrote an article related to them that was published in a major journal. Occasionally, he crossed the boundary between his hobby and ministry commitments. When he needed to take photos of his caterpillars at strategic moments, meetings and appointments could wait! Even though hobbies need to be kept in perspective, they can become important means of coping in other cultures.

Be Patient with Your Family and Your Colleagues

No one is perfect. When people are trying to live together in stressful situations, there is sure to be frustration and conflict. A healthy dose of humility and patience will go a long way toward calming these storms. Arthur Judson Brown (1950, 241) tells a delightful story about what can happen when temperaments collide: "'You should learn to

---

SIDEBAR 11.8
TEN GENERAL RULES FOR DEALING WITH CONFLICT

D. Elmer (1993, 180--81)

1. Ask whether this is worthy of attention or should be let go.
2. Make your approach one of concern for the person and the preservation of the relationship.
3. Seek understanding through inquiry before forming judgments and making accusations (blaming).
4. Separate facts from rumor, partial information, feelings and interpretation.
5. Consider how much stress the relationship can bear; this will help you tell how much time and sensitivity will be required.
6. Put yourself in the other person's place and try to appreciate his or her perspective on the matter.
7. Address behaviors rather than motivation.
8. When you detect tense emotions or defensiveness, back up and give assurances of friendship and your desire to understand.
9. Frequently acknowledge and summarize what the other person has said to assure accuracy of understanding of both parties.
10. Believe a win-win resolution is possible if both parties can remain calm, understand each other's interests and negotiate with integrity and fairness.

PRINCIPLES FOR CROSS-CULTURAL CONFLICT RESOLUTION

When in a two-thirds world situation, consider the following:

1. The degree to which shame, face and honor are core cultural values will determine how important it is to use an indirect method.
2. If the other person has had extensive exposure to Western culture, sensitive directness may be acceptable, understood and not offensive.
3. All forms of confrontation should occur in private, if possible, so as to minimize any loss of face.
4. Familiarize yourself with stories, parables, fables, legends and heroes of a culture in order to appropriately interpret their use in conflict situations.
5. Understand the various indirect methods used in the two-thirds world and be alert to which ones are used and under what circumstances.
6. Build a close relationship with a host-country person who will be able to help you interpret confusing situations.
7. Ask God for help in understanding and applying unfamiliar conflict resolution.

---

control your temper as I do,' said the phlegmatic missionary to one who had spoken too vehemently in the heat of a debate. 'Control my temper!' was the reply; 'I control more temper in a day than you do in a month.'"

LEARN TO HANDLE CROSS-CULTURAL CONFLICT

Not all the conflicts you experience will be within your family or missionary community. You will sometimes find yourself caught up in disagreements and clashes with national coworkers or friends and acquaintances within the broader culture. Very often, these tensions and stresses grow out of differences in worldviews, values, and norms, which we discussed earlier. Duane Elmer provides helpful rules and principles for handling interpersonal and cross-cultural conflict. Some general rules for dealing with conflict are listed in sidebar 11.8.

ACCEPT YOUR LIMITATIONS

You will never make a "perfect" adjustment to the culture. However long you are in the country, however hard you try, there will always be gaps between where you are and where you would like to be in your relationships, role fulfillment, and culture and language acquisition. You are growing and becoming; you are on a journey. God is not finished with you yet.

DO NOT HESITATE TO GET PROFESSIONAL HELP

Missionaries live in the midst of high stress, many losses, and numerous challenges. If you, a family member, or a colleague are not functioning well, and you believe the problem may be depression or burnout, do all you can to enlist the needed professional help for yourself or for others.

TAP YOUR SPIRITUAL RESOURCES

Last, but certainly not least, remember that God does not expect you to cope with cultures by yourself. He is beside you, smiling with you and crying with you along your journey. The spiritual formation issues we talked about in chapter 4 are crucial to your being at home in the culture.

SUMMARY

One of the most spectacular attractions that visitors to the Amazon Basin enjoy is the "meeting of the waters." This is the point near the city of Manaus where the sandy, gray-blue waters from the Rio Solimões and the darker, murky waters from the Rio Negro meet with such force that they stay separated for more than six miles before joining together. If you are sailing down the middle of the river, the waters you see on one side of the boat will be strikingly different from those on the other side.

This tropical phenomenon provides a helpful metaphor in understanding what happens when you cross cultures. You may have passed your whole life in your first culture, or at the most ventured out of it for short visits to ethnic urban neighborhoods, a backpacking adventure in Europe, or a short-term missions trip with a church youth group. Your life journey has had ebbs and flows and meandered at times, but nothing up to this point has compared with your arrival in a new culture for a long-term missions assignment.

The currents of your two cultures are colliding with such force that you may feel you are in a lifeboat that is about to capsize.

Your identity is at stake. In your home culture, you knew who you were. You knew the language, understood the culture, and could cope with the everyday demands of living. You had friends and understood your cultural roles. Now that you are in the midst of swift and changing cross-cultural currents, three options are open to you. One temptation is to retreat to the sandy, gray-blue waters of your first culture. You will take forays into your new culture to make a stab at studying the language and become a bit involved in ministry.

> *Ten-year-old Johnny and his parents had just returned for a home assignment in the United States after a term of service in the Republic of the Congo. On a visit to a supporting church, Johnny was welcomed to a Sunday school class. "Johnny," the teacher asked, as she was introducing him to the other children, "Where would you rather be, in the United States or in the Congo?" Johnny didn't have to think long before he blurted out his answer: "I would rather be in an airplane!"*
>
> Source unknown

But as soon as these interludes are over, you will scurry back to the safety and comfort of your expatriate network. There you will chat and share deeply with your missionary colleagues before you log on to your computer to keep in touch with friends you left behind or escape to the Web for music, movies, and news from your homeland.

Another option that you may try is throwing over your first culture by steering your boat over into the waters of your new culture and "going native." This may sound good and even fit your idealized missionary image. The problem is that it does not work. Even if you spend the rest of your life in your adopted culture and reach top levels on the culture and language acquisition scales, your national cohorts will still be aware of your other-culture identity. Your accent, habits, and some of your values will give you away. More seriously, you may be setting yourself up for severe trauma. You cannot toss your first culture into the river without throwing your selfhood, identity, heritage, and life history overboard with it.

When we resist either retreating to our first culture or going native and make a firm commitment to stay in the middle of the stream, our bicultural identity begins to emerge. We are becoming more and more comfortable in our second culture and more and more accepting of our first-culture roots. We have deep friendships and fulfilling ministries in both cultures without deriving our full identity from either of them. Both of our cultures are equally comfortable, rewarding, and satisfying to us (and also equally frustrating, exasperating, and upsetting at times). When we are here, we want to be there, and when we are there,

---

CASE STUDY:
WHAT HAS HAPPENED TO OUR DREAMS?

P. G. HIEBERT (1985, 64–65; used with permission)

Paul G. Hiebert has provided this vivid description of what it can be like to live in the midst of lost cues. After you have read this case study, explain what this family is experiencing in the light of the "Everything Is Beautiful" and "Disenchantment" stages of culture shock. Then identify understandings related to worldview, values, and norms that could help this family adapt to the culture.

We are all excited and a little fearful when we enter a new culture. When the letter of appointment arrives, our level of personal satisfaction is high. . . . Our dreams have come true. This is what we have been planning and training for over the past few years.

The farewell at the church is even more satisfying. All our lives we may have occupied the pews but now we are center stage. Even the pastor takes second place. The good-byes at the airport are even more exciting, a sweet mix of sad partings and the thrill of new adventure.

Landing in a strange city abroad, our satisfaction is still high. We are tired from the flight, but there is the excitement of

new sights and strange customs. We are really here. We can hardly believe it!

We stop at a restaurant and order lunch. But when it comes, we recognize only half of it as food. The other half looks inedible—like worms or even ants. Hungry, we stop at the market and ask for some oranges, but the woman in the stall does not understand us. We suddenly realize that all people do not speak English. Desperate for something to eat, we point like children to our mouths and stomachs and then to the oranges. When the vendor finally understands and gives us fruit, we face another problem. How are we going to pay for it? We cannot understand her, and the new coins make no sense to us. Finally, in desperation, we hold them out and let her take what she wants. We are sure we are being cheated. To make matters worse, the children nearby are making fun of us, obviously amused that these wealthy and educated people cannot speak a language any local three-year-old knows well. Inside we are angry and want to tell them how learned we really are, but to no avail. Our education is of little use to us here.

> The next day our host sends us across town on a bus, with instructions to get off after five miles at the stop with a big brown house on the left and a small green one on the right. We set out confidently, but a few stops later we see a big brown house on the left, and a small green one on the right. We know we must go further, but every stop thereafter is the same. Suddenly we are afraid of getting lost, but we cannot turn back now. We have visions of spending the rest of our lives riding around a strange city in a bus.
>
> Later we get sick and are taken to a local doctor. We are afraid, for are not all foreign doctors witch doctors? Can they really cure us?
>
> As anxieties multiply, we seem to get little done, beyond keeping ourselves alive. Everything is strange, everyone looks alike, we have few friends to whom we can turn for help, and we cannot admit defeat and go home. Unlike the tourists, we cannot even go to the local Hilton and its familiar settings. What has happened to our dreams?

we want to be here. Shared cultural patterns and affinities, which John and Ruth Useem describe as the "third culture," develop among people who have become immersed in two or more cultures (Useem and Hill Useem 1967). Staying in the middle of the stream is the most difficult and stressful of our three options. At the same time, it is the healthiest and offers the most possibilities for long-term adaptation and effectiveness in cross-cultural settings.

In our next chapter, we will look at some of the specific issues involved in culture and language acquisition.

223

12

Culture and Language Acquisition

> Soon after Roberto di Nobili arrived in India in 1606, "it became clear to him that . . . the attempts of missionaries to persuade their converts to adopt Portuguese ways had imposed a fatal barrier . . . and would have to go. If he wished to win the Brahmans for Christ, he must, as far as was possible, become a Brahman for their sakes."
>
> Stephen Neill (1984, 280–81)

Historian Stephen Neill provides a vivid account of the culture and language acquisition ventures of Roberto di Nobili.

His first appointment was to the Fisher Coast, where, with his inborn facility for learning languages, he acquired in seven months reasonable fluency in the form of the Tamil language which was spoken in those parts. Then came the appointment to Mathurai, which was reached on 15 November 1606. There a young Hindu elementary school teacher agreed to serve as Nobili's instructor in his further study of the Tamil language; at the end of a year Nobili was able to express himself as fluently and correctly in high Tamil as though it had been his native language. During this time a close friendship sprang up between the two young men, and the teacher was prepared to discuss with his pupil Indian ways and usages and those things in the imported Portuguese way of life which from the Indian point of view were insupportable. The list was almost endless—almost everything that the Portuguese did was objectionable to the high-caste Hindu. They wore leather shoes—no high-caste Indian may touch anything that comes from a dead animal. They ate with knife and fork, which to the Hindu is disgusting. They drank wine and ate meat; worst of all they ate beef—a habit practised by one of the very lowest of the separated communities. (Neill 1984, 280–81)

Di Nobili's perceptive cultural insights, combined with his persistence in developing fluency in the language, have made him a model for missionaries in succeeding generations.

Culture and language acquisition go hand in hand. You will not be at home in the culture without communicating well in the language, and your communication through language will be ineffective if you are not immersed in the culture. Language learning, relationships, cultural adjustments, and cultural understandings are all intertwined. They grow and develop together, as can be seen in table 12.1.

Each of the first three levels in the table includes low, mid, and high ranges. Detailed descriptions for both culture and language acquisition are provided for all four levels. The ultimate goal is to form deep relationships that result in a high degree of oral and social proficiency (naturalness) gained through an integrated understanding of culture and language (language levels based on *ACTFL Proficiency Guidelines–Speaking* available at www.actfl.org).

While we are functioning at a basic level of culture and language acquisition, we are learning words and short phrases, making concrete observations, adjusting in small ways to the culture, and beginning to develop relationships. As we progress, we are able to use declarative statements and questions from daily life, can understand what people are doing and saying in varied social situations, and are able to engage in banter and small talk. Even though we still experience frequent discomfort, we are beginning to adjust to the culture. Then, as we become more capable in the language, we learn to tell stories, grasp implicit meanings in the situations around us, and talk about our dreams and goals. At this level, we have meaningful relationships and are comfortable in almost any cultural situation. As our proficiencies continue to grow over time, we may become acculturated to a level of near-native comfort. We can use extended discourse, appreciate and use a variety of literary genres, speak and write without repetitive patterns of error, and engage in in-depth investigation of abstract issues.

Our purpose in this chapter is to introduce you to cultural, linguistic, and nonverbal competencies you will need to develop; attitudes, traits,

TABLE 12.1

CULTURE/LANGUAGE ACQUISITION LEVELS

(ADAPTED FROM NEW TRIBES MISSION 2006; USED WITH PERMISSION)

1. Basic (Novice)	**Culture:** Material and concrete objects in a situation	**Language:**
		Use words and short phrases
	Visible characteristics	
	What can be directly observed	
	Many acquaintances and beginning relationships	
	Little adjustment to culture	
2. Progressing (Intermediate)	**Culture:** Human and social	**Language:**
	What people are doing/saying in the situation	Use sentences, questions from daily life
	What can be learned from simple conversation and Q/A	
	Growing relationships (banter and small talk)	
	Beginning to adjust to culture; still frequent discomfort	
3. Capable (Advanced)	**Culture:** Implicit	**Language:**
	What is underlying the situation and related situations	Use paragraphs, narratives, and descriptions
	What can be learned from texts and follow-up interviews	Speak in the past, the present, and the future
	Many meaningful and comfortable relationships	
	Comfortable in most cultural situations	
4. Proficient (Superior)	**Culture:** Abstract issues	**Language:**
	What can be learned from in-depth investigation	Uses extended discourse
	Deep relationships	Many genres mastered
	Acculturated to level of near-native comfort	No patterns of error

and values that will be helpful; and ways in which you can take charge of your culture and language acquisition program.

DEVELOPING COMPETENCIES

Linguistic and nonverbal competencies are not acquired in a vacuum. They are permeated with the culture in which they are being developed and are interwoven with the missionary's efforts to get around, connect with people, and handle his or her missions assignment. We discuss these cultural competencies below.

SIDEBAR 12.1
WORSHIPING THE GOD WHO COMMUNICATES

Lois McKinney Douglas

One cannot approach the study of language without a sense of awe and wonder as we worship the God who communicates. Take time to read the Scripture passages below quietly and prayerfully, listening to God's voice speak through his creation, the incarnate Word (Jesus Christ), the written Word (the Bible), the Holy Spirit, and the promise of a future kingdom.

- The Genesis account of creation is a record of God's communicative acts. When God spoke, the heavens, the earth, and all living things were created. Through his words, his special creation of human beings was mandated.

   God *said,* "Let us make man in our image" . . . male and female he created them. God blessed them and *said* to them, "Be fruitful and increase in number; fill the earth and subdue it." (Gen. 1:26–28)

- The book of Hebrews reminds us that God continued to speak through the Old Testament prophets and through his Son. We hear God's voice through his creation, the incarnation, and the promises of the future kingdom.

   In the past God *spoke* to our forefathers through the prophets at many times and in various ways, but in these last days he has *spoken* to us by his Son, whom he appointed heir of all things, and through whom he made the universe. (Heb. 1:1–2)

- The incarnation of the Word of God in Jesus Christ expresses the depth of God's desire to communicate with us and to show us what he is like.

   In the beginning was the Word, and the Word was with God, and the Word was God. . . . The Word became flesh and made his dwelling among us. (John 1:1, 14)

- The Bible, the Word of God, was written by

   . . . men [who] *spoke* from God as they were carried along by the Holy Spirit. (2 Pet. 1:21)

Cultural Competence

GETTING AROUND

You will not be able to survive long in your new surroundings unless your culture and language skills enable you to buy food and medicines, eat out, fill your gas tank, ask for services and pay for them, ask for directions, use the local currency, make bank transactions, read package labels, mail a letter, make a telephone call, go to a doctor or a dentist, get your hair cut, or take care of residence permits. Even though the people who live in the context handle these and scores of other tasks with ease, they can create all kinds of anxieties and questions for a newcomer. Even in the midst of your self-doubts and uncertainties, it is important to get

---

SIDEBAR 12.2

LANGUAGE IS AT THE HEART OF WHAT IT MEANS TO BE MADE IN GOD'S IMAGE

Lois McKinney Douglas

Consider the following things that language enables, and then discuss the questions below. Through language:

- We can connect with the outside world. Whether we are talking about the weather with a stranger or sharing deeply with a close friend, we can reach out to others and acknowledge they are there.

- We can share experiences, seek information, exchange ideas, express opinions, and let our feelings be known. Through these verbal activities, interpersonal relationships are nurtured and deepened.

- We can recall the past, interact with the present, and anticipate the future together. Historical continuity, purpose in each moment, and an eschatological hope emerge.

- We can listen to God and respond to his voice. The Bible is full of examples of people listening and responding when God speaks: Abraham (Gen. 12:1–5), Moses (Exod. 3:1–4:17), Isaiah (Isa. 6), Paul (Acts 9:1–19), and many others.

REFLECTION AND DISCUSSION

1. Why did God give us the gift of language?
2. How does our use of language separate us from the rest of God's creation?
3. In what ways can we use this special gift for his glory?

---

involved in these activities and learn to function well in the culture as quickly as possible.

CONNECTING WITH PEOPLE

From the moment you arrive in your host country, you will need the culture and language skills to connect with people. You will want to learn the everyday polite phrases that correspond to "Please," "Thank you," "I'm sorry," and so on. You will want to be able to introduce yourself to people and respond to introductions. You will want to engage in simple conversations that will help you become acquainted with people and allow them to know you.

Before long, you will become frustrated with this superficial kind of communication and want to go deeper. You will want to share your story with people and listen to their stories as they share them. You will want to develop some trusting and close relationships, so that you and your friends can share your joys, struggles, doubts, worries, successes, and failures with one another. Cultural issues may emerge at this point as well. A common complaint people from other cultures have is that, on the surface, North Americans are usually extremely open and friendly, but at a deeper level, they resist committed, long-term, reciprocal relationships with people who are different from them. Learn to let people into your life!

As you connect with people, you will want to share your love for Jesus and your journey with him through the years. You will want to encourage your Christian friends and let them encourage you. You will try to develop meaningful relationships with secular people and those from other religions as well. And you will want to do this in an atmosphere of mutual sharing. Many find evangelism through friendship to be far more effective than structured plans for "witnessing." Once again, cultures vary greatly. Be sensitive. Ask questions. Listen and learn.

Handling Your Missions Assignment

Many of the readers of this book are looking forward to missions assignments in another culture. Some may want to be involved in evangelism, church planting, discipling, and leadership development efforts. The vision of others may be to help churches act out their social concern through medical work, education, agriculture, or community development. Still others may be committed to bivocational ministry, serving Christ by bringing their professional or business activities and their missions commitment together.

Regardless of the form and shape of your intercultural ministry, it will involve some combination of higher-level intercultural competencies in teaching, preaching, writing, encouraging, helping, explaining, and resolving conflict. Your values, expectations, and practices related to these ministries are almost certain to be different from those of your national coworkers and people among whom you want to minister.

- An experienced international theological educator began a pastors' seminar in Hong Kong with breakout groups in which the participants were asked to create lists of needs they saw in their churches. She instantly lost rapport. They had not come to this seminar to talk to one another. They had come to hear an "expert" assess their needs.

- A church planting missionary in Latin America was ineffective in his ministry and eventually returned to the United States. The reason? He had not been able to develop a Latin rhetorical style in his preaching. Worshipers found his quiet speech and content-filled, expository sermons boring. They wanted their pastor to sound excited, shout at times, and use broad gestures.

229

There are, of course, many positive experiences that can be shared. Over time, the overwhelming majority of intercultural workers adapt well to differences in ministry expectations and develop the competencies and skills that enable them to engage in effective intercultural ministries.

Language Competence

Acquiring a language involves formal, sociolinguistic, discourse, and strategic competencies (Dickerson 2004, 3–4; Sawyer and Smith 1994, 300–306). As you read about these competencies in the sections below, you will become even more aware of how completely interwoven language and culture learning are.

FORMAL LINGUISTIC COMPETENCE

Formal linguistic competence involves proficiency in forming words, structuring sentences, reproducing sounds and intonations, developing an adequate vocabulary, spelling correctly, and writing clearly (Dickerson 2004, 3–4). These skills are foundational. We cannot get very far in intercultural communication without them.

The Ephraimites discovered how important pronunciation can be. Forty-two thousand of them were killed because they were unable to distinguish an s sound from a sh sound (Judg. 12:1–6). Even though we are not likely to be put to death because of our poor pronunciation or grammatical constructions, we will still limit the effectiveness of our ministry if we make people struggle to understand us. At the very least, we will have some humorous or embarrassing moments. For example, a missionary in China while at a restaurant with some friends wanted to ask for a refill of her tea. She used the common Chinese phrase ging win to call the waiter. He blushed but did not come over. The missionary continued to call ging win until a Chinese person sitting nearby leaned over and said, "You are asking him to kiss you!" She had used the correct sounds but the wrong tones. Even intonation is important in being understood.

One sunny afternoon, a mother mouse and her little mice left their hole to go out for a walk. Suddenly, as they were happily sniffing and zigzagging their way down the path, a stealthy tomcat appeared out of nowhere and was ready to pounce on them. The mother mouse, staying calm and in control, responded with a loud "ARF!! ARF!! ARF!!" The startled cat fled away. "See, my children," the mother mouse said when the cat was out of sight, "I wanted you to see how important it can be to learn a second language!"

Source unknown

230

Good pronunciation skills should be developed early in your language learning experience. If you wait until you speak fluently, it will be very difficult to change the bad habits you have learned.

Global communication through the Internet and mushrooming publishing ventures around the world are making proficiency in writing, as well as speaking, more important. On one occasion, at a writer's workshop for theological educators and expatriate missionaries, the instructor submitted 250-word excerpts from the self-instructional texts the participants were writing to a "CLOZE" test, designed to assess the naturalness of their writing styles and vocabularies. Every fifth word (including prepositions and articles) was omitted from the selected excerpts. Then target-language speakers filled in the blanks with the words they thought belonged there. When the results were analyzed, there was a bimodal distribution. The national educators were clustered on the "high" end of the naturalness curve, and their missionary counterparts at the "low" end. Happily, several of the missionaries were indistinguishable from their host-cultural counterparts in their ability to write naturally. With a modicum of ability and perseverance over an extended period of time, most second-language learners can develop adequate, or perhaps even superior, formal linguistic skills.

SOCIOLINGUISTIC COMPETENCE

Sociolinguistic competence involves learning the socially accepted norms of a culture in greeting people, using forms of address, expressing emotions, keeping the conversation moving, interrupting, and maintaining rapport (Sawyer and Smith 1994, 300–306). The story in sidebar 12.3 is one of the hundreds of true stories that could be told to illustrate how this kind of competence expresses itself in intercultural relationships.

Sociolinguistic competence develops as we learn, often by trial and error, the kinds of behaviors that are expected in specific social contexts. Along with other language competencies, their acquisition continues throughout our cross-cultural sojourn.

DISCOURSE COMPETENCE

Competence in discourse begins with naturalness and correctness of speech, but it does not stop there. It also involves making culturally appropriate changes in your style of communication as you move from conversing to writing letters, lecturing, praying, telling stories, writing poetry, or preparing articles for professional journals.

One of the more interesting and culturally relevant aspects of discourse competence is storytelling. Large portions of the Scriptures are narrative. They tell the stories of creation; the fall; the flood; the patriarchs; the exodus; the kingdom of Israel; the division of the northern

---

Sidebar 12.3
Getting the Job Done

Early one morning, a missionary in an African country hurried to a publishing center to get a "rush" job done. He nodded quickly as he walked past the receptionist/secretary, went straight to the printing press operator, and blurted out his request. "Would it be possible to have one thousand copies of this brochure ready for me by this afternoon?" "Yes," the operator responded coolly, "I will get them done." The missionary was taken aback for a moment by the icy response. But then he realized that he had made a social blunder. He was acting like the manager of a business firm in a task-oriented country where "time is money" and getting right to the point is expected. So he started over and tried to repair the damage. "I'm sorry," he apologized to the printing press operator. "I was in such a hurry to take care of this job that I didn't ask you how you are doing. Is your wife well? Are your children well? And how is your father's health?" The worker smiled, shared family news, and then reciprocated with similar questions for the missionary. After sharing an update on his own family, the missionary reiterated his request for the print job. Both of the men smiled and shook hands before he left the shop.

---

and southern kingdoms; the captivity; the return from exile; the birth, life, death, and resurrection of Jesus, the Messiah; and the history of the New Testament church.

Even today, especially in traditional cultures, people use stories that have been transmitted from generation to generation to connect with their past. Understanding these cultural stories is basic to appreciating their values and worldviews. Stories are also used to communicate in everyday situations. A visitor at African congresses and consultations will be sure to observe national leaders using stories to clinch their point. The Africans often laugh and clap to express their approval, while many of the expatriate missionaries are baffled by what is going on. In many contexts, listening to others tell their stories and telling your own stories become essential communication skills.

Strategic Competence

Strategic competence involves your ability to adjust your language on the spot to enhance effectiveness or to modify communication when it breaks down. It includes such skills as controlling the volume and rate of speech, paraphrasing, and using circumlocution when your vocabulary doesn't allow you to express yourself directly (Dickerson 2004, 3–4; Sawyer and Smith 1994, 300–306).

I (Lois) began to learn circumlocution skills during the early months of my language and culture learning experience in Portugal. On one occasion, I needed paper clips. While I was on my way to the office supply store, I realized that I didn't know how to ask for them in Portuguese. So when I got there, I went to a clerk and struggled to explain what I wanted. "I need some small metal objects that are shaped like this," I said in Portuguese, as I drew a picture on a notepad. "They are used to hold pieces of paper together." *"Pois não"* (of course), the clerk responded with a nod and a smile. *"A senhora deseja clipes"* (you want clips—pronounced CLEE-pees!).

Nonverbal Competence

DIVERSITY OF NONVERBAL COMMUNICATION

Examples such as those in sidebar 12.4 can go on and on. Some scholars suggest that as much as 93 percent of meaning in a conversation may be conveyed nonverbally (Dodd 1998, 134). A bit of reflection on the diversity of nonlinguistic communication tends to confirm this assertion. Dodd (1998, 133–51) provides an overview of nonverbal communication categories. Four of these are illustrated in sidebar 12.4 on the following page. The head of state's gesture was badly misunderstood because of differences in the meaning of body language, or kinesics. The university couple's and their host culture friends' efforts to adjust to each other's concepts of lateness illustrate chronemics, or perceptions related to time. It was proximics, the physical space between the North American missionary and his European friends, that made him feel uncomfortable after a church service. The missionary's inappropriate hugging reflected differences in haptics, or touching behavior.

Dodd's categories include additional forms of nonverbal behavior (1998, 133–51). Oculesics (facial expressions) communicate. Smiling does not always mean happiness, openness, and friendliness. In some Asian cultures, smiling and laughing can reflect embarrassment. Not looking people in the eye, especially when social status differences are involved, is sometimes considered respectful. The tendency in some Middle Eastern cultures to gaze intensely during conversation can be interpreted by outsiders as staring. Some Europeans and Asians think that the North American habit of revealing emotions so openly through facial expressions is immature and childish. Yet even in cultures where facial expressions are controlled, subtle changes in expression in the eyes and movements of the forehead, cheeks, jaws, and lips can still be observed and interpreted.

Sensorics, or communication through the senses, are important. Responses to sound, taste, textures, colors, temperature, odors, and so on, are culturally conditioned. Most youth cultures respond positively to loud contemporary music, amplified by electric guitars and punctuated by

233

SIDEBAR 12.4
THE IMPORTANCE OF KNOWING NONVERBAL COMMUNICATION PATTERNS

As you read the following real-life examples, consider the importance of taking the time to learn nonverbal communication. What steps can you take to begin this process when you enter a new culture?

- A head of state was riding in a motorcade in a foreign country. He looked from side to side, smiling broadly and with his hand raised high and two fingers curled into a circular pattern. The crowds of people along the route were waving, smiling, and even laughing as the vehicles rolled by. This national leader thought his finger gesture was telling the crowd that things were "Great!" However, within the culture, the gesture was interpreted as obscene. A large photograph on the front page of the country's newspapers greeted their readers the next morning, and the incident triggered laughs and jokes for days to come.

- When a university professor from the United States was on an extended assignment in Brazil, he and his wife decided to join the Rotary Club as a means of reaching out into the community. Members took turns hosting meetings in their homes. When the couple attended their first meeting, they arrived promptly at the scheduled time, only to find that the hostess was still taking a bath and the housekeeper was busy preparing the refreshments. The couple quickly adjusted and began arriving an hour or so later at the meetings. When their turn came to entertain, they were still getting dressed and arranging the chairs in the living room when the doorbell rang. The whole group was arriving! Word had gotten around that Americans were punctual, so they decided to respect their friends from the States by being on time.

- A North American missionary in a European country could not get over feeling uncomfortable when he was conversing with people after a church service. He would find himself moving back a step or two to be at a more comfortable distance, only to see his conversation partner take steps forward to close the gap.

- A missionary in a South American country returned to her home church in the United States for the first time after four years away. She embarrassed herself, and made her pastor's face turn red, by giving him a big Latin hug when they greeted.

drum combos. When this kind of music is played and sung in a church, some older people attend a parallel traditional service, take earplugs with them, or even stay home! Smells communicate. On one occasion, American university students in a graduate residence hall launched a protest because of the strong garlic smell that permeated the building when some of the international students were cooking. Colors are important too. Some North Americans and Northern Europeans feel that paint colors used on Mediterranean and Latin American homes are gaudy and sometimes clash. On the other hand, many Latin Americans and

Southern Europeans find the colors of their northern neighbors' homes to be far too subdued, unimaginative, and even depressing.

The Importance of Nonverbal Communication

By this point in our discussion, you are probably becoming aware of how much of what we understand, feel, and experience when we are interacting with other people depends on nonverbal communication. In interpersonal and intercultural interaction, much more than cognitive content is being exchanged (Singeles 1994, 282–84; Dodd 1998, 134–35). When we are in social settings, subtle (and sometimes not so subtle) changes in facial expressions, eye contact, posture, body movements, and the raising and lowering of our voices betray our attitudes and emotions.

- You may be bored while you are listening to a class lecture. Without being aware of it, you are likely to be slumped back in your chair, losing eye contact with the instructor, and daydreaming or muffling your yawns.
- On the other hand, you may be participating in a stimulating group discussion. Your interest in what is going on and even your thoughts and feelings become apparent as you lean forward, smile or frown, nod or shake your head, and gesture during the course of the discussion.
- Perceptions of status and power or access and approachability are also communicated nonverbally. A professor standing behind a lectern facing students seated in rows sends a very different message than he or she conveys by sitting in a circle with them.

There are some specific ways in which verbal and nonverbal communication interact (Singeles 1994, 282–84; Dodd 1998, 135). First, nonverbal messages enhance and complement verbal messages. When you greet a friend you are waiting for at a restaurant by rising, shaking his hand, and asking him how he is, and he answers, "I'm tired," you will be more likely to believe him if he sighs and collapses into his chair before you have time to sit down again.

At the same time, a nonverbal message can contradict, modify, or create dissonance with a verbal one. If your friend says, "I'm tired," as he smiles, gives you a firm handshake, sits down erectly, and starts sharing exciting news with you, his verbal message of tiredness will come across as unbelievable. Nonverbal messages may also substitute for verbal ones. Your friend may say nothing about being tired, but his message comes across clearly as he yawns, stretches, slides down into

235

his chair, and keeps letting his eyelids drop during your conversation. Additionally, a nonverbal message can repeat a verbal one. When your friend puts his hand over his mouth in a yawn gesture as he says, "I'm tired," his gesture reinforces his verbal message.

Nonverbal communication is especially important in synchronizing conversation and other social interaction. Eye contact, sitting forward, nodding in agreement, shaking your head in disagreement, and raising and lowering your voice are some of the nonverbal messages that interact with the verbal messages being sent. Attitudes such as liking or disliking, involvement and attention, confidence, status and respect, and self-presentation are also communicated in nonverbal ways. Finally, nonverbal communication is extremely important in communicating emotion. Even without wanting to, people often let us know nonverbally when they are hurt or angry, elated or depressed, confident or afraid, happy or sad, eager or reluctant, interested or bored.

The discussion above has made it quite apparent that culture and language acquisition and the acquisition of nonverbal competencies go hand in hand. Our communication skills will be incomplete unless we develop all three.

UNDERSTANDING YOURSELF

Culture and language acquisition happens from the inside out. Your expectations, motives, and attitudes may get in the way or spur you on. Your personality type, thinking styles, and preferred learning strategies also influence the way you approach the task. No two culture and language learners are alike. We trust that, as you recognize yourself in this discussion, you will be able to adjust the suggestions that follow later in the chapter to the uniqueness of your own personality.

Previous Experiences

Language acquisition must begin with expectations of success. If you are filled with anxiety and have visions of failure, it is important to identify possible sources of these negative feelings.

Your previous attempts at culture and language learning may be getting in the way. If you had an interesting, creative teacher when you studied a language in school or enjoyed learning some basic phrases and gestures that helped you to connect with others while you were on a summer missions team, you are probably looking forward to immersing yourself in a new language and culture. But if, on the other hand, your memories of previous language learning consist largely of boring translation exercises in school situations or frustrating attempts to communicate with people you could not understand, you may find yourself

236

dreading, or at least being extremely anxious about, more culture and language study. You must not allow these experiences to create negative expectations. Culture and language acquisition does not have to be drudgery. It can be exciting, challenging, and even fun.

Anxieties

You may also be concerned about trying to learn a language and enter a new culture as an adult. Obviously, the process is not the same as it is for a young child. You have to work at using new grammatical structures, acquiring a new vocabulary, and reproducing strange sounds. It is difficult to intuit and mimic what is going on around you in ways that a child can. And you do not have proud parents, grandparents, older brothers and sisters and other family members, friends, and nursery school teachers who are eager to cheer you on!

But being an adult has its upside as well. You can concentrate for longer periods of time, analyze grammar, make generalizations, and understand sociolinguistic and other cultural factors that are woven into language learning. You can map your own strategies and set your own goals. And most important, you can keep working hard over an extended period of time.

Researchers in second-language acquisition have shown that almost anyone can learn a second language. While some people are quicker than others, the rest of us cannot use our age or our lack of natural ability as excuses for not launching our language study and expecting some degree of success. Take heart—God has endowed you with the ability not only to acquire a second language but also to use this gift to reach the minds and hearts of the people with whom he has called you to work (Dickerson 2004, 1).

Motives

When we are crossing cultures with the gospel, we need to be especially careful of our motives. Are we acquiring the culture and language *primarily* as instruments for preaching, teaching, evangelizing, and planting churches? Do we tuck our sermon notes and our second-language use into our briefcases as we leave the site of our ministry and find ourselves feeling eager to retreat to our familiar surroundings, where we can enjoy time with our families, colleagues, and friends in the expatriate community? What proportion of our social needs is met through interaction in our second culture? And what about our relationships? Do they extend beyond our ministry contacts? Are we friends to the people God puts within our sphere of influence, even if they reject our message? Does our use of the second language reflect our commitment to identification,

---

SIDEBAR 12.5
1 CORINTHIANS 13: A MISSIONARY VERSION

McCracken (1979; used with permission)

I may be able to speak fluently the language of my chosen field
    and even understand its culture,
        but if I have not love, the impact of my speech is no more for Christ than that
        of a businessman who comes to exploit the people.
I may have the gift of contextualizing God's word when I deliver it to my hearers.
    I may have all knowledge about their customs,
        I may have the faith needed to combat witchcraft,
            but if I have no love, I am nothing.
I may give everything that I have to the poor, to the hungry in the favelas (slums),
    I may even give my life for them,
        but if I have no love, this does no good.
Love is . . .
    thinking in their thought patterns,
        caring enough to understand their worldview,
            listening to their questions,
                feeling their burdens,
                    respecting them,
                        identifying with them in their need,
                            belonging to them.
Love is eternal.
    Cultures pass away.
        Dynamic equivalents will change because cultures change.
            Patterns of worship and church administration will need revision.
                Languages will be altered over time.
                    Institutions will be replaced.
                        . . . Because these are not reality.
Since I am finite, I can only study how to express the Message cross-culturally,
    trying to free it from my cultural bias.
I am able to do this only in a limited way,
    but I pray that the Spirit will use my life to show Christ to those with whom I
    work.
Meanwhile, these remain . . .
    Identification,
        Contextualization,
            and
                Love,
                    BUT THE GREATEST OF THESE IS LOVE.

contextualization, and love? You may want to take time to meditate on
Jean McCracken's missionary paraphrase of 1 Corinthians 13 (sidebar
12.5) before you continue reading this chapter.

Attitudes

It is easy to let stereotyping and prejudice get in the way of culture and language learning. A missionary in Francophone Africa did a good job of learning French in Paris and yet never became fluent in a tribal language. The underlying reason was that he valued the French language more. He felt it was useful to know and prestigious in other contexts. The tribal language seemed inferior and not really all that necessary to learn. The effectiveness of his ministry was severely limited by his lack of fluency in the local language.

Other factors can also affect the language's prestige. Standardization of language use through the media has an impact. Historic or contemporary conflicts between cultures can get in the way. A perceived loss in the vitality of a language can occur in tribal situations in which the trade language or national language is making inroads into the use of the local language. Similarly, in immigrant communities, the second and third generations are often reluctant to retain and use their parents' or grandparents' language. Another interesting phenomenon is "code switching," in which ethnic groups use dialects within their own context that are different from those they use with out-groups (Dodd 1998, 124–26; Gudykunst et al. 1989, 145–62).

Personality Type

Personality factors play an important role in culture and language acquisition. One of these is your tendency toward introversion or extroversion. If you are an extroverted, outgoing, risk-taking kind of person who is energized by social interaction, you will probably develop sociolinguistic competencies in a second language more readily than your more reserved colleagues will. However, you may find your motivation to keep working on the language lessening as your social needs begin to be met. This is sad, because you may rob yourself of the grammatical accuracy and extensive vocabulary you need and find yourself on a plateau in your language acquisition competencies. Your challenge will be to keep on stretching and growing.

Now, let us suppose that you are more introverted. You enjoy the challenges of formal linguistic analysis and the intricacies of discourse competence. But you have to force yourself to get out, mix with people, and relate to the culture around you. You find it hard to develop sociolinguistic skills and want to be sure of yourself before you communicate to avoid mistakes and embarrassment. If you can jump over these hurdles, your persistence and carefulness may, in the long run, allow you to become an even more effective culture and

---

SIDEBAR 12.6
A "GOOD" LANGUAGE LEARNER

adapted from Dickerson (2004, 5--6)

The following are attributes of good language learners. Choose the one that might be most difficult for you personally and discuss steps you can take to improve.

1. From the beginning, good language learners work to gain acceptance in their new culture.
2. Good language learners are highly motivated individuals who have positive attitudes toward their new language and culture.
3. Good language learners are also good culture learners.
4. Good language learners know themselves.
5. Good language learners know how to manage their emotions.
6. Good language learners make their mistakes work for them.
7. Good language learners assume responsibility for their own learning.

---

language learner than your more extroverted colleague. And there is further encouragement for you: you may find that your control and reserve are more acceptable in some cultures than your colleague's extroversion is.

Thinking Style

People bring different thinking styles to their language study. Some learners are more "linear" thinkers. They use systematic approaches to language learning. They spend hours at a time memorizing vocabulary and days on end working on verb tenses or practicing difficult sounds. They may be frustrated by exceptions to grammatical rules. (Every language has them!) Their discourse competencies may develop quite readily.

Other learners are more global and intuitive thinkers. They would rather read a story than analyze grammar. They would rather learn vocabulary by immersing themselves in the culture than by spending hours analyzing word meanings. They guess at sounds and "feel" the grammar. The flow of conversation is much more interesting to them than the structures and rules of the language.

Remember that we are not talking about fixed patterns. Women often see themselves as global and intuitive. Yet many have learned to write impressively linear research papers and theses. And in off-guard moments, linear thinkers can actually enjoy poetry and stories. Your culture and language learning experience will be more effective if you incorporate elements from both of these styles.

240

Preferred Learning Strategies

Culture and language learners develop different strategies. One important difference is that some prefer to listen and speak while others want to read and write. If you are a listener and speaker, you will probably want to practice with a coach or spend time on interactive oral language–learning Web sites. If you are a reader and writer, you will enjoy surfing the Web for good reading material; surrounding yourself with newspapers, books, and magazines in your new language; and trying your hand at exchanging e-mail with your second-culture friends.

Once again, some cautions are in order. Listeners must learn to read, and readers must learn to listen. Recognize your preferences and capitalize on them, without neglecting the other skills that you need. And in the midst of media resources that you have access to, remember that a patient "real, live" coach who will listen to you, read with you, interact with you, correct you, and encourage you is still your best language learning resource. We talk more about this below.

Your Commitment

In the midst of the frustrations triggered by not being able to communicate and the enormity of the task you have undertaken, you may find yourself getting discouraged. You may even feel like giving up. It is at moments like these that your firm commitment will come to the rescue. Betty Sue Brewster describes this kind of commitment as a settled decision on the part of language learners that they want and need the language, they want to involve themselves with the people, they are willing to be vulnerable and let others help them, and they will reach out to people different from themselves, enter their world, and persevere in acquiring their language (2000b, 862).

TAKING CHARGE

You are responsible for your own culture and language acquisition. If you expect programs prescribed by mission agencies or language schools to provide ready-made answers to all your needs, you are likely to be settling for mediocrity and boredom. Effective culture and language learning is active and proactive. Before you leave on your assignment, you will want to gather information about your new home and find opportunities for direct exposure to the culture and language. When you arrive at your destination, you should be creative and flexible in finding a language school, developing relational networks, exploring your surroundings, enlisting a coach, and becoming a participant observer in new social situations.

Before You Leave

INFORMATION GATHERING

The technology explosion gives you immediate access to answers to many of the questions you have about living abroad. While you are sitting in front of your computer, you can learn about your target country's history, geography, politics, economics, health services, and education system. You can discover its literature, music, and art. Your awareness of the country's social issues and concerns can grow. Interaction with the religious systems, beliefs, worldviews, values, and norms of your new culture are possible.

Even if your computer skills are not all that great, you are not doomed to cultural incompetence. The resources available in libraries and bookstores are sometimes even more valuable than information on the Web. The medium is not important. What is important is that you do what you can to acquire some understanding of your host culture before you leave your homeland. Efforts made while you are getting ready to go are likely to smooth out transitions, make your initial cross-cultural experiences more enjoyable, and contribute to your long-term intercultural effectiveness.

EXPOSURE TO THE CULTURE AND LANGUAGE

Bookstores, libraries, and the Internet are not the only ways to prepare for your cross-cultural experience. They may even get in the way if they keep you from more direct kinds of exposure to the culture and language. If you are in a university community, you may be able to develop interpersonal relationships with students or professors from your target culture. Or perhaps there are culture and language courses you can attend. Before you enroll in one of these, make sure it is being taught by a native speaker and that the focus is on speaking and cultural acquisition skills, not just on reading and translation exercises.

If you live in a culturally diverse environment, such as an urban center, you may discover an ethnic neighborhood where people from your future culture live. Be sure to visit their restaurants, shops, special cultural events, and perhaps their temples, mosques, synagogues, or churches. Short-term missions trips and other brief cultural emersion experiences can also be helpful.

A "LEARNING HOW TO LEARN" COURSE

A "learning how to learn" course will help you get off to a good start in acquiring a second language. It can be especially useful for people who have less than stellar language aptitudes (that includes most of us!) or who are going to be tackling a particularly difficult language. Two recommended programs that have sites on the Web are the Institute for

Cross-Cultural Training (ICCT), offered by the Billy Graham Center of Wheaton College (www.wheaton.edu/bgc/icct), and PILAT (Program in Language Acquisition Techniques), available through Mission Training International (www.mti.org/pilat). There are others. Many mission agencies have developed their own courses. Some businesses, government agencies, and relief and development programs offer them as well. As you evaluate these programs, remember that their purpose is to help you to acquire knowledge, attitudes, and skills related to culture and language learning. They are not focused on specific contexts or languages.

When You Arrive

When you arrive in your new culture, you will be greeted by a variety of resources for culture and language learning. Among these are language schools, relational networks, and your local surroundings.

FINDING A LANGUAGE SCHOOL

Language schools come in many forms, shapes, and sizes. Some are large, perhaps regional in scope, and may serve several denominations or mission agencies. They may have highly developed structures and many resources. Others are smaller, often serving a particular agency or group. They may be less structured and offer more limited resources. There are also programs that link students with tutors and university programs and provide counseling and supervision along the way. These all have strengths and limitations that you will want to consider.

You may ask how important it is to go to a language school. In spite of their limitations and imperfections, they can be extremely helpful to most learners, providing them with the structure, information, resources, and collegiality that will help them to stay motivated and disciplined and ultimately to succeed in reaching their language acquisition goals. Most people find it more difficult to achieve superior levels of sociolinguistic and discourse competencies without this kind of environment.

Betty Sue Brewster (2000b, 552–53) has identified areas of concern in evaluating a language school: its learning philosophy; its curriculum; the training, experience, and attitudes of the teachers; instructional methods; class size; emphasis on conversation and communication; attention given to culture learning and involvement; location; the dialect being taught; expected outcomes; the school's reputation; flexibility in dealing with differences in ability and learning styles; preparation for continued independent learning; contact hours; length of program; and cost. Brewster stresses that the greatest benefit from the course accrues to those who are fully engaged in the process, participating actively and willing to try new skills and accept correction. They will be disciplined,

---

SIDEBAR 12.7
RESOURCES FOR LANGUAGE LEARNERS

Lonna J. Dickerson, Institute for Cross-Cultural Training (ICCT) (n.d.)

Of the hundreds of available resources to help you become a better language learner, here are two easy-to-read books and one CD-ROM program. These books are written for those who want to learn a second language but know little about how to go about the process other than taking a course and hoping that their needs will be met. In these books, you can find practical guidance for becoming a more self-directed learner who is increasingly able not only to learn more effectively in the classroom but also to learn successfully from ordinary native speakers. While the CD-ROM program is primarily for language learners who want expert advice throughout their learning process, it also offers a broad range of practical guidance for language coaches/facilitators.

Joan Rubin and Irene Thompson, *How to Be a More Successful Language Learner*, 2nd ed. (Boston: Heinle & Heinle, 1994).

A foundational "must read" for every language learner and language coach/facilitator. Provides a very readable and relatively short overview of the language learning process including important issues you need to understand to become an effective self-directed learner.

Terry Marshall, *The Whole World Guide to Language Learning* (Yarmouth, ME: Intercultural Press, 1989).

Written for independent language learners, this book shows you how to learn at your own pace through involvement with ordinary native speakers in the local community. It includes guidance for finding a native-speaker helper (a "mentor") and using a Daily Learning Cycle.

LinguaLinks Library Version

CD-ROM from the SIL International (www.sil.org/lingualinks).

A rich source of ideas and information on all aspects of language learning. Seven major sections (bookshelves) are included: Anthropology, Language Learning, Linguistics, Literacy, Sociolinguistics, Consulting, and General Reference. Indispensable for language coaches/facilitators and also highly useful for learners who will take the time to ferret out information to help themselves become more successful self-directed learners. Updated and expanded yearly. You may also purchase separately the Language Learning bookshelf on a CD-ROM.

---

making an ample investment of their time and energy in the course. They will spend their time outside the classroom relating to people in the language group and, where possible, living with a local family.

If you cannot find a good language school or want to supplement your "formal" language learning experiences, consider taking advantage of the resources suggested in sidebar 12.7. You may also find Tom and Elizabeth Brewster's *Language Acquisition Made Practical* (1976) and Donald N. Larson's *Guidelines for Barefoot Language Learning* (1984) helpful.

DEVELOPING YOUR RELATIONAL NETWORK

Culture and language acquisition experiences go beyond interacting with your colleagues and instructors in a language school. You will be interacting with people in other contexts as well. To begin with, there is your family, your roommates, or a host-culture family you live with. You attend church activities, including worship, prayer, study, and social events. You may be involved in evangelistic or social outreach projects. You develop relationships with neighbors and other people in the community. These kinds of opportunities can enrich and enhance the structured activities you are involved in. They can also provide the friendship, support, and encouragement you need in the midst of your cultural transitions and adaptations.

EXPLORING YOUR SURROUNDINGS

There are almost limitless resources for culture and language learning in the village, town, or city where you will be living. How can you discover these? Where can you start? One approach is to take a walk. Using your home or the language school as a hub, spiral outward, and with a small notepad and pen or pencil in your hand, make a list of social settings that look interesting to you. An open-air market, a bus terminal, a coffee shop across from a soccer field, or a religious bookstore are examples of some of the possibilities.

As you begin to understand the language, you will want to keep abreast of local events. Perusing local newspapers, posters plastered on walls, and brochures that are thrown into your yard will help you to know what is going on. So will the blaring loudspeaker announcements from trucks rolling by. There may be a special sale, a musical concert, a holiday parade, an exhibit in a local museum, or a political rally. These kinds of experiences can be valuable both in language acquisition and in helping you to appreciate and identify with the culture.

WORKING WITH A COACH

Your culture and language learning experience will be far more enjoyable and effective if you can enlist a coach to work alongside you. This person should be someone who can encourage you, correct your mistakes, get you in touch with resources, help you assess your progress, and assist you in projecting your learning goals and plans. Your language school, a host-culture friend, or a mission colleague will probably be able to get you in touch with the right person. Your coach should be a native speaker of the language who knows the culture well and is committed to working with you over an extended period of time.

245

BECOMING A PARTICIPANT OBSERVER

Participant observation is a method used in ethnographic research. It involves the systematic observation of human cultures, aspects or dimensions of a culture, or specific social situations. Used less formally, elements of the method can be extremely helpful in culture and language learning. Here are some tips and suggestions.

Be flexible in scheduling your visits to social settings. In some cases, you may want to visit a site every week, or perhaps several times a week, over a period of time. In other situations, visiting at regular or irregular intervals over several months or even a year or more may be more workable. Sometimes there will be single events that you do not want to miss. Be flexible and creative in adapting to opportunities as they come along.

Have a clear plan for every visit. Work with your coach in advance on the words, phrases, and sentences that will help you to communicate within the social setting you have chosen. Anticipate what kinds of people are likely to be there, activities they will be involved in, and questions you can ask to trigger a conversation. If you have decided to go to the coffee bar across from the soccer field, you will need to learn how to greet the server and ask for black coffee with just a bit of sugar, along with a special pastry that you like. You must remember to hold the pastry in your hand with a paper napkin. It is likely that you will run into soccer fans while you are there, so working on vocabulary and questions related to the team or an upcoming game will be useful.

Prepare the questions that will help you to understand and interpret what you are observing in the social situation. While you are in an open-air market, you will probably want to ask yourself who the people are and why they are there. Are they all buying produce? What other reasons are there for being there? What underlying dynamics and meanings do you see?

Take notes and keep a journal. If possible, jot down some key words and phrases during your visits to the site to jog your memory afterward. As soon as you get home, take time to make a journal entry. Describe what happened with as much detail as you can. Include your questions and attempts to interpret what was going on. Reflect on what you learned through your successes and failures in conversation and social interaction. Each visit, try to go a little deeper in uncovering cultural values, meanings, and norms. Debrief your journal entries with your coach, and work with him or her in developing strategies that will help to deepen your cultural understanding and improve your communication skills during future visits to the site.

246

And Down the Road . . .

The day will come when your language and culture skills will have developed to the point that your primary focus will shift to ministry. This does not mean that you will put participant observation skills aside, or quit working on your sociolinguistic, discourse, and strategic competencies. You will want to keep developing your communication and cultural skills throughout your sojourn in the culture.

Full-time involvement in ministry will involve changes in your language and culture acquisition strategies. You will probably want to enlist at least one friend or colleague who will keep correcting your choice of words, pronunciation, and grammar when he or she is with you. This person can also help you to be aware of sociolinguistic and cultural norms you may be violating. While I (Lois) lived in São Paulo, my secretary filled this role. Several years later, when I made a return visit to Brazil, we went to a restaurant together. Throughout the entire table conversation, my former secretary was still correcting my speech and behaviors! Reading local newspapers, browsing in bookstores, surfing cultural Web sites, and watching national television will also be helpful. Be sure to keep asking questions about social interactions that are new to you or that you are not sure you understand.

If your ministry involves written communication or speaking in formal contexts, you will need continual help. Ask competent friends and colleagues to smooth out the style of your lectures or sermon notes, correct manuscripts before you submit them for publication, and make lists of repeated mistakes you make during oral presentations.

> *The most important factor in gaining fluency, if not mastery, of a foreign language, is consistency in learning over time. After years of pre-field preparation, followed by one or two years in intensive foreign language learning, many missionaries are eager to dispense with further study. They cannot wait to plunge into their long anticipated ministries. However, while most missionaries are able to begin using limited language skills early in their career, real language mastery will take much longer. It will require continued effort to acquire active use of new vocabulary, advanced grammar, colloquial patterns, idioms, etc. These outcomes will only happen with plenty of practice, continual effort to have mistakes corrected, and more study. Only time will show whether one's language skills have continued to improve, or have instead plateaued.*
>
> Mark Dominey, OMF International (personal communication, 2005; used with permission)

247

Culture and language learning will go on and on. We never stop learning and growing in our first language; our second language experience should be the same. If you would like to use proficiency scales to measure your progress, you may want to consult the "Skill Descriptions" that have been developed by the US government's Interagency Language Roundtable (www.govilr.org) or the Proficiency Guidelines provided by ACTFL, the American Council of Teachers of Foreign Languages (www.actfl.org). Terry Marshall's revision and narrative descriptions of these skills are also helpful (Marshall 1989, 40–47), as are New Tribes Mission's language levels based on the ACTFL guidelines (table 12.1).

SUMMARY

Above all, in the midst of your efforts to achieve ever-higher levels of competency in communication and social skills, remember that they will add up to nothing unless they reflect Christ's love. Before you go on to the next chapter, take time to read Jean McCracken's paraphrase of 1 Corinthians 13 (sidebar 12.5) once again. Ask God to fill you with his love for the people around you, helping you to think in their thought patterns, to care enough to understand their worldview, to listen to their questions, to feel their burdens, to identify with them in their need, and to belong to them. This is what missions is all about. It means loving God with all our heart, soul, mind, and strength, and loving our neighbor as ourselves. Culture and language acquisition flow out of this love.

CASE STUDY:
IN THE MARKETPLACE

Lois McKinney Douglas

Marge Sanders and her husband have been on a mission assignment in Brazil for a little more than a year. She has turned her regular visits to an open-air market into a culture and language learning experience. On this occasion, she and her household helper, Maria Alves, have partially filled a large shopping bag with oranges, tomatoes, and lettuce. We encounter them at a banana stall. There are at least eight different kinds of bananas to choose from.

Marge has learned to identify most of them. She likes the "apple bananas" best.

Marge decides to save time by leaving Maria to finish the banana transaction while she buys beans. She has to ask Maria where the bean stall is. Maria answers with an intermediate distance word that enables more precise communication than the English words "here" and "there."

On her way to the bean stall, Marge's neighbor, Eulália, sees her at a distance and gestures to ask her to come over to talk. The gesture is similar to the one used to wave good-bye in North America, but Marge has learned to interpret it correctly and goes over to greet her friend. They embrace loosely but warmly, with arms on each other's shoulders, while they kiss each other lightly on both cheeks. Marge uses a different form of address with Eulália than she does with Maria. With Maria, she uses the common word for "you." But because of Eulália's age and social status, and because she has not known her long, Marge greets her with the formal terms, "Dona" and *a senhora*. At some point, as their friendship deepens, they will agree to address each other less formally.

After chatting for a while, Dona Eulália suggests that they get a *cafezinho*, a small cup of strong coffee. They go to a nearby coffee bar and continue conversing. When the attendant starts to pour her coffee, Marge uses a gesture with her thumb and forefinger to tell him that she just wants half a cup. The women part company, kissing on both cheeks again. As she walks away, Dona Eulália calls back to Marge, gesturing with her fingers clasped and her hand held close to her ear to ask Marge to give her a phone call when she gets home.

When Marge finally gets to the bean stall, she is once again faced with a choice, this time among several different kinds of beans. She opts for *feijão preto*, the small black beans her family likes best. She mentally translates pounds to kilos to determine how much to ask for and struggles a bit in selecting the right bills and coins for her purchase. She would like to bargain for a lower price, but her language and culture skills are not quite up to this yet.

After finishing her purchase, Marge returns to the banana stand, where Maria is visiting with a friend who came by. When Maria sees Marge, she and her friend quickly kiss to say good-bye, and the two women head home.

After they get back, and the produce is cared for, Marge picks up her journal, goes to the veranda, rests back comfortably in a lounge chair, and begins to reflect on her trip to the market.

REFLECTION AND DISCUSSION

Put yourself in Marge's position:

1. What would she record in her journal about her trip to the market? Include her thoughts and feelings as she interacted in this social setting.
2. What goals and strategies will she want to develop for her next visit?

Now, imagine you are Marge's culture and language coach:

1. What is your assessment of her progress?
2. In what areas would you like to see her keep learning and growing?

249

PART 4

Missionaries and Their Lives

13

Women in Missions

It is amazing how one can get such a false idea as that not all God's children should use all their powers in all ways to save the lost world. There
are, so to speak, many people in the water about to drown. A few men are
trying to save them, and that is considered well and good. But look, over
there a few women have untied a boat also to be of help in the rescue,
and immediately a few men cry out; standing there idly looking on and
therefore having plenty of time to cry out: "No, no, women must not help,
rather let the people drown." What stupidity!

Fredrik Franson (in Nilsen 1956, 26)

HISTORICAL OVERVIEW

At the beginning of the modern missions movement, most women went
to the field to accompany their husbands. They were the wives of missionaries, not missionaries themselves. Their role was to be homemakers
and mothers who reached out to local women and girls. Sometimes the
wife felt overwhelmed and lonely in attempting to handle these responsibilities by herself, so she and her husband enlisted a single woman to
serve alongside her.

Opportunities

As the "faith mission" movement began to emerge during the nineteenth century, new opportunities opened up. J. Hudson Taylor, founder of China Inland Mission (now OMS International); Fredrik Franson, founder of The Evangelical Alliance Mission (TEAM); and others recruited women to evangelize, teach, and preach. When the casualties of the Civil War left many women widowed or without prospects of marriage, and denominational boards still were not willing to send them overseas for direct work, they began to found their own boards. These women raised funds over and above the denominations' regular budgets, founded women's missionary training colleges, and mobilized more than one hundred thousand local church "auxiliaries" as home bases for education, prayer, and funding. Three million active women raised funds to build hospitals and schools around the world, pay indigenous female evangelists, and send single women across cultures as missionary doctors, teachers, and evangelists. By the early decades of the twentieth century, women in the mission force outnumbered men by two to one. Then, during the 1920s and 1930s, women's sending agencies were persuaded to merge with denominational boards, and their opportunities for direct mission work gradually diminished (Kraft and Crossman 1999, 13–17).

During the same period, the work of evangelical women on the mission field began to flourish. Many were motivated by the urgency of the times. Their strong premillennial conviction that the gospel must reach the ends of the earth before the return of Christ spurred them on. These women began joining other faith missions such as Africa Inland Mission and Central American Mission. Since these missions prioritized evangelism over educational and medical work, women with little formal education or economic status were often accepted, as long as they were willing and able to raise their own financial support. Other women were motivated to cross cultural boundaries by the holiness movement and its emphasis on the good news of salvation and sanctification. Women within this tradition usually served under Wesleyan denominations, such as the Church of the Nazarene, the Church of God (Anderson, Indiana), and the Assemblies of God. The Keswick movement, which emphasized gradual growth toward Christian maturity, attracted women from Reformed traditions (Robert 2002, 13–16).

Some women went beyond activism to make contributions to the development of mission theories through their letters, diaries, and, later on, biographies and periodical literature. Gender-based social concerns and emphases emerged. They concentrated on personal and ethical aspects of missions related to witnessing and working toward the reign of God. Issues such as foot binding, female infanticide, child marriage, and opportunities for advanced education were high on their agendas. Their focus on schooling provided acceptable roles for them as teachers, enabling them to break down cultural prejudices toward Christianity and challenge non-Christian worldviews. One of these women was Eliza Agnew, who dedicated her life to serving as principal of a girls' boarding school in Ceylon.

Holistic concerns also led women into healing ministries. One of these was physician Nancy Monelle Mansell, who, appalled by the mortality rate of child brides in India, led a petition drive to the Indian parliament to raise the age of marriage to twelve. "[W]omen physicians interpreted their task holistically. They prayed with patients and conversed with them about their spiritual states as well as healed their bodies" (Robert 1996, 414). Without the contributions of these kinds of women, the historical record of North American missions would be distorted and partial. Their mission theory has provided a glimpse of the church that goes beyond being an institution to become a way of life (409–18).

Problems and Challenges

The life and work of these missionaries were filled with problems and challenges. Some accompanied their husbands into missions out of duty rather than a sense of personal vocation. Dorothy Carey followed her husband, William, to India, even though she was afraid to go. Tragedy followed: she was overwhelmed by cultural stress and, after the loss of a five-year-old son, eventually succumbed to psychosis and death (Tucker 1988, 15–17).

At the other end of the spectrum, some women married so that they could be missionaries:

> Narcissa, the daughter of Judge Stephen Prentiss, was a teacher before she met Marcus [Whitman], but she was not fulfilled. She had heard the story of the Nez Perce Indians in the far West who had pleaded that someone be sent to bring them the "Book of Life," and she desired more than anything else to answer that plea. The American Board was actively seeking missionary volunteers—single men or married couples. Single women were not eligible. For Narcissa, marriage was the only answer to her dilemma. (Tucker 1988, 51)

Women and children were especially vulnerable to disease and death. Many women had large families. Ministering and caring for a family in the midst of a difficult climate and the stresses of culture left many of them drained physically and emotionally. Rosalind Goforth and her husband, Jonathan, traveled as a couple in an effective evangelistic ministry

255

in China. Five of their eleven children died in infancy or early childhood (Tucker 1988, 34–35).

Both married and single women faced discrimination. Women were often appointed as only associate missionaries and found ministries closed to them. They were usually in situations in which neither married nor single women had voices on mission councils. A single woman's support level was often less than a single man's. But in the midst of discrimination, some advocates spoke out forcefully for women in missions.

The problems women have faced in missions fade into insignificance when we know and recognize the heritage they have left for us. Margaret Kraft and Meg Crossman encourage today's missionaries to study these women of greatness and to be inspired by their pioneer spirit to make their own contribution to current and future generations:

> We can study women of greatness who served in Christ's cause and claim them as our role models. From Mary Slessor, single woman pioneer in Africa, to Ann Judson of Burma and Rosalind Goforth of China, wives who fully served; from Amy Carmichael of India to Mildred Cable in the Gobi Desert; from Gladys Aylward, the little chambermaid determined to get to China, to Eliza David George, black woman missionary to Liberia; from translator Rachel Saint to medical doctor Helen Roseveare; from Isobel Kuhn and Elisabeth Elliot, mobilizing missionary authors, to Lottie Moon, pacesetting mission educator; from simple Filipino housemaids in the Middle East to women executives in denominational offices to unsung Bible women in China, the roll is lengthy and glorious!
>
> The roll is, however, incomplete, expectantly awaiting the contribution of current and future generations. . . . Women, stirred by the task that lies ahead, can mobilize, devoting their skills, their accessibility, their knowledge, their tenderness, their intuitiveness, their own distinctive fervor to the work. The pioneer spirit, full of dedication and faithfulness, which women throughout history have shown, will set the standard. The task is too vast to be completed without all of God's people! (Kraft and Crossman 1999, 17)

THEOLOGICAL DEBATES

Women's roles in ministry, marriage, and singleness have been hotly debated over the last several decades. Sometimes situations have become ugly as tempers have flared, scathing articles have been written, and churches and denominations have split. On one side of the heated discussions are *complementarians*, who believe that women may speak, sing, pray, ask questions, and perhaps even debate in church-sponsored situations, but that they are not allowed by the Scriptures to be pastors, hold other ruling offices, preach in church services, or teach men (Culver 1989, 25). Within the home, a wife should voluntarily submit to her husband's leadership and see her role as humbly serving and helping him by being a homemaker and raising children. Single women should submit to the authority of male church leaders and family members in their vocational and personal decisions.

On the other side of the debate are *egalitarians*, who believe that the Bible teaches the fundamental equality of women and men. Husbands and wives are equal partners in the home. Within the Christian community, there is no indication that spiritual gifts are gender-specific. Women are encouraged to exercise all their gifts in all the church's ministries and leadership roles. The starting point is creation. Both men and women were created in the image of God (Gen. 1:26, 28) and became the same flesh (Gen. 2:18–23). The fall resulted in the subordination of women (Gen. 3:16), and the new creation in Christ restored women to equality (Gal. 3:28).

Attempts to interpret 1 Timothy 2:11–15 illustrate some of the dynamics in this ongoing debate. Complementarians see the interpretation of this text as clear and straightforward. We are told that a woman must be silent and learn in quietness and full submission. Paul does not permit a woman to teach or have authority over a man. This precludes women from roles of public ministry in the church in which they would teach or lead men. Paul bases his argument on creation. Adam was formed first, then Eve. Adam was not the one deceived; it was the woman. There is something about woman's nature that showed her to be more susceptible to temptation through deceit than was man (Culver 1989, 36). Based on Paul's teaching here and in other parallel passages, such as 1 Corinthians 11:11–14, complementarians conclude that the mandate to be silent applies to all times and all places. It is transtemporal and transcultural.

But egalitarians will say it is not that simple. Paul passed up more common Greek words for authority (*exousiazo* and *kyrieuo*) and used *authenteo*, a word that likely had a negative meaning of domineering or lording it over someone. Women were being prohibited not from leading but from exercising an inappropriate style of leadership.

When Peter addressed the crowd on the day of Pentecost, he reminded them that they were seeing Joel's prophecy that both men and women would prophesy being fulfilled (Acts 2:17–21). We know from other New Testament passages that women did teach and lead in the New Testament church. Philip had four daughters who prophesied (Acts 21:9). Priscilla and her husband, Aquila, co-led a house church (1 Cor. 16:19). Euodia and Syntyche were Paul's yokefellows, contending by his side for the gospel (Phil. 4:2–3). Phoebe was a deaconess (Rom. 16:1). There were other women who worked hard with Paul in ministry (Rom. 16). With respect to creation, Paul balances his argument that woman came

257

from man and was created for man (1 Cor. 11:8–9) with a reminder that man is also born of woman (1 Cor. 11:12). Based on these biblical data, egalitarians suggest a localized and contextual interpretation of the 1 Timothy 2:11–15 text.

To explore the complementarian perspective further, we suggest reading *Recovering Biblical Manhood and Womanhood* (Piper and Grudem 1991) and exploring the Council on Biblical Manhood and Womanhood Web site (www.cbmw.org). For a better understanding of the egalitarian viewpoint, read *Discovering Biblical Equality: Complementarity without Hierarchy* (Pierce and Groothuis 2004) and visit the Christians for Biblical Equality International Web site (www.cbeinternational.org).

InterVarsity has also published *Women in Ministry: Four Views* (Clouse and Clouse 1989). The continuum of positions presented in this book extends from the *traditional view*, which holds that the Scriptures do not allow a woman to pastor, preach, or hold other leadership roles; to the *male leadership view*, which supports limited involvement of women in church ministries under the direction of a male senior pastor; the *plural ministry view*, which affirms the ministry of all believers, including women, and identifies arguments over ordination as the root problem; and the *egalitarian view*, which fully supports the ministry of women in any kind of service for which God has endowed them and to which they feel called. The presentation of each view is followed by responses from people who hold other positions (1989, 20).

ROLE EXPECTATIONS

Unfortunately, the divisive issues we discussed above are not just abstract theological topics that are interesting to reflect upon, or North American concerns that we can leave behind when we go to our field of service. Role expectations for women in their ministries, marriages, or single lives are so deeply enmeshed in our sending cultures, churches, and agencies that we take them along with us on our overseas assignments. There they are acted out among our field teams, in our ministry outreach, and in our adaptations to the broader culture around us.

Ways in which your personal convictions and role expectations are supported or challenged within your mission contexts are extremely important. If you affirm women's full participation in ministry and equal partnership in marriage, you will likely be frustrated if your sending churches, mission agency, field team, and the national churches do not support these views. If, on the other hand, you believe women should serve in supportive roles, you may be uncomfortable with roles where more is expected.

Divergent viewpoints on women's roles in missions affect both men and women. Even in situations where men are the dominant decision makers, all missionaries have a stake in the outcomes. It is important that missionaries' personal views converge with those of the sending and the host country institutions to which they will be relating. There are many stories of confusion and conflict when role expectations are not met. Some of these are presented below.

Ministry Roles

SENDING CHURCHES

Churches sometimes do not know what to do when a missionary woman they are supporting visits them. Informal social gatherings, small group meetings, outreach activities, and missions banquets are usually enjoyable. If conflicts in role expectations occur, they are more likely to be related to public ministry. The church may have a policy of not allowing women to speak from the pulpit or to adult groups composed of both men and women. Even capable women who are effective public speakers and have made an impact on overseas missions are sometimes relegated to the children's church, while a young man who is leaving on his first missions assignment is invited to speak from the pulpit during the morning service. Missionary wives, many of whom have much to share, become accustomed to being quickly introduced before their husbands bring the message.

> Larry, Audrey, and their two children were visiting one of their sending churches after a four-year term on the mission field. Both had spent two years studying the language and culture. Both had developed ministry plans and were planting a church. His gift was evangelism. She discipled believers. Both were raising their young family. (Downey 2005, 66)

Here is how the pastor introduced them:

> We are very pleased to have a missions report this morning. Larry is here to share with us about his ministry. His wife and two children were able to join him as well. Larry, come share with us what the Lord is doing in your ministry. (Downey 2005, 66)

Occasionally, there is a clash between the missionary's field ministry and the expectations of a church at home. Lois experienced this during the unforgettable speaking engagement described in sidebar 13.1.

SENDING AGENCIES

Happily, many missionaries work in situations in which relationships between the home office and their field team are good. Area directors encourage and counsel missionaries when they visit the field. They are

259

SIDEBAR 13.1
ARE YOU TEACHING ONLY WOMEN?

McKinney Douglas (1975, 79)

The pastor's greeting was as icy as the Midwestern U.S. roads my car had been skidding on while I was trying to find his church. I suspected that he had invited me to his study for something more than the usual prayer-before-the-meeting with the visiting missionary speaker.

I was right. We had scarcely sat down when he displayed the publicity material he had received from my mission.

"I just wanted to clarify a couple of things before the service," the pastor began, clearing his throat. "In the first place, I noted that you are teaching in a seminary in Brazil. Am I right in assuming that you are teaching only women?"

"In most of my courses I teach both men and women," I admitted rather meekly.

"Then I can only conclude that you and your mission have deliberately chosen to disobey God's command that women are not to teach or have authority over men."

I knew that it wouldn't help to point out that women taught and prophesied in the early church (Acts 18:24–26; 21:8–9; 1 Cor. 11:5), so I just went on listening.

"The reason I wanted to talk to you before the meeting," the pastor continued in a somewhat kinder tone, "is to make two requests. First, I noted that one of your missionary activities has been training Sunday school teachers. I would prefer that you tell our people about this aspect of your work and not mention your involvement in the seminary. Secondly, I must ask you to avoid any teaching or exhortation from the Word of God. What I want from you is strictly a report of your work."

Since I was considerably more compliant then than I am today, I conformed to the pastor's requests. I was careful not to mention to either him or the congregation that many of the Sunday school teachers I had been training were also men!

---

aware of the impact their policies can have on missionaries and the host country churches. In their administrative role, they sometimes go a second mile in creating space for a woman to work, interpreting her ministry to the mission board and churches back home and being open to changes she may suggest. In its newsletters and reports, one agency constantly praised three of its female missionaries; one was directing a hospital, the second a literature program, and the third a theological education association. These women were reporting directly to the home office rather than to their field councils. The intent was to free them from the mission's field structures and give them more space for their ministries.

Another incident humorously illustrates a mission agency's openness to change. When the field director visited her field, a missionary gently confronted him: "I have just reread the mission policy manual. It is full

---

SIDEBAR 13.2
NOW A SEMINARY GRADUATE CAN TAKE OVER

Lois McKinney Douglas

Following is a true story of a mission that found itself needing to interpret the ministry of a woman who was an extremely effective church planter to a home board and supporting churches that did not understand or approve of her role. How would you advise the field team and the mission agency?

Her mission was proud of Sarah Frances. She was a singular person. She learned auto mechanics on one of her home assignments so she could take care of her vehicle when she was miles from nowhere on precarious roads in a remote area of the South American country in which she was serving. Some male missionaries took their cars to her for maintenance and repair. She spent her career planting churches in remote, barely accessible places where missionary families would find it hard to serve. Her strategy was

to go to a village at the invitation of an evangelical family and work with them in conducting meetings in their home. They had worship services, prayer meetings, and Bible studies. She waited for ordained pastors to visit for baptisms and serving communion. After a period of two or three years, there was usually a thriving, self-sustaining congregation. That was the point at which Sarah Frances moved on. "Now a seminary graduate can take over," she would say. "They don't need me here anymore."

The field team and the mission agency never knew what to do. They were impressed and even thrilled by what was happening. But how could they communicate all of this to their home board and constituent churches, which might be shocked and scandalized to see a woman in this role?

---

of gender-biased language. Every other sentence uses "missionary, he . . ." The director reflected a moment and then said, "I think you are right. Would you be willing to go through the manual and edit it? I'm quite sure the board will approve." So the missionary accepted the challenge, and gender-biased elements were removed. With one exception. In the doctrinal statement, one of the affirmations was: "All men are sinners." With tongue in cheek, the missionary made a note in the margin: "This is fine just like it is!"

The relationships between sending agencies and field teams can be smooth and comfortable as long as there is a fundamental agreement between them in their expectations regarding women's roles. But agencies and fields are dynamic and changing, and role expectations often change as well. A large denominational mission recently swung from supporting mutual submission in marriage and a broad spectrum of opportunities for a woman in ministry toward a restrictive position in which a woman is expected to find fulfillment in submitting to her husband's leadership and serving as his helper in the home. Some long-term missionaries who could not accept the direction their mission was heading have resigned or been dismissed.

Another factor that affects women in relation to evangelical sending agencies is a "glass ceiling." Women often constitute a small minority of mission executives and board members and also tend to be underrepresented in intermission and international associations and commissions. Women who have "crashed through the ceiling" have interesting stories to tell. On one occasion, a woman who was attending an invitation-only missions consultation found herself alone with ninety-nine men. At the refreshment table, one of the men approached her with an intended compliment: "You ladies have done such a good job of preparing for us. Thank you so much." At another gathering, this time a planning retreat for the board of a missions association, only one woman was listed among the plenary speakers. Her topic? "What Mission Leaders' Wives Need to Know" (Zoba 2000, 45).

Women can face other awkward situations in consultations and meetings. For example, what do they do at mealtime? They can tag along with colleagues they know, but at these kinds of gatherings, mealtimes are for networking. So they exercise other options. One is to arrive late and join a table with a man or two they know. This sometimes works, but on other occasions the nonverbal communication comes through clearly: this is a private men's discussion, and they would rather not have a woman barging in. Another option is for the woman to arrive early and wait for others to join her. This one can also backfire. She can easily find herself sitting alone during the entire meal.

There are some encouraging exceptions to this pattern of male dominance. One of these is SIM International. Women comprise about two-thirds of their mission force. The mission actively promotes their participation on the board of governors, in area councils, and in other leadership roles. Single women direct missions in India and Ghana, and a married woman is director of Sudan. "By limiting half of the evangelical force that has legitimate spiritual gifts, we're not hurting women so much as the cause of Christ. . . . We've got all kinds of opportunities, and we desperately need women to take them," says Jim Plueddemann, former general director of SIM (Zoba 2000, 45–47).

FIELD TEAMS

Relationships within a field team are sometimes extremely close. The missionaries become brothers and sisters to one another and aunts and uncles to the children, almost as if they were an extended family. When there are emergencies and crises, they are there for each other. In everyday living, they support and encourage one another. They often work as compatible colleagues in a broad range of ministries.

All of this does not necessarily mean that the team is free from problems in defining women's roles. Subtle and not so subtle differences in expectations can be shattering. One example occurred on a field where men comprised the executive committee, and field decisions were made when they went on retreats together. The practice functioned until the treasurer was ready to go on home assignment, and the most qualified person to take over his job was a woman. The executive committee asked her to do the accounting and bookkeeping and send reports to them without being named treasurer. She and her husband said she would accept the position only if she were designated treasurer and made a part of the committee. There was no other choice. They accepted her, even though it meant an end to their all-male retreats.

Another case of conflicting role expectations occurred when a missionary arrived on a field to work with churches. She was greeted at the airport by a male missionary who grumbled: "I thought we asked the mission not to send us single women." Instead of becoming defensive or taking the next flight back to the States, she accepted a teaching position in the field's missionary children's school, where she put her heart into teaching and encouraging missionary parents. Within a year or two, there was not a missionary on the field who did not love and respect her. Later she was invited to work in church-related ministries and even became a member of the field executive committee.

Host Churches and Cultures

Women in missions quickly discover that role expectations go beyond those of sending churches, mission agencies, and field teams. The cultures they enter create opportunities and limitations related to their ministries as well. The dedication of some female missionaries to ministries among nationals has become a part of missions folklore. One of these is Eliza Agnew (1807–83), who arrived in Ceylon (now Sri Lanka) in 1839 to serve as principal of a girls' boarding school, where she served until retirement without returning home. She became revered because of her dedication to education, itinerant ministries in churches, and visits to the homes of her former students. Although she never married and had no children of her own, her obituary praised her as "'the mother of a thousand daughters.' All of her pupils loved her as a mother, and nearly all of them claimed her as their mother in Christ, and she was permitted to see their children to the third generation walking in the ways of the Lord. She probably led more brides to the marriage-altar than any other person living" (Beaver 1968, 79).

Women have often become mentors of national teachers, pastors, and evangelists. One of these was Malla Moe, a Norwegian immigrant to the United States, who after being recruited by Fredrik Franson, spent

263

fifty-four years in Swaziland as an extremely effective church planter, preacher, and evangelist. In spite of her domineering and demanding personality, Moe identified closely with the culture and was deeply loved by Africans. One colleague who observed a farewell gathering just before her first furlough recognized that she had won the hearts of the people. "Grown men cried like children, over the entire room there was a deep heart rending cry as if the heart would break. Many were the prayers that were offered for her soon return to them" (Tucker 1988, 95).

Sometimes expatriate women have even been able to transcend the hostilities of two groups at war.

> Such was the case with Rose Lambert who served for twelve years as a pioneer Mennonite missionary in Turkey. It was a terrible time of starvation and massacre caused by the war between the Turks and Armenians. Rose was a nurse and the matron of an Armenian orphan school. The city was full of typhoid fever and processions continually marched to the graveyard. Rose did not discriminate between Armenians and Turks, caring for all who needed her. Then she herself became ill with typhoid. After it became peaceful enough for her to travel, she relocated to a lower altitude to recover, [leaving behind her the deep respect of both parties in the conflict]. (F. F. Hiebert 1999, 23)

In some contexts, of course, a woman working with men or even relating to men is subject to taboos. "Things she would do at home— smiling and chatting with a man behind her in a grocery line, or looking in the eyes of men she passes on the street, or simply answering a question from a taxi driver—are all considered in her host country as come-ons and invitations to sexual relationship" (Eenigenburg 2001, 481). "Yet in a nomadic Muslim group in Sub-Saharan Africa, a single woman is effectively training Imams (Islamic teachers) in the Gospel. They perceive her to be non-threatening, 'just a woman'" (Kraft and Crossman 1999, 16).

Even in contexts where women find their ministry accepted, role identification can be confusing. While I (Lois) was a missionary in Brazil, I enjoyed affirmation and respect from the national men with whom I worked. Yet, at the same time, some of the expatriate missionaries were convinced that a single woman had no place there. I was looked upon within the culture as a potential mistress for a married man. I was puzzled enough by this anomaly that I resorted to an ethnographic study of women's roles within the culture. Roles were identified ranging from normative (daughter, wife, mother, matriarch), to accepted (nun, single professional, unmarried aunt), tolerated (mistress), or rejected (prostitute). As I looked at myself in relation to these roles, I began to understand my cultural identity. I was old enough to be a grandmother in a culture where age is respected. My choice to remain single so that I could dedicate myself to God's work was valued by my Catholic friends, who saw me as a nun, and by many evangelicals who had been influenced by the broader culture. My graduate degrees and professional role enhanced my social respectability. In other words, I was a matriarchal, professional nun!

Missionary Wives' Roles

Sometimes the "super mom syndrome" gets exported to the mission field. The missionary wants to be a caring, supportive wife to her husband, a good homemaker and mother, and perhaps even a homeschool teacher of her children. Of course she also wants to be active in a church, get to know neighbors and shopkeepers, become involved in some community activities, and have an intense and fulfilling ministry that goes beyond supporting what her husband is doing.

At the other end of the spectrum are wives who retreat from the culture into their home, the expatriate community, the missionary children's school, and an English-language church that serves the international community. Even though these women may have been on the field for years, some of them never learn the local language well or feel at home in the culture. They are often unhappy, and when they open up, they may tell you candidly that they are in the country because of their husband's ministry. If they had a choice, they would return home.

Between these two extremes, of course, are the hundreds of married missionaries who succeed in juggling multifaceted role expectations and are finding fulfillment as wives, mothers, and involved participants in ministries within the culture.

These women are not sorting out their roles in a vacuum. Field teams and sending agencies have their own expectations. Sometimes the wife is told that she is a full-time missionary and expected to make fieldwork her primary concern. She may be encouraged to send her children to a boarding school and turn her home care over to household helpers, so that she can devote her full attention to ministry. Other agencies may move in the opposite direction, expecting the wife's ministry to be serving and supporting her husband and taking the full responsibility for the home and the children.

Karol Downey (2005, 66–74) underscores the ambiguity and complexity of married women's roles in missions. The expectations may be unclear. They may not even have a job description, and when they do, it is likely to separate homemaking and parenting (being a wife) from "ministry" (being a missionary). Integrated ministry expectations are needed. All that we do, whether washing dishes, reading the Scriptures, visiting a neighbor,

---

SIDEBAR 13.3
PRISON MINISTRY IN MOZAMBIQUE

Zoba (2000, 41)

"Personally, I'm more interested in the historical missionary women who were failures," says Karen DuBert, who serves with TEAM in Mozambique with her husband, Phil. "I guess that's because sometimes I feel like a failure. We don't really have our role [as missionary wives] designed; we have to make it for ourselves."

Karen, a stay-at-home mom, has built many female friendships in the port city of Quelimane. Along with an Argentinian missionary friend named Silvia, she visits women in the town jail to teach them the Bible. One woman had stolen a pair of shoes and sat in jail for 13 months before she was brought to trial.

Another woman who was being beaten by her husband defended herself by cutting him with a razor, which required him to get eight stitches. The judge sentenced her to two-and-a-half years in jail.

"There is a lot of injustice going on for everybody," says Karen, "but the women especially have much less chance of being looked out for. A lot of times someone in the court is waiting for a bribe, and these women don't have enough money, so they just sit there."

She and Silvia began showing up in court, pressing court-workers (and anybody who would listen) to put these women's trials on the docket and move up the dates. The woman who cut her husband had waited in jail for a year before the court sentenced her. She had become a Christian through their ministry, and Silvia and Karen went to the judge and vouched for her. Silvia asked if she could take responsibility for her and take her home as hired help. The prison director said she could, and she was released under Silvia's care after serving one year of her sentence.

---

or planting a church, is to be done for God's glory (Col. 3:23–24). Clearer definitions will contribute to a better balance between home and ministry and encourage both husbands and wives to get involved in running the home, raising children, and sharing in each others' ministry. The full participation of both spouses in all facets of ministry will be facilitated by taking advantage of household help and teaching children to get involved in both home and ministry as well. You will enjoy the story of a stay-at-home mom who has succeeded in bringing these facets of her life together in a prison ministry in Mozambique (sidebar 13.3).

The kind of partnership we have been talking about assumes a healthy marriage. Most missionary marriages are impressive. The couple expresses dedication to God, each other, and the children. But, at the same time, one of the major problems missionary couples face is their relationship to each other. The reasons for this are not hard to see. Modern social problems have made an impact.

Today's missionaries grew up in a culture where living together outside marriage was commonplace. Often their own homes were fractured through divorce, and perhaps their parents have new partners. Once they are on the field, missionaries face in-service problems. They sometimes try to model a "perfect" marriage and are afraid that being open about their marital problems may destroy their witness. If they are in a culture where privacy is not valued, it is hard for them to find time to be alone. Frequent travel by one or both of the partners can mean coping with separations.

Personal development is also important in marriage. Unrealistic expectations can get in the way. There can also be overdependency, with expectations that the spouse will meet all of the partner's psychological needs. Add to this list sexual problems that may be aggravated during cultural adjustments and anxieties about child-related matters, and it is easy to see how marriage relationships can become both the major problem and the greatest joy in a missionary couple's life (Foyle 2001, 165–81).

In the midst of the conflicting role expectations missionary wives face, Dana Robert reminds us that the ideal of the Christian home remains a powerful witness for Christ:

> Over the past two centuries the missiology of the Christian home has functioned as a justification for the participation of women in mission, as a gender-based evangelistic strategy and a foundation on which to construct the liberation and leadership of women in society. The ideal of the Christian home, with its promise of male-female partnership and its family-centered ethic, remains a powerful witness to Christ, especially in patriarchal cultures. Women around the world have seen in the Christian home a concrete embodiment of the better life promised by the Gospel—a place in which children are secure, and women and girls are respected, valued and educated. (Robert 2005, 326)

It is this kind of vision that brings home and ministry together in missions.

Single Missionaries' Roles

The lives of the women described in Frances Hiebert's quote on the next page were distinguished by both self-reliance and reliance on God. They experienced stresses and adjustments created by the conflict between their missionary vocation and the social expectations of marriage and motherhood. They were exemplary in their willingness to serve in areas of hardship, positive attitudes toward education, close ties to nationals, and sensitivity to cultural role expectations. They had unique

267

> *Young women today very badly need role models that single women missionaries of the past can provide. "Model" may not be the first word that comes to mind in considering these women. Their clothes often were out of fashion and cosmetics were usually an unaffordable, unnecessary luxury.*
>
> *No, most single women missionaries could hardly have been called fashion models. Rather, the modeling they did was of a much more significant kind. Their commitment to the Great Commission and the leadership they provided in the spread of the Gospel makes them model Christian apostles. Their feet may have been cracked and calloused in their worn-down sandals, but they were the beautiful feet of those who bring good tidings of the Gospel of Peace. We still need feet like these today.*
>
> F. F. Hiebert (1999, 2)

opportunities and restrictions due to their female, single status and often had problems with sending agencies and other missionaries (F. F. Hiebert 1999, 2).

In this section, we take a closer look at single women in missions by examining singleness in the light of Scripture and then discussing three recurring issues that these women face: living arrangements, relationships, and loneliness.

SINGLES AND SCRIPTURE

Sermons on singleness are few and far between. This may be because marriage is considered the norm toward which all singles are aspiring. God created humans as both male and female (Gen. 1:27–29), and he made them become one flesh (Gen. 2:18–25). Wholeness, completeness, unity, and companionship are good and are expressed through marriage. But does this mean that single people are incomplete? Jesus and Paul never married, and they both encouraged a voluntary choice to be single for a period of time for those who are able to accept it. Singleness can free people from constraints on their time, facilitate a simpler lifestyle, and enable an undistracted focus on serving God. There is no indication in these passages that these kinds of single people are less whole and complete than their married counterparts (Matt. 19:11–12; 1 Cor. 7).

The completeness we are talking about can be illustrated by an arithmetical model. In a ½ + ½ = 1 marriage, two incomplete persons expect marriage to make them whole and complete. In a 1+1 = 2 marriage, they never become united as one. In either case, the marriage is likely heading toward disaster. It is in a 1 x 1 = 1 marriage, in which two complete persons are brought together in Christ, that true unity in marriage can occur. Extending the model a bit further, a person who has chosen to voluntarily stay single in order to serve Christ is whole and complete in him as well, so the issue becomes our completeness in Christ, rather than our marital status.

LIVING ARRANGEMENTS

We can create a long list of single missionaries' living arrangements when they cross cultures. There are still situations in which they are placed in pairs in mission housing with no choice of who their partners will be (F. F. Hiebert 1999, 25). Among other options are living alone or with others in women's dormitories, rooming houses, high-rise apartments, duplexes, or single-family homes. They may live in mission-owned property, rented housing, or in some cases, where field policies and their financial resources allow it, they may buy their own homes.

Sidebar 13.4 describes some of my own (Lois's) housing adventures. God has helped me to keep growing in cultural sensitivity, flexibility, and relational skills in the midst of these very diverse circumstances. *Cultural sensitivity* enabled me to agree to having an older live-in housekeeper in Portugal; to come to grips with the conflicting values related to space, privacy, and noise levels in northeast Brazil; and to understand the economic inflation and currency exchanges that forced me out of my south Brazilian apartment. I also needed the *flexibility* to accept a live-in housekeeper in Portugal when I would rather have lived alone; to leave doors open, settle for cramped spaces, and tolerate high noise levels and a lack of privacy in northeast Brazil; and to move from a pleasant high-rise apartment into a house with twelve other women when inflation devalued my dollars in south Brazil. A third factor that helped was *warm relationships*. I have had a lifetime pattern of living in the midst of students who are preparing for ministry. Over the years, God has allowed me to become a "mother" and mentor to many of them.

RELATIONAL ROLES

The relationships of single women in missions contexts are complex. Their singleness affects the role perceptions and expectations of both their expatriate and their national colleagues.

Roles in the Missionary Community

"Roles" are intentionally used in the plural here. Single women will need to discover roles in relation to husbands and wives on the field, both individually and as couples. There will also be role expectations in their relationships to missionary children. Social gatherings, business meetings, and other group activities create still different sets of expectations. Sociologists John Useem and Ruth Hill Useem (1967) conducted extensive research related to expatriate communities overseas over a

269

SIDEBAR 13.4
A PLACE TO CALL HOME

Lois McKinney Douglas

Most single missionaries have housing adventures to recount. Three of Lois's stories are told below. As you read them, try to identify factors that can help single missionaries adjust to the kinds of situations she describes.

When I was a missionary in Portugal, northeast Brazil, and south Brazil, my housing situations could not have been more varied.

PORTUGAL

When I arrived in Portugal, as the only single woman with our mission, I had passed the housemate stage and wanted a home of my own. But I was told that if I lived alone, I would be perceived as a mistress of one of the male missionaries. I would need to live with a family or another single woman.

Frustrated, I decided to explain my dilemma to a top national leader. He thought for a moment and came up with a solution: find an elderly live-in housekeeper. Her presence would dispel doubts about what was going on in my home. I took his advice, and despite my initial embarrassment at the prospect of being waited on hand and foot, I employed Senhora Natividade. The

arrangement worked. The neighbors warmly accepted my single identity. They even called me "a menina da Senhora Natividade" (Natividade's little girl!).

NORTHEAST BRAZIL

When I was teaching in a seminary in the northeast Brazilian interior, I had a comfortable but very small and open apartment next to the women's dormitory. Because sounds carried, the students knew what I was doing twenty-four hours a day. I sometimes felt like screaming because of the cramped living quarters, lack of privacy, and noise level. But the perception from the seminary women was different. Over and over, they asked me how I could stand living alone in such a big house!

SOUTH BRAZIL

The one-bedroom apartment in a high-rise building in São Paulo, five blocks from the seminary where I taught, was pleasant. I often invited students over for pizza. Since most of my waking hours were spent in my seminary office, the apartment became a place for rest and relaxation.

---

period of several decades. Two of the many commonalities these communities shared was the loss of their extended families back home and a need to create substitute families in their new cultures. Understanding these dynamics can be helpful to a single missionary as she attempts to discover her roles.

Couples. A couple's relationship to a single missionary can sometimes be motivated by pity and a desire to take care of this poor young woman who is alone in a foreign country. By being aware of the problem and

But a year before I was planning to leave for home assignment, out-of-control inflation hit, and the landlord needed to triple my rent under a new contract or ask me to move out. My monthly allowance arrived in badly devalued dollars, so I couldn't afford the higher rent. I had to find another living arrangement. So, when a short-term librarian from the States returned home, I moved into the comfortable room she had occupied in a house with twelve other seminary women. It was fun, in spite of having to share a single bathroom and kitchen with all twelve of them.

TODAY

Now, as the retired widow of a Canadian Brazilian who spent over forty-five years in Brazil as a professor of physics in state universities and in service to a campus student ministry, I am living in our master bedroom, now transformed into a kitchenette apartment, in the family home that has become a campus student center.

God has been my home during my lifetime of comings and goings (Ps. 121).

taking creative initiatives, the single missionary can go a long way toward changing these perceptions. For example, she can encourage reciprocity by inviting the couple to her home regularly instead of always getting together in theirs and can demonstrate self-reliance by finding a local plumber to fix a leaky pipe rather than expecting a male missionary to do this for her (Foyle 2001, 151).

Husbands. A single missionary often works in seminaries, hospitals, or other institutions with missionary husbands. They may spend many hours each day together. If these relationships are to be healthy and happy, the boundaries need to be clearly defined. These men are brothers in an extended field family and colleagues at work. Sharing ideas and visions related to ministry, cultural and social reflections, mission agency policies, and field-related and missiological concerns and topics of a similar nature is appropriate. Intimate discussions and suggestive nonverbal behaviors must be avoided. Missionary colleagues must respect each other as they would their own brothers and sisters.

Wives. Similarly, the single missionary's relationships to wives in the mission will be the most fulfilling if she sees them as sisters, trusted friends, and coworkers. This means that she will communicate both verbally and nonverbally that she respects their marriages, values their friendship, and appreciates the contributions they are making through their homemaking, child rearing, and field ministries. She will be sensitive to feelings of jealousy and anxiety wives may have because she is working with their husbands.

Children. Single women are likely to find themselves in the satisfying role of being an "auntie" to missionary children. They can cultivate this relationship and free up parents for periods of time by playing with

271

them, taking them on outings, or inviting them to their home to read books, visit, and eat cookies. Not all single women are in situations where they can spend time with missionary children, but those who are able to often develop lasting relationships with grateful parents and happy "nieces and nephews." In the process, they are also enriching their own lives.

Missionary Gatherings. Field missionaries gather frequently for social times, business meetings, and prayer and study groups. Some of these gatherings are for missionaries only; others include national friends and coworkers. It is a good idea to keep the "missionaries only" get-togethers to a minimum. In many parts of the world, missionaries are working in partnership and often under the leadership of national churches. Meeting alone sends the wrong message.

Single women who participate in missionary gatherings find themselves in conflicting roles. At social get-togethers, the husbands and wives often form separate groups. The single women are often more interested in the men's discussions of missions strategy than they are in the women's conversations about a child's cold or a new recipe. Yet they realize that it is important to use these times to deepen relationships with the wives on the field by entering into their world. On the other hand, some of the wives are as bored with superficial conversations as the single women are, and are glad for extra support in bringing up more stimulating topics to talk about.

When the field is having a business meeting or involved in a study conference, the single missionary's role changes. She is an involved member of the ministry team. It is best for her to sit by herself near the front, with a pad and pen, exercising her role as a full participant in discussions and decision making. On one occasion, when an experienced missionary was addressing a women's gathering, she included some tongue-in-cheek and admittedly stereotypical advice on how to handle themselves in largely male meetings: Speak directly to the point; men may ramble, but you cannot. When you are upset about something, get angry; do not cry. Men can understand your anger; they do not know what to do with tears. Try to sound as if you are using linear logic. Keep emphasizing that "the first point is . . ." and "the second point is . . ." Your presentation may not hang together all that well, but men are not always that tight in their logic either. The important thing is to sound logical!

To end on a more serious and positive note, it is important to reemphasize our discussion earlier in this chapter. Even though single women and married women are still small minorities in leadership roles in evangelical missions, more opportunities have opened up for them in recent decades, especially in areas involving work with women, cross-cultural communication, literature, education, lifestyle, urban ministries, and mission specialization (Tucker 1987, 73). Their challenge is to buy up the opportunities that are there, rather than become angry or withdrawn because of obstacles that are in their way.

Roles among Nationals

In some cultures, a single woman in missions creates a social peculiarity that nationals have a hard time interpreting. They may assume that the woman is single because her parents did not try to find a husband for her or perhaps did not offer a large enough dowry (Foyle 2001, 142). When they do begin to understand her roles, she often becomes their deeply respected friend and partner in ministry. She is their teacher, but on other occasions she is a learner. They mentor and support each other as they work and serve together. Over time, as they share joys and sorrows, victories and disappointments, comprehension and misunderstanding, conflicts and reconciliation, lasting friendships develop.

The experience of many single missionaries is that they develop more bonded relationships with nationals than they do with expatriate missionaries. A missionary in southern Europe has happy memories of camping trips she took with four national friends and an especially close relationship with one of them who became her mentor and confidante. During her years in the country, her relationships kept deepening and widening. At the farewell gatherings before she returned to North America, she was overwhelmed by the outpouring of love and appreciation from her host country friends.

COPING WITH LONELINESS

Most single missionaries experience feelings of loneliness, at least occasionally, and maybe much of the time. Being surrounded by married couples on field teams and among national coworkers can exacerbate these feelings. Having other single women on the field does not always help. Marjory Foyle provides some practical suggestions for coping with loneliness:

- Single missionaries should not let themselves become overly dependent on others for either emotional support or help with everyday living. Dependency gets in the way of healthy, reciprocal relationships with national and missionary colleagues and undermines self-confidence. They will feel better about themselves and free up their colleagues to relate to them as equals when they are able to function independently.
- Singles should avoid sharing too much. When they are lonely, it is natural to unload all they are thinking, feeling, and doing when

they are with people. This is healthier than keeping things inside, but it can quickly tire and "turn off" people around them. Instead of pouring out everything on everyone, they should ask God to lead them to one or two confidantes—people with whom they will be able to share deeply and regularly over a period of time. When this happens, they will find themselves freed from a compulsion to unload everything on everyone.

- Conversely, it is important for singles not to isolate themselves. When they are feeling lonely, it is important to get out of the house and get involved in people-oriented, creative kinds of activities. These can be found among national and missionary colleagues, in the churches, and by venturing out into the community. Keeping busy and reaching out can help to break a pattern of isolation.
- Most importantly, singles need to learn the difference between loneliness and solitude. Loneliness is being unhappy at being alone with yourself. Solitude is being happy because you are alone with God, experiencing his love and presence, and allowing these to overflow into your love for others. (Foyle 2001, 151–54)

Sometimes people wonder if any good can come out of singleness, and I want to assure them that it can. . . . Our Lord was the best example [of this]. He loved people, his disciples, parties, flowers, birds, fishing, the sea, and his surrogate family in Bethany. Although his life was tough as he went toward the cross, he never seemed to lose his love and zest for human life, going from hours of prayer with God back to meet the people who needed his help. We can share some of this, so that our lives of personal sexual denial as single workers in his kingdom can be as full of dedication, love, fun, and fulfillment as his was. (Foyle 2001, 162)

MEN AND WOMEN TOGETHER

This chapter has been written for both men and women. All of us, regardless of our gender, can thank God for the ways in which he has used women and men as his servants and messengers across the centuries and continues to use them today. Men and women are together in mission, encouraging and enabling each other to exercise all the gifts that God has given them in cross-cultural ministries.

It is true that men are more likely to be in leadership roles and decision-making positions than women are. Thus they will often have opportunities to help their wives and female colleagues find fulfilling avenues of service and provide counsel along the way. Many women who have been missionaries remember with gratitude the men who took time to coach them, encourage them, and open doors for them. Lois shares recollections of two of these in sidebar 13.5. But this mentoring is not all in one

SIDEBAR 13.5
MENTORS: OPENING DOORS AND GIVING GUIDANCE

Lois McKinney Douglas

I look back with gratitude to my mentors.

While I was a new missionary teaching in a seminary in Portugal, my colleague Art Brown was unobtrusively opening more doors for me, by telling a pastor he thought I would be able to help in his church, or suggesting to the national church board that I would be a good director for the children's camp. At the same time, he was checking up on me. "What are you doing in the church?" he would ask. "I'm keeping busy working with young people and women," I would respond rather proudly. "That's fine," Art continued. "But who is your counterpart? Who are you training? Your job is not to do these things by yourself. It is to train others."

Another mentor was Ted Ward. He first met me when he came to Brazil to conduct a workshop on theological education by extension (TEE), while I was teaching in a seminary there and getting ready to leave for a home assignment. On my return to Brazil, I was looking forward to a full-time ministry in TEE and wanted to use my time in the United States for further graduate study in education. Ward, who was then a professor at Michigan State University, paved the way for me to enter a doctoral program with a research fellowship. As the director of my program, he was able to get me a grant for fieldwork related to my dissertation. Then, when my program was completed and I was returning to Brazil as a missionary, he wrote to my mission, encouraging them to do all they could to open doors for my ministry. Later, we became colleagues at Trinity Evangelical Divinity School.

I had other patient mentors during my missions career. A director of a seminary confided years later that he found that the best way to get me to do something was to put obstacles in my way. A regional director of my mission, who had become a friend after I came back to the States to teach missions, said with a smile, "You'll never know how many times I had to stick up for you through the years!"

direction. As women become more prominent in leadership roles, they too are being sought out as role models, advocates, and mentors by both male and female colleagues. Men and women are together in mission.

SUMMARY

We began this chapter by quoting Fredrik Franson. After coming full circle in our discussion, we return to his challenge: "People are drowning, and the efforts of both men and women are needed. All of God's children should use all their powers in all ways to save a lost world" (Tucker 1988, 97).

14

Missionary Families

Anxieties for parents and children are far less if we use our second cultural context to better understand our first cultural context.

Ted Ward (1989, 57)

When a married couple heads for the mission field, children are never far behind. Families engaged in international missions have made their contribution since the first century and remain the nucleus of the missionary force today. Success in missions should not be defined by the father's ministry or the parent's ministry or the well-being of the children. Rather, success should be measured by the well-being of the whole family in the midst of effective participation in the Great Commission. In this chapter we address common issues faced by parents and children involved in cross-cultural ministry.

PARENTS IN MISSIONS

We begin this chapter by asking some key questions that parents will want to discuss as part of their pre-field preparation.

Closely related to the definition of ministry is the stage of life of the family. Having one or two preschoolers in the home demands different time commitments and efforts from the parents than does having two teenagers. Recognizing the continually changing stages in the life of the family will help the husband and wife know that the roles they take today will change shortly. Possibly what is most important for parents is what Carol Herrmann (1997) discovered in her research on MKs, which is that dads and moms who are not just present but who really love each other, and express that love openly, help make it possible for their young children to develop into quality adults.

The expectations and ministry roles of husbands and wives in various stages of life find their foundations in a theology of the family. Nancy Narramore, a professor at Biola's Rosemead School of Psychology, likes to ask her students: Has the family articulated a theology of family? Does it promote family *and* missions? Family *or* missions? Family *in* missions?

For Kelly and Michele O'Donnell, a healthy family is "one which can use cross-cultural challenges to stimulate family solidarity, as well as draw upon family strengths to increase the effectiveness of its ministry and adjustment. Adequate preparation, a family system which fosters spiritual and emotional health, and an organizational structure sensitive to the development needs of the family are necessary to encourage the growth and unique contribution of each family member" (1988, 141).

Parental goals set within the parameters of biblical principles will attempt to balance family unity and developmental changes over time with cultural adjustment and family-oriented ministry in a foreign setting.

CHILDREN IN MISSIONS

MK, TCK, or MCK?

Children add a new dimension and dynamic to international ministry. Two widely recognized terms have emerged to capture this elite community who, willingly or unwillingly, have spent a significant part of their lives outside their passport culture: MK (missionary kid) and TCK (third culture kid). John and Ruth Hill Useem coined TCK in the 1960s to refer to those who found themselves together in a different culture creating their own community.

Evangelicals have since captured and expanded the term beyond the concepts initially implied in TCK and MK. For example, the *T* in TCK refers to the third of three cultures: the home culture, the host culture, and the resulting culture

> *I'm not quite at home anywhere.*
> *I'm a little at home everywhere.*
> Pearl Buck (cited in
> Plueddemann 1994, 331)

that blends elements of both home and host cultures. After living abroad, a child is soon in the position of not feeling at home in either the passport culture or the host culture. Instead, he or she becomes a combination of the two. TCK is also a broader term, moving beyond MK to include the children of those not associated with missions, such as children of diplomats, businesspeople, those serving in the Peace Corps, military personnel, and so on. Perhaps we need a new term to match twenty-first-century realities, such as MCK (multiple culture kid).

In today's globalized world and with the growing number of bicultural marriages, missionary children living abroad are often exposed to multiple cultures of peers, teachers, and nationals on a daily basis. As a result, they become a blend of many cultures. Some have expanded their definition of TCK to incorporate the new reality. In this chapter, we use the terms MK and TCK interchangeably.

The MK and Education

One of the major reasons for a family's premature departure from the mission field is the education of children. The time comes sooner or later when parents must answer the question, "How will we educate our children?" Some believe it is their godly responsibility to do so and that sharing responsibility with others to raise one's children is unbiblical, so they choose homeschooling. Others choose the same option not on a theological basis but simply because they believe that this is the best way to educate their children.

Still others do not feel they have the gifts, organization skills, or patience to teach their own children, so they select a boarding school, or an international school, or a national school, or a satellite cluster. This is especially true once their children reach the secondary level, where courses broaden and deepen, and extracurricular group activities, such as drama, service programs, and sports are desired. Because of the geographic distance between residence and the school, many parents and children experience separation for significant periods for the first time. But before we develop this section, a brief overview of the development of education for TCKs may prove helpful.

In the eighteenth and nineteenth centuries, children were often sent home for schooling. Lacking good schools and health facilities abroad, not to mention the long, arduous journey to and from the field, parents felt that education in the passport culture was in the best interest of the overall welfare of the children. The many graves of children, such as the two children (and wife) of Adoniram Judson (1788–1850), stand as stark testimonies of the harshness of the times. Diseases and death were the norm.

The pain of long years of family separation was something expected of God's choice servants during that era. After all, David Livingstone was

278

away from his family for some sixteen years. Regardless of the expectations, the pain of such separation was inevitable. Hudson Taylor was determined to change the painful family separations (for more details, see Danielson 1984). His revolutionary idea envisioned that missionary children be educated *on the field of service* rather than in the culture of citizenship. The first MK primary school began in Chefoo, China, in 1881 and produced qualified students in the seven-month school year who often skipped a grade once they returned home. High schools, however, would not appear on the field scene until after World War II. Until the early 1960s, most TCKs would remain in their passport culture for high school.

The Chefoo school became the forerunner for all future MK schools, both primary and secondary. Today, there are over 140 schools in eighty different nations. Some of these are Alliance Academy (Ecuador), Black Forest Academy (Germany), Dalat School (Malaysia), Faith Academy (Philippines), Kunming International Academy (China), Morrison Christian Academy (Taiwan), Pan American Christian Academy (Brazil), Rift Valley Academy (Kenya), and Tambo School (Bolivia).

The late 1970s and early 1980s saw another major change introduced in the education of TCKs. What some had labeled a "fad" soon turned into a mainstream, mature movement. Homeschooling, challenging the secularization and mendicancy of American education on the mainland, soon found its way into the mission community, but for different reasons. What brought about this change? A number of issues converged.

Parents, often having more formal education than their earlier counterparts, went to the field older and with more children. Boarding schools were not cheap, especially on a missionary budget. Homeschooling provided a way to reduce expenses. But there was also a theological component for some, focused on the family. A theology of the family began to reign during that era with the goal of keeping the family together. Many parents felt that they were solely responsible before God to educate their children (Deut. 6:4–9). Not to do so would be to abdicate parental authority and responsibility. Children must be safeguarded and socialized into a value system that recognizes Scripture as the final word for life and service. Those best suited to accomplish this are naturally the parents.

Critics argued that homeschooling advocates took parental responsibility too far, forgetting the shared responsibility of God's extended family. By allowing children to determine the agenda and geography for ministry, parents minimized their faithfulness to the Great Commission while creating smothered kids (SK) through overprotection. Comfort took precedence over cost, the critics said.

As in the beginning of most new movements, the first responders tended to be black-and-white in their responses and actions. Over time, participants in the homeschool movement recognized the need for partnerships with MK boarding schools and mission agencies to complement the areas they could not adequately provide, such as testing student achievement and grade level and providing student group activities and teachers who serve satellite clusters of homeschoolers.

Because of the educational level and differences in curriculum content, few parents chose to send their children to national schools even though ministry opportunities and group activities abound in these schools. It should also be noted that pre-university schooling remains available in the United States even though few missionaries choose to leave their children behind in such schools.

Pros and Cons of TCK Education Options

There is no single schooling option that is right for every parent and every child. Each TCK educational option has its pros and cons. Many family considerations, therefore, must be addressed if the right choice at the right time in the right place is to be made. Some of these considerations include the personalities of parents and children, the opinions of every family member, the stage of life, the teaching abilities of parents, the expectations of the mission agency, and the geographical location of the ministry. To help provide answers for the missionary family, we identify some of the central pros and cons of each TCK educational field option.

MK BOARDING SCHOOLS

The MK boarding school offers a number of advantages to the missionary family (see table 14.1; discussion in Pollock and Van Reken 1999 informed this discussion significantly). These schools teach the boarding student to develop self-reliance and independence. They also provide a means to develop relationships with peers, dorm parents, missionary parents, and faculty and staff from around the world that will remain for a lifetime. Academic excellence tends to prevail. With low faculty-to-student ratios, one-on-one faculty time with students is the norm.

Boarding students are usually well prepared for the rigors of academic life when they return home to primary or secondary schools or college. Boarding schools also provide numerous extracurricular activities, such as organized sports, dramas, clubs, music, and field trips. The boarding student's time is extremely structured, offering little free time. Rules and regulations provide secure boundaries for students, preparing them for the total freedom they will experience upon graduation. Selfless dorm parents can become the surrogate dad and mom, providing the boarder with encouragement, correction, love, and individualized attention. Last,

TABLE 14.1
BOARDING SCHOOLS

Pros	Cons
• Builds self-reliance	• Long separations from parents and siblings
• Cosmopolitan faculty and student body	
• Builds lifelong relationships	• Multiple new adjustments
• Offers academic excellence	• Cocoon from real world and nationals
• Relevant curriculum for passport country	• Rules and regulations can promote current or future rebellion
• Extracurricular activities provided	
• Dorm parents can become surrogate parents	• Dorm parents' theology, values may differ
• Rules and regulations can provide security	• Income-earning job opportunities virtually nonexistent
• School becomes intermission center	• Expensive
	• Little family ministry potential
	• Time highly structured

the school often serves as a center for intermission activities, providing opportunities for fellowship and cross-pollination.

On the negative side of the ledger, long separations from parents and siblings are part of the package for this option. This, along with the new context, results in a host of adjustments for boarding students, putting them on a steep learning curve. Separation from parents and siblings minimizes the possibility of family ministry or of the nationals seeing the family in action on a consistent and realistic basis. The compound-type structure of the facilities often places boarding students in a cocoon, sheltering them from the real world, not to mention the daily lives of the nationals who surround them. Opportunities to earn income through a regular job, particularly career related, are virtually impossible. A highly regimented routine and numerous regulations may cause some students to rebel immediately or bury their frustrations. Years may pass before the resulting buried anger spews to the surface. Dorm parents may have different theology, values, and decision-making patterns from those of the actual parents, adding to the boarding students' ongoing adjustments. Parents must be alert to the philosophies that drive the school and the dorm parents.

HOMESCHOOLING

Those who choose homeschooling must also recognize its positive and negative aspects. On the positive side, the TCK remains at home, where family values can be taught and walked. In that each student has particular study needs, curriculum that matches these needs can be purchased, making learning easier and more enjoyable for both student

TABLE 14.2
HOME SCHOOLS

Pros	Cons
• TCK remains with family	• Lacks socialization among peers
• Can match curriculum with student's needs	• Minimal healthy competition
	• Minimal extracurricular group activities
• Moderately inexpensive	• Reference tools minimal compared to library sources
• Family ministry possible	
• Interaction with nationals natural	• Parents may have weak teaching skills
• Creates individual discipline	• Parent-child tensions

and teacher. The cost of homeschooling tends to be much cheaper than for boarding schools. In that the TCK lives at home, natural family ministry opportunities with nationals abound. Homeschooling is great for producing disciplined students. TCKs often line out the days' activities, schedule the times to complete each assignment, and make sure they keep pace with the curriculum daily and annually.

But homeschooling also has its weaknesses. Without student peers, socialization takes a hit as does healthy competition. Extracurricular group activities also suffer in this model. While the Internet (if consistently available), books on CDs, and DVDs are quickly bridging this gap, most families will not have the library at their fingertips that a boarding school student has. Parent-student relationships are critical to the success of homeschooling. If personalities collide, education will probably suffer, and stress levels will certainly rise. The same is true if the parent's teaching skills, organizational skills, and/or patience are issues. Both parents and students may wish for more time away from each other. Students who favor certain subjects over others may spend a disproportionate amount of time in those areas, neglecting other subjects. Outside help may be necessary to test levels of academic achievement.

SATELLITE SCHOOLS

A growing number of missionary parents have selected satellite schooling, often sponsored by mission agencies or boarding schools, as a means to educate their children. This model allows the TCK to remain at home yet provides parents without sufficient teaching and/or organization skills a specialist with the requisite skills in a slightly more formal context. Parental participation remains but is complemented. Group activities with peers can improve as multiple families cluster their children. Students receive parental values and the professionalism of the teacher in a tight teacher-to-student ratio. The one-room schoolhouse immortalized in the expansion of the American West is back.

TABLE 14.3
SATELLITE SCHOOLS

Pros	Cons
• Student lives at home	• Electronic tutors predominate
• Parental participation maintained	• High attrition of teachers
• Improved structured peer activities	• Teacher must often handle multiple grade ranges
• Professional teacher	
• Professional outsider organizes curriculum	• Minimal library sources
	• Labor-intensive for sponsors

As with all other models, satellite schooling has inherent weaknesses. Teaching is often relegated to CDs, DVDs, and the computer with minimal library resources. This type of teaching takes its toll on teachers, with many leaving their posts prematurely. In that the grade levels may be multiple, the teacher must be knowledgeable in a wide range of curricula. It also requires much sacrificial work on the part of the sponsoring institutions.

NATIONAL SCHOOLS

Another model to consider is local national schools. Positively, the TCK again can remain at home under the influence of parental values. In countries that have strong national schools, this is an excellent way to go. The TCK will learn culture and language deeply and build strong relationships with peers and their families, making ministry opportunities numerous and natural. They will truly become TCKs in the broadest sense, teaching parents better pronunciation of the language, more exact terminology, and hidden nuances of the culture. National schools also tend to be less expensive than the other options.

Negatively, the student without some knowledge of culture and language before starting school will be placed in an extremely tough situation. Not all children can survive the sink or swim approach. This would be particularly so in cases where anti-Americanism prevails. They will, however, eventually learn the local culture and language, sometimes so well that some may reject the passport culture entirely. Even if they don't reject the passport culture, some TCKs may want to marry a national. Parents who chose national schools must be ready for such inevitable outcomes.

Although some national schools may have good teachers, others will be substandard. Teaching standards and styles may vary from those of the passport culture. For example, rote memory may be preferred over careful analysis; compliance to the teacher may be preferred over challenging the teacher; story may be preferred over propositions. The

283

TABLE 14.4
NATIONAL SCHOOLS

Pros	Cons
• Student lives with parents	• Teaching level may be substandard
• Learns culture and language	• Curriculum may not match that of passport country
• Builds deep relationships with nationals	
• Strong schools in some countries	• Teaching styles will differ
• Inexpensive	• Strong anti-American nationalism

curriculum may also differ from that of the passport culture, making the return home for further schooling difficult for the TCK.

INTERNATIONAL SCHOOLS

The final model we consider is the international school. On the pro side, this model often makes it possible for the student to live at home with his or her parents while attending school. It also provides exposure to a wide ethnic range of peers and personnel. Facilities and technology tend to be state of the art. Specialized courses and programs abound, providing students depth in areas of particular interest. Some international schools offer the demanding international baccalaureate (IB) degree that is recognized for university admission around the world. IB is normally earned in the last two years of secondary education.

On the con side, the price tag for such quality education does not come cheap. Parents sending children to international schools may be in for sticker shock. Standards of conduct and ethics are often based on secular moorings. Like public schools in the United States, religion is often viewed unfavorably. Parents must be alert to the philosophy that drives the international school. The curriculum, teaching styles, testing (entrance and courses), and grading may all differ from that of the passport culture, emphasizing different national values. High transition of students is normal as Dad and Mom are moved to another new location. Making and losing friends is an every-year occurrence.

So what is the global nomadic parent to do? The choices are multiple, all with long-term implications for the parents, the children, and the ministry (see Haile 2006). Stories abound of choices made that did not work out. But does that necessarily mean the model itself was bad, or that it did not work in a specific situation? Would a combination of options throughout the stages of primary and secondary education be the best for all? We would agree with David Wickstrom when he says that "no schooling option is perfect" (1994, 387). A helpful source is the Association of Christian Schools International (www.acsi.org/web). It

TABLE 14.5
INTERNATIONAL SCHOOLS

Pros	Cons
• Student lives with parents	• Expensive
• Cosmopolitan faculty and student body	• Usually driven by secular standards
• Offers academic excellence	• Curriculum may differ from that of pass-port country
• State-of-the-art technology and facilities	
• Smorgasbord of special programs	• High student transition

also has an e-journal, ACSI World report (www.acsi.org/web2003/default.aspx?ID=1609).

TCK Research

Even though thousands of TCKs lived and studied abroad in the first fifty years of the twentieth century, only five reentry studies were conducted (Austin and Jones 1987). Six more appeared in the 1950s and 1960s. In the 1970s, scholarly research on TCKs burst on the scene. The early 1990s produced the results of a major study conducted on adult TCKs (ATCKs) published through Newslinks, the newspaper of International Schools Services.

The first international MK conference, International Conference on Missionary Kids (ICMK), took place November 5–9, 1984, in Manila. The purpose of this historical gathering was to change attitudes toward boarding schools, address the role of itinerant teachers, recruit and train dorm parents, and alleviate negative aspects of growing up as an MK by providing more effective caregiving. One major outcome of this conference was the creation of reentry seminars for adults and MKs (for an excellent source, see Gordon 1993). This conference continues to meet periodically at various locations around the world. Sidebar 14.1 offers a helpful letter written from an MK to help other MKs face the realities of reentry.

Present research on today's TCKs shows little change in reentry issues from those faced by ATCKs of the 1980s. In 1984 at the first ICMK in Manila, Clyde Austin (1986) cited data from twenty-seven different studies of TCKs. In sum, Austin noted that their reentry resulted in (1) the most difficult adjustments being social adjustments (dating, self-consciousness, different moral standards, fast pace); (2) moderate difficulty in personality identity (low self-concept) and religious experience (lack of commitment to the local church, rejection of evangelistic goals of parent's ministry while retaining their social values); (3) good adjustment in financial and vocational areas; and (4) excellence in academic achievements.

285

The results of research studies and the opinions of the authors about TCKs may be helpful. But most helpful will be the voices of TCKs themselves. We present below quotes collected from this generation of TCKs gathered through an informal study as they responded to several questions we asked. We do not condone some of the language or activities even though they are reality for some of the authors. Following are the questions and selected answers that they would like you to read.

What did you experience positively and negatively while living abroad?

- I LOVED living there! I never minded the "danger" or "third world-ness" that some Americans fear. Negatives: hard to come back to the USA because I felt like an outsider, I had a hard time meeting with other MKs because they were always complaining and talking about how Californians and other Americans were so ignorant and dumb and hooked on fashion—it was hard to want to be with MKs or Americans—I just didn't feel like I fit in.
- I learned how simple life can be.
- Probably the most difficult and negative part of being an MK is always having to move. There is the frustration with having to make friends who you know you will soon leave. Then there is the heart-wrenching task of saying good-bye and moving on, or seeing your closest friends have to move on while you stay behind. I know that MKs fear change, but at the same time if things stay the same for too long they get antsy and feel like they need a change. Losing friends and continually being uprooted from your world and comfort is the most difficult part, but it is just part of the price that we have to pay.
- I'm a little cynical, having seen both sides of the coin in a lot of circumstances.
- I'm not very good at growing attached to people. Part of that is being an introvert, but moving back and forth between two islands every six months did not help. So even though I value my ability to just pick up and leave and adjust to a new place and people in a matter of days, I feel like I don't love people because I never let myself grow dependent on them. I never invest, never put down roots or long-term plans for the future.
- It has given me a broader perspective on life and made me want to join missions and live overseas for the rest of my life.
- I never felt "abandoned for the ministry," but rather privileged to be a part of it. . . . Through my nomadic life I think the Lord has

SIDEBAR 14.1
OPEN LETTER TO CLASSMATES

Dear Classmates,

"Reentry" is one of those words that makes most MKs flinch when they hear it. It is one of those cruel words that forces us to face reality. It is a term we all must come to grips with, for if we try and pretend that we don't have to go through reentry into our home culture we are only fooling ourselves, and whether we want to or not, we will be forced to integrate back into society.

To survive we can't just hole up in our houses on the Internet and have a fruitful existence serving the Lord most fully, although that may be the easiest route. We can't live in the past hanging onto our old relationships like they are all we have left. Deep down I think we as humans realize that we need to have a place to call home. And this call from the soul is what tears many of us apart, as we do not know who we are and where home is. We are not natives of our beloved country, but at the same time we differ from those in our passport country. We are of mixed race in the heart and mind, where it really matters.

We fear being the outcast at our new school. No one wants to be the strange kid from that weird country that no one

can pronounce or tell you where it is. We have all been in that situation and it hurts. Who likes having the nickname
_____. Not many people that I know. That is why we are so scared to leave our little haven of friends and fellowship. We shy away from meeting new people because we know that a good-bye is unavoidable. If we stop giving our heart away it can't be broken, but at the same time it can't grow and that is the risk we take with reentry. We hang onto what we no longer have and think that we can be happy. We cry ourselves to sleep because no one understands, and it feels like no one even tries to comprehend what our lives are like. Yes it's hard, but we must overcome. We must not become slaves to our fear of being different. Because the fact is whether or not we like it, we will always be different and that is awesome. Though it is hard, it is the torch we have been called to carry. And we can't let that torch go out, or no one will ever be able to see the great world outside of them.

We are called to be eye-openers. Young men and women who are not afraid to step forward and proclaim the need for the gospel around the world and at the same time encourage other

Continued

impressed me with what it means to be a pilgrim and stranger in this world.

* Growing up on the mission field . . . I have learned the importance of family, deep relationships, and God. I've realized that he is the sole constant around the world. I have grown to love the beauty in nature and the importance of diversity. . . . I realize the vast need for missionaries and the lack of support from today's first world church. Really being a missionary kid is who I am outside of being a child of the King.

287

Christians to know that the word of God is going out and people are coming into the kingdom in flocks and droves. Man, that's quite a responsibility. I don't believe that sulking about having to leave our home was one of the things we were to help accomplish. No, that's just the opposite. We have to be proud of our heritage. I understand that that is hard and many days we will feel like an outcast, and I guess that for the rest of our lives we will in some sense be outcasts. But I want to be an outcast for Jesus Christ if that's what he called me to be, because he knows what he's doing so much more than I.

Having just come back to the States for college I have been struggling with the whole idea of reentry. I see that there will be part of me that will never be completely understood except by other MKs, but God gave these words to me. "Open your eyes for you are not alone." At first I was just like OK, whatever that means, but as I dwelled upon his words I realized the power and the truth of them. I have to let it go, all of it. That doesn't mean forgetting about my years as an MK in _____, but it means being willing to move on. I have to stop holding on

to my selfish desires. I have to open my eyes to see what God has for me and be a part of this body of believers wherever I am. I need to find other men of God to fellowship with at my college. I must have other believers to sharpen me and push me. So I don't know about you, but I am going to stop holding on to the past. Because it will never satisfy me like it did. I am going to open my eyes and find those who I can help. I want to leap out in faith and be who God wants me to be here in the United States. I still get down and miss my friends, but it is all bringing me closer to my Father and it will do the same for you.

"Reentry" is no longer a word to fear but a word to revel in. We have a chance to take our past and affect the history of our nation. We can bring a wealth of knowledge and experience that others can only dream of. We can play a large part in the body of Christ wherever God has us. We just have to be willing to let go. I pray that you will do this. That you will open your eyes and let God reveal what he has for you.

Your Classmate,

xxxxxxxxx

- I learned to travel by myself and now I can travel the world and know that I will be OK.
- MKs are smarter (homeschooled), wiser (well-rounded worldview), more creative (making something from nothing), more practical (not concerned with the superfluous items of life and living), and more capable of having a good time with little technological assistance. MKs in general are the best world citizens you'll meet. But of course, there are some devastating exceptions.
- I try to practice self-reliance, for I see great potential for disaster in trusting others and the systems of others. I want to fix all the problems in the world, and I think I can, but I know I can't.
- I am more globally aware, for example, my homepage for my Internet browser is CNN-International.

If you could talk to the new generation of MKs headed overseas, what would you like to tell them?

- You don't have to hate it to stay true to your home country. Try to think of it as a different place, and it can become a new home. Home number two. Try to look at things as fascinating.
- Make the most of your experience. Dive in . . . learn the language, culture, befriend the indigenous peoples. Be flexible. Look at change as an adventure, rather than an inconvenience. . . . See this not just as your parents' work, but as the family's. Rejoice that the Lord has counted you worthy, not just your parents, to encounter what you will for the sake of his name! . . . Don't shy away from building relationships for fear of saying good-bye.
- Don't head overseas expecting a stereotype, for the local culture or for the missionary community.
- If I could talk to every kid who's going overseas because his parents decided to go missionary, the main thing I'd tell them would be to get some humility, because if you walk around with an arrogant attitude you won't change or learn or grow at all, and there's no way living in the US can possibly prepare a kid for the real world. I went to school with all the other missionary kids at the missionary base. . . . The place was really strong on academics and all that, but I've learned that that's all schools are good for, academics. Anyway, the public schools here are worse, so I've got no cause to complain.
- My life's been pretty heavy with negative experiences. Not fitting in with nationals for eleven years is a lot tougher than not fitting in with people here . . . not fitting in is probably the reason I'm a schizoid now. It was only during the last year I was there that I figured out how things worked . . . and that was only because I started to break away from what my parents taught me. They raised me as a typical American kid in a third world island nation, and during that last year when I started figuring things out I tried my best to forget everything that they taught me.
- Positive experiences . . . wandering through the jungle, living off the land, learning how to take care of myself . . . experimenting with the local recreational drugs, dating an Asian, a British girl, and another American girl. . . . I wouldn't trade those experiences for anything.
- Don't focus on what you might be missing in the US, but on what you are blessed with that many will never get.
- Dive in deep wherever you go . . . make the most of the time you have wherever you are. . . . You are a missionary just as much as

---

SIDEBAR 14.2
TWO DIFFERENT LIVES

Author unknown

Soon,
We will leave this place
To return
To somewhere
That I call home;
To a place
Hiding in my memories;
To something
That I knew
In times past.

But I am sure
That there has changed,
So has here

And so have I.
In my fantasy
I return
To my life there
As if time had not gone by
While I was gone.

For I live two different lives—
My life here
And my life there,
And neither one mixes,
And to each one
The other
Is only a dream.

---

your parents so make a difference for the kingdom. . . . When you leave the mission field be proud of your past and don't be afraid to share it.

How were you schooled? How well did it prep you for today's reality?

- This first year in college I have felt so far ahead of the rest of my American friends in terms of study habits, overall knowledge and preparation, and also my ability to read, write, and comprehend literature. . . . My teachers were my friends as well as my instructors. They taught me to be a lifelong learner and instilled in me the desire to learn more about our world and to never settle for mediocrity but to strive for excellence in everything I do. . . . My teachers taught me to think for myself, to challenge authority, and to go above and beyond just the grade.
- Boarding school made me independent, and so I wasn't homesick in college and could do stuff myself.
- I only wish I had spent some time at a national school, to fully round out my experience. Homeschooling fostered an independent learning style. Boarding school fostered social skills and challenged me to step outside my comfort zone in some things to try experiences I would never have had living with my parents—plays, sports, speech tournaments. High school in the US showed me the Lord's

faithfulness to provide friends wherever I went and the importance of Christians in the US.

- Growing up in a Christian home I learned to love God and put him first, but it was boarding school that made me make my faith my own. In boarding school sometimes there was no one but God to go to. I love the Lord with all my heart and desire to serve him for the rest of my life.
- I was mostly homeschooled up until ninth grade. . . . I continue to be a self-starter, a disciplined, hard-working, overcome-the-problem person.

How has your experience impacted your spirituality? View of parents? Missions? Missionaries? TCKs? Supporting churches?

- I knew many MKs. There seemed to be three different reactions to their parents being missionaries: (1) They felt on board with it and felt they were also there to minister to the "locals." This often seemed to give them a "better than thou" attitude at school and out in public with [nationals]; (2) They resented their parents for yanking them out of their home. This is more common with older kids. These MKs were bitter, and I think their parents' involvement in the church and ministry overseas turned them away from God; and last, (3) (this is where I fall in) They were glad to live there, and enjoyed the experience, but were neither involved in nor left out of their parents' ministry.
- I have incredible respect for my parents.
- I love the fact that I was, am, and will forever be an MK. If there is any better life, I can't think of it.
- I think teaching on the local church was a weak part of my childhood. We went to church, but I knew missions more than I really grasped "local church." I have learned about it now in college, so serve and love the body.
- Some churches we went to we were welcomed with open arms, asked to speak in groups, homes, from the pulpit, etc. Other times we were strangers and would have members, upon hearing we were supported by the church, exclaim, "Wow! I didn't know our church supported missionaries!"
- My parents are awesome. . . . I hope to be just like them. . . . I want my future family to stick together like my parents did, spending lots of time with the kids and teaching them well about life and how to live it.
- Missions . . . are in need of a new start.

- I've seen some overly involved churches, who thought the missionaries were overseas to accomplish the kingdom work of that church rather than the Lord's kingdom work, and I've seen some very removed churches, who thought participation in the Great Commission could be checked off their "list of how to be a good Christian" with writing a check every month.

- We have a bond that other Americans don't just "have." I can meet an MK from Africa, Europe, or Asia, countries with different languages and different cultures and still find so many very great things we have in common.

- I want to be a missionary. I don't think there is a better job on earth.

- My mom suffered a lot with having us away. She still cries every time we have to leave. I think they are very strong, but they still feel every pain.

- If you grew up as a "good kid" with a "do-able standard," you will struggle with self-righteousness.

- My parents are the most amazing people I know. . . . I have seen them go through hard situations and still be faithful and never doubt that God will provide.

- I love them [nationals] and desire for them to know the Savior. They are people too and nothing can make me so mad as racism, especially going through immigration back into the States.

- I want my kids to grow up as MKs. They are a weird bunch but a lot of fun, and I'm so glad that I grew up overseas.

- I think more people should be missionaries for life. The short-term missions movement has boomed recently, but at the same time the number of career missions has drastically fallen. . . . More people need to be willing to commit their whole lives to serving God overseas.

- I miss being on the field. I miss the automatic purpose and intentionality that comes with it. I miss seeing God in more miraculous settings (because the people of other cultures tend to believe he'll work in those ways more often). Perhaps some day I'll have the privilege of joining an overseas mission field.

- While I was raised by my parents, going to the missionary school and doing youth group, I was constantly bombarded by Christianity, Jesus, the Holy Spirit, the Ten Commandments, blah blah blah. I must have been saved like seventeen times. It's only now that I'm in a godless environment that I realize for myself the value of having values and beliefs. I was born a Christian, raised a Christian,

292

schooled a Christian and all that crap, but after so much it all just started to sound stale and boring. I knew every parable, every Old Testament story, I'd read the Bible through two times, I'd memorized Scripture every week since preschool, but it didn't mean anything. I didn't see how any of it had any value aside from keeping me out of hell. Things are different now that I'm in a mostly atheist environment. Man, this is taking a long time. I'll end by saying that I'd rather be back in _____, and sooner or later I'm going back no matter what. There's no way I'm staying in this dead country.

- I'm planning to go myself [as a missionary] in a couple years. Does that answer the question?

TCK Wrap-up

Stories and stereotypes of TCKs prevail. Some depict these global nomads correctly while others perpetuate myths, such as the following:

- Boarding schools destroy all TCKs.
- God always protects TCKs from the flaws of workaholic parents.
- TCKs do not struggle with academics.
- Pre-teen field arrivals always adjust better than post-teen field arrivals.
- The mission field, including TCK dorms, is free of expatriate pedophiles.

Fortunately, scholarly research continues to differentiate myth from reality. New research has also raised new questions. How long does it take TCKs to adjust upon reentry to the passport culture? Are we producing professional fakers? Why does it usually take TCKs longer to graduate from college? How do personal-familial sacrifice, the Great Commission, and children converge? Should children determine where parents minister geographically? Should children be reverenced or respected? What percentage of TCKs have been sexually abused while on the field? How do parents, schools, and agencies try to protect children from such predators? What is the impact of major crises such as kidnappings, tsunamis, terrorism? Many other questions are currently being studied, and many more will be in the future, providing the missionary family correctives, challenges, and hope.

SUMMARY

Judith Lingenfelter, of the School of Intercultural Studies, Biola University, quips that "the two goals (raising children and doing ministry) are not incompatible, or God wouldn't have granted children to missionaries at all." Since God has blessed some parents with children, he will surely direct those families in ways that will meet family needs as well as the needs of a lost world.

In the end, those who become good at saying good-bye, but never used to it, may be the best prepared segment of society to impact a globalized world for Christ at home and abroad. Success in missions must include the success of its future generation.

15

Crises in Missions

A mighty fortress is our God,
A bulwark never failing;
Our helper he amid the flood
Of mortal ills prevailing.
For still our ancient foe
Doth seek to work us woe—
His craft and pow'r are great,
And, armed with cruel hate,
On earth is not his equal.

Did we in our own strength confide,
Our striving would be losing,
Were not the right man on our side,
The man of God's own choosing.
Dost ask who that may be?
Christ Jesus, it is he—
Lord Sabaoth his name,
From age to age the same,
And he must win the battle.

Martin Luther (1483–1546),
translated by Frederick H. Hedge

After posting his ninety-five theses on the door of Wittenberg's Castle Church
in October 1517, Martin Luther faced many years of trials and persecution.

[However], despite . . . continual threats to his life and freedom, and times of intense spiritual battle, [he] came to know better than most the gracious power of God's sheltering hand. . . . Many who suffered for their faith during that time found solid comfort in Luther's words of faith and praise.

Brown and Norton (1995, Oct. 31)

E ven though over five centuries have passed since Luther wrote "A Mighty Fortress," it continues to provide encouragement and challenge for missionaries and other faithful Christians who are serving God in the midst of poverty, natural disasters, pandemics, and violence. In this chapter, we examine these crises, our responses to them, and the toll they take on God's faithful witnesses who are serving him in difficult situations.

A HURTING WORLD

A Precious Moments figurine sits on my (Lois's) desk. It is the sculpture of a small child dressed in a doctor's white coat holding a stethoscope against a world globe that has a long fissure and a Band-Aid on it. The expression on the little doctor's face combines deep worry and sadness. Then, if you turn the statuette over to look at the underside of its base, you see the inscription: "Jesus is the Answer."

Yes, Jesus is the answer to the hurts of our world. He uses us as his messengers of love and compassion in the midst of the poverty, disasters, diseases, and conflicts that are tearing it apart.

Poverty

Global poverty is with us everywhere and all the time. It is like a silent, chronic illness that does not go away. However, even while the wealthiest nation continues to struggle with pockets of poverty, "material and economic development has been very unevenly distributed throughout the world. The richest 20% of the world's people consume about 80% of its resources whilst the poorest struggle to survive with unclean water, inadequate food, shelter, education and health care" (WVA 2003d, 1).

When people are chronically hungry, they feel weak and lethargic, their ability to work productively is chronically reduced, and their life expectancy is lowered (WVA 2003a, 1). Sidebar 15.1 offers some grim statistics.

Global Concerns

Exploitation of the environment, diminished water supplies, malnutrition, a lack of immunizations, and special needs confronting girls

296

SIDEBAR 15.1
HUNGER FACTS

World Vision of Australia (2003a). Data from Food and Agricultural Organization of the United Nations (FAO), 2002. The State of Food Insecurity in the World, 2002 (www.fao.org) and World Food Programme, 2003. Focus on Women (www.wfp.org).

The facts below are not just cold information. Do not allow yourself to read them only with your mind. Let your heart get involved as well as you feel, pray, and even cry while reflecting on the needs of a hurting world.

- Every day, 25,000 people die from hunger and poverty.
- Nearly three-quarters of the world's poor and hungry live in rural areas in the developing world.
- Between 50 and 60 percent of the 12 million child deaths each year are related to malnutrition.
- More than 2 billion people suffer from micronutrient deficiencies including anemia, iodine deficiency, and vitamin A deficiency.
- Seven out of ten of the world's hungry are women and girls.

and women are among the pressing issues that we face when we try to respond to global poverty.

ENVIRONMENTAL PROBLEMS

Environmental problems contribute substantially to global poverty. Among these are deforestation, overexploitation of fish stocks, dumping toxic wastes into the ocean, industrial pollution, and global warming. Poverty causes people to put pressure on the environment by having many children, overexploiting soils and forests, imposing changes without valuing traditional knowledge about how to protect the environment, and failing to provide adequate waste-disposal services. Soil erosion, salination, shortages of wood for fuel, overcrowding and poor sanitation in urban areas, the impact of floods and other natural disasters, war, and political unrest are felt more by the very poor (WVA 1998, 1–2).

WATER

Water is a basic survival issue. All major ecosystems and living organisms depend on it; human beings are no exception. Health, food production, and economic development depend on it. "Clean water is not an infinite resource. There is a fixed amount which cannot be increased, yet it is constantly under threat from overuse and pollution. Despite improvements about one-sixth of the world's population doesn't have access to safe water and half do not have access to adequate sanitation. Australians use a million litres of water per person per year while those in water scarce places such as the Middle East have access to less than one thousand litres per person per year" (WVA 2000, 1).

CHILDREN

The world's children suffer the most in situations of poverty. Millions die each year. Most of these deaths are from hunger because their families are too poor to feed them. The result is malnutrition and related illnesses that take their lives in early childhood (WVA 1999, 1). Malnutrition is not the only reason children die prematurely. Often their lives are shortened by contagious diseases such as measles, whooping cough, tetanus, polio, tuberculosis, hepatitis B, and diphtheria. "With immunisation, children can be protected from all of these killer diseases. Children in the developing world are ten times more likely to die from vaccine-preventable diseases than those in developed countries" (WVA 2003b, 1).

We have heard these kinds of reports and statistics so often that we develop an immunization of our own—we no longer hear them or respond to them. It often takes heart-wrenching personal experiences in our lives for the reality to set in. My own (Lois's) life-transforming experience as a missionary in poverty-ridden northeast Brazil is related in sidebar 15.2.

GIRLS AND WOMEN

Girls and women are especially hard hit by poverty. Girls are often denied education. They are needed at home, and it costs too much to send them to school. Parents are afraid that education will make them less marriageable, too opinionated, and expose them to the dangers of traveling and being taught by male teachers (WVA 2003c, 1).

Sometimes there are also gender-based health issues. If food is scarce and preventive health care involves time, travel, and money, parents may feed girls less and make less effort to seek medical care for them than they do for their male children (WVA 2003c, 2).

The feminization of poverty also extends to economic issues:

> The majority of the 1.5 billion people living on 1 dollar a day or less are women. In addition, the gap between women and men caught in the cycle of poverty has continued to widen in the past decade. . . . Worldwide, women earn on average slightly more than 50 per cent of what men earn.
>
> Women living in poverty are often denied access to critical resources such as credit, land and inheritance. Their labour goes unrewarded and unrecognized. Their health care and nutritional needs are not given priority, they lack sufficient access to education and support services, and their participation in decision making at home and in the community are minimal. Caught in the cycle of poverty, women lack access to resources and services to change their situation. (UN 2000, 1)

298

SIDEBAR 15.2
WHAT DO YOU DO WHEN A LITTLE GIRL DIES?

Lois McKinney Douglas

As you read this example, consider the relationship between evangelism and social responsibility.

One morning very early, in my apartment in a poverty-ridden area of northeast Brazil, I woke up to ear-piercing cries coming from the little house across the street. I had heard this kind of sobbing before and knew what had happened. I dressed quickly and ran over to where a crowd was already gathering. A little five-year-old girl named Eulália had just died.

A doctor told me during the wake later that morning that there was no reason Eulália should have died. A combination of malnutrition and parasites had killed her.

During the funeral later that same day, we sang a children's chorus about what a wonderful place heaven will be, and how good it will be to see the Savior there.

I felt my heart being torn apart and found myself asking questions I had never asked before. I was glad that Eulália had loved Jesus and was now in heaven and that her whole family had been evangelized through our mission's work. But was evangelism enough? Should we not also be helping northeastern Brazilian churches do something about the heartbreaking poverty that makes funerals of little children like Eulália an everyday occurrence? Should we not be encouraging Brazilian Christians to work toward societal change in the midst of the gross inequalities in the distribution of wealth that cause little girls like Eulália to die?

REFLECTION AND DISCUSSION

What can we do or should we do to help little girls like Eulália not only to sing songs about heaven but also to live a full and happy life here on earth?

Listening and Responding

Happily, many Christians around the globe are listening to the world and its needs. Hundreds of churches, missions, microenterprises, health initiatives, community development programs, and other creative initiatives have resulted from their concern. Among the most visible of these are international organizations dedicated to relief and development such as World Concern, TearFund, World Relief, and World Vision International.

World Concern (www.worldconcern.org) has been providing disaster response and community development programs for more than fifty years to the world's poorest people in Africa, Asia, and the Americas. It works closely with local communities to eliminate core causes of poverty, with an emphasis on livelihood training, literacy, and education; access to clean water, food, and health care; disaster assistance; and special initiatives. Its goal is to reach seven million people by 2010.

299

TearFund (www.tearfund.org) is largely supported by individuals and churches in the United Kingdom. It works with local partners in more than seventy countries in community development projects. Its workers are also involved in disaster prevention and relief. They speak out, tackling the underlying causes of poverty by attempting to persuade governments and institutions to act on the behalf of poor people, by giving them a chance to own their own land or to start a business.

World Relief (www.wr.org) enables North American evangelical churches and their indigenous partners in local churches around the world to serve those who are hurting and to confront disaster, deprivation, and disease in response to the poverty and suffering around them. Together these churches are saving lives and restoring hope through microenterprise development, child survival initiatives, HIV/AIDS education, child development, disaster response, agriculture, refugee care, immigrant assistance, trafficking victim protection, and other efforts.

World Vision International (www.wvi.org) works to promote the material, emotional, social, and spiritual well-being of all people. It has had a special concern for children. In 2006, it became involved in the Global Call for Action against Poverty (GCAP) and has been identified with campaigns for increased contributions of richer countries to poor ones, accelerated and deepening debt relief efforts for the poor countries, loans to these countries judged solely by their poverty reduction and economic growth, and greater fairness in the international trading system.

Regardless of where we serve or what our primary mission may be, we will find ourselves surrounded by global concerns. We will not be able to—nor will we want to—drown out these cries from a hurting world. Jesus's compassion for the multitude caused him to heal their sick and give them food. We will want our ministries to flow out of his love and compassion (Matt. 14:14) as we minister holistically to people in need.

Natural Disasters

While this chapter was being written, reports of natural disasters continued to be the top stories on radio, TV, the Internet, and in newspaper headlines. Jesus predicted that there would be great earthquakes, famines, and pestilences in various places before he returned (Luke 21:11). The church is living in the midst of these natural disasters, which are crying out for its concerted response:

- The December 2004 Indian Ocean tsunami was the deadliest in recorded history. It killed hundreds of thousands of people over an area ranging from the immediate vicinity of the quake in Indonesia,

Thailand, and the northwestern coast of Malaysia to thousands of kilometers away in Bangladesh, India, Sri Lanka, the Maldives, and even as far as Somalia, Kenya, and Tanzania in eastern Africa.

- Flooding in Mumbai, India, in July 2005 left over seven hundred dead. In November of the same year, many villages turned into islands due to heavy rains caused by low pressure areas formed in the Bay of Bengal.
- In August 2005, Hurricane Katrina caused catastrophic wind and flood damage along the Gulf Coast, breaching the New Orleans levees and resulting in the loss of almost two thousand lives. Long-term economic and environmental effects, along with looting and violence, were left in its aftermath.
- In October of this same year, a massive earthquake rocked Kashmir and the region around it, causing devastation to the land, the loss of tens of thousands of lives, and displacement of great numbers of people.

Evangelical relief organizations, such as those mentioned above, have become increasingly well equipped to make rapid emergency responses when disasters strike. World Relief has offices in ninety-six countries and is building up the local relief capacity. It is able to have relief staff at disaster sites within hours, and Global Rapid Response Teams of relief experts on site twenty-four to seventy-two hours after the onset of a disaster. During the Indian Ocean tsunami, it was able to launch simultaneous relief efforts in four countries. It is also pre-positioning relief supplies and services on three continents and working on efforts to mitigate and prevent the tragic effects of disasters from happening (World Vision International 2005, 1).

At the other end of the spectrum are local churches that are finding opportunities to serve when disasters strike. Carey Wallace offers a vivid description of the response of local churches to the 1999 earthquake in northwestern Turkey. We start with his account of the earthquake itself: "In the dead of night, it must have seemed like an act of God. From miles below the earth, ancient rocks groaned with inhuman voices. On the frail surface, steel twisted and shrieked, glass shattered, concrete crumbled like sand. For a moment, silence. And then the human voices: whispers, whimpers, shouts and cries—the people of heavily populated, industrial northwestern Turkey, waking at 3 a.m. on Tuesday, August 17, 1999, to the end of their world" (Wallace 2000, 35).

During the first days after the disaster, relief workers flooded in from around the world with cranes, trucks, medications, water, tanks, food, and other emergency supplies. World Vision, World Concern, and the

TearFund partnered with World Relief, channeling funds to them as they began to collaborate with local churches in disaster relief. One of these was in the province of Izmit. The entire local church (consisting of a family of four!), in spite of experiencing severe restrictions on their ministry, approached the governor to volunteer their help. The governor gave them a plot of land and a couple of vehicles and asked them to provide tents, sanitation, food, security, and medical treatment for five thousand people. This was a key moment, the first sense of the legitimization of the Turkish church in the twentieth century.

The pastor of the Istanbul Presbyterian Church also saw opportunities for grace in the midst of this tragedy. With over a hundred members, it was one of the largest national churches in the country. This small body of believers carried out an astonishing relief effort. They gave unceasingly in aiding funeral preparations, food and water distribution, and providing an open-air hospital and warm clothing. They built relational bridges as they worked within the parameters of Turkish organizations and laws. The pastor had a dinner for all the people who had worked with the church during the relief effort where he was able to explain the faith of his church to the people, and a great many were able to hear the gospel.

At the same time, a long-term sister-church relationship was being established between the Istanbul church and a Presbyterian church in Ann Arbor, Michigan, which sent three of their members to Turkey to work alongside the local believers. Their commitment was qualitatively different: they were bringing with them to the other nation not just their deeds but also their hearts. It is this heart exchange among the world's peoples that can make a difference for eternity (Wallace 2000, 35–37).

Pandemics

Pandemics are as old as history. Pharaoh and the people of Egypt suffered multiple plagues when Pharaoh refused the Lord's command to let the Hebrews go into the desert to worship him (Exod. 7:14–11:9). Later Moses warned the Israelites that the Lord would send upon them the same kinds of diseases and disasters that they had dreaded in Egypt if they did not follow the law and revere his name (Deut. 28:58–63).

There have been many other tragic plagues across the centuries. A disease that was later confirmed to be typhoid fever killed a quarter of the Athenian troops and a quarter of the civilian population during the Peloponnesian War (430 BC). It was possibly smallpox brought back from the Near East that caused two plague outbreaks in Rome (AD 165–80 and AD 251–66). During the height of the second outbreak, five thousand people a day were said to be dying. Bubonic plague broke out during the rule of Justinian (starting in AD 541) and later returned to Europe at the beginning of the 1300s as the tragic Black Death that killed twenty million people in six years, a quarter of the total population. There have been repeated pandemics of cholera, influenza, and typhus as well. Today, there are serious concerns about the Ebola virus, SARS, Avian flu, and, sadly, HIV/AIDS, which has become a full-blown twenty-first-century pandemic.

The spread of HIV/AIDS is rampant. It is estimated that 50 million people will be infected by the year 2010. Much is at stake in the way we respond to the challenges this creates for Christian missions. "A crisis on this scale is a crisis for the whole of humanity. Every one of us is implicated in it, whether we like it or not. Everyone has played a part in creating the conditions in which the epidemic spreads. Everyone suffers as the human community loses so many of its young, creative, and productive members. Everyone is at risk of being infected, although risks vary greatly. Everyone faces the questions raised by onset of the pandemic about what it means to be human" (Ross 2004, 338).

Kenneth R. Ross discusses four dimensions of a Christian response to the questions that the HIV/AIDS pandemic raises: justice and compassion, new frontiers for faith, sexual power and politics, and the need to practice presence (2004, 337–48).

Responding with justice and compassion means involvement in social action. The global economy needs to be challenged. National governments and international monetary organizations must relieve poor countries of the burden of unpayable debts and dedicate a portion of their budget to international development. The availability of antiretroviral drugs also must be addressed. "Even with recent price cuts, [these] drugs remain unaffordable for the vast majority of the people in 'the south'" (Ross 2004, 340).

The church must be challenged to move toward new frontiers of faith: "In the church we proclaim ourselves together as members of the body of Christ. 'If one member suffers, all suffer together with it' (1 Cor. 12:26). In the context of the HIV/AIDS epidemic, it means that no member of the church can be unaffected while so many brothers and sisters are infected with the virus. If one has AIDS, we all have AIDS. The virus has infected our body. It is a crisis that involves the whole membership of the church" (Ross 2004, 340).

Living out our identification with those who are suffering means repenting of our silence, stigmatization, and abandonment of them by talking openly about AIDS in our Christian worship and teaching, actively reaching out to hurting people, and allowing them to experience the length and width and height and depth of Christ's love (Eph. 3:18).

303

If we are to find convincing answers to the profound questions the HIV/AIDS pandemic raises for church and mission, issues of gender and sexual behavior must be addressed. "Gender-based power leads to sexual behavior that makes women and girls particularly vulnerable to HIV/AIDS. In many societies women face a style of male power that restricts their capacity to protect their sexual health. They are not expected or permitted to exercise choice with regard to when, how, and with whom to have sex" (Ross 2004, 342).

Women can become infected by a husband they trusted or become victims of sexual violence and rape. Male attitudes related to masculinity that sometimes include valuing multiple sexual partners and unprotected sex become part of the equation. "If individual attitudes need to undergo radical change, then so do social and economic structures. Migrant working, limited economic opportunities and cultural sexual practices all contribute to establishing patterns of behavior that lead to the spread of HIV and AIDS" (Ross 2004, 344).

At the most basic level of our discussion, Christian missions is at stake. There is a need to *practice the presence of Christ*.

> In today's context, this means taking HIV and AIDS into the vocabulary of the church. Then its worship and witness will signal that those infected or affected by the epidemic are affirmed, accepted, and embraced rather than being judged or excluded. . . .
>
> There is a need to think critically and act decisively with regard to the social location of the church. The incidence [of HIV/AIDS] is highly concentrated in the poorer sections of the world community. What is more, it is the weakest and the most vulnerable within poor communities who are the most likely to be infected. . . . The solidarity with the poor in which the church finds its identity needs to find fresh expression in face of the reality of the epidemic. . . .
>
> In offering presence in the context of HIV/AIDS, the church has the capacity to be there when death approaches . . . in the desolating silence of approaching death . . . [the] assurance that in death, as in life, we belong to Jesus Christ liberates us to live every minute to the full, with a sense that the victory of Easter Day will be ours even if there are times that the darkness of Easter Saturday seems to fall upon us. (Ross 2004, 345–46)

As we end this section, take time to read sidebar 15.3, which tells the story of an African girl who discovered the victory of Easter Day in the midst of her own deep suffering.

Violence

Violence is a sweeping term that covers aggressive and abusive acts ranging from domestic violence and street violence to global wars and

> ## SIDEBAR 15.3
> ## GOD LOVES US AND LEADS US
>
> *Ross (2002, 41)*
>
> Recall some of your experiences of God's love and guidance in the midst of difficult and painful times. Then put yourself in the place of the thirteen-year-old girl whose story is told below. How could she still say, "God loves us and leads us," while she was facing such heartbreaking circumstances?
>
> The courage and faith we encounter as we enter into solidarity with individuals and communities facing HIV/AIDS can open up new depths to Christian faith. Scottish visitors to Africa encountered a thirteen-year-old girl whose mother and father had died. She was solely responsible for two younger brothers and had given up school to care for them. After the death of their parents, relatives had come and removed everything from the house, even the animals.
>
> When visited by a church member, who was moved to tears, the girl said: "Please don't cry for us, because you make us feel hopeless. Even without anything, the Lord is sustaining us. I have seen the hand of the Lord leading us."
>
> When asked how she manages, she responded: "God loves us and leads us."

terrorism. Without minimizing the tragedy of violence at any level or our commitment to missions at every level of need, this section of the chapter focuses on the implications of Islamic terrorism for concerned governments, Muslim-Christian relations, and Christian missions. We rely on J. Dudley Woodberry's (2002) article in *Evangelical Missions Quarterly* to guide our discussion. He begins with his reflections after he and his wife had been evacuated from Pakistan:

My wife, Roberta, and I had just been evacuated from Peshawar, Pakistan—the birthplace of the Taliban and Osama bin Laden's main conduit to the world. As we waited in Thailand with other Christian aid workers among Afghans, to see if we could return, we walked along the beach. Dark storm clouds were clustering around a crescent moon (the symbol of Islam) as boats moved out for the night of fishing. The scene started my reflection on the gathering storm in Afghanistan and the Muslim World: How do terrorism and the Taliban relate to Islam? What grievances drive the terrorists and their admirers?

During a service on world Communion Sunday, a day after we arrived in the United States, we learned that bombs were falling on Afghanistan. As the round loaf of bread was broken, symbolizing Christ's broken body, I also thought of our broken world. As the cup was poured, commemorating his shed blood, I also thought of the blood being shed right then in Afghanistan, a land that had been our home. Each bomb landed on or near a place where we had been. Some craters were in the actual dirt where we had walked.

When we turned on our car radio, we heard a recording of Bin Laden calling on all Muslims to join a Holy War against the infidel West, especially Americans. Yet Muslims had been our hosts during our years of living in Afghanistan, Pakistan, Lebanon, and Saudi Arabia, and our ministry had made us guests for shorter periods in most Muslim lands. Again questions arose: What are the implications for concerned governments, Muslim-Christian relations, and for missions? (Woodberry 2002, 66–67)

What follows here is a summary of Woodberry's responses to the questions he raises.

How does terrorism relate to Islam? Muslims are not all fundamentalists and terrorists. Some are peaceful, others are militant. Both of these positions are justified by recitations in the Qur'an by Muhammad from Allah to meet needs as they arose. During the Middle Ages, Muslim governments were more tolerant of Jews and Christians than the crusading Christian governments were of Jews and Muslims. Today, militants tend to lump all Americans together as Christians and see them as unjust oppressors and infidels. Dying as martyrs in a struggle to overcome God's enemies assures them of having their sins forgiven, avoiding purgatory, abiding in paradise, and receiving a crown of honor. Today, without the diplomatic or military power to engage in "traditional" warfare, they resort to suicide bombings and other acts of terrorism (Woodberry 2002, 67–69).

What grievances drive the terrorists and their admirers? High on the list of grievances are the Jewish occupation of what the Palestinians consider to be their land and the incursions of Israel into Lebanon. They are also concerned about the modernist Muslim states that compromise Islamic laws by adopting Western law codes. More fundamentally, the Muslim world feels the humiliation of no longer being empires and superpowers. There has been a power shift to the "Christian" West that "has corroded morality with the flow of alcoholism, drugs, materialism, sexual promiscuity and arrogance" (Woodberry 2002, 69–71).

What are the implications for concerned governments? Woodberry suggests that concerned governments work toward conflict solutions that maximize justice, focus on relief and development, and keep as low a profile as possible in nation building. They should remember that resorting to military action creates new martyrs and kills civilians (2002, 71–72).

What are the implications for Muslim-Christian relations? We must work on underlying issues by helping to heal the festering wounds in the Muslim community and communicate our support for them in many moral issues. We need to avoid stereotyping Muslims, develop attitudes of mutual empathy and forgiveness, and learn to communicate and work together (Woodberry 2002, 72–73).

What are the implications for missions? Christian missions in Muslim contexts will involve learning from experiences in the "fiery furnace" (compare with Dan. 3:17–30) and seeing how God in Christ reaches militant fundamentalists (compare with Saul's experience on the Damascus road; Acts 9:1–19). We need to be aware of the "domino" effect: when "there are local friendly Christians, there is receptivity to the gospel, which in turn can lead to the persecution of Christians" (Woodberry 2002, 74). There is "the obvious need to redouble our efforts to distinguish between Christian faith and Western culture through the contextualization of word and deed and raising up of more non-Western missionaries" (ibid.). We must continue to give attention to developing appropriate forms of witness in the midst of the cycles of suppression and freedom that we encounter in the Muslim world and help moderate Muslims reason with extremists. Above all, we must remember that God has given us a ministry of reconciliation. Woodberry recalls visiting "the worship of new believers in a country in western Africa where two ethnic groups that had been killing each other on the streets were eating and worshipping together because they were one in Christ" (75).

Woodberry concludes his article with a challenge: "I described [above] how Roberta and I . . . walked the beach in Thailand and began reflecting on the questions above as we saw storm clouds gathering around the crescent moon. By the time we returned, darkness had settled in. But lights now appeared on each fishing boat to light the places where they worked until dawn came—and we knew a little better what we needed to do" (2002, 75).

A DANGEROUS WORLD

In September 1955, three missionaries to Ecuador, Jim Elliot, Nate Saint, and Ed McCully, were searching for unreached tribes when they discovered the Waorani (called by them the Aucas, which is a pejorative term best not used today). "For three months they dropped gifts weekly from the air to the Aucas. In January 1956, with two more companions, Robert Youderian and Peter Fleming, the five established a beachhead on the Curaray River near the Auca territory. One friendly contact with three Aucas took place at their river encampment. Then on January 8, 1956, they were attacked and speared to death" (Howard 2000, 309).

More than fifty years later, the stories of these missionary martyrs and others like them continue to motivate believers from around the world to commit themselves to taking the gospel to hard-to-reach peoples.

They often live among small and hurting groups of believers in the midst of danger, persecution, and the ever-present possibility of martyrdom. "Current estimates are that roughly 150,000 Christians are martyred each year. . . . Some project that the numbers will increase to 600,000 by AD 2025, given current trends in human rights abuses and growth of militant religious systems" (Tallman 2000, 602).

Reports in newspapers, journals, and on the Internet underscore the vulnerability of foreign missionaries serving in contexts of violence. A quick search uncovers some of their stories: "Missionaries Face Violence in Haiti," "New Tribes Missionaries Kidnapped in the Philippines," "American Missionary Murdered in Uganda," "Four U.S. Missionaries Killed in Iraq," "Three Killed, One Injured in Attack on Baptist Hospital in Yemen," "Missionaries May Be Target of FARC Guerrillas." And the list goes on and on.

In the following paragraphs, we discuss important issues raised by persecution and martyrdom, especially as these relate to missionaries and missions. First, we try to define martyrdom and through this process discover that the concept is deeper and broader than we had imagined. Next we provide a brief overview of persecution and martyrdom in the Scriptures, the Roman Empire, the Persian Empire, and the Islamic world. This biblical and historical perspective will help us to reflect on a nagging "Why?" question: Why are Christians persecuted and martyred? Finally, we suggest ways in which missionaries and missions agencies can respond to persecution.

What Is Martyrdom?

Martyrdom is derived from the Greek word *martyrus*. The verb form, *martyreo*, integrates concepts of truth and Scripture into its meaning. It is closely associated with "witness." Jesus was a witness to the truth (Matt. 26:65; Mark 14:63; Luke 22:71); the apostles were sent as his witnesses to the ends of the earth (Acts 1:8). The meaning of "martyr" is extended still further to include Christlike values such as faithfulness, truth, witness, and simple lifestyle (Tallman 2000, 602).

Thus the concept of martyrdom goes well beyond being killed for a cause or belief. It includes all that God has done through the life, death, and resurrection of Jesus Christ, in the church, and in our individual lives. It includes bearing up under persecution in the name of Jesus Christ and being willing to lose our lives for his sake (Nazir-Ali 1999, 56). The Orthodox Church recognizes this broader definition by distinguishing three kinds of martyrdom: "white" martyrdom involves giving up wealth and adopting a contemplative lifestyle; "green" martyrdom demands living simply in order to experience God more deeply and share him with

308

others; and "red" martyrdom involves shedding your blood and giving your life for Jesus (57–58).

Persecution and Martyrdom Are Not New

The Beatitudes in Matthew 5 include a special blessing for those who were being persecuted. Jesus told them to rejoice and be glad (Matt. 5:10–12). He spoke these words knowing that some of his closest disciples would become martyrs. Herod commanded that James be put to death with a sword (Acts 12:2). Peter was arrested, put in prison, and awaiting the same fate, when, through the prayers of the church and the miraculous intervention of an angel, he was released. It was Herod who was struck down (Acts 12:1–23). Jewish persecution resulted in Paul's being arrested and transported to Rome. While he was there, Jews in Rome, his escorts, and the whole palace guard heard the gospel (Acts 28:17–30; Phil. 1:12–14; Moreau 2000a, 746–47). Later, Paul was also put to death.

During the earliest decades of Christianity, the Roman rulers looked upon the new movement as a subsect of Judaism. Then, in AD 64, a devastating fire destroyed large parts of Rome. Although some suspected that the Emperor Nero himself had set the blaze, he blamed it on Christians. Smoldering suspicion and hostility toward Christians were fanned to a flame by the accusations and sparked almost 250 years of persecution. With varying degrees of intensity, Christianity was considered illegal and Christians a threat to the state. Throughout the period, waves of hostility were followed by temporary reprieves. Then, in AD 313, Constantine issued the Edict of Milan, which bestowed imperial favor on Christianity and affirmed its legal status. This prepared the way for the recognition of Christianity as the religion of the empire by the latter part of the same century (Moreau 2000a, 747). In the midst of this victory of the church, Lesslie Newbigin reminds us that "the Roman imperial system was not won by seizing the levers of power: it was won when the victims [who were about to be fed to the lions] knelt down in the Coliseum and prayed in the name of Jesus for the Emperor. The soldiers in Christ's victorious army were not armed with the weapons of this age; they were the martyrs whose robes were washed in blood" (1989, 210).

The impact of Constantine's affirmation of Christianity overflowed into the Persian Empire. When the Persian king Shapur II sent a delegation to visit him, they brought news of the Christian population in their land. Constantine sent a letter back to the king: "I profess the Most Holy Religion [Christianity]. . . . Imagine, then, with what joy I heard news, so much in line with my desire, that the fairest provinces of Persia are to a great extent adorned by the presence of . . . Christians. . . . I commend these people to your protection" (cited in Nazir-Ali 1999, 57).

But during the year before Constantine died, war broke out between the Persians and the Romans. Sixty to seventy years of violent persecution of Christians followed. At least 190,000 were killed. Thousands more were left homeless, deprived of their property or exiled (Nazir-Ali 1999, 57–58).

Persecution and martyrdom are taking place in the Islamic world as well. It is difficult to turn on a TV, access a news site on the Internet, or pick up a newspaper without being overwhelmed by the reports of violence and persecution targeting Christians, Jews, and even more moderate Islamic sects. These current events are a continuation of a centuries-old history of violence. During Muhammad's lifetime, Muslims, Christians, and Jews lived together in the Arabian Peninsula. The Prophet had cordial relationships with Christians and even made treaties with them. But after his death, word spread that he had said there should be no other religion except Islam. Under Caliph Umar, both Jews and Christians were expelled. Later, in conquered countries where Islamic law was imposed, even though Jews and Christians were considered *dhimmi*—protected people for whom Muslims had responsibility—they were denied basic rights as citizens and had severe restrictions placed on their witness. Persecution broke out from time to time during the ensuing years and then largely disappeared during the Ottoman Empire (1299–1922) and for several decades after its dissolution. Recent events in the Islamic world have returned Christians to their unequal status and allowed them to become targets of persecution once again. Conflicts and violence have caused many thousands of Christians to lose their lives and countless others to be forced from their homes and livelihood (Nazir-Ali 1999, 58).

Why Are Christians Persecuted and Martyred?

There is no single answer to this "Why?" question. Sometimes there is ideological opposition to the Christian message. Missionaries and church members suffer prejudice, discrimination, imprisonment, torture, and even death because they are naming the name of Christ and propagating their faith in contexts where this is considered blasphemy or heresy. This kind of persecution is more likely to occur when there is a Christian witness over a long period of time, conversions are occurring, and groups of believers are beginning to form. Paul's ministry is a good example of this process. Persecution mushroomed and spread as news of conversions resulting from his witness and encouragement of new believers followed him from place to place.

Political issues are often intertwined with persecution. Missionaries and other outsiders may be seen as intruders and troublemakers when they enter an unreached region with their message. Their public witness may be considered a political crime. Those who accept their message may be seen as disloyal to their country and rejecting their own culture. These political and ideological issues can become so intermingled that it is hard to separate them. It is even more difficult to answer the "Why?" questions they raise. An incident from Iraq illustrates this point.

On March 15, 2004, five Southern Baptist aid workers were shot, and four of these killed, in the northern city of Mosul in Iraq. Why? A coworker of Karen Watson, who was one of the four who died, believes that it was because "Karen loved people. . . . She was there because she wanted to make a difference. . . . She just wanted to give her life sharing God's love with the Iraqi people. So that's what she did" (Bridges 2004, 2).

At its core, our answer to the "Why?" question is intricately linked to God's desire to win glory for himself in all things (Ramstad 2004, 469–70): "The persecution of his people is one means by which he does this. . . . As Paul wrote, '. . . I have lost all things. I consider them rubbish, that I may gain Christ. . . .' This single-minded devotion to gain Christ is what God will use to overcome the world. In Mark 13:9 Jesus says, 'But be on your guard; for they will deliver you to courts, and you will be flogged in the synagogues, and you will stand before governors and kings, *for my sake as a testimony to them*' [emphasis added]. So persecution is for Jesus's sake to win him glory, and as a testimony of the gospel to the persecutors (1 Pet. 4:12–16)."

What Can Missionaries Do When They Are in the Midst of Persecution?

Ramstad (2004, 471–72) offers helpful counsel to missionaries and other believers when they are suffering persecution. The following discussion draws upon his suggestions.

Resilience is important. When danger, suffering, persecution, and even death are all around us, we may find ourselves feeling anxious and tense, and as if we are falling apart physically, emotionally, and spiritually. When this happens, it is important for us to rebound as quickly as we can. God has given us the resources we need. As we put on his armor—the belt of truth, the breastplate of righteousness, the shield of faith, the helmet of salvation, the sword of the Spirit (the Word of God), and the gospel of peace as our sandals—we will be able to hold our ground and remain standing in the midst of the spiritual battle (Eph. 6:10–18).

If we have experienced severe psychological trauma, we may need professional therapy to help heal our wounds (posttraumatic stress disorder is discussed in the next section). Regardless of how hurt or afraid

311

we are, or what it may take to get us going again, we must allow God to heal us and strengthen us.

Christians serving in the midst of persecution need to learn to trust in God and not themselves. When Peter, James, John, and Andrew asked Jesus what the signs of the end of the age would be, his answer was: "You must be on your guard. You will be handed over to the local councils and flogged in the synagogues. On account of me you will stand before governors and kings as witnesses to them" (Mark 13:9). The disciples must have been anxious and afraid at such an overwhelming prospect, because Jesus quickly reassured them that they were not alone: "Whenever you are arrested and brought to trial, do not worry beforehand about what to say. Just say whatever is given you at the time, for it is not you speaking, but the Holy Spirit" (Mark 13:11).

Another challenge to believers in the midst of persecution is to persevere, to not give up. Hebrews 11 ends with a vivid description of faithful witnesses who have gone before us: "Some faced jeers and flogging, while still others were chained and put in prison. They were stoned; they were sawn in two; they were put to death by the sword. They went about in sheepskins and goatskins, destitute, persecuted and ill-treated—the world was not worthy of them. They wandered in deserts and mountains, and in caves and holes in the ground" (vv. 36–38).

Hebrews 12 begins by challenging believers who are surrounded by such a great "cloud of witnesses" to get rid of the weights and everything that gets in the way or entangles us. Then we must persevere—not growing weary, not losing heart, and not giving up, regardless of how difficult things become—as we run the race before us. Jesus is our example. He willingly suffered persecution and death because of the joy that was waiting for him at the right hand of God (Heb. 12:1–3). Joy is waiting for us as well. When our suffering and persecution are over, we will be able to enjoy an eternity in the presence of our risen Lord, praising him along with the multitude who came out of great tribulation and have washed their robes and made them white in his blood.

Times of persecution allow us to gain new depths of experience in God's Word. Martin Luther was a timeless example of this. We began this chapter with the first two stanzas of "A Mighty Fortress Is Our God." In excerpts from later stanzas of this same hymn, we catch a glimpse of Luther's celebration of the truth of the Scriptures in the midst of Satanic attacks and even facing possible martyrdom:

> And though this world, with devils filled,
> Should threaten to undo us;
> We will not fear, for God hath willed
> His truth to triumph through us.

Let goods and kindred go,
This mortal life also;
The body they may kill:
God's truth abideth still,
His kingdom is forever.

Martin Luther (1483–1546),
translated by Frederick H. Hedge

The story of Stephen's martyrdom (Acts 6:8–7:60) adds three more elements of faithful witness in the face of persecution. First, he was courageous and uncompromising in communicating his message. When he was dragged before the Sanhedrin by an angry crowd that was accusing him of blasphemy, the high priest asked him if the charges were true. Stephen responded with a strong defense of his message through the Old Testament Scriptures and then accused his accusers: "You stiff-necked people, with uncircumcised hearts and ears! You are just like your fathers. You always resist the Holy Spirit. . . . And now you have betrayed and murdered [the Righteous One]" (7:51–52).

In the midst of persecution, Stephen also experienced the presence of the resurrected Christ. While the crowds were furious and gnashing their teeth at him, "Stephen, full of the Holy Spirit, looked up to heaven and saw the glory of God, and Jesus standing at the right hand of God. 'Look,' he said, 'I see heaven open and the Son of Man standing at the right hand of God'" (7:54–56). While they were stoning him, Stephen prayed, "Lord Jesus, receive my spirit" (7:59). Then, while he was dying, he added a third element to his witness: he prayed for forgiveness for those who were taking his life as he "fell to his knees and cried out, 'Lord, do not hold this sin against them.' When he had said this, he fell asleep" (7:60).

Learning to be resilient when we fall down, trust God when we are afraid, get rid of things that entangle us, persevere in the midst of difficulty, gain depth in God's Word, be courageous in our witness, experience Christ's presence in the darkest hour, and forgive those who persecute us does not happen overnight. We cannot wait until we are in the midst of persecution to become concerned about these areas of Christian growth and maturity. We must allow God to begin preparing us now, so that when we may be asked to face danger, suffering, or even death, we will be faithful and steadfast witnesses.

A HEAVY COST

Serving in the midst of danger and hardship can involve a heavy cost for missionaries, relief workers, local Christians, and others who

313

become directly involved in crises. All too frequently, they are forced to evacuate, with their homes and possessions left behind. There are also tragic instances of kidnapping, rape, or murder. Exposure to these kinds of dangers and traumatic events make many missionaries vulnerable to special forms of stress, including burnout and posttraumatic stress disorder (PTSD). The following discussion is largely a summary of Marjory F. Foyle's treatment of these topics in her must-read book *Honourably Wounded: Stress among Christian Workers* (2001, 201–21).

Burnout

Foyle begins her discussion of burnout by challenging the traditional belief that full commitment to missions means being willing to "burn out for God." Thousands of fully committed missionaries are happy, fulfilled, and successful in their ministry. The real source of burnout is not commitment; it is overwork. Missionaries deplete their physical and mental resources as they allow their personal values, along with those of the missionary community and the broader society, to impose unrealistic expectations on their ministry.

"Brownout" may be a more accurate term than "burnout" to describe what happens when missionaries become exhausted. They have not been destroyed by a fire that has left only ashes in its wake. Rather, their power supply has dimmed and is becoming depleted. They cannot function at full force anymore. However, since "burnout" is a more common term than "brownout" for the missionary's diminished energy and ability to cope, Foyle continues to use it.

There are several different causes for burnout. *Wear and tear* are important among these. They can be particularly severe in situations of danger, when missionaries are sometimes called on to work far beyond their own human resources.

> The important thing to remember is that this [wear and tear] is a potentially dangerous situation, and that we need to ask God to show us what steps to take to curtail it as soon as possible. This principle is very important in disaster areas. The team has to work full stretch for a long time to bring some order into the situation, to organise how the relief is distributed, and to cope with ever-increasing needy people with limited resources. Workers in this situation have told me how guilty they felt when management sent them off duty to a reasonable bed and adequate food and water. Yet without this "rest therapy" they would burn out prematurely. I believe firmly that we should take breaks from the situation, even if the cover we leave behind is not really numerically adequate. (Foyle 2001, 205–6)

314

Even though Jesus lived in the midst of suffering, danger, and facing his own impending death, Foyle has the impression that he was very careful with his strength:

> I think he used the house in Bethany as a sort of [electric socket] where he could go and relax and recharge his batteries. Similarly, his common use of flowers, fish and birds as examples in his stories may well indicate that he used his times on the mountains not only for prayer but also to wander around looking at natural history. . . . We know he got tired just like we do. "Jesus, tired as he was from the journey, sat down at the well" (John 4:6). But possibly one of the reasons he never burned out was because he was very sensible, and sat down whenever he could. For example, the sermon on the mount was to be a very long one, so he made himself comfortable by sitting on the hillside before he began. (Foyle 2001, 206)

Physical illness can contribute to burnout. Unless there are emergencies that no one else can handle, it is extremely important to take time off for rest and recuperation when you are ill. This is especially necessary if you have a viral infection.

Overwork is a major cause of burnout. Some highly conscientious people run on overload. They continually take on more work than they can handle. Some of them are "workaholics." Their sense of fulfillment and satisfaction comes through work, and their self-confidence is bound up with success. They drive themselves to prevent failure. Even though others advise them to cut back and take care of other areas of their lives, they continue to be controlled by work. If you recognize yourself in this profile, allow Jesus to teach you to slow down and enjoy other things. He was on the most important mission in the history of humankind, but, even so, as we noted above, he was never in a hurry.

Foyle offers advice for people who must report to workaholics on a regular basis. Discuss your situation with the team leader and make it clear to your superior that you need time off to keep functioning. If you are overworked and in charge of a project, develop your delegating skills and learn to leave some things undone. If serious frustrations with your assignment continue, try to find ways to make what you are doing more interesting and make a point of taking regular "pajama days" when you depressurize by doing whatever you want to (other than work!). If you see no way out, consider whether you should stay where you are, and, if so, how long. If you do decide to leave, try to create or wait for a natural transition rather than leaving abruptly.

Sometimes missionaries bring psychological baggage with them that contributes to burnout. They may not have come to terms with inferiority feelings that grew out of sibling rivalries, being put down by parents or teachers, or being in homes where there were constant quarrels and violence or no religious faith. These experiences may have left them with a feeling of guilt and believing that no one loves them. Some antidotes to help you handle inferiority feelings are refusing to live with "if onlys" (if only I had been . . .) and learning to forgive yourself rather than judge yourself for being less than perfect. "Remember that anything unpleasant we learn about ourselves is the door to a new creation, a new possibility of a new kind of life. . . . Build up the areas in which you are even mildly gifted and pay some attention also to the weaker ones. You will be surprised what God can do for you" (Foyle 2001, 215).

Posttraumatic Stress Disorder (PTSD)

Trauma occurs when missionaries get caught up in wars and natural disasters or in localized but equally traumatic occurrences such as armed robberies, rapes, and kidnappings. Some mission agencies conduct special predeparture courses to prepare overseas workers for these possibilities. The emphasis is on being proactive: making sure that finances will be immediately available in case of evacuation, knowing how to make your house into a safe shelter if a war begins, notifying authorities, living circumspectly until it is safe to leave, and being alert to risks of kidnapping.

After a traumatic event happens, it is important to be on the alert for your own initial reactions, as well as for trauma symptoms among your team and other people around you. Watch for fear, anxiety, and hyperactivity, followed by a loss of energy, insomnia, repeated images of the trauma scene, guilt about not doing what one should have done, a sense of total shock, and bereavement reactions. If full-blown PTSD develops, the initial symptoms will be prolonged and new ones will develop. This fuller picture can develop immediately, within a few days, or, rarely, after several months. It can include startled reactions to noises that resemble the initial trauma-inducing ones, irritability, anxiety, poor concentration, and sometimes depression. There can also be flashbacks when something triggers memories of the event. Sleep can be greatly disturbed—whether from inability to fall asleep or from nightmares that make it impossible to go back to sleep. The long-term sufferer may resort to avoidance, retreating from situations that may remind him or her of the original event, such as social gatherings in which conversation about it is likely to occur.

When crises arise, it is important to get help to those who are suffering from trauma as quickly as possible. Team leaders need to do what they can, whether or not they have the necessary preparation and training. Many mission agencies now have mental health personnel who can get into the area fairly quickly, or care for people as soon as they get out.

316

There is also often a third tier of workers who can come in to take over where the first two tiers leave off by assessing the needs for treatment and evacuation, facilitating group meetings for support and mutual sharing, and getting permission from those who need future care to discuss the requirements with the local doctor and/or their mission agency.

Good things can emerge from an experience of PTSD:

One is that you have opportunity not only to look the current episode in the face but also to deal with older problems that may be making the PTSD more severe. Never forget that people may emerge stronger on the other side of the illness, despite the possibility of certain aspects of their health being a little damaged. If we end up like weakened Jacob leaning on his staff, we will be enabled to continue to worship God, and our illness makes no difference to our relationship with God. He never lets us go, however awful we feel, and will actually use the weakness we experience to enhance our relationship with him and to increase enormously the help we can give other people. (Foyle 2001, 221)

SUMMARY

We began our chapter with the first two verses of Martin Luther's great Reformation hymn "A Mighty Fortress." Now we will end with a loose paraphrase of the last two verses:

Even though it would be easy to let this troubled, devil-filled world undo us, we are not afraid. We can put up with Satan's rage, because we know that, through Jesus Christ, his doom is certain. Jesus is on our side. Through him we have been given the Holy Spirit's gifts. This knowledge and faith enable us to give up earthly possessions, our families, and even our lives for him. Remember that our bodies are only temporal; they can be killed in the midst of conflict and violence. God's truth and his kingdom abide forever. They are eternal.

Then, as we gain courage and strength from this glimpse of God's kingdom and of the great cloud of witnesses who have surrounded us throughout biblical and church history (Heb. 11; 12:1), and who continue among us in the midst of today's missions crises,

let us throw off everything that hinders and the sin that so easily entangles, and let us run with perseverance the race marked out for us. Let us fix our eyes on Jesus, the author and perfecter of our faith, who for the joy set before him endured the cross, scorning its shame, and sat down at the right hand of the throne of God. (Heb. 12:1–2)

CASE STUDY:
MINISTRY IN THE MIDST OF CONFLICT:
A STORY FROM ANGOLA

LOIS MCKINNEY DOUGLAS

Read the story below. After you have done so, discuss what missions in the midst of crises and suffering mean in terms of personal attitudes and commitments and in terms of outreach and ministry.

Analzira was a student of mine at a theological seminary in São Paulo in the late 1970s.

Years later, I was with her in São Paulo again at COMIBAM, the Iberian-American Missions Congress. We met for dinner and talked late into the evening, without even pulling away from our conversation for a scheduled meeting. I just said "we" talked. It would be more accurate to say that I heard Analzira pour out the most incredible story of missionary commitment that I had ever heard in a firsthand encounter.

Analzira was a registered nurse and a Christian educator when a group of Angolan pastors visited Brazil. For many years Analzira had believed God was calling her to Angola, and she was overjoyed that these church leaders were in her country. She made an appointment to see them.

The pastors were so impressed by her commitment and capabilities that they invited her to come to Angola to reopen their seminary. It had been closed when missionaries from the north had pulled out during the upheavals of independence and civil war. Analzira's home church in Brazil commissioned her, and she left for her adopted country with only her suitcase. There was no way for foreign currency to be sent to Angola at that time. Angolan churches promised to provide her food and lodging.

She funded the reopening of the seminary by teaching nursing part-time at a government hospital in the town where the school was located. "Reopening the seminary" was not as easy as it sounds. The buildings, furniture, library books, and other supplies were just as the earlier missionaries had left them. However, by this time they were covered with tropical mold and rust. She spent weeks cleaning things up while at the same time developing a curriculum and preparing for classes.

Finally the seminary was reopened, and thirty students preparing for ministry arrived. At first she was the director, registrar, treasurer, dean, and only professor. Gradually, she was able to enlist and develop a national and expatriate staff for a thriving seminary.

I was excited and thrilled by Analzira's accomplishments, but that was just the beginning of her story. Her town was caught in the middle of the conflict between the government army in the north and the UNITA rebel forces in the south. Every time the rebel forces surged north or the government forces pushed south, she and her colleagues were caught in the middle of the conflict.

She told about
- the outside walls of her home being riddled with pockmarks from bullets,

and spending time under her bed to have some protection when fighting broke out;

- a period of several months in which she, along with the other local residents, survived on locally grown produce, mustard greens, and manioc mush, because all the roads out of the town had been cut off by land mines;
- the bouts with malaria she had, one so severe that she had to be taken

to the hospital, where there was no food or water. The local believers came in several times a day to keep her supplied.

I couldn't sleep that night when I got back to my hotel room. The tears kept flowing. This is what missions in the midst of crises and suffering is all about.

16

Reentry

As dangerous as it may seem to orbit in a space shuttle, 135 miles above the earth at a speed of 18,000 miles per hour, it is relatively risk free . . . compared to the risks involved in rocketing the shuttle up into space in the first place, and most certainly compared to the risks involved in bringing it back down to earth. . . . It is no mistake that the word re-entry is also applied to the experience returning missionaries must go through as they make the adjustment from life on the mission field back to life at home. Like the astronaut guiding his craft back into the earth's atmosphere, returning missionaries must negotiate many potential hazards. . . . If [the process] is not handled correctly, [they] may barely escape with [their] emotional well-being and faith intact.

Peter Jordan (1992, 13)

W hen the modern missions movement began to emerge at the turn of the nineteenth century, questions about the missionary's reentry were seldom asked. The commitment was for a lifetime. Friends and family waved good-bye at the docks as the missionary sailed off to sea, knowing that long years would pass before they would see each other again. In some cases, missionaries spent their lifetime overseas without ever returning home. The questions we try to answer in this chapter were almost never raised. When God called a

---

SIDEBAR 16.1
"THE LORD WILL WATCH OVER YOUR COMING AND GOING"

Psalm 121

Take a few moments to sing this Psalm in your heart before you go on with the chapter.

I lift up my eyes to the hills—
    where does my help come from?
My help comes from the LORD,
    the Maker of heaven and earth.
He will not let your foot slip—
    he who watches over you will not slumber;
indeed, he who watches over Israel
    will neither slumber nor sleep.
The LORD watches over you—
    the LORD is your shade at your right hand;
the sun will not harm you by day,
    nor the moon by night.
The LORD will keep you from all harm—
    he will watch over your life;
the LORD will watch over your coming and going
    both now and forevermore.

---

person to a distant land, there was no turning back. Returning permanently to your homeland before you died, or at least were elderly or in poor health, meant turning your back on God's will.

Today, much has changed. A trip by ship sometimes took several months. Now a flight to anywhere in the world takes only hours. Exchanges of boat mail used to take many weeks or even months. Now there is instant e-mailing, chatting, and even free phoning on the Web.

The lives of missionaries have become fast paced and constantly changing as well. Missionaries who spend their lifetime in a single place have become few and far between. Even if they serve with the same mission agency for their entire career, they are likely to have a variety of assignments and serve in more than one culture.

Even though the form and shape of our commitment to missions keeps changing as the world whirls faster and faster, its essence is still the same. Missions still means participating in *missio Dei*, what God is doing in the world through his church, and following him with confidence and assurance, knowing that he will "watch over [our] coming and going both now and forevermore." This quotation is from the last verse of Psalm 121, sometimes called the Pilgrim's Psalm. The people of

Israel sang it as they ascended to Jerusalem to celebrate feasts and holy days. Christian missionaries across the centuries have echoed its words as they have gone to all nations and peoples as heralds of the gospel.

REENTRY TAKES ON DIFFERENT FORMS AND SHAPES

As missionaries come and go more frequently, reentries to their home countries are taking on different forms and shapes. Some come back for home assignments with plans for returning to the field. Others reenter church- or missions-related ministries in their homeland, move on to a different vocation, or retire. Still others leave prematurely, before they had planned to, and sometimes before they were expected to by their mission or church. These different scenarios create different expectations and needs.

Returning for a Home Assignment

Home assignments used to be called "furloughs." This older term is seldom used anymore, largely because it is not a good descriptor. It creates expectations of a leave from active service. This is not what happens when missionaries return home. They quickly discover that responsibilities during their home assignments are every bit as demanding as those they left behind in their host countries. There are sending agencies who require reports. Support needs to be raised, and church relationships need to be reactivated. Personal and family matters need attention. And in the midst of all of this, missionaries need time for study, not to mention time to relax and slow down.

Scheduling home assignments has become more flexible. A traditional pattern was four years abroad and a year back home. Now, some missionaries return annually for three-month periods to accommodate their children's education on the field. They are also likely to extend their home assignments occasionally to care for family and health issues that have come up or to have some extra time for academic work. Let us look at some of the activities that keep missionaries busy while they are back home.

REPORTING BACK

Mission agencies, churches, and individuals who have been praying for the missionaries, supporting them financially, and receiving their e-mails and newsletters are eager for face-to-face meetings with them when they return. Mission agencies often expect formal debriefings with executives and board members. Some provide reentry seminars, medical examinations, and psychological counseling for the returnee. Churches usually want their returning missionaries to meet with missions committees. Individuals who have been supporting them will want to be brought up-to-date as well.

RAISING ADDITIONAL SUPPORT

Sometimes returning missionaries find their support base eroded by the escalating cost of overseas living. Other times the initial support that was promised before they left for the field never materialized. In still other instances, church or individual supporters were committed for only a single term and decide not to continue. Support raising is "people raising" (Dillon 1993). It involves praying, e-mailing, and enlisting friends. Face-to-face contacts with churches and interested people are far more effective in encouraging financial support than the occasional news that reaches potential supporters while missionaries are away.

REACTIVATING CHURCH RELATIONSHIPS

Your contacts with churches cannot stop with support raising. You will want to renew friendships and get acquainted with new people. Try to catch up with what has been happening in their lives and share what has been happening to you. You may be invited to preach, teach, visit small groups, or participate in evangelistic and social outreach activities as you visit churches. These opportunities allow you to minister to those who have been ministering to you.

CARING FOR PERSONAL AND FAMILY MATTERS

Personal and family matters can be time-consuming and stressful while you are on home assignment. Perhaps an elderly parent needs help, or your oldest child is getting settled in a university. Maybe your family has medical needs. Complicated legal or financial matters may need to be resolved. And even without these urgent kinds of needs, the visits you make to families and friends can involve long car trips and lots of activity. When these kinds of concerns are added to a long list of other responsibilities, it is no wonder that returning missionaries feel stressed out and exhausted at times. We talk more about reentry stress later in this chapter.

STRETCHING AND GROWING

The knowledge explosion will affect your home assignment. A few years overseas is enough to make you feel out of touch, or even obsolete, in your ministry and profession. Your long-term effectiveness will often depend on carving out periods of time during your home assignment that are dedicated to stretching and growing. Professional meetings, academic courses, libraries, and bookstores provide resources that can help you. The discipline, financial costs, and extra energy these efforts involve are more than worth the effort. It is important for sending agencies and supporting churches to facilitate these opportunities. The ongoing effectiveness of their missionaries is at stake.

RESTING, RELAXING, SLOWING DOWN

Talking about resting, relaxing, and slowing down may seem almost laughable after you have read through this long list of home assignment responsibilities. You may be thinking that more activities will just make matters worse. But remember that rest and relaxation are not just "add-ons." They are enablers and facilitators. It is essential to get away from the pressures from time to time. Visits with friends and families do not count. You will need some quiet moments for just you. Try to plan ahead for these times, even before you leave the field. Otherwise, it is too easy to let them get crowded out.

KNOWING GOD BETTER AND LOVING HIM MORE

Spiritual formation does not stop while you are on home assignment. You will want to have frequent times alone with God and practice being mindful of his presence while you are in the midst of busy activity. Short retreats, or even longer ones, are important. Allow God to turn your stressful home assignment into a time when you are learning to know him better and love him more. Reviewing the discussion of spiritual formation in chapter 4 from time to time during your reentry will provide challenges and suggestions to help you keep growing.

Returning to Stay

On one occasion in the early 1980s, a missionary resigned from an overseas missions agency after over twenty years of service to teach missions in an evangelical university. Some supporters were shocked. They felt that returning to the sending country meant leaving a missions vocation. Even though the missionary had returned to prepare others for missionary service, it was difficult for them to believe that leaving a field-based assignment to serve at home could possibly be God's will.

Now, two decades later, such comings and goings are widely accepted in the missions world. Not all missionaries serve overseas for a lifetime. Many of them reenter after *planned* periods of time abroad, ranging from summer experiences to short terms, longer terms, repeated assignments, and retirement at the end of a lifetime missions career. Other reentries are *unplanned*. Missionaries come back because of family concerns, political turmoil, decisions made by mission agencies or national churches, ministry opportunities that open up for them in their home country, or, sadly, because of unresolved conflicts and other personal problems. We describe these different scenarios below.

AFTER PLANNED PERIODS ABROAD

Planned periods of time abroad take on many forms and shapes. There can be short-term, longer-term, and repeated assignments. A church youth group may spend a summer rebuilding homes in a devastated area. University students may spend their summer in cultural exchange programs, such as the one described in the case study "Coming Home from Poland." A librarian from an evangelical college may dedicate her sabbatical to training a national staff for an overseas seminary library. A high school teacher may accept a two-year contract at a missionary

---

CASE STUDY:
COMING HOME FROM POLAND

ANGEL LEIGH GRANT, UNIVERSITY OF MASSACHUSETTS (USED WITH PERMISSION);
HTTP:/HOME.SNU.EDU/~HCULBERT/RE-ENTRY.HTM

I spent five weeks in Poland with an InterVarsity short-term missions program. Three of those weeks were in Wisla, a village in the mountains near the Czech border. Our "cultural exchange camp" included thirty Polish university students. They were very excited about the chance to study English with native speakers and to learn about life in America.

We each had two or three Polish roommates. Almost immediately, several began asking questions about God. Others were fascinated by the worship times to which we invited them on Sunday nights. They often wanted to continue praising God after our worship had officially ended. They even initiated some impromptu worship on other nights of the week!

"I am intrigued by you Americans," my Polish roommate Anna told me. "There's something special about your faith. I can feel it when you are singing."

Several Bible studies started up in Poland as well. "My roommates were the ones who initiated the Bible study," said Jeanna Leigh Allen, my prayer partner. "I don't know about at your school, but at UMPI [University of Maine at Presque Isle], no one would ever say to me, 'Hey, do you want to get together and read the Bible?'"

"I was floored by what God did there," another teammate, Amy Sparks, a senior at Milligan College in Tennessee, said to me. "I never thought that the Poles would be so eager to listen and to learn."

The openness of the Polish students made returning to campus difficult for me. Back at school, everyone—me included—has their own agenda. No one has time to sit and talk like we did in Wisla.

As school started, I found myself wondering if I was selfish because of all the

Continued

children's school. A medical doctor may take a leave from her practice to spend several months working in a refugee camp. A pastor may return to his church in the United States after leading seminars for national pastors and counseling missionaries during a period of time abroad. A businesswoman may make a midcareer decision to take her expertise overseas by contributing to economic development efforts and getting involved in evangelistic outreach.

What all these people have in common is their commitment to a specific mission for an agreed-upon period of time. Some renew their contracts and stay longer, but others choose to return home, at least for a while. It is not unusual for such people to keep repeating short-term assignments across the years.

FOR RETIREMENT

Retirement for missionaries usually means a change in status and source of income. They are no longer directly supported through missions, churches, and individual donors. Instead, their financial needs are met through government and private retirement plans, including those

Coming Home—Continued

time I spent sitting in classes. It felt as if I was studying just for my own sake. I couldn't see how the path I was on was going to benefit anyone else. I wanted to be back in Wisla with the teammates I had grown to love dearly. I wanted to be back there sharing God's love with people who were willing to learn about him.

When I returned to the States, almost everything I saw reminded me of something that had happened in Poland. I needed to talk about my experience but I didn't feel the other Christians I knew could understand because they hadn't been there. I feared that people were tired of hearing me talk about my trip.

I came home wanting God to do wonderful things on my campus. Still, I wasn't ready to throw myself into any campus group because leaving Poland was hard. The truth is, I hadn't wanted to come home at all.

In Poland, I saw God's Holy Spirit work miraculously in ways I'd never seen before. Back home in my everyday routine, that

wasn't the case. For one thing, I could often get through a day at school without talking to God. In Poland the things I saw God doing drove me to my knees many times each day. Those differences caused me to struggle in my relationship with God.

Talking to my teammates from the trip helped tremendously in the readjusting process. I discovered that all of us had experienced similar emotions and difficulties. As we came back to the States, we all felt that we had changed somehow. We were not the same people who had left our home country five weeks earlier.

Time and prayer have helped me to re-enter life at school. Still, I wonder if I could have better prepared myself for the re-entry. What could I have handled differently? How can I use my summer experience to be even more effective as a witness on my campus and as an encouragement to other Christians?

set up by their missions. Sometimes these sources are supplemented through savings and income from continued ministry activities.

As long as their health permits, these retired missionaries are likely to keep busy. Spending the rest of their lives reading, watching television, chatting with friends, and pursuing hobbies is not appealing to most of them. And even if they could afford it, they are usually not interested in taking Caribbean cruises or living in upscale retirement communities.

CASE STUDY: TWO REENTRIES AND MULTIPLE RETIREMENTS: A MISSIONARY'S STORY GOES ON AND ON

H. WILBERT NORTON

As you read the Nortons' story that follows, ask yourself what kept them going on and on. In what ways do their lives provide a model for you?

First Reentry (June–July 1945)

After a term in Congo was extended to five years by the war, we were in the capitol city, Kinshasa, trying to return to the United States for home assignment. However, no freighter captain would take on families. While we were wondering what to do, we met U.S. Army air personnel who were en route to South Africa. They said they would pick us up and fly us north to Liberia on their return trip. When we finally made it to Liberia, we found that a Pan American Clipper had been put in service between Liberia and Brazil. We waited our turn for a flight and arrived in Natal, Brazil, only to find that air travel to the States was backlogged. But there was space in the officers' quarters of a U.S. Army troop ship to accommodate our family and some others. So we spent ten days on a "Caribbean cruise" via Puerto Rico to New Orleans.

As we stepped ashore, a band was playing marches to welcome the soldiers home. The traffic and the hordes of people, apparently unconcerned for anybody but themselves, was too much for us. We felt like flotsam and jetsam, unnecessary and unwanted. I really wanted to push my family on the ship and head back to Africa!

Second Reentry (December 1949)

Back in the Congo for a second term, my wife, Colene, became ill. The medical director of the hospital in Kinshasa advised returning to the States by boat because he thought an ocean voyage would assist her recovery by providing rest and relaxation. So, for two weeks we plowed through Atlantic storms while I was trying to keep an eye on three boys and care for Colene. Just before sunset on a cold December evening, the ship docked at a refueling coal yard in Philadelphia. We had a severe

Continued

327

Options for these retirees are varied and complex. Some decide to continue living in their adopted countries. Others find themselves involved in churches, educational institutions, or mission agencies in their homeland. Some continue in full-time ministries. One of these is H. Wilbert Norton, who at age ninety-one is still involved in writing projects. You will enjoy reading about his experiences in the case study "Two Reentries and Multiple Retirements: A Missionary's Story Goes On and On."

Retired missionaries face special kinds of reentry issues. They often have inadequate incomes and living arrangements. They can feel lonely

Two Reentries—Continued

case of culture/weather shock! In God's providence, we were later directed to the medical services we needed and Colene's case was diagnosed and treated.

Trinity (1950–64) and Wheaton (1965–80)

The second reentry led to our call to Trinity International University, founding the missions program there, and being able to secure a choice spot for a new campus during the period I served as president. After fourteen years at Trinity, I was invited to start the missions program at Wheaton Graduate School and, during the last nine years, to serve as dean.

Shattering the Stereotypes (1980–83)

As we were facing retirement at age sixty-five, the Nigerian general secretary of the Evangelical Church of West Africa invited Colene and me to join him in beginning a second seminary for a denomination of two million believers in two thousand churches, five hundred of which had no pastor. We accepted the challenge, and in the midst of adaptation to an urban African culture totally different from the bush culture we had known among the Ubangi tribe in the Congo, the Jos ECWA Seminary was born. It continues to prosper, providing strong leadership for local churches and the national denomination—an amazing work of the Lord!

CAMEO (1983–89) and Reformed Theological Seminary (1989–2003)

My appointment as executive director of the Committee to Assist Ministry Education Overseas (CAMEO), sponsored by two associations of evangelical mission agencies, began while I was still in Jos and continued after I went to Reformed Theological Seminary in 1989. I was involved with this seminary for almost fourteen years, first in helping the Jackson, Mississippi, campus to develop a doctoral program, and later at the new campus in Charlotte, North Carolina, teaching missions to MDiv students.

A Long Journey

As we journeyed across the Atlantic in December 1949, I had in mind going into tree farming. I was washed up. My career was gone. But the Lord had promised he would always be with us (Matt. 28:20). God was working in us (Phil. 2:13)—regardless of age, status, culture, or church—and meeting all our needs in the process (Phil. 4:19). The reality of God's grace (2 Cor. 8:9) has been clearly evident and the benediction of Hebrews 13:20–21 has been humbly experienced through the decades for his glory! Amen!

and find it difficult to "find their niche" in social situations that have changed. Eventually, some will have health needs that involve long-term care. In the midst of these kinds of difficulties, they share stories of God's faithfulness. When the Gehmans returned to the United States after thirty-seven years of missionary service, they found that they would need double the income they had in Kenya. Even so, in their own words, they can say with the hymn writer, "All I have needed thy hand hath provided; Great is thy faithfulness, Lord unto me." "We never lacked anything we needed when serving in Africa and God is providing for us in retirement in the States. The rich experience of serving cross-culturally is a far greater reward than the monocultural life of most affluent Americans. It is amazing what little we need to enjoy life. Africa taught us much in this regard" (Gehman 2005, 175–76).

Unplanned Reentries

Not all reentries are expected. Sometimes reentries are caused by unplanned events related to family concerns, political crises, church and mission agency decisions, new ministry opportunities at home, and unresolved conflicts and personal problems that occur.

FAMILY CONCERNS

Family concerns may bring missionaries home early. They may have come back to be with elderly parents or help a child to make the transition to a university in his or her home country. Sometimes they come back because they are struggling with depression and burnout or have other health issues to face. These kinds of reentry events can be extremely disruptive to the family's field ministries and their plans for the future.

POLITICAL CRISES

Many missionaries are living in the midst of political, religious, and social conflict. Security checkpoints along streets and highways, verifications of personal documents, riots, gunfire in the distance (or perhaps close by), disruptions of church services by authorities, and searches of their homes and workplaces have become a part of their daily life.

> *After we returned home [from overseas], my seven-year-old daughter said out of the blue over a bowl of cereal one morning, "Dad, we are not missionaries anymore."*
> *I replied, "No honey. What do you think about that?"*
> *After all my futile attempts to make sense out of the overwhelming transition, she said it best: "It doesn't matter if people call me a missionary or not. I will always be a missionary on the inside."*
> Steve Hunter (2005, 154)

329

Then, at some point, everything falls apart, and their country's embassy orders them to prepare for an immediate evacuation. So the missionaries stuff their most important belongings in bags and say hasty good-byes to their friends, ministries, and the country in which, in spite of the stresses and uncertainties, they have learned to feel at home.

SENDING CHURCH, MISSION AGENCY, AND NATIONAL CHURCH DECISIONS

Decisions made by sending churches, mission agencies, or ministry leaders on the field can also bring unplanned changes in a missionary's career. A sending church may discontinue financial support, or a mission agency or field conference may decide to withdraw from the field. One new missionary arrived in the country she was adopting to be greeted by the news that the mission team had initiated a plan for withdrawal from the field!

MINISTRY OPPORTUNITIES AT HOME

Some missionaries return because of ministry opportunities that open up in their country of origin. They may be invited to serve in the home office of their mission agency, or perhaps they want to get involved in local church ministries, urban missions, or ethnic outreach. An invitation to teach in a theological school or university may have brought them back. They may find themselves gravitating toward chaplaincy, medicine, publishing, agriculture, or other professions that fit their training and skills. There are scores of ways in which these post-career missionaries continue to serve Christ when they return to their countries of origin.

UNRESOLVED CONFLICTS AND PERSONAL PROBLEMS

This section must end on a sad note. Not all missionaries return home after an agreed-upon period of service or because of understandable changes in their lives. They come home before they had expected to, and before missions and churches believe that they should. They may be returning because of marriage or family conflict, inadequate commitment, or an immature spiritual life. The presenting issue may have been an immoral lifestyle, problems with peers, problems with local leaders, a lack of job satisfaction, dismissal by an agency, inadequate supervision, poor cultural adaptation, language problems, lack of home support, or disagreement with an agency (Brierley 1997, 92–94). The attrition that results from these kinds of problems and conflicts has serious consequences for both missionaries and missions.

These realities underscore the importance of prospective and newly appointed missionaries doing all they can, through their spiritual, personal, and ministry readiness, to ensure that they will not become a

SIDEBAR 16.2
THE COST OF ATTRITION

Graham (1987)

Following is a list of some costs of attrition. What might you add to this list?

1. Lost souls are not reached.
2. Churches go unplanted.
3. "Windows of opportunity" are lost.
4. Missionaries experience a sense of failure.
5. Marriages/families experience stress.
6. Stewardship of resources is poor.

dropout statistic. Missions, churches, and theological schools also have crucial roles to play. They must provide member care at every stage of missionary preparation and service, including efforts toward restoration when things fall apart on the field. The ReMAP II study, launched by the World Evangelical Alliance Missions Commission in 2002, concluded that "good practice" agencies

> expect well-trained missionary candidates and apply careful candidate selection. They have effective leadership and good interaction with their missionaries. They exercise a lean, quality administration with a servant attitude and flexible structures. They provide their missionaries with opportunities for continuous training and development of new gifts. They also encourage missionaries to improve their ministries and their agency's operations and structures. . . . These agencies have maintained their missionaries' commitment, loyalty and vision. They are blessed with highly experienced and dedicated staff. (Blocher 2005, 236–37)

Whether missionaries return home after a short term or because of new opportunities, family circumstances, health needs, or retirement—or even when they have been restored after problems on the field—they become God's special emissaries. Their overseas assignments have transformed them into world Christians with a contagious love for missions that continues to infect families, friends, and churches, both in their homeland and abroad.

REENTRY IS STRESSFUL

By the time you have read this far, you will have become keenly aware that not all cross-cultural adjustments are related to entering another culture. For many people, the shock of coming back home after immersion

331

> *A conversation overheard between a mission executive and a recently returned missionary:*
> "You seem to have landed with both wheels on the ground," said the mission executive. "Are you kidding?" the missionary responded. "We crashed and burned and were left for dead on the runway."
> Livingstone Huff (2002, 81–82)

in a second culture can be every bit as traumatic as crossing cultures was in the first place. The initial excitement and euphoria of returning home is usually short-lived. It is not long before returning missionaries begin to feel out of place and disoriented. They sometimes become confused, disillusioned, angry, frustrated, and judgmental. Huff (2002) has called this the "crash-and-burn" syndrome.

Most people do not talk much about crashing and burning as they reenter their home country, perhaps because of embarrassment. It seems obvious that entering another culture is difficult. But finding it stressful to come back home? There must be something wrong. Psychologist Clyde N. Austin (1987, 72) has called this reluctance to talk about reentry adjustments "the conspiracy of silence." When people do open up and talk about reentry, what sorts of experiences do they share? The case study relating Dan and Joyce's story gives an example. (The structure of this section has been adapted from C. N. Austin 2000.)

CASE STUDY: DAN AND JOYCE

LOIS MCKINNEY DOUGLAS

The following story provides a composite example gleaned from many missionaries' experiences. While you are reading it, focus on the adjustments to lifestyle differences, conflicting values, changes, and losses they are experiencing. Then try to integrate these factors into the discussion of reentry stressors below.

Dan and Joyce Williams and their children, Karen and Ken, have just come home from a two-year assignment to a mission hospital in Indonesia. Dan, a hospital administrator, was helping the hospital to set up a state-of-the-art record-keeping system. Joyce, a laboratory technician, helped to develop an in-service technician's training program.

After struggling with some initial frustrations and setbacks, Dan was able to work with the national and expatriate staff in introducing useful improvements in the way patient, inventory, and accounting records were kept. He felt quite satisfied with what he had been able to accomplish.

Joyce is a natural teacher. She thrived on her training role in the laboratory and developed some close friendships with her national counterparts. She enjoyed the slower pace of life.

Twelve-year-old Ken and ten-year-old Karen attended the missionary children's school adjacent to the hospital property. Ken spent his free time collecting insects and reading about them. Outgoing Karen became a friend to everyone at the school, at the hospital, in the Indonesian church, and in the village just down the road.

There was a big send-off for the family when they were ready to return to the States. A large crowd of people from the church, the school, the hospital, and the community came. The family was showered with gifts, praise, and expressions of friendship.

Now they have been back in the States for two months. Listen as they talk about the reentry stresses they are facing.

Dan's Story

When everyone told me there would be some adjustments to Indonesia, I'd say, "Of course. Now tell me something new." I expected things to be difficult, and they actually turned out better than I had imagined they would. Our family had an incredible time overseas. If we had the opportunity, we'd go back in a minute.

But coming back home has been something else. I can't believe the stress we've been under. If someone took time to measure it, I'm sure they'd find us going off the top of one of those stress scales. I'm usually an easygoing kind of guy. But lately I've been irritable, tense,

keyed up, and even yelling at Joyce and the kids.

There have been tensions from a lot of different quarters. I was on a leave of absence from my job at Central Hospital, so I figured I could move right back into it. I did get my job back. Same title, even a raise. But while I was gone, a young MBA right out of business school brought in some sophisticated software that wasn't even available two years ago. The whole institution is moving into newer technology than I've worked with. I know I'll catch up again in a few months, but right now, I feel useless and hopelessly out of date.

We had really looked forward to getting back to our home church. Even that has been a disappointment at times. Sure, they had a big reception for us the first Sunday morning we were back, and they even gave us fifteen minutes to talk about our overseas experiences. But then it was back to business as usual. Both Joyce and I have learned to talk about Indonesia only when asked, and then to limit ourselves to short answers to questions.

I have been put back on the church board of trustees. They're probably sorry by now. I can't seem to control my anger in the meetings. The first time I exploded was when they wanted new padding for the pews. I lost my temper again when they wanted to upgrade a sound system that is still working well. And I really started climbing walls when they wanted to enlarge and reconfigure the parking lot. When I see them spending so much money on our church facilities, I can't get the picture of our village church in Indonesia with its thatched roof and wooden slabs for seats out of my mind.

All the time I was gone, I looked forward to seeing my brother and his

Continued

Dan and Joyce—Continued

family again. My brother and I have always been close. I had so many experiences I wanted to share with him. He and his family came to visit about a week after we got back. I asked him how the family was. He said, "Fine." He asked me how Indonesia was. I said, "Fine." And then we watched the Bears game on television. We spent three hours sitting next to each other and had nothing to talk about. I felt as if he were a stranger. There was no way of sharing my Indonesian experiences with him.

My relationship with Joyce and the kids isn't as good as it was in Indonesia. I've already fallen back into my old habit of bringing work home from the office with me. Our family life seems to have fallen apart. In Indonesia, all four of us sat around the table every night for dinner. It was a special time that we all looked forward to. Now Karen stays after school for club and sports activities, Joyce is out almost every night for something with the PTA or at church, and Ken can hardly be dragged away from his books and computer.

I worry about the kids. I never worried about them while we were in Indonesia because they were so protected. But now they're constantly being exposed to the drug culture. I remembered the States as such a good place to live. But now I'd rather raise the kids in Indonesia any day. Any day . . .

Joyce's Story

Coming back to the States has certainly not been easy. It has taken its toll on our whole family. Dan has been uptight on his job. He's been hard to live with at home. He's even exploded a few times in church business meetings.

How am I doing? Well, one thing is sure. I don't act out my anger like Dan does. I keep it inside. The result? Tension headaches, mild depression.

I don't want to go back to work just yet, but I'm going to have to soon. We can't handle mortgage payments on a single salary. I checked out my old laboratory job, but they told me there were no openings. Not surprising. My boss was extremely unhappy when I quit to go overseas.

I really don't know how I could handle a job right now on top of everything else. I haven't been able to cope well since we've been back. Our family has so little time together now. I especially miss the times of sharing Dan and I had in Indonesia. We both cared so much about the hospital. We would talk about our experiences until late into the night. Since we've been back, all four of us have been going in different directions.

I find myself trying to play Super Mom, and I don't like it. I just can't seem to get back into things. The whole family needed clothing, so I went shopping. I had to buy in a hurry. The prices were absurd. And I didn't know enough about what's in style to make good choices for the children. They've been complaining ever since.

And then there was the first trip to the supermarket. I didn't know how to act. You'd think I'd just arrived from Mars. The store lights seemed too bright. There were too many people and too much confusion. I was overwhelmed by so many new products and brand names. The food prices seemed much higher than I had remembered them. Then I got to the checkout counter. The cashier and the line of people behind me became impatient while I was trying to figure out how to slide my credit card through the automated approval box.

I don't even look forward to going to church. People don't relate to us in the same way they used to. The morning Dan and I spoke, we both came down hard on materialism. One of our friends told us we had offended some people. And the youth pastor hasn't spoken to me since I confronted him about the church contributing to the breakdown of the family by keeping the kids busy every night of the week. Strange. I didn't used to notice these kinds of things. Now I feel as if I'm marching to a different drummer.

Both of the children have had a hard time reentering school. Ken has buried himself in his books. That makes him into a good student, but I'm worried about his social development. He seems lethargic and withdrawn. He got angry with his Dad and me the other day when we encouraged him to get involved in sports or some other group activities.

Karen complains about stomachaches. She cries for her friends in Indonesia before she goes to sleep at night. She overheard the two most popular girls in her class at school talking behind her back about the cheap-looking bargain jeans she was wearing.

I have to drag the children to church. They don't like the worship services. They don't have any close friends. The youth group has been hard for them to break into. It hurts me to see my family struggling so much.

Lifestyle Adjustments

The returning missionaries in our case studies found themselves struggling with lifestyle issues. Dan and Joyce were facing higher mortgage payments than they had anticipated; Susan (see the case study at the end of the chapter) does not have enough money for a dependable car. These problems are echoed by others. "How did everything get so crazy and so fast and so expensive?" one returning missionary exclaimed. "[But we knew that] if we didn't jump in midstream, we were not going to make it. We went into debt for the first time in our married life. After buying a house, two cars and furniture, I could not sleep at night for two months" (Hunter 2005, 152). Financial problems are not the only lifestyle changes confronting returning missionaries. They find themselves trying to adjust to a faster pace of life while they are relearning how to shop at the supermarket, pay tolls, and handle dozens of other daily activities that have changed while they were away.

Conflicting Values

Reentry adjustments go much deeper than the getting around and financial survival issues we have just discussed. They involve clashes in inner values. "[These] may occur between homecomers and receivers in bewildering areas: material possessions, family life, racial prejudice, national priorities in politics and ecology, and Christian community conflicts" (C. N. Austin 2000, 1). All three people in our cases found

335

their values in conflict with the culture they were reentering. Dan lost his temper when he realized how much the church was spending on its building. Joyce did not want to pay exorbitant prices for designer jeans. Susan (see below) cried over dog food commercials and was angered by the lack of concern for social justice.

Changes inside You and around You

A principal reason for reentry shock is not hard to uncover: you have changed; your home culture has changed; your family, friends, and church have changed.

YOU HAVE CHANGED

You are not the same person who left on an overseas assignment a few years ago. You have come in contact with other worldviews, other values, and other lifestyles. You have developed friendships with people from another culture. The dynamics of intercultural interaction have changed you. You do not even eat, dress, or act like you did. Yet people remember you as you were before you went overseas. They do not know how to deal with the new you. In some ways, you seem like a stranger to them.

YOUR HOME CULTURE HAS CHANGED

In a fast-paced society, it is hard to keep up with what has been going on even while you are there. The culture you are returning to is not the same one you have left. New TV shows, slang, styles, technology—and countless other changes—have appeared while you were gone. Even values are changing. You may feel as if you are emerging from a time capsule that has suddenly catapulted you into the future.

Marjory F. Foyle, a missionary who ministers internationally as a psychiatrist and counselor, describes a personal experience:

> After four years in a small town area of Nepal where there were no wheeled vehicles, I returned to London and went out on a public bus. I noted all along the roads big orange globes flashing, and finally turned to a lady beside me and asked what they meant. She looked at me in absolute astonishment and said in the local slang, "Where you been living, ducks, on the moon?" They apparently marked zebra crossings, places for pedestrians to cross the road safely. . . . The key expression to use [at times like this] is "silly old me, but I'm learning!" Then everyone laughs with you and not at you. (Foyle 2001, 223–24)

YOUR FAMILY, FRIENDS, AND CHURCH HAVE CHANGED

Remember that life has not been standing still for anyone while you have been away. Those closest to you have been living very full lives. A lot has happened. There have been births, deaths, weddings, job changes, educational opportunities, vacations, and illnesses. These kinds of experiences have changed your family, friends, and church. They are not the same as they were when you left. Changes in the church can be especially difficult to cope with: "[M]issionaries may find, to their shock, frustration and amazement, that they may be totally unfamiliar with the routines, practices, music, and interests of their home church. In fact, depending on how long they have been overseas, they may not even know on a personal basis the pastor or many of the people at their home church. The missionary has returned home to discover that he or she is a stranger in a strange land" (Huff 2002, 83).

Grief and Loss

When you abruptly find yourself in the changed context you used to call "home," you are almost sure to find yourself grieving over what you left behind. It is a reverse bereavement reaction, as friends, home, job, church, educational system, food, and climate have been lost again. The host country you have left now feels like home, and your home culture feels like the host country (Foyle 2001, 223).

Sometimes your bereavement reaction may be mixed with guilt and sadness. Things may not have turned out as you had planned on the field. You had dreams of fulfillment, accomplishment, happy relationships, and spiritual growth. But things fell apart. Your time abroad was filled with psychological stress, conflicts, disappointment, and frustration. These have left you hurting and grieving (Huff 2002, 84–85). Even if you felt at home in your adopted culture and would go back today if you could, you will likely be grieving over your losses. There are so many of them! On the field your identity was intact. You had a ministry, social roles, a professional status, and support networks that included friends, churches, and mission and community activities. Now these are gone, and for the moment at least, there is nothing to replace them.

It is important to mourn these losses. You must allow yourself to feel the sadness, grief, pain, and homesickness. But there is another side to this process, best captured through the Portuguese word *saudades*. This single word blends losses and sadness with joyful, happy, tender memories, heartfelt nostalgia, sweetness, and healing. This is exactly what God wants to happen to us during our reentry.

What Can Help to Lessen Stress?

Even though reentry stress is inevitable, its impact will be lessened if we leave and reenter well, enlist supportive friends, engage in participant observation, and learn from critical incidents.

337

Leaving Well

In the midst of the chaos and confusion of transition, it is important to leave the field well (Hunter 2005). *Reconciliation* is important. Do your part in smoothing out strained relationships and resolving tensions before you leave. Be sure to say *thank you*. Tell others that you have appreciated their friendship and enjoyed working with them. Do not bypass *good-byes* to people, pets, places, and possessions. These are essential elements of closure and moving on. In the midst of all these separations, you will also need to focus on the *reentry* that lies just ahead. Try to recall what things were like when you left your home country and anticipate how they may have changed. Take time to process your field experiences (struggles and successes, what you have learned, how you have changed) and start thinking about what you want to say to friends, supporters, churches, and agencies back home. Remember to take photos and keepsakes with you. They will provide a comforting and reassuring reentry bridge for both you and those with whom you share them when you return (Koteskey 2006, 39–43).

Reentering Well

You have survived the good-byes and the trip back to your sending country. There are several things you can do to lessen the initial stresses of reentry. If possible, try to avoid major speaking responsibilities or other commitments during your first weeks back. You need time to decompress. Continue to process what has happened. Review and revise your thoughts about what you want to share with your mission, supporters, churches, and friends. Unpack and get settled as quickly as you can. Even if you are in a temporary living arrangement, it will be reassuring to be in a comfortable place that you have made your own. Take care of immediate personal needs. These can range from medical concerns and psychological counseling to getting a car and buying clothes.

Enlisting Supportive Friends

It does not take many weeks in your home country before you realize that when most people ask you what it is like to be back home, they are looking for a thirty-second, upbeat sound bite for an answer. But thanks to God's providence, you will be likely to find at least one friend who is eager to listen to you and help you. When you share with this person, try not to spend a lot of time chatting about external experiences. Share your deepest feelings and responses to what is going on. What is happening to you? How does it make you feel? Be sure that the conversation goes both ways. You will probably discover that your friend is frustrated by some of the same issues that you are. You can provide mutual support for each other by exploring the meanings behind what is happening.

ENGAGING IN PARTICIPANT OBSERVATION

Most of the adaptation hints that were shared in the "At Home in the Culture" chapter apply to cultural reentry as well. You will want to revisit social settings you knew well before you left home to discover ways they have changed since you were away.

A good starting place is to walk around your neighborhood and drive through other areas of your town or city that were familiar to you. What are some of the changes you see? You may find some of them quite overwhelming. The historic town center you remembered has been replaced by a new shopping mall. The Greek restaurant you enjoyed has gone out of business. Your physical surroundings are not the same as those you left.

Next, make visits to the supermarkets, along with the furniture, clothing, office supply, and information technology stores. How have the services and products changed since you were away? What do these changes reveal about interests and values? Talk to a friend about what you observe and how you feel.

Get into the media. If you have not been surfing the Web for home news while you were away, this would be a good place to start. But also take time to read the newspapers, watch television, and browse in bookstores to get a feel for what people are interested in and talking about. How are they interpreting and responding to current events? What kinds of attitudes and beliefs do they reveal? How are they responding to politics and foreign policy?

Come closer to home. Try to interpret what is going on in your church, mission, and denomination. Find out what is happening in your children's schools and other institutions that are becoming a part of your life again. Listen to conversations around you for clues about underlying changes.

LEARNING FROM CRITICAL INCIDENTS

You will likely find yourself reacting emotionally to situations and people around you. Perhaps you jump to quick and irrational conclusions about what is going on. It is important to allow yourself to feel. When you are alone, or with a close friend or your spouse, let yourself cry or get angry as often as you need to. But do not stop there. L. Robert Kohls (2001, 137–38) has suggested a three-step formula that can calm us and bring us back to rationality on these occasions:

1. *Describe* (if only to yourself) the situation. What do you actually see happening?
2. *Interpret* what you see. What do you think about the situation?
3. *Evaluate* the situation. How do you feel about what has taken place?

When we know God is with us in the midst of changes and "critical incidents" we can add another question:

4. How is God revealing himself to us, and working out his purpose in our lives, through these difficult experiences?

SUMMARY

The suggestions we have made above can be useful in handling reentry stress. They can go a long way toward helping you to make lifestyle adjustments, handle the tensions created by conflicting values, and cope with the losses and grief you are experiencing because of changes that occurred while you were away. But by themselves, all these good strategies are not enough. Ultimately, your help will come from the Lord. He will not let your foot slip; he will keep you from all harm; and he will continue to watch over you in the midst of all of your comings and goings, during the rest of your life and throughout eternity. Take time to sing Psalm 121 (sidebar 16.1) in your heart again as you conclude this chapter.

CASE STUDY: SUSAN'S ADJUSTMENT

LOIS MCKINNEY DOUGLAS

The following story provides a composite example gleaned from many missionaries' experiences. While you are reading it, focus on the adjustments to lifestyle differences, conflicting values, changes, and losses they are experiencing. How might you respond to her perspective?

Susan was invited by a Brazilian seminary to train a national library staff.

With a master's degree in library science and another one in theology, capped off by ten years of library experience in the States, she brought a near-perfect blend of gifts, education, and experience to her work.

She did a good job of entering into the culture. During her three years on the field, she became fluent in Portuguese. She spent her weekends assisting a community development project in a slum area. This was a consciousness-raising experience for her. Her eyes were opened to the needs of the urban poor.

Socially, Susan spent far more time with Brazilians than with her North American compatriots. One reason was that she was the only single woman on the field with her mission. Another was that most of the married missionaries lived in another part of the city. But the main reason was choice. She genuinely enjoyed her Brazilian friends.

But her time in Brazil was brought to an abrupt end when word came that her elderly mother had fallen, broken her leg, and was no longer able to care for herself. Susan was the only child, so she hurried back to the States to help her mother.

Let Susan tell the rest of her story:

Returning to the States right now has been one of the most difficult adjustments I have ever had to make. I was becoming fluent in the language. I was beginning to see some results from my work on the field. I was developing some close friendships. I had begun to fall in love with Brazil. Then I needed to come back to the States, at least long enough to help make plans for my mother and decide what the next step in my life should be.

You wouldn't believe how busy I've been since I've been back. With the full responsibility for my mother, plus housekeeping and paying bills, I haven't had a minute to myself. I finally found a nursing home for Mother that she and I feel good about. I helped her move in last weekend, and she seems to be doing well.

Now that she's settled, I will have more time to get in touch with my feelings. Reentering the States after spending time in a São Paulo slum has been almost more than I can cope with. I find myself crying a lot and feeling angry at the social injustices I see here in my home country.

The hardest thing to handle is materialism. The other day I saw a TV commercial for dog food. As I looked at those shiny-coated pooches on the screen, I thought of a little girl from the slums I had seen dying of malnutrition. I shut the TV off and began sobbing. It must have been fifteen minutes before I could stop.

I'm sure my mother's illness has made me more sensitive than I would normally be. One of the things I'm appalled by is the lack of care and services for the elderly in our country. My mother's financial resources will be used up in less than a year. Then she will have to go on Medicaid.

Social injustice has even invaded my home church. A Hispanic family visited last Sunday. No one except me even spoke to them. I overheard one woman whisper to another, "I hope they don't decide to start coming here regularly." Then yesterday, a letter to the editor of the local paper urged the county to keep out additional low-cost housing. It was signed by a prominent member of our church! How can Christians be so blind? Someone has to start speaking up.

But I'm afraid that someone who speaks up won't be me. At least not right now. My schedule over the next few months won't leave time for activism. My mission board has a full speaking schedule lined up for me. I'm really dreading this. For one thing, I've been going through a kind of spiritual dry spell since I've been back. When I was in Brazil, I found so much comfort and joy in daily Bible reading. Now I feel like I'm just going through the motions.

Another problem I'm facing in going on a speaking tour is that the church services

Continued

here seem so stiff and formal. After three years of Latin American worship, I don't even know how to act. I forgot where I was the other day and gave the pastor a big Brazilian hug. He pulled away, and his face turned red. Mine did too!

At least speaking won't fill up my whole home assignment. A graduate school near my mother's nursing home has a program in community development. I'm planning to work in some study time there.

All of these plans depend on my car holding up. I had so little money in my mission vehicle allowance that I had to settle for a very used vintage model with 90,000 miles on it and in need of a lot of repair. It's traumatic under the best of conditions to drive on North American expressways after being away for so long. My driving style has become very Latin. I keep looking at my rearview mirror to see whether a police car is following me.

These external adjustments aren't nearly as difficult as the internal ones. I've been very lonely since I've come back. My three closest friends all got married while I was away. Their interests and my interests have changed. Even my friend who is still single seems distant. The other day, I was groping for an English word while we were talking. She was irritated and told me to quit calling attention to myself and reminding people that I can speak a second language. That really hurt.

I just got a letter from the president of the seminary I worked with in Brazil. He thanked me for my help with the library and told me everyone was counting the days until I got back. They aren't the only ones! After all my good experiences in Brazil and my bad ones since I've been back, I wonder if I can ever fit into my own culture again.

17

What's Next?

The trouble with our times is that the future is not what it used to be.

Paul Valery (Quotesandsayings.com n.d.)

Question: "How do you get God to laugh?" Answer: "Tell God your plans."

Yiddish saying

Christian witness is always lived out in social environments influenced and shaped by local and global economics, politics, and religions. Cross-cultural Christian workers do not live or serve in a vacuum. What global trends can cross-cultural Christian workers expect to impact their lives and ministries in the early twenty-first century (for in-depth discussion, see especially Pocock, Van Rheenen, and McConnell 2005)? How will a shrinking, "flat world" (Friedman 2005) that, according to Warren Bennis (2001), "has no shelf life" due to accelerated change, challenge global missions? How will a growing global migration challenge existing lifestyles and ministries? How will formal and nonformal missions training and education adapt to these trends?

In a world that differs greatly from the worlds that Lois served in her generation or my (Tom's) family served in our generation, your generation can be assured of several things. The Creator knows the end from the beginning and, unlike us, is not surprised by anything that happens. For him there are no surprises. Nor does he change in the midst of rapid change for "Jesus Christ is the same yesterday and today and forever" (Heb. 13:8). In this closing chapter we identify some key trends that will impact the lives and ministries of cross-cultural Christian workers and discuss some possible implications.

TREND 1: GLOBALIZATION CREATES WINNERS AND LOSERS

The interconnectedness of the world does not, however, mean that everyone wants to participate in a democracy, wear Western clothes, eat at McDonalds, drink Coke, visit Disney World, or sing country music. Nor does it necessarily result in economic equity. The gap between the rich and poor will continue to grow. All this will result in miniaturization, that is, the strong surge of nationalism and tribalism. Heightened resistance to the perceived encroachments on their way of life will become the norm for these people. For certain parts of the world, communism will see a resurgence. The same will be true for theology. New theologies will be popularized and/or former ones revised. Globalization tends to create "haves" and "have nots," resulting in each side digging its trenches deeper.

Implications for future cross-cultural workers: Those cross-cultural Christian workers coming from the West will for the most part, rightly or wrongly, be identified with the advocates of globalization, that is, the "haves," especially if they are white. A good dose of humility and patience will be necessary, as well as a lifestyle that challenges the accepted stereotype. Make sure you understand the pros and cons of capitalism as well as other economic systems that will govern daily life. Be open to having Western theology challenged and expanded. Be a learner-leader.

TREND 2: IT IS AN URBANIZING WORLD

The year 2000 saw the world reach a 50/50 percent breakdown between urban and rural. In 1900, only 12 percent of the world lived in cities. By 1950, 30 percent did.

Cities grow for many reasons, one of which is the infusion of those coming from rural areas. That means that many people in the city still have a rural mentality even though they live in an urban environment. These individuals typically send money back to rural areas, make periodic visits to the countryside, and receive visiting family and friends from rural areas. Another reason cities grow is the influx of ethnic immigrants, creating a mosaic of peoples often living in close proximity.

Implications for future cross-cultural workers: The accelerated move to the cities has tremendous implications for today's cross-cultural Christian workers. Growing cities require missions personnel who can become gracious residents in a variety of settings. Workers who can be involved in holistic ministries will be needed to address critical social needs, such as HIV/AIDS, addictions (drugs, alcohol, pornography), unemployment, as well as spiritual needs. Those astute in issues related to ethnic diversity will also be in demand, not only for personal family members, but also for ministries as well. The mentality of the audience, whether rural or urban, as well as the ethnicity of those being reached must be discerned so that appropriate communication can take place. Due to the high expense of land, creative ways to secure a place of worship will be necessary if the house church model is not used.

When the Steffens went to the Philippines, "real" missionaries worked in rural areas. With the push to reach the cities in the 1980s, "real" missionaries went to the urban settings. What advocates of each trend often failed to realize was the interconnectedness of the urban and the rural. We need prepared personnel who can develop and implement integrated strategies that take advantage of these natural social highways between the cities and the countryside.

TREND 3: THE UNITED STATES–LED "WAR ON TERROR" WILL CHALLENGE MISSIONS FOR SEVERAL DECADES

Islamic radicals (and certainly not all Muslims), bound by hate and history, guided by an apocalyptic interpretation of the Qur'an, and led by a leader who places faith over fortune, will continue to challenge the "decadent" West (and fellow Muslims who side with the West) with a generation socialized to die for the holy cause. From children (through cartoons) to adults, a glorified culture of death is taught and celebrated. A once-glorious empire that led the world is now determined to reinstate itself no matter what the sacrifice or how many more generations it will take. Death is not an issue, nor is time. Heated rhetoric taught through certain imams and flamed by low employment provides a ready military force. A holy jihad by this minority is underway to purge Muslim sacred lands of hundreds of years of domination and humiliation by arrogant infidels, most recently the United States ("The Big Satan"), Israel ("The Little Satan"), and their supporters—including those Muslims who do not stand against them. When flash-point events happen, we can expect to hear a global call for jihadists dedicated to Allah to join the sacred battle zone.

Implications for future cross-cultural workers: Cross-cultural Christian workers in the twenty-first century, no matter where they serve, can expect to experience terror and face persecution. In the wired world, nothing is secret, anywhere, anytime. In the Google world, secrecy is nonexistent as everything and everyone can be investigated.

Some will give their lives, joining the elite forerunners mentioned in Hebrews 11. Others will serve under unrelenting stress even as they befriend those God has prepared for his kingdom. Through teaching, consulting, business, community development, and a host of other ventures, committed Christian workers will be called to match the dedication of those advocating a culture of death and determined to reinstate a new global kingdom.

Today's cross-cultural Christians will need a well-defined and lived theology of violence that addresses persecution and terror. Like first-century followers of Christ, twenty-first-century workers will experience persecution. And like first-century followers of Christ, twenty-first-century workers must learn how to pray. They may also need to become bi-vocational like first-century rabbis.

TREND 4: SLAVERY IS ALIVE AND WELL

When slavery is defined as "forced labor without pay under threat of violence" (www.iabolish.org/slavery_today/primer/index.html), estimates go as high as 27 million people being enslaved globally. Internationally, 600,000 to 800,000 are trafficked annually, 80 percent of these being women and children. Every continent except Antarctica has slavery. Some of the hotspots include the United States (sexual, domestic, garment-worker, and agricultural slaves), Brazil (families work the rain forest at gunpoint), Albania (organized crime traffickers trick teenage girls into prostitution), Mauritania (black Africans bought and sold by Arab Berbers), Pakistan (children forced to weave carpets), India (indebted children roll cigarettes), and Thailand (sex slaves for tourists). Sidebar 17.1 points out the differences between slavery in the past and slavery in contemporary settings.

Implications for future cross-cultural workers: The world stands in need today of a modern-day William Wilberforce (1759–1833), actually many of them. Wilberforce ("The Liberator"), a deeply religious man, fought a lifetime to abolish slavery throughout the vast British Empire (the 2007 movie *Amazing Grace* recounts his story). Three days before he died, the House of Commons passed the bill abolishing slavery. Those who challenge human trafficking today, such as International Justice

---

SIDEBAR 17.1
SLAVERY: PAST AND PRESENT

www.garstangfairtrade.org.uk/slavery_today.htm

OLD SLAVERY	NEW SLAVERY
• Legal ownership	• Legal ownership usually not asserted
• High purchase cost	• Very low purchase cost
• Low profits	• Very high profits
• Shortage of potential slaves	• Glut of potential slaves
• Long-term relationship	• Short-term relationships
• Ethnic differences important	• Ethnic differences less important
• Slaves maintained	• Slaves disposable

Mission, must expose the current global situation, work with governments to abolish it, and provide long-term ministry to those fortunate to be freed.

TREND 5: ETHNIC AND INDIGENOUS MISSIONS WILL PROLIFERATE, PARTICIPATE, AND PARTNER

On the home front, the 30,000 to 35,000 American Hispanic churches will emerge to play an effective, long-term, holistic, cross-cultural role in global missions. Sparked by the terror of 9/11, the devastating tsunami in Indonesia, and the fury of Katrina on the Gulf States, American Hispanic churches discovered that cross-cultural ministries in word and deed were possible without the permission of or funds originating from Anglo churches.

Spirit-led and faith-based, these brave servants launched into the choppy seas of cross-cultural ministries only to discover that they too were not only capable players but also necessary participants to help other denominations and Christian groups to meet the vast human and spiritual needs of the victims. They realized that they could now participate in strategic missions, not just be sent to their home countries because they knew the culture and language. No longer would they have to join Anglo agencies and become marginalized or patronized in order to serve globally.

The Hispanic churches also learned that through what Kelly McClelland calls "contextual church partnerships" (personal communication, 2006) they could learn the needed "hows" of effective cross-cultural ministries as well as ways to keep their personnel on the field long-

347

term. Look for American Hispanic churches to join their brothers and sisters from Latin America, such as COMIBAM, Recursos Estratégicos Globales, and other groups, in long-term, contextual, holistic global missions. Look also for numerous former "receiving" nations to become strong "sending" countries, with their own training centers, trainers, and support systems.

Implications for future cross-cultural workers: For years, Westerners took up the pioneer role, following the example of the apostle Paul, who went where the gospel was yet to be heard (Rom. 15:20). And for the most part, they were successful, giving birth to strong national churches around the world. The pioneer role, generally, certainly not totally, is now taken up by the nationals who desire to expand God's kingdom locally and globally. What are some of the implications for those heading into missions?

While some will still want to concentrate on reaching unreached peoples, a great number of new personnel will be required to facilitate rising national movements that have or will launch into cross-cultural missions. From Hispanics, African Americans, and First Nations peoples in North America, to Africans, Chinese, Indians, Koreans, Latinos, and Filipinos abroad, those who have the gifts and skills to facilitate missions movements will be greatly needed.

The facilitator role is broad in application, including such ministries as church planting, film, comics, digital books, community development, and information technology. Through partnerships and networks, Western Christian workers provide dedicated national workers with whatever it takes to make them effective in their service, whether among their own people or cross-culturally.

Does your spiritual gift inventory and skill set push you toward facilitator roles? Do you get excited if those you train can do it better than you? If so, can you take up this role in humility? One without the other will not work. The facilitator role also assumes that you have some experience in the ministry areas you will facilitate. What pre-field cross-cultural ministry experience can you gain so that when you arrive you speak from experience?

Another outcome of the proliferation of others into missions will be multinational teams. Multinational teams will call for workers who can not only minister cross-culturally but also work with teammates from different cultures in loving relationships that glorify God (John 13:35). Before joining a multinational team, learn not only their philosophy of ministry but also what lingua franca is used by the team, how conflict is resolved, how raised finances are dispersed among teammates, and how work and play are defined (see M. S. Harrison 1983; Roembke 2000).

TREND 6: MINISTRIES TO CHILDREN WILL PROLIFERATE

The mission world, which has tended to focus on reaching adults, will now (rightly) turn its attention to children as well. With one-sixth of the world's children living in crisis, it will attempt to address critical social and spiritual issues faced by those who represent the future. Some of the glaring social issues include HIV/AIDS, abandonment, being sold as sex slaves or placed as combatants in military conflicts, high suicide rates, and one child death from hunger every seven seconds. This generation of cross-cultural Christian workers, like Jesus, will prioritize ministries to children.

Implications for future cross-cultural workers: Cross-cultural ministry teams will want to include those capable of ministering to children with a variety of needs. These teammates must be able to handle stories of years of heartbreak and hate as they will hear and see the results of the depths of evil. But they can become the moms and dads that many of these children never had, showing them the love of Christ.

TREND 7: LARGE MISSIONAL CHURCHES WILL MULTIPLY IN NORTH AMERICA

Thankfully, a significant number of churches are (re)discovering the missional nature of the church and desire to use their talents, treasures, and vacations to spread the gospel around the world through ordinary people. One such example, as noted earlier in the book, is Rick Warren's PEACE plan. The Saddleback Church has chosen Rwanda to become the first purpose-driven nation through implementation of the PEACE plan, which relies on programs such as church planting "in a box" and community development "in a box."

Other PEACE plans and "in-a-box" programs will proliferate. Will these well-intentioned missional megachurches take advantage of the lessons learned by years of missionary experience, or will they go it alone? Will the global McDonaldization of "proven programs" be the best way to reach the world? Which parts of the world? What level of missiological astuteness is required to contextualize the plans for specific audiences? Some will learn fast. Others will die a quick death, such as Bruce Wilkerson's Dream for Africa (DFA) begun in Swaziland (2002–5).

Implications for future cross-cultural workers: Missions that results in genuine Christian movements requires much more than people, finances, and a plan. It requires strong relationships with the indigenous people, which takes time to develop. It requires incarnation as modeled by Jesus's coming to this earth and residing in the context in which he would serve. Time together with the indigenous people will raise in the recipients questions that require answers rather than presupposed questions introduced by outsiders, which may not scratch where they itch. It will require building strong partnerships with those (locals and expatriates) who understand the context and are not just missional but also missiologically astute. And while it can and should use amateurs, it will require more than amateurs.

Missions in this century requires people who desire to spend time building and maintaining strong relationships, learning about the needs from the perspective of the indigenous people, and partnering with them and others to develop solutions that result in long-term transformation glorifying the King of kings.

TREND 8: SHORT-TERM MISSIONS WILL MATURE AND MULTIPLY

The tremendous influx of short-termers has impacted not only career Christian workers but nationals as well. As the movement matures, more attention must be given to assure long-term impact through short-term efforts. For example, if a person with linguistic limitations spends only a few weeks in a location, he or she will find it quite difficult to build quality relationships. In collective societies where relationships rule, where the amount of time spent with someone signifies the level of intimacy, where privacy is virtually unheard of, ministry effectiveness is impaired. Nationals cry out, "Make room for us in your hearts" (2 Cor. 7:2; see sidebar 11.6).

For many Western expatriates, particularly for those coming from broken families, relationships do not carry the same value. Individualism, privacy, and independence seem normal, even valued. Such normality, however, tends to distance the short-termers from those they have come to reach because intimacy expectations differ. Transforming discipleship often results through meaningful relationships; therefore quality relationships are not optional. Relationships, to a great extent, determine results.

Becoming cognizant of the limitations of short stays, short-termers need to intentionally seek ways to make sure that the relationships they have started with nationals continue long after their departure. Will this include the long-termers, who often provide entrée into a community and ongoing follow-up after departure?

> *According to the National Study of Youth and Religion, 29 percent of three thousand U.S. teens age thirteen to seventeen have been on a religious mission trip at least once in their life. Eighteen percent have been on two or more mission trips or service projects, and 10 percent have been on three or more mission trips or service projects.*
>
> www.youthandreligion.org/ news/2004-0811.html (August 24, 2006)

Another area of growth will be in the area of ministry expectations. In *Serving with Eyes Wide Open*, Dave Livermore (2006) raises a central question: "Do we do at home what we travel over seas and mountains to do?" Senders will raise the bar in training (culture and language acquisition requirements) and ministry experience for those who desire to participate in short-term trips (see Steffen 2001, 213–30).

With an estimated 1.6 million short-termers going out internationally from US churches in 2005, a significant amount of funding once tagged for long-term ministries has been siphoned from their side of the ledger, making them an endangered species (see Priest et al. 2006).

Implications for future cross-cultural workers: Those seeking to minister cross-culturally in specific ways should take advantage of every opportunity to do the same type of ministry on the home front before going cross-cultural. Gain whatever experience you can here. When you cross cultures, ask nationals and expatriates how this type of ministry will have to be contextualized for the audience so that it can be understood and reproduced. Once there, begin building those friendships. When you return home, make sure you keep up with the e-mails you promised. Relational-oriented societies' understanding of friendship demands it.

TREND 9: FUNDING FOR LONG-TERM MISSIONARIES WILL SLOWLY DRY UP

With many North American churches making missions a low priority, with the increase in short-termers eating up a growing percentage of the mission budget, with it taking around two years to raise needed support, career missionaries are seeking alternative ways to pay the bills. Some will start Great Commission companies. Others will take up professional roles that provide a paycheck. As the resources dry up in the local churches, the fulfillment of the Great Commission will continue because creative career-bound cross-cultural Christian workers will discover alternative support models. And these models may take them even closer to the people they wish to reach for Christ, even as it moves them further away from those who could back them through prayer and finances. Move over fully paid positions; bivocationalism is back!

Implications for future cross-cultural workers: How will you secure financial support? Do you have a skill set that could provide you a living? Should you? In some parts of the world hostile to Christianity, there is no choice. Yes, your preparation time will expand, but so will your ministry opportunities and your time with nationals as you work beside them day by day. Remember, you have some excellent New Testament bivocational models: Paul, following the rabbi model, was required to learn a trade (Acts 18:3; 1 Cor. 4:12; 2 Thess. 3:7–9), and Priscilla and

351

Aquila were also tentmakers as they planted three churches in three different areas (Acts 18:3, 26; Rom. 16:5; 1 Cor. 16:19). Should you become totally self-supporting, do not forget to secure prayer support from friends associated with churches.

TREND 10: MINISTRY POSSIBILITIES WILL PROLIFERATE

What does a cross-cultural Christian worker do? The answer to this question will expand far beyond the stereotypical roles of evangelists or church multipliers. Some workers will include TESOL teachers, businesspeople, ethnoartists, ethnomusicians, medical personnel, curriculum developers, Web developers, technicians, Bible translators, consultants, lawyers, and mass media personnel. A rediscovered understanding of a "theology of work" will widen the scope of legitimate ministry possibilities (see Stevens 1991; Yamamori and Eldred 2003). Genuine ministry will be seen as using God's gifts and talents through the power of the Holy Spirit to make a difference in the world. This makes the personnel possibilities multiple and the time frames unlimited.

Implications for future cross-cultural workers: With new definitions will come new concerns. Will each specialist seriously strategize ways to integrate "making disciples"? Will business personnel develop a ministry plan that integrates with their business plan? Will TESOL teachers have a ministry plan that integrates with lesson plans? Will Bible translators also assist in the planting of multiplying holistic communities of faith that use the translation? Will as much energy be dedicated to spiritual transformation as to social transformation?

If cross-cultural workers continue to be influenced by the Enlightenment, making it possible to bifurcate ministry from work or other activities, rather than take a first-century holistic view of the world that made such distinctions impossible, then the debate of primacy (e.g., evangelism trumps work or social efforts) will continue.

If, however, these workers view the Bible as a sacred storybook and believe that all the books and letters must be taken seriously to define both mandates, then primacy will no longer be the issue. The issue will be *ultimacy.* Starting points may differ, as evident in Jesus's ministry and throughout Acts, where sometimes miracles preceded the message or vice versa, but ultimacy calls for both to eventually be covered. Ministry integration without compromising either mandate will be one of the chief challenges of the twenty-first century. Your view of the Bible, work, and the world will determine the outcome to this fifty-plus-year debate (see Wright 2006, 265–323 for an excellent discussion on primacy and ultimacy).

A second concern will be the wisdom of sending amateurs to participate in missions. Does a few hours studying TESOL, buying some textbooks, and heading for a distant part of the world qualify you as a TESOL teacher? Does a trip overseas to start a business with little or no experience in business at home qualify you to start a business in a different culture? Does your love for music or art qualify you as an ethnomusicologist, ethnodoxologist, or ethnoartist? Does receiving a few cognitive-focused seminars on church multiplication from a training institute qualify you as a cross-cultural church multiplier or facilitator?

The growing practice of commissioning shallowly trained and inexperienced personnel is what Ralph Winter calls the "re-amateurization of missions" (1996). This legitimate concern, however, is not new. The Moravians and the Basel Mission preferred qualified professional recruits because "[s]uch work calls for specialists and professionals rather than for clerical amateurs. When the latter [amateurs] dabble in it, they often bring harm to both the mission and economic activities" (Danker 1971, 136–37). J. I. Packer raised a similar concern: "The blunderings of sanctified amateurism, impervious to the need to get qualified in the area where one hopes to function, are neither good Christianity nor good business" (1990, 24). Genuine dedication, availability, or brief training does not necessarily translate into missionary astuteness.

One of Clint Eastwood's famous movie lines is appropriate to the discussion: "A man [and, we would add, a woman] has to know his [her] limitations." Participation in missions by amateurs is healthy, but it does have its limitations. We think it was Mary Wong who wisely pointed out that the "best witness is professionalism." Will amateurs do all they can through networks and partnerships with the experienced to demonstrate professionalism in their specific field? When practitioners and professionals fulfill their role responsibility, short-term or long-term, God is glorified and his kingdom is expanded.

TREND 11: LIFE EXPERIENCE WILL BE APPRECIATED AND APPROPRIATED

Unlike former times when mission agencies refused to accept those who had reached a certain chronological age, churches and agencies of the twenty-first century will welcome those with life experience. Intergenerational teams will become the norm. This will be a learning process for some coming from age-based grades in school and Sunday school. Others, however, will not find it difficult and will enjoy the contributions that different generations bring to ministry. In societies where age matters, nationals will give greater credence to those intergenerational teams with some gray-haired members. The twenty-first century will see the largest number ever of well-educated, healthy, wealthy, young retirees to participate in global missions from the West.

Implications for future cross-cultural workers: Become involved in intergenerational activities now. Learn from the life experiences of others. Let their wisdom gained through heartaches and joy become part of you. To help anticipate possible reactions of other generations to your thinking and actions and to understand yourself better, study the history that helped develop the values of different generations: veterans, boomers, Xers, Nexters (see Zemke, Raines, and Filipczak 2000).

Trend 12: E-care Will Become Recognized as a Legitimate Form of Member Care

While certainly not the only means of member care, e-mail together with Internet telephony will become a fast, immediate, personal, and inexpensive means to identify, clarify, and rectify issues faced by individuals on the field. While not substituting for on-site visits, e-care will make the time between such visits strong opportunities for ongoing personal growth.

Implications for future cross-cultural workers: Assuming you reside in an area where the electricity usually works, you can expect frequent check-ins from those responsible for your oversight. Through Skype, video calls are now possible and cheap. Reaching the emotional state that Lottie Moon came to at the end of her ministry no longer has to happen. Help is only a fingertip away.

Trend 13: Storytelling and Symbols Will Increase in Importance

Storytelling will become a legitimate means to communicate all aspects of a holistic Christianity globally in missions circles. Once considered a mode of communication primarily for children, story has been rescued for the adult Western world as well, thanks in part to the postmodern world. Expect mission personnel to become competent storytellers in all aspects of holistic ministries. Human stories will be used to teach about HIV/AIDS, community development, evangelism, discipleship, church multiplication, theology (focused on Bible characters), business, the disabled, and so forth.

Nor will the role of symbols be overlooked. For example, with inexpensive video cameras, every person can become a video producer. No formal schooling is necessary. Leading church ministries in the United States are already taking advantage of video-sharing sites such as YouTube .com to get their messages out to a broader public (see, for example, www .youtube.com/watch?v=8RtfNdg1fQk). In addition to videos, media such as paintings, sculptures, comics, landscape art, architecture, and digital novels will engage a welcoming world. Digital media will break down previous barriers of distribution, making it inexpensive to blitz a large audience with immediate impact. Integrated stories (verbal) and symbols (visual) will make a strong comeback, wedding imagination with reason, thereby enhancing communication for a global postmodern world that prefers visual literacy. Even so, will the creative producers be aware of the cultural differences of symbols (and stories), not assuming that what's understood by their culture will automatically be understood in the same way by another?

Implications for future cross-cultural workers: Learn how to tell engaging stories. For evangelism, use the stories of Bible characters to teach abstract, propositional concepts. The story of Adam can teach about sin, the fall of humankind, and God's promise. Noah's story offers critical insights on judgment, obedience, and hope. Abraham's extended saga teaches not only justification by faith but also forgiveness, restoration, and God's provision.

The adept cross-cultural servant will also learn how to use symbols to communicate (tablet, throne, cross). You can also do this for ministry or a discipline specialty. Your ability to tie stories and symbols together will have a definite impact not only on comprehension but also on your audience's ability to communicate to others what they have learned.

TREND 14: BIBLE TRANSLATION WILL INCLUDE THE "REST OF THE STORY"

For decades most Bible translators have begun in the New Testament, often with Mark. Only 426 of the 2,400 language groups that have portions of the Bible today have a full Bible. Of the 1,700 translations under way presently, some 500 of them are estimated to be full Bible projects.

Various reasons have been given for skipping over 75 percent of the sacred story (Old Testament), such as (1) the Old Testament is too long; (2) the Gospels are shorter to translate; (3) there are too few qualified Bible translators; and (4) completing one of the Gospels makes evangelism possible. Today, a growing number of translators recognize, thanks in part to chronological Bible teaching and the recognition of the story nature of Scripture (having a beginning, middle, and end), that the New Testament, the last 25 percent of the story, requires a firm foundation to help avoid faulty results, such as syncretism. Without at least some Old Testament, the New Testament will not make sense. More and more Bible translators will discover that it is best to begin at the beginning, rescuing the literary nature of the sacred storybook while providing a total way of life to transform recipients.

Implications for future cross-cultural workers: Several things may be pointed out. First, learn the Old Testament: know the key characters and the historical sweep that it covers, be able to write the theme of the Old Testament in a sentence, and be able to tell the Old Testament in a story. From evangelism to discipleship to Sunday sermons, most Christians from the United States have been taught from the New Testament with only a token tip of the hat to the Old Testament. This must change if we are to take seriously the literary nature of the Bible (see Ryken 1984).

TREND 15: EDUCATION FOR MISSIONS WILL BE MODIFIED DRAMATICALLY

Mission education will not necessarily be tied to the prestigious seminaries, colleges, or universities in the twenty-first century. In a globalized, blogisphere world, small can emerge big. Some, therefore, will reject formal education entirely, relying on searches, Web-based repositories, blogs, and chat rooms to gain needed information in a fast, immediate, and inexpensive way. Taking years to gain an "education" that will soon be outdated (a new generation of thinking takes place every five years presently) and spending the exorbitant amount of money necessary to earn a degree just do not seem to make sense. So far this view represents only a minority, but that minority is growing. These individuals prefer to collaborate and connect rather than be commanded or controlled; they prefer to work on a vertical level rather than a horizontal one.

Megachurches and consortiums of churches take another approach, educating their personnel often with little attention given to accreditation or missiology. Their theology, typically systematic and devoid of the Bible narratives that inform theology, will be strong but often presented from the narrowness of a Western perspective. Topics relevant in many parts of the world tend to be overlooked because they are perceived as nonissues in North America. These may include visions, dreams, demons, spirits, manna, the evil eye, healings, spiritual guidance, shamanism, ancestor veneration, polygamy, justice, poverty, economics, and politics.

One reason for this may be that the textbooks being studied by teachers and students in formal and nonformal settings are often woefully inadequate for missions training. For example, in fifty-seven chapters spanning 1,290 pages, Wayne Grudem's *Systematic Theology* does not include key terms such as "*missio Dei*," "mission," "justice," "missions," the "kingdom of God," or non-Western topics in the chapter titles. The same is true of Millard Erickson's *Christian Theology*, which contains fifty-nine chapters spanning 1,302 pages. Erickson does include, however, "Social Sin" (17 pages) and the "Role of the Church" (17 pages). This raises an interesting question for twenty-first-century missions: Although the Bible is complete, are our theological categories still lacking?

356

Implications for future cross-cultural workers: In the formal educational setting, particularly on the graduate level, residential programs are already being supplemented by online courses, virtual classes, and one- to two-week modular courses on and off campus. Students will prefer to complete degrees that offer them multiple choices for completion: online, modular, campus, extension, and distance education campuses. They will also demand opportunity to immediately apply what they are learning. Reflection praxis, or classroom instruction followed by extended time for practice, will rule the day for some. This may lengthen the time to graduation, but an appreciation for lifelong education will offset the negatives.

Wise graduate schools will take advantage of modular and other distance education options to take their programs to the students rather than requiring students to come to North American campuses. Numerous benefits will result if they do so. Among others, they will reduce the cost of formal education, keep cross-cultural Christian workers on the field (benefiting family stability and agencies by filling leadership roles), reduce the brain drain of nationals who decide to stay in North America after completing their degrees, provide opportunity for immediate application of learning, and keep faculty on the cutting edge and more global in perspective.

The Bible will become a better-taught story because the curricula will continue to become more relevant for intended audiences. Traditionally Bible curricula from the West were taken to the rest of the world and translated verbatim. These "global" curricula (one-for-all) were considered applicable for the world. While some missions still follow this practice, among many in the majority world this has resulted in a negative reaction and calls for establishing local contextualized curricula (for each unique setting). Each people group deserves its own curriculum. This type of demand may work well when working with specific people groups, but the urban setting presents a much more complex world that demands a different approach. "Glocal" curricula (one-for-some) will meet the needs of a "multifaceted cultural mosaic." Globalization creates the need for a glocal Bible curriculum that can reach a broad urban audience.

With focus given to the 10/40 window and secularized countries, such as those in Europe, many more students will prefer to double major on the undergraduate level. They will recognize the need not only for mission-related topics, but a professional skill set as well. Schools that offer cross-disciplinary courses will flourish.

Another reaction will be the preference of some for nonformal training over formal education. This often means a shorter, less-expensive course of study, narrower in scope but touching specifically on relevant topics

357

and issues. In a world of "over-choice," this approach keeps a student focused like a laser beam on the necessities rather than possibilities and peripheries.

Whether through formal or nonformal means, each set of teachers will face students who will be theologically challenged. The uniqueness of Christ, hell, the Great Commission, Old Testament characters, to cite just a few topics, will require major rework.

What are the implications for today's missionaries-in-progress? Most importantly, you need to know the Bible. Make sure you understand the key teachings of Scripture. As you do this, make sure your understanding of the sacred storybook goes beyond Western theology. If you have a specific people group in mind that you desire to work with, begin to identify the non-Western theologies that will require answers, and then search for solutions. Learn to develop a curriculum that speaks to an intended cross-cultural audience rather than transport your own classes from the West. If you are presently an undergraduate student, a good question to consider is your major. Is it sufficient preparation for your future, or should you go for a double major? Identify the blogs that address your future cross-cultural ministry. As you plan your lifelong education career, consider the variety of quality opportunities now available on the field.

SUMMARY

Missionaries ministering in the twenty-first century can expect to serve in an atmosphere of constant change. Missions will be conducted everywhere, in every way, by everyone. This will demand lifelong learning and lifelong humility. Are you ready to join in the journey? The ride will be exciting, demanding strong faith, passion, patience, character, and a lot of hard work, but it comes with present and eternal rewards. Begin with strong, thorough pre-field and on-field preparation so that you can finish well. Our hope is that your generation will far surpass the behavior and efforts of previous generations. We believe it can and will.

Appendix

Helpful Web Sites

The following Web sites are intended to help you explore some of the topics and groups mentioned in the book. They do not include search engines, which should always be part of your initial efforts to learn more about the topic you are exploring. Note that all URLs are assumed to start with http:// unless otherwise noted.

ASSOCIATIONS AND SOCIETIES

Aotearoa New Zealand Society for Mission Studies (ANZAMS)	www.missionstudies.org/anzams
American Society of Missiology	www.asmweb.org
Association of Professors of Mission	www.asmweb.org/apm
British and Irish Association for Mission Studies (BIAMS)	www.martynmission.cam.ac.uk/BIAMS.htm
EFMA	www.community.gospelcom.net
Evangelical Missiological Society	www.emsweb.org
Fellowship of Missions	www.fellowshipofmissions.org
Gospel and Our Culture Network	www.gocn.org
IFMA	www.ifmamissions.org
International Association for Mission Studies	www.missionstudies.org
MisLinks Mission Societies	www.mislinks.org/research/societies.htm

BOOKS

Evangelism and Missions Information Service (EMIS)	bgc.gospelcom.net/emis
Intercultural Press	www.interculturalpress.com
MARC Resources	www.mislinks.org/info/books.htm
MisLinks Books Online	www.mislinks.org/info/books.htm
MisLinks Publishers	www.mislinks.org/info/publishers.htm
Missionary E-Texts Archive	www.missionaryetexts.org
Orbis Books	www.orbisbooks.com
William Carey Library	www.missionbooks.org
YWAM Books	www.ywam.org/books

BUSINESS AS MISSION

Business as Mission Blogspot	businessasmission.blogspot.com
Business Professional Network	www.bpn.org
EC Institute	www.ec-i.org
Global Opportunities	www.globalopps.org
Integra Venture	www.integra.sk
Scruples	www.scruples.net

CHURCH PLANTING

A Church Planter's Paradise	www.church-planting.org
Church Multiplication Associates	www.organicchurchplanting.org
Global Church Advancement	www.gca.cc
House Church Central	www.hccentral.com
Resources for Cross-Cultural Church Planting	www.ideateam.org

DIRECTORIES

Education and Training

Indigenous People's Technology and Education Center (I-TEC)	www.I-TECusa.org
INSIGHT	www.uscwm.org/insight
Institute for Cross-Cultural Training	www.wheaton.edu/bgc/ICCT
MisLinks Schools and Training Programs	www.mislinks.org/research/progs.htm
Missiology.org	www.missiology.org
Mission Training International	www.mti.org
Perspectives Study Program	www.perspectives.org

Evangelism

Bulletin of Web Evangelism	guide.gospelcom.net/resources/bulletin.php
Gospel.com	www.gospel.org
Lausanne Committee for World Evangelization	www.lausanne.org
MisLinks Evangelism	www.mislinks.org/church/evangelism.htm

Fund-Raising

Ask a Missionary	www.thejourneydeepens.com/askamissionary.asp
The Body Builders (Support-Raising BootCamp)	www.thebodybuilders.net
MisLinks Fundraising	www.mislinks.org/practical/funds.htm
People Raising	www.peopleraising.com

Journals

Connections	www.wearesources.org
eJournal: *Global Missiology*	www.emqonline.com
Evangelical Missions Quarterly	www.GlobalMissiology.net
International Journal of Frontier Missions	www.ijfm.org/archives.htm
Journal of Asian Mission	www.apts.edu/jam
Lausanne Occasional Papers	www.lausanne.org/Brix?pageID=12890
MisLinks Periodicals page	www.mislinks.org/research/periodicals.html
Missiology: An International Review	www.asmweb.org/missiology.htm
Mission Frontiers	www.missionfrontiers.org

Member Care

Cares	www.cares.ca
Eastern South America Member Care Services	ministryserver.com/others/esac/ESAcare.htm
Global Member Care Resources	www.membercare.org
Interaction International	www.tckinteract.net
Mental Health Resources for Cross-Cultural Workers	www.crossculturalworkers.com/ebooks.htm
MisLinks Member Care	www.mislinks.org/practical/membcare.htm
Missionary Care	www.missionarycare.com

Missionary Kids and Families

Families in Global Transition	www.figt.org
International Society for Missionary Kids	www.ismk.org
MisLinks MK Weblinks	www.mislinks.org/practical/mk.htm

361

MK Connection	www.mknet.org
MK Planet	www.mkplanet.com
Mu Kappa	www.mukappa.org
TCK World	www.tckworld.com

Mobilization

AD 2000 and Beyond Movement	www.ad2000.org
Adopt-A-People Clearinghouse	www.adoptapeople.org
AIMS (Accelerating International Mission Strategies)	www.aims.org
Antioch Network	www.antiochnetwork.org
Finishers Project	www.finishers.org/core.html
Initiative 360	acmcnetwork.com
National Short Term Mission Conference	www.nstmc.org
Short-Term Evangelism/Missions	www.STEMmin.org
Student Mobilization	www.stumo.org
Transforming Teachers	www.transformingteachers.org
Urbana	www.urbana.org

News and Information

Brigada Today	www.brigada.org
Global Prayer Digest	www.global-prayer-digest.org
Lausanne WorldPulse	www.lausanneworldpulse.com
MisLinks Missions News Sources	www.mislinks.org/practical/news.htm
Operation World	www.operationworld.org
Persecuted Church	www.persecutedchurch.org

Relief and Development

Association of Evangelical Relief and Development Organizations	www.aerdo.net
MAP (Medical Assistance Programs)	www.map.org
MisLinks Relief and Development Organizations	www.mislinks.org/practical/rdorgs.htm
World Vision International	www.wvi.org

Research Centers

Barna Research Group	www.barna.org
Billy Graham Center Archives	www.wheaton.edu/bgc/archives/archhp1.html
Caleb Project	www.calebproject.org
Centre for Evangelism & Global Mission	www.cegm.org.au

Network for Strategic Missions	www.strategicnetwork.org
Overseas Ministries Study Center	www.omsc.org
Oxford Centre for Mission Studies	www.ocms.ac.uk
U.S. Center for World Mission	www.uscwm.org

Reference List

Adams, Robert McAnally. N.d. "Christian Quotations of the Day for January, 2002." http://cqod.gospelcom.net/cqod0201. htm#q020125 (accessed March 30, 2006).

Adeney, Bernard T. 1995. *Strange Virtues: Ethics in a Multicultural World.* Downers Grove, IL: InterVarsity.

Adorno, Theodor, et al. 1982. *The Authoritarian Personality.* New York: Norton.

Allen, Catherine. 1980. *The New Lottie Moon Story.* Nashville: Broadman.

Allen, Roland. 1962. *The Spontaneous Expansion of the Church and the Causes Which Hinder It.* Grand Rapids: Eerdmans.

Anderson, Darrell. N.d. "Define Your Terms." http://simpleliberty.nfshost.com/main/ define_your_terms.htm (accessed February 9, 2007).

Anderson, Gerald H. 1998. *Biographical Dictionary of Christian Missions,* gen. ed. Gerald H. Anderson, s.v. "Kane, J(ames) Herbert." Grand Rapids: Eerdmans.

Anderson, P. A., M. L. Hecht, and S. A. Ribeau. 1989. "The Cultural Dimensions of Nonverbal Communication." In *Handbook of International and Intercultural Communication,* ed. Molefi Kete Asante

and Willam B. Gudykunst, 163–85. Newbury Park, CA: Sage.

Anderson, Sherry Ruth, and Paul H. Ray. 2001. *The Cultural Creatives: How Fifty Million People Are Changing the World.* New York: Three Rivers Press.

Austin, Clyde N. 1986. "Interpersonal Stresses from Living in a Cross-Cultural Environment." In *International Conference on Missionary Kids (1984): New Direction in Missions,* ed. Paul Nelson, 132–48. West Brattleboro, VT: ICMK.

———. 1987. "Cross-Cultural Re-entry." In *Intercultural Skills for Multicultural Societies,* ed. Carley Dodd and Frank Montalvo, 70–82. Washington, DC: SEITAR.

———. 2000. "Missionary Reentry." *Resources Newsletter* (July). Missions Resource Network. http://www.mrnet.org/ Content/Documents/Library/Missionary %20Clyde%20Austin.pdf (accessed August 24, 2006).

Austin, Clyde N., and Billy Van Jones. 1987. "Reentry among Missionary Children: An Overview of Reentry Research from 1934–1986." *Journal of Psychology and Theology* 15 (9): 315–25.

Austin, Thomas L. 2000. *Evangelical Dictionary of World Missions,* ed. A. Scott

Moreau, s.v. "The Missionary Call." Grand Rapids: Baker Academic.

Baker, Dwight P. 2000. "Resources for Mission Facilitators." *The Covenant Quarterly* 58 (2): 3–16.

Baker, Karle Wilson. N.d. "Courage." http://www.geocities.com/heartland/lane/2470/courage.htm (accessed March 26, 2006).

Banister, Doug. 2004. *We're All in the Family Business: A Story about Faith, Work and Destiny*. Kingston, TN: William & Warren.

Barclay, William. 1975. *The Letter to the Romans*. Edinburgh: Saint Andrew Press.

Barna Group. 2005. "Americans Donate Billions to Charity, but Giving to Churches Has Declined." http://www.barna.org/FlexPage.aspx?Page=BarnaUpdate&BarnaUpdateID=187 (accessed January 18, 2007).

Barnett, Betty. 1991. *Friend Raising: Building a Missionary Support Team That Lasts*. Seattle: YWAM.

Barrett, David B., George M. Kurian, and Todd M. Johnson. 2001. *World Christian Encyclopedia: A Comparative Survey of Churches and Religions in the Modern World*. 2nd ed. New York: Oxford University Press.

Barry, William A., and William J. Connolly. 1982. *The Practice of Spiritual Direction*. New York: Seabury Press.

Beaver, R. Pierce. 1968. *American Protestant Women in World Mission*. Grand Rapids: Eerdmans.

———. 1976. "The American Protestant Theological Seminary and Missions: An Historical Survey." *Missiology: An International Review* 4 (January): 75–87.

Bennis, Warren G. 2001. "The Future Has No Shelf Life." In *The Future of Leadership: Today's Top Leadership Thinkers Speak to Tomorrow's Leaders*, ed. Warren G. Bennis, Gretchen M. Spreitzer, and Thomas G. Cummings, 3–13. San Francisco: Jossey-Bass.

Biber, Douglas, Susan Conrad, and Geoffrey Leech. 2002. *Longman Student Grammar of Spoken and Written English*. Harlow, Essex, UK: Pearson ESL.

Blocher, Detlef. 2005. "Good Agency Practices: Lessons from ReMAP II." *Evangelical Missions Quarterly* 41 (April): 228–37.

Bonhoeffer, Dietrich. 1949. *The Cost of Discipleship*. New York: Macmillan.

Boomershine, Thomas E. 1988. *Story Journey: An Invitation to the Gospel as Storytelling*. Nashville: Abingdon.

Bosch, David J. 1982. "Theological Education in Missionary Perspective." *Missiology: An International Review* 10 (January): 13–34.

———. 1991. *Transforming Mission: Paradigm Shifts in Theology of Mission*. Maryknoll, NY: Orbis.

Bourdieu, Pierre. 1977. *Outline of a Theory of Practice*. New York: Cambridge University Press.

"Brainy Quote." N.d. http://www.brainyquote.com/quotes/authors/d/dwight_d_eisenhower.html (accessed June 19, 2007).

Brewster, Elizabeth S. 2000a. *Evangelical Dictionary of World Missions*, ed. A. Scott Moreau, s.v. "Bonding." Grand Rapids: Baker Academic.

———. 2000b. *Evangelical Dictionary of World Missions*, ed. A. Scott Moreau, s.v. "Language Schools." Grand Rapids: Baker Academic.

———. 2000c. *Evangelical Dictionary of World Missions*, ed. A. Scott Moreau, s.v. "Second Language Acquisition." Grand Rapids: Baker Academic.

Brewster, Tom, and Elizabeth S. Brewster. 1976. *Language Acquisition Made Practical: Field Methods for Language Learners*. Colorado Springs: Lingua House.

Bridges, Erich. 2004. "Why?" *Florida Baptist Witness* (March 25). http://www.floridabaptistwitness.com/2863.article.print (accessed January 15, 2007).

Brierley, Peter W. 1997. "Missionary Attrition: The ReMAP Research Report." In *Too Valuable to Lose*, ed. William D. Taylor, 228–37. Pasadena, CA: William Carey Library.

Brierley, Peter, and Heather Wraight. 1998. *Atlas of World Christianity: A Complete Visual Reference to Christianity Worldwide, Including Growth Trends into the New Millennium*. Nashville: Thomas Nelson.

Brislin, Richard. 1981. *Cross-Cultural Encounters: Face-to-Face Interaction*. Boston: Allyn & Bacon.

Brown, Arthur Judson. 1950. *The Foreign Missionary: Yesterday and Today*. New York: Revell.

Brown, Donald E. 1991. *Human Universals*. Philadelphia: Temple University Press.

Brown, Robert K., and Mark R. Norton, eds. 1995. *The One Year Book of Hymns*. Wheaton: Tyndale House.

Burnham, Gracia, with Dean Merrill. 2003. *In the Presence of My Enemies*. Wheaton: Tyndale House.

———. 2005. *To Fly Again*. Wheaton: Tyndale House.

Bush, Luis. 2003. "The AD 2000 Movement." In *Between Past and Future: Evangelical Mission Entering the Twenty-first Century*, ed. Jonathan J. Bonk, EMS Series 10, 17–36. Pasadena, CA: William Carey Library.

Bush, Luis, and Lorry Lutz. 1990. *Partnering in Ministry: The Direction of World Evangelism*. Downers Grove, IL: InterVarsity.

Cable, Mildred, and Francesca French. 1946. *Ambassadors for Christ*. Chicago: Moody.

Camp, Bruce. 2003. "A Survey of the Local Church's Involvement in Global/Local Outreach." In *Between Past and Future: Evangelical Mission Entering the Twenty-first Century*, ed. Jonathan J. Bonk, EMS Series 10, 203–47. Pasadena, CA: William Carey Library.

Camps, A., L. A. Hoedemaker, and Marc R. Spindler. 1995. *Missiology: An Ecumenical Introduction*. Grand Rapids: Eerdmans.

CardWeb.com. 2002. "Minimum Payments (3/7/02)." http://www.cardweb.com/cardtrak/news/2002/march/7a.html (accessed January 18, 2006).

———. 2006. "Debt Levels 5/30/2006." http://www.cardweb.com/cardtrak/news/2006/may/30a.html (accessed January 18, 2006).

Chole, Alicia Britt. 2000. *Until the Whole World Knows: Discovering Our Part in the Plan near God's Heart*. Rogersville, MO: Onewholeworld.

Christian History Institute. 1996. "What Happened This Day in Church History: October 7, 1873: Extraordinary Lottie Moon Reached China." http://chi.gospelcom.net/DAILYF/2001/10/daily-10-07-2001.shtml (accessed March 30, 2006).

Clouse, Bonnidell, and Robert G. Clouse, eds. 1989. *Women in Ministry: Four Views*. Downers Grove, IL: InterVarsity.

Cohen, Jeffrey. 2002. *Economic Development: An Anthropological Approach*. Walnut Creek, CA: Rowman & Littlefield.

Collard, Dianne B. 2004. "The Role of Visual Art in the (Free) Evangelical Churches of Germany and Spain." DMiss diss., Biola University, School of Intercultural Studies.

Conn, Harvie M. 2000. *Evangelical Dictionary of World Missions*, ed. A. Scott Moreau, s.v. "Migration." Grand Rapids: Baker Academic.

Cook, Harold R. 1954. *An Introduction to the Study of Christian Missions*. Chicago: Moody.

———. 1971. *An Introduction to Christian Missions*. Chicago: Moody.

Covell, Ralph R. 2000a. *Evangelical Dictionary of World Missions*, ed. A. Scott Moreau, s.v. "Faith Missions." Grand Rapids: Baker Academic.

———. 2000b. *Evangelical Dictionary of World Missions*, ed. A. Scott Moreau, s.v. "Kane, J. Herbert." Grand Rapids: Baker Academic.

Covell, Ralph, and Marshall Shelley. 1982. "Permanent or Temporary?" *Wherever* 6 (Spring): 8–9.

Crouch, Andy. 2004. "The Emergent Mystique: The 'Emerging Church' Movement Has Generated a Lot of Excitement but Only a Handful of Congregations: Is

It the Wave of the Future or a Passing Fancy?" *Christianity Today* 48 (November): 36–41.

Culver, Robert D. 1989. "A Traditional View: Let Your Women Keep Silence." In *Women in Ministry: Four Views*, ed. Bonnidell Clouse and Robert G. Clouse, 25–52. Downers Grove, IL: InterVarsity.

Danielson, Edward E. 1984. *Missionary Kid (MK)*. Pasadena, CA: William Carey Library.

Danker, William J. 1971. *Profit for the Lord: Economic Activities in Moravian Missions and the Basel Mission Trading Company*. Grand Rapids: Eerdmans.

DeCarvalho, Levi. 2001. "What's Wrong with the Label Managerial Missiology." *International Journal of Frontier Missions* 18 (3): 141–46.

Demarest, Bruce. 1999. *Satisfy Your Soul: Restoring the Heart of Christian Spirituality*. Colorado Springs: NavPress.

Dickerson, Lonna J. N.d. "Resources for Language Learners." http://www.wheaton .edu/bgc/ICCT (accessed March 27, 2006).

———. 2004. *Planning for Success in Language Learning*. Wheaton: Institute for Cross-Cultural Training, Billy Graham Center, Wheaton College.

Dillenberger, John. 1999. *Images and Relics: Theological Perceptions and Visual Images in Sixteenth-Century Europe*. New York: Oxford University Press.

Dillon, William P. 1993. *People Raising: A Practical Guide to Raising Support*. Chicago: Moody.

Dodd, Carley H. 1998. *Dynamics of Intercultural Communication*. 5th ed. Boston: McGraw-Hill.

Dollar, Harold G. 2000. *Evangelical Dictionary of World Missions*, ed. A. Scott Moreau, s.v. "The Fruit of the Spirit." Grand Rapids: Baker Academic.

Downey, Karol. 2005. "Missionary or Wife? Four Needed Changes to Help Clarify the Role of a Missionary Wife." *Evangelical Missions Quarterly* 41 (January): 66–74.

Dye, T. Wayne. 1974. "Stress-Producing Factors in Cultural Adjustment." *Missiology: An International Review* 2 (January): 61–77.

Easterling, John. 2000. *Evangelical Dictionary of World Missions*, ed. A. Scott Moreau, s.v. "Deputation." Grand Rapids: Baker Academic.

Eddy, Daniel C. [1854]. *Daughters of the Cross: Or Woman's Mission*. http://www .gutenberg.org/dirs/etext05/7dcrs10.txt (accessed March 30, 2006).

Eenigenburg, Sue. 2001. "Women Muslims, Converts, Missionaries: Dealing with Fear." *Evangelical Missions Quarterly* (October): 480–85.

Eire, Carlos M. N. 1986. *War against the Idols: The Reformation of Worship from Erasmus to Calvin*. New York: Cambridge University Press.

Eldred, Ken. 2005. *God Is at Work: Transforming People and Nations through Business*. Ventura, CA: Regal.

Elmer, Duane. 1993. *Cross-Cultural Conflict: Building Relationships for Effective Ministry*. Downers Grove, IL: InterVarsity.

Elmer, Muriel I. 1986. "Intercultural Effectiveness: Development of an Intercultural Competency Scale." PhD diss., Michigan State University.

———. 1988. "The Intercultural Competency Scale: A Description of the Factors and the Total Score. Form E." Unpublished manuscript.

Engel, James F., and William A. Dyrness. 2000. *Changing the Mind of Missions: Where Have We Gone Wrong?* Downers Grove, IL: InterVarsity.

Erickson, Millard J. 1992. *Christian Theology*. Grand Rapids: Baker Academic.

Escobar, Samuel. 2000. "Evangelical Missiology: Peering into the Future at the Turn of the Century." In *Global Missiology for the Twenty-first Century*, ed. William J. Taylor, 101–22. Grand Rapids: Baker Academic.

———. 2003. "Migration: Avenue and Challenge to Mission." *Missiology: An International Review* 31 (1): 17–33.

Fernando, Ajith. 2002. *Jesus-Driven Ministry.* Wheaton: Crossway.

Ferris, Robert W. 2000. *Establishing Ministry Training: A Manual for Programme Developers.* Pasadena, CA: William Carey Library.

Finger, Thomas N. 1985. *Christian Theology: An Eschatological Approach.* Vol. 1. Nashville: Thomas Nelson. (Reprinted as part of 2 vols.: 1987–1989, Scottdale, PA: Herald.)

Finney, Paul Corby. 1999. *Seeing beyond the Word: Visual Arts and the Calvinist Tradition.* Grand Rapids: Eerdmans.

Foster, Richard J. 1988. *Celebration of Discipline: The Path to Spiritual Growth.* Rev. ed. San Francisco: Harper & Row.

———. 1998. *Streams of Living Water.* San Francisco: HarperSanFrancisco.

———. 2003. "A Pastoral Letter from Richard J. Foster." http://www.renovare.org/readings_heart_to heart_2003_May.htm (accessed August 24, 2006).

Foyle, Marjory F. 2001. *Honourably Wounded: Stress among Christian Workers.* Wheaton: Evangelical Missions Information Service.

Friedman, Thomas L. 2005. *The World Is Flat: A Brief History of the Twenty-first Century.* New York: Farrar, Straus & Giroux.

Friesen, Garry, with J. Robin Maxson. 1988. *Decision Making and the Will of God: A Biblical Alternative to the Traditional View.* Portland, OR: Multnomah.

Galli, Mark. 2004. "Baptism + Fire: Suffering May Build Character, but Ultimately It's Not about Us." *Christianity Today* 48 (December): 38–40, 42.

Garrison, David. 2003. *Church Planting Movements.* Midlothian, VA: Witgake.

Geertz, Clifford. 1973. *The Interpretation of Cultures.* New York: Basic Books.

Gehman, Richard J. 2005. "Transitioning Cross-Culturally—to the Good Old USA." *Evangelical Missions Quarterly* 41 (April): 174–78.

Glasser, Arthur F., with Charles E. Van Engen, Dean S. Gilliland, and Shawn B. Redford. 2003. *Announcing the Kingdom: The Story of God's Mission in the Bible.* Grand Rapids: Baker Academic.

Godfrey, W. Robert. 1996. "The Reformation of Worship." In *Here We Stand: A Call from Confessing Evangelicals,* ed. James Montgomery Boice and Benjamin E. Sasse, 157–72. Grand Rapids: Baker Academic.

Goldschmidt, Walter. 1966. *Comparative Functionalism.* Berkeley: University of California Press.

Goldsmith, Marshall, Beverly Kaye, and Ken Shelton, eds. 2000. *Learning Journeys: Top Management Experts Share Hard-Earned Lessons on Becoming Great Mentors and Leaders.* Palo Alto, CA: Davies-Black.

Goodenough, Ward. 1957. "Cultural Anthropology and Linguistics." In *Report of the Seventh Annual Round Table Meeting on Linguistics and Language Study,* 167–73. Washington, DC: Georgetown University.

Gordon, Alma Daugherty. 1993. *Don't Pig Out on Junk Food: The MK's Guide to Survival in the U.S.* Wheaton: Evangelical Missions Information Service.

Graham, Thomas. 1987. "How to Select the Best Church Planters." *Evangelical Missions Quarterly* 23 (January): 70–79.

"Grand Rapids Report: Evangelism and Social Responsibility: An Evangelical Commitment. 1982. Consultation on the Relationship between Evangelism and Social Responsibility (1982: Reformed Bible College, Grand Rapids, MI)." 1982. Lausanne Occasional Papers 21. Wheaton: Lausanne Committee for World Evangelization.

Grenz, Stanley J., and Denise Muir Kjesbo. 1995. *Women in the Church: A Biblical Theology of Women in Ministry.* Downers Grove, IL: InterVarsity.

Groothuis, Douglas. 2000. *Evangelical Dictionary of World Missions,* ed. A. Scott Moreau, s.v. "New Age Movement." Grand Rapids: Baker Academic.

Grudem, Wayne. 1994. *Systematic Theology: An Introduction to Biblical Doctrine.* Grand Rapids: Zondervan.

Gudykunst, William B., Stella Ting-Toomey, Bradford J. Hill, and Karen L. Schmidt. 1989. "Language and Intergroup Communication." In *Handbook of International and Intercultural Communication*, ed. Molefi Kete Asante and William B. Gudykunst, 145–62. Newbury Park, CA: Sage.

Gudykunst, William B., Stella Ting-Toomey, and Tsukasa Nishida. 1996. *Communication in Personal Relationships across Cultures*. Newbury Park, CA: Sage.

Guillemets, Terri, ed. N.d. "The Quote Garden." http://www.quotegarden.com (accessed March 26, 2006).

Guthrie, Donald. 1983. *The Pastoral Epistles: An Introduction and Commentary*. Grand Rapids: Eerdmans.

Guthrie, Stan. 2000. *Missions in the Third Millennium: Twenty-one Key Trends for the Twenty-first Century*. Carlisle, Cumbria, UK: Paternoster.

Haile, Dorothy. 2006. "Where Are We Going in MK Education?" *Evangelical Missions Quarterly* 42 (4) (October): 462–70.

Hall, Dave. 2000. "Ten Reasons Why Every Church Planting Team Needs a Worship-Arts Leader." *Evangelical Missions Quarterly* 36 (January): 50–53.

Harrison, Eugene Myers. 1954. "Giants of the Missionary Trail: William Carey, the Cobbler Who Turned Discoverer." http://www.wholesomewords.org/missions/giants/biocarey2.html (accessed January 17, 2007).

Harrison, Myron S. 1983. *Developing Multinational Teams*. Manila: OMF.

Harvey, Richard S. 2000. *Evangelical Dictionary of World Missions*, ed. A. Scott Moreau, s.v. "Jew, Judaism." Grand Rapids: Baker Academic.

Herrmann, Carol Bernice. 1997. "Foundational Factors of Trust and Autonomy Influencing the Identity-Formation of the Multi-Cultural Life Styled MK." PhD diss., Northwestern University.

Hesselgrave, David. 1978. *Communicating Christ Cross-Culturally*. Grand Rapids: Zondervan.

———. 1994. *Scripture and Strategy: The Use of the Bible in Postmodern Church and Mission*. Pasadena, CA: William Carey Library.

Hiebert, Frances F. 1999. "Single Women in Mission." Unpublished research data for Doctor of Ministry in Missiology, Trinity Evangelical Divinity School.

Hiebert, Paul G. 1976. *Cultural Anthropology*. Philadelphia: Lippincott.

———. 1982. "The Flaw of the Excluded Middle." *Missiology: An International Review* 10 (January): 35–47.

———. 1984. "Critical Contextualization." *Missiology: An International Review* 12 (July): 287–96.

———. 1985. *Anthropological Insights for Missionaries*. Grand Rapids: Baker Academic.

———. 1999. *The Implications of Epistemological Shifts*. Valley Forge, PA: Trinity Press International.

———. 2000a. *Evangelical Dictionary of World Missions*, ed. A. Scott Moreau, s.v. "Folk Religions." Grand Rapids: Baker Academic.

———. 2000b. "French Structuralism and Modern Missiology." A paper presented at the Christian Perspectives on Anthropological Theory at Biola University, La Mirada, CA, April 6–8.

Heibert, Paul G., R. Daniel Shaw, and Tite Teinou. 1999. *Understanding Folk Religion: A Christian Response to Popular Beliefs and Practices*. Grand Rapids: Baker Academic.

Hill, Harriet. 1993. "Lifting the Fog of Incarnational Ministry." *Evangelical Missions Quarterly* 29 (October): 262–69.

Hinson, Glenn E. 1971. "1–2 Timothy and Titus." In *The Broadman Bible Commentary, Vol. 11*, ed. Clifton J. Allen, 299–376. Nashville: Broadman.

Hoke, Steve, and William Taylor, eds. 1999. *Send Me! Your Journey to the Nations*. Pasadena, CA: William Carey Library.

Howard, David M. 2000. *Evangelical Dictionary of World Missions*, ed. A. Scott Moreau, s.v. "Elliot, Philip James (1927–56)." Grand Rapids: Baker Academic.

Howard, Lucy Hamilton. N.d. "Her Lengthened Shadow." http://imb.org/main/give/page.asp?StoryID=5551&LanguageID=1709 (accessed June 28, 2007).

Huff, Livingstone. 2002. "Avoiding the Crash-and-Burn Syndrome." *Missiology: An International Review* 30 (January): 80–89.

Hunsberger, George R. 2000. *Evangelical Dictionary of World Missions,* ed. A. Scott Moreau, s.v. "The Gospel and Our Culture Network." Grand Rapids: Baker Academic.

Hunter, Steve. 2005. "Coming Home: Heartache, Hope and Helpful Hints." *Evangelical Missions Quarterly* 41 (April): 150–54.

Hyatt, Irwin. 1976. *Our Ordered Lives Confess: Three Nineteenth-Century American Missionaries in East Sahntund.* Cambridge, MA: Harvard University Press.

"Instant Wisdom." N.d. http://instantwisdom.bravepages.com/topics/know.htm (accessed March 27, 2006).

Iyer, Pico. 1988. *Video Night in Kathmandu: And Other Reports from the Not-So-Far East.* New York: Random House.

Jaffarian, Michael. 2004. "Are There More Non-Western Missionaries than Western Missionaries?" *International Bulletin of Missionary Research* 28 (3): 131–32.

Jenkins, Philip. 2002. *The Next Christendom: The Coming of Global Christianity.* New York: Oxford University Press.

Johnson, Paul I. 2006. *More Than Money . . . More Than Faith: Successfully Raising Missionary Support in the Twenty-first Century.* Enumclaw, WA: Pleasant Word.

Johnson, R. Park. 1998. *Biographical Dictionary of Christian Missions,* ed. Gerald H. Anderson, s.v. "Brown, Arthur Judson." Grand Rapids: Eerdmans.

Johnson, Todd. 2006. "Missiometrics 2006: Goals, Resources, Doctrines of the 350 Christian World Communions." *International Bulletin of Missionary Research* 30 (1): 27–30.

Johnstone, Patrick. 1993. *Operation World: The Day-by-Day Guide to Praying for the World.* 5th ed. Grand Rapids: Zondervan.

Johnstone, Patrick, and Jason Mandryk. 2001. *Operation World.* 6th ed. Carlisle, Cumbria, UK: Paternoster Lifestyle.

Jordan, Peter. 1992. *Re-entry: Making the Transition from Missions to Life at Home.* Seattle: YWAM.

Kane, J. Herbert. 1975. *The Making of a Missionary.* Grand Rapids: Baker Academic.

———. 1980. *Life and Work on the Mission Field.* Grand Rapids: Baker Academic.

———. 1986. *Understanding Christian Missions.* Grand Rapids: Baker Academic.

Kelsey, Morton T. 1975. *God, Dreams and Revelation.* Minneapolis: Augsburg.

Kohls, L. Robert. 1996. *Survival Kit for Overseas Living.* 3rd ed. Chicago: Intercultural Press.

———. 2001. *Survival Kit for Overseas Living.* 4th ed. Yarmouth, ME: Intercultural Press.

Koteskey, Ronald L. 2006. *What Missionaries Ought to Know.* N.p.: privately published. Available at www.missionarycare.com.

Kraft, Charles H. 1979. *Christianity in Culture.* Maryknoll, NY: Orbis.

———. 1996. *Anthropology for Christian Witness.* Maryknoll, NY: Orbis.

———. 2000. *Evangelical Dictionary of World Missions,* ed. A. Scott Moreau, s.v. "Culture Shock." Grand Rapids: Baker Academic.

Kraft, Marguerite, and Meg Crossman. 1999. "Women in Mission." *Mission Frontiers* 21 (August): 13–17.

Kroeber, A. L., and Clyde Kluckhohn. 1952. *Culture: A Critical Review of Concepts and Definitions.* New York: Vintage Books.

Lai, Patrick. 2005. *Tentmaking: Business as Missions.* Waynesboro, GA: Authentic.

Lake, Kirsopp, trans. 1913. "The Epistle to Diognetus." In *The Apostolic Fathers,* 2:359–61. Cambridge: Harvard University Press.

371

Larsen, David L. 2001. *Biblical Spirituality*. Grand Rapids: Kregel.

Larson, Donald N. 1984. *Guidelines for Barefoot Language Learning*. St. Paul: CMS.

Latourette, Kenneth Scott. 1971. *A History of the Expansion of Christianity*. Vol. 3. Grand Rapids: Zondervan.

Lausanne Committee for World Evangelization. 1974. "The Lausanne Covenant." http://www.lausanne.org/lausanne-1974/lausanne-covenant.html (accessed June 19, 2007).

————. 1983. *Co-operating in World Evangelization: A Handbook on Church/Para-Church Relationships*. Lausanne Occasional Papers 24. Wheaton: Lausanne Committee for World Evangelization.

Lewis, James F. 2000. *Evangelical Dictionary of World Missions*, ed. A. Scott Moreau, s.v. "Hinduism." Grand Rapids: Baker Academic.

Lingenfelter, Sherwood G. 1992. *Transforming Culture*. Grand Rapids: Baker Academic.

————. 1996. *Agents of Transformation: A Guide for Effective Cross-Cultural Ministry*. Grand Rapids: Baker Academic.

Lingenfelter, Sherwood G., and Marvin K. Mayers. 2003. *Ministering Cross-Culturally: An Incarnational Model for Personal Relationships*. Grand Rapids: Baker Academic.

Livermore, David A. 2006. *Serving with Eyes Wide Open: Doing Short-Term Missions with Cultural Intelligence*. Grand Rapids: Baker Academic.

Livingstone, W. P. 1916. *Mary Slessor of Calabar: Pioneer Missionary*. London: Hodder & Stoughton.

Lo, James. 2004. "The Pressure to Lie." *Evangelical Missions Quarterly* 40 (October): 362–66.

Lundy, David. 1999. *We Are the World: Globalization and the Changing Face of Missions*. Cumbria, UK: O.M. Publishing.

Luzbetak, Louis. 1988. *The Church and Cultures: New Perspectives in Missiological Anthropology*. Maryknoll, NY: Orbis.

Mangalwadi, Vishal. 1999. *The Legacy of William Carey: A Model for the Transformation of a Culture*. Wheaton: Crossway.

Marshall, Terry. 1989. *The Whole World Guide to Language Learning*. Yarmouth, ME: Intercultural Press.

Maslow, Abraham H. 1999. *Toward a Psychology of Being*. 3rd ed. New York: John Wiley & Sons.

Mayers, Marvin K. 1987. *Christianity Confronts Culture: A Strategy for Cross-Cultural Evangelism*. Grand Rapids: Zondervan.

Mbiti, John S. 1970. *African Religions and Philosophy*. New York: Doubleday.

McCracken, Jean. 1979. "1 Corinthians 13: A Missionary Version." *Evangelical Missions Quarterly* 15 (July): 151.

McGavran, Donald A. 1970. *Understanding Church Growth*. Grand Rapids: Eerdmans.

————. 1988. *Effective Evangelism: A Theological Mandate*. Phillipsburg, NJ: Presbyterian & Reformed.

McIlwain, Trevor. 1965–92. *Building on Firm Foundations*. 9 vols. Sanford, FL: New Tribes Mission.

McKinney Douglas, Lois. 1975. "Are You Teaching Only Women?" *INTERLIT* 12 (4): 79.

————. 2002. "My Pilgrimage in Mission." *International Bulletin of Missionary Research* 26 (4): 174–77.

————. 2006. "Globalizing Theology and Theological Education." In *Globalizing Theology*, ed. Harold A. Netland and Craig L. Ott, 267–87. Grand Rapids: Baker Academic.

McKnight, Scott. 2004. *The Jesus Creed*. Brewster, MA: Paraclete Press.

McLoughlin, Michael C. R. 2000. "Back to the Future of Missions: The Case for Marketplace Ministry." *VOCATIO* (December): 1–6.

McManus, Erwin. 2002. *Seizing Your Divine Moment: Dare to Live a Life of Adventure*. Nashville: Thomas Nelson.

McQuilkin, J. Robertson. 1984. *The Great Omission: A Biblical Basis for World Evangelism*. Grand Rapids: Baker Academic.

———. 2000. *Evangelical Dictionary of World Missions*, ed. A. Scott Moreau, s.v. "Commitment." Grand Rapids: Baker Academic.

Merton, Thomas. 1958. *Thoughts in Solitude*. New York: Farrar, Straus, & Cudahy.

Metcalf, Samuel F. 1993. "When Local Churches Act like Agencies." *Evangelical Missions Quarterly* 29 (July): 142–49.

Miley, George. 2003. *Loving the Church . . . Blessing the Nations: Pursuing the Role of Local Churches in Global Mission*. Waynesboro, GA: Gabriel.

Moffett, Samuel H. 2005. *A History of Christianity in Asia*. Maryknoll, NY: Orbis.

Moll, Rob. 2006. "Missions Incredible." *Christianity Today* 50 (March): 28–34.

Moreau, A. Scott. 2000a. *Evangelical Dictionary of World Missions*, ed. A. Scott Moreau, s.v. "Persecution." Grand Rapids: Baker Academic.

———. 2000b. "Putting the Survey in Perspective." *Mission Handbook: U.S. and Canadian Ministries Overseas 2001–2003*, ed. John A. Siewert and Dotsey Welliver, 33–80. Wheaton: Evangelism and Missions Information Service.

———. 2004. "Putting the Survey in Perspective." In *Mission Handbook 2004–2006: U.S. and Canadian Protestant Ministries Overseas*, 19th ed., ed. Dotsey Welliver and Minnette Northcutt, 11–64. Wheaton: Evangelical Missions Information Service.

———. 2007. "Putting the Survey in Perspective." In *Handbook of North American Protestant Missions 2007–2009*, ed. Linda Weber, 11–75. Wheaton: Evangelism and Missions Information Service.

Moreau, A. Scott, Gary Corwin, and Gary McGee. 2004. *Introducing World Missions*. Grand Rapids: Baker Academic.

Muck, Terry C. 2000. *Evangelical Dictionary of World Missions*, ed. A. Scott Moreau, s.v. "Buddhism." Grand Rapids: Baker Academic.

Mulholland, Kenneth. 1996. "Missiological Education in the Bible College Tradition." In *Missiological Education for the Twenty-first Century: The Book, the Circle and the Sandals*, ed. J. Dudley Woodberry, Charles Van Engen, and Edgar J. Elliston, 43–53. Eugene, OR: Wipf & Stock.

Murdock, George P. 1945. *The Common Denominator of Culture in Ralph Linton: The Science of Man in the World Crisis*. New York: Columbia University Press.

Myers, Bryant. 1999a. *Walking with the Poor: Principles and Practices of Transformational Development*. Maryknoll, NY: Orbis.

———. 1999b. *Working with the Poor: New Insights and Learnings from Development Practitioners*. Monrovia, CA: World Vision.

Nanda, Serena. 1994. *Cultural Anthropology*. Belmont, CA: Wadsworth.

Nanus, Burt. 1992. *Visionary Leadership*. San Francisco: Jossey-Bass.

Nazir-Ali, Michael. 1999. "Martyn and Martyrs: Questions for Mission." *International Bulletin of Missionary Research* (April): 56–60.

Neely, Alan. 2000. "Missiology." In *Evangelical Dictionary of World Missions*, ed. A. Scott Moreau, 633–35. Grand Rapids: Baker Academic.

Neill, C. Stephen. 1975. *A History of Christian Missions*. Middlesex, UK: Penguin.

———. 1984. *A History of Christianity in India: The Beginning to AD 1707*. London: Cambridge University Press.

Netland, Harold A. 1994. "Theology and Missions: Some Reflections on an Ambivalent Relationship." *Trinity World Forum* 19 (3): 1–4.

———. 2001. *Encountering Religious Pluralism: The Challenge to Christian Faith and Mission*. Downers Grove, IL: InterVarsity.

Newbigin, Lesslie. 1989. *The Gospel in a Pluralist Society*. Grand Rapids: Eerdmans.

Niebuhr, H. Richard. 1951. *Christ and Culture*. New York: Harper and Row.

373

Nilsen, Maria. 1956. *Malla Moe*. Chicago: Moody.

Nouwen, Henri J. M. 1995. "Moving from Solitude to Community to Ministry." *Leadership* 20 (Spring): 81–87.

———. 1999. *The Return of the Prodigal Son: A Story of Homecoming*. New York: Continuum.

Oberg, Kalvero. 1960. "Cultural Shock: Adjustment to a New Cultural Environment." *Practical Anthropology* 7 (July–August): 177–78. Cited in Kohls 2001, 94.

O'Donnell, Kelly S., and Michele Lewis O'Donnell, eds. 1988. *Helping Missionaries Grow: Readings in Mental Health and Missions*. Pasadena, CA: William Carey Library.

Olsen, Ted. "Go Figure." 2005a. *Christianity Today* 49 (June): 24.

———. "Go Figure." 2005b. *Christianity Today* 49 (December): 22.

Opler, Morris E. 1945. "Themes as Dynamic Forces in Culture." *American Journal of Sociology* 51: 198–206.

Packer, J. I. 1990. "The Christian's Purpose in Business." In *Biblical Principles and Business: The Practice*, ed. Richard C. Chewning, 16–25. Colorado Springs: NavPress.

Patterson, George, and Richard Scoggins. 2001. *Church Multiplication Guide: Helping Churches to Reproduce Locally and Abroad*. Pasadena, CA: William Carey Library.

Pentecost, Edward C. 1982. *Issues in Missiology: An Introduction*. Grand Rapids: Baker Academic.

Peoples, James, and Garrick Bailey. 2005. *Humanity: Introduction to Cultural Anthropology*. Belmont, CA: Wadsworth.

Peters, George. 1972. *A Biblical Theology of Missions*. Chicago: Moody Press.

Peterson, Eugene H. 1997. *Leap over a Wall: Earthy Spirituality for Everyday Christians*. New York: HarperCollins.

Phillips, Barbara. 1996. *City Lights*. 2nd ed. New York: Oxford University Press.

Pierce, Robert W., and Rebecca Merrill Groothuis, eds. 2004. *Discovering Biblical Equality: Complementarity without Hierarchy*. Downers Grove, IL: InterVarsity.

Pierson, Paul E. 2000. *Evangelical Dictionary of World Missions*, ed. A. Scott Moreau, s.v. "Moravian Missions." Grand Rapids: Baker Academic.

Piper, John. 2004. *Why I Don't Desire God: How to Fight for Joy*. Wheaton: Crossway.

Piper, John, and Wayne Grudem, eds. 1991. *Recovering Biblical Manhood and Womanhood*. Wheaton: Crossway.

Plueddemann, Carol Savage. 1994. "Review of *Don't Pig Out on Junk Food: The MK's Guide to Survival in the U.S.*" *Evangelical Missions Quarterly* (July): 331–32.

Pocock, Michael, Gailyn Van Rheenen, and Douglas McConnell. 2005. *The Changing Face of World Missions: Engaging Contemporary Issues and Trends*. Grand Rapids: Baker Academic.

Pollock, David C., and Ruth E. Van Reken. 1999. *The Third Culture Kid Experience: Growing Up Among Worlds*. Yarmouth, ME: Intercultural Press.

Prescott, Ian Charles Herbert. 2001. "Creative Access Mission in East Asia." DMiss diss., Fuller Theological Seminary, School of World Mission.

Priest, Robert J., Terry Dischinger, Steve Rasmussen, and Steve Brown. 2006. "Researching the Short-Term Mission Movement." *Missiology: An International Review* 34 (4) (October): 431–50.

Program in Language Acquisition Techniques (PILAT). http://www.mti.org/pilat (accessed March 27, 2006).

Putnam, Robert, and Lewis Feldstein. 1975. *Better Together: Restoring the American Community*. New York: Simon & Schuster.

———. 2003. *Better Together: Restoring the American Community*. New York: Simon & Schuster.

Quotesandsayings.com. N.d. "Quotes and Sayings." http://www.quotesandsayings.com/gatoz.htm (accessed March 25, 2006).

Ramstad, Mans. 2004. "Persecution: A Biblical and Personal Reflection." *Evangelical Missions Quarterly* (October): 468–75.

Reich, Robert B. 2001. *The Future of Success.* New York: Alfred A. Knopf.

Renovaré. N.d. http://www.renovare.org (accessed March 26, 2006).

Rickett, Daniel. 2000. *Building Strategic Relationships: A Practical Guide to Partnering with Non-Western Missions.* Pleasant Hill, CA: Klein Graphics for Partners International.

———. 2002. *Making Your Partnership Work.* Spokane: Partners International.

Ridderbos, Herman N. 1975. *Paul: An Outline of His Theology.* Grand Rapids: Eerdmans.

Robert, Dana L. 1996. *American Women in Mission: A Social History of Their Thought and Practice.* Macon, GA: Mercer University Press.

———. 2002. "Historical Themes and Current Issues." In *Gospel Bearers, Gender Barriers: Missionary Women in the Twentieth Century,* ed. Dana L. Robert, 1–28. Maryknoll, NY: Orbis.

———. 2005. "What Happened to the Christian Home? The Missing Component of Mission Theory." *Missiology: An International Review* 33 (July): 325–40.

Roembke, Lianne. 2000. *Building Credible Multicultural Teams.* Pasadena, CA: William Carey Library.

Ross, Kenneth R. 2002. *Following Jesus and Fighting HIV/AIDS: A Call to Discipleship.* Edinburgh: Saint Andrew Press.

———. 2004. "The HIV/AIDS Pandemic: What Is at Stake for Christian Mission?" *Missiology: An International Review* 32 (July): 337–48.

Rubin, Joan, and Irene Thompson. 1994. *How to Be a More Successful Language Learner.* 2nd ed. Boston: Heinle & Heinle.

Rundle, Steve, and Tom Steffen. 2003. *Great Commission Companies: The Emerging Role of Business in Missions.* Downers Grove, IL: InterVarsity.

Russell, Walt B., III. 1988. "An Alternative Suggestion for the Purpose of Romans." *Bibliotheca Sacra* 145 (578): 174–84.

Ryken, Leland. 1984. *How to Read the Bible as Literature.* Grand Rapids: Zondervan.

Sawyer, Mark, and Larry E. Smith. 1994. "Approaching Cultural Crossover in Language Learning." In *Improving Intercultural Interactions,* ed. Richard W. Brislin and Tomoko Yoshida, 300–306. Newbury Park, CA: Sage.

Schein, Edgar. 1985. *Organizational Culture and Leadership.* San Francisco: Jossey-Bass.

Scherer, James. 1984. "The Future of Missiology as an Academic Discipline in Seminary Education: An Attempt at Reinterpretation and Clarification." *Missiology: An International Review* 13 (October): 445–60.

———. 1987. "Missiology as a Discipline and What It Includes." *Missiology: An International Review* 15 (October): 507–22.

Schreiter, Robert J., ed. 2001. *Mission in the Third Millennium.* Maryknoll, NY: Orbis.

Sells, Ben. 2004. "Student Debt: A Hurdle Too High for 'Impact' Missionaries." *Mission Frontiers* (July–August): 8–9.

Shaw, R. Daniel, and Charles Van Engen. 2003. *Communicating God's Word in a Complex World: God's Truth or Hocus Pocus?* Lanham, MD: Rowman & Littlefield.

Shenk, Wilbert R. 1996. "The Role of Theory in Mission Studies." *Missiology: An International Review* 24 (January): 31–45.

———, ed. 2004. *North American Foreign Missions, 1810–1914: Theology, Theory, and Policy.* Grand Rapids: Eerdmans.

Shetler, Joanne, with Patricia Purvis. 1992. *And the Word Came with Power: How God Met and Changed a People Forever.* Portland, OR: Multnomah.

SIL International. N.d. "Lingua Links Library." http://www.sil.org/lingualinks (accessed March 27, 2006).

Singeles, Ted. 1994. "Nonverbal Communication in Intercultural Interactions." In

Improving Intercultural Interactions, ed. Richard W. Brislin and Tomoko Yoshida, 268–94. Newbury Park, CA: Sage.

"Slavery: Past and Present." N.d. http://www.garstangfairtrade.org.uk/slavery_today.htm (accessed January 30, 2007).

Smallbones, Jackie L. 1995. "Spiritual Director, Mentor and Christian Educator." *Christian Education Journal* 16 (Fall): 37–44.

Snow, Donald B. 2001. *English Teaching as Christian Mission: An Applied Theology*. Scottdale, PA: Herald.

———. 2006. *More Than a Native Speaker: An Introduction for Volunteers Teaching English Abroad*. Alexandria, VA: Teachers of English to Speakers of Other Languages.

Spiritual Formation Forum. N.d. http://www.spiritualformationforum.org (accessed March 26, 2006).

Spradlin, Byron. 2005. "Review of *Taking It to the Streets: Using the Arts to Transform Your Community*, by Nathan Corbitt and Vivian Nix-Early." *Evangelical Missions Quarterly* 41 (January): 130.

Spurgeon, C. H. N.d. "Everyday Religion." http://www.puritansermons.com/spurge6d.htm (accessed June 28, 2007).

Steffen, Tom A. 1993. "Urban-Rural Networks and Strategies." *Urban Mission* 10 (October): 37–42.

———. 1997. *Passing the Baton: Church Planting That Empowers*. La Habra, CA: Center for Organizational and Ministry Development.

———. 1998. "Foundational Roles of Symbol and Narrative in the (Re)construction of Reality and Relationships." *Missiology: An International Review* 26 (October): 477–94.

———. 1999. *Business as Usual in the Missions Enterprise?* La Habra, CA: Center for Organizational and Ministry Development.

———. 2001. "Caring for GenXers." In *Caring for the Harvest Force in the Twenty-first Century*, ed. Tom A. Steffen and F. Douglas Pennoyer, EMS Series 9, 213–30. Pasadena, CA: William Carey Library.

———. 2005. *Reconnecting God's Story to Ministry: Cross-Cultural Storytelling at Home and Abroad*. Rev. ed. Waynesboro, GA: Authentic Media.

Stevens, Paul. 1991. *The Other Six Days: Vocation, Work, and Ministry in Biblical Perspective*. Grand Rapids: Eerdmans.

Stott, John. 1975. "The Lausanne Covenant: An Exposition and Commentary." Lausanne Occasional Papers 3. Wheaton: Lausanne Committee for World Evangelization. http://community.gospelcom.net/Brix?pageID=14323 (accessed June 28, 2007).

Taber, Charles R. 2000. *World, to Save the World: The Interface between Missiology and the Social Sciences*. Harrisburg, PA: Trinity Press International.

Tallman, J. Ray. 2000. *Evangelical Dictionary of World Missions*, ed. A. Scott Moreau, s.v. "Martyrdom." Grand Rapids: Baker Academic.

Taylor, William D., ed. 1994. *Kingdom Partnerships for Synergy in Mission*. Pasadena, CA: William Carey Library.

———. 2001. "Culture and Knowing God." Plenary presentation at the Second International Spiritual Formation Conference at Dallas Theological Seminary, May 17–19.

Telford, Tom. 1998. *Missions in the Twenty-first Century: Getting Your Church in the Game*. Wheaton: Harold Shaw.

Tienou, Tite. 2000. *Evangelical Dictionary of World Missions*, ed. A. Scott Moreau, s.v. "African Traditional Religion." Grand Rapids: Baker Academic.

Tippett, Alan R. 1987. *Introduction to Missiology*. Pasadena, CA: William Carey Library.

Tournier, Paul. 1962. *Guilt and Grace*. New York: Harper & Row.

Trans World Radio. N.d. "MemCare by Radio: Combating Loneliness in Central Asia." http://www.twr.org/give/projects/memcare_radio (accessed June 28, 2007).

Tucker, Ruth A. 1987. "Female Mission Strategists: A Historical and Contemporary

Perspective." *Missiology: An International Review* 15 (January): 73–89.

———. 1988. *Guardians of the Great Commission: The Story of Women in Modern Missions.* Grand Rapids: Zondervan.

United Nations. 2000. Division for the Advancement of Women, Department of Economic and Social Affairs. Based on "Review and Appraisal of the Implementation of the Beijing Platform for Action: Report of the Secretary General" (E/CN.6/2000/PC/2). http://www.un.org/womenwatch/daw/followup/session/presskit/fsl.htm (accessed August 30, 2006).

Useem, John, and Ruth Hill Useem. 1967. "The Interfaces of a Binational Third Culture: A Study of the American Community in India." *Journal of Social Issues* 23 (Spring): 130–43.

U.S. Government Interagency Language Roundtable. N.d. http://www.govilr.org (accessed March 27, 2006).

Van Engen, Charles. 1996. *Mission on the Way: Issues in Mission Theology.* Grand Rapids: Baker Academic.

———. 2000. *Evangelical Dictionary of World Missions,* ed. A. Scott Moreau, s.v. "Postmodernism." Grand Rapids: Baker Academic.

Vardell, Douglas J. 2000. *Evangelical Dictionary of World Missions,* ed. A. Scott Moreau, s.v. "Image of God." Grand Rapids: Baker Academic.

Verkuyl, Johannes. 1978. *Contemporary Missiology: An Introduction.* Grand Rapids: Eerdmans.

Wallace, Carey. 2000. "Devastation in Turkey: The Church Responds." *Mission Frontiers* 22 (January): 35–37.

Walls, Andrew F. 1996. *The Missionary Movement in Christian History: Studies in Transmission of Faith.* Maryknoll, NY: Orbis.

Waltke, Bruce K. 1995. *Finding the Will of God: A Pagan Notion?* Grand Rapids: Eerdmans.

Wan, Enoch. 2003. "Mission among the Chinese Diaspora: A Case Study of Migration

and Mission." *Missiology: An International Review* 31 (1): 35–43.

Ward, Ted. 1989. "The MK's Advantage: Three Cultural Contexts." In *Understanding and Nurturing the Missionary Family,* ed. Pam Echerd and Alice Arathoon, 49–61. Pasadena, CA: William Carey Library.

Warner, Timothy M. 2000. *Evangelical Dictionary of World Missions,* ed. A. Scott Moreau, s.v. "Spiritual Warfare." Grand Rapids: Baker Academic.

Weber, Linda, ed. 2007. *Handbook of North American Protestant Missions 2007–2009.* Wheaton: Evangelism and Missions Information Service.

Welliver, Dotsey, and Minnette Northcutt, eds. 2004. *Mission Handbook 2004–2006: U.S. and Canadian Protestant Ministries Overseas.* 19th ed. Wheaton: Evangelical Missions Information Service.

Welliver, Dotsey, and Minnette Smith, eds. 2002. *Directory of Schools and Professors of Mission and Evangelism 2002–2004.* Wheaton: Evangelism and Missions Information Service.

Wickstrom, David L. 1994. "The Right Stuff in Boarding School Staff." *Evangelical Missions Quarterly* 30 (October): 376–88.

Willard, Dallas. 2002. *Renovation of the Heart: Putting on the Character of Christ.* Colorado Springs: NavPress.

———. N.d. "Spiritual Formation: What It Is and How It Is to Be Done." http://www.dwil lard.org/articles/artreview.asp?artID=58 (accessed April 4, 2005).

Winter, Ralph D. 1970. *The Twenty-five Unbelievable Years, 1945 to 1969.* South Pasadena, CA: William Carey Library.

———. 1996. "The Re-Amateurization of Missions." *The Occasional Bulletin of the Evangelical Missiological Society.* http://www.missiology.org/EMS/bulletins/winter.htm.

———. 1997. "Six Spheres of Mission Overseas." *Mission Frontiers Bulletin* (November–December): 5.

———. 1999. "The Convergence of Theology and Missiology: Will This Happen in the Third Millennium?" A paper presented at the EMS/SW meetings, Biola University, La Mirada, CA, April 23.

Woodberry, Dudley J. 2000. *Evangelical Dictionary of World Missions*, ed. A. Scott Moreau, s.v. "Islam, Muslim." Grand Rapids: Baker Academic.

———. 2002. "Muslim Missions after September 11." *Evangelical Missions Quarterly* 38 (January): 66–75.

World Vision of Australia (WVA). 1998. "Poverty and the Environment." http://www.wvi.org/wvi/develop/development_issues.htm (accessed August 29, 2006).

———. 1999. "The State of the World's Hungry Children." http://www.wvi.org/wvi/develop/development_issues.htm (accessed August 29, 2006).

———. 2000. "Water: A Precious Resource." http://www.wvi.org/wvi/develop/development_issues.htm (accessed August 29, 2006).

———. 2003a. "Food for the World—Enough for Everyone?" http://www.wvi.org/wvi/develop/development_issues.htm (accessed August 29, 2006).

———. 2003b. "Immunisation—Shots of a Life-Saving Kind." http://www.wvi.org/wvi/develop/development_issues.htm (accessed August 29, 2006).

———. 2003c. "Nurturing Girls—Nurturing Change." http://www.wvi.org/wvi/develop/development_issues.htm (accessed August 29, 2006).

———. 2003d. "Participatory Development: Power to the People." http://www.wvi.org/wvi/develop/development_issues.htm (accessed August 29, 2006).

World Vision International. 2005. "Relief." http://www.wvi.org/wvi/relief/relief.htm (accessed August 29, 2006).

Wright, Christopher J. H. 2006. *The Mission of God: Unlocking the Bible's Grand Narrative*. Downers Grove, IL: InterVarsity.

———. 2007. "An Upside-Down World." *Christianity Today* 51 (January): 42–46.

Yamamori, Ted, and John Warton. 2004. *General Forum Orientation: Historical Overview*. Audiotape of lecture at Kingdom Business Forum, Atlanta, April 2004.

Yamamori, Tetsunao, and Ken Eldred, eds. 2003. *On Kingdom Business: Transforming World Missions through Kingdom Entrepreneurship*. Wheaton: Crossway.

Yancey, Philip. 1983. "Finding the Will of God: No Magic Formulas." *Christianity Today* 27 (September): 24–27.

Yohanan, K. P. 1986. *The Coming Revolution in World Missions*. Altamonte Springs, FL: Creation House.

Youngren, J. Alan. 1981. "Parachurch Proliferation: The Frontier Spirit Caught in Traffic." *Christianity Today* 25 (November): 38–39.

Zemke, Ron, Claire Raines, and Bob Filipczak. 2000. *Generations at Work: Managing the Clash of Veterans, Boomers, Xers, and Nexters in Your Workplace*. New York: Performance Research Associates.

Zoba, Wendy Murray. 2000. "A Woman's Place." *Christianity Today* 44 (August): 40–48.

Scripture Index

379

14:14 300
19:11–12 268
19:29 202
22:34–40 67
22:37–40 50
26:65 308
28:18 80
28:18–20 130
28:19 80, 81
28:20 80, 203, 328

Mark

3:13 57
6:7 210
6:9 211
10:29–30 202
12:28–34 67
13:9 311, 312
13:11 312
14:23 211
14:63 308
16:15 80, 81

Luke

1 52
1:24–2:35 5
2:36–38 5
3:19 5
4:26 5
4:38 5
6:12 72
6:12–19 72
6:13 76
6:17–18 79
7:11–12 5
7:36–50 5
8:3 5
8:19–20 5
8:22–25 68
10 32
10:5 106
10:25–28 67
10:38–42 5
11:27–28 5
11:31 5
13:10–17 5
14:28–30 162
15:8–10 5
17:32 5
18:1–8 5
18:9–14 67
18:29–30 202
21:1–4 5
21:11 300
22:13 211
22:19 211
22:56–57 5
22:71 308
23:27 5
23:49 5
23:55 5
24:10 5

24:30 211

John

1:1 227
1:12–13 78
1:14 227
3:16 81, 121
8:2–11 66
13:14 210
13:35 348
14:2 203
20:21 80
20:30 52

Acts

1 52
1:3 4
1:4–8 80
1:5 4
1:8 4, 33, 81, 308
1:26 211
2:1–4 80
2:17 52
2:17–21 257
2:38 210
2:44–45 211
3:1 210
4:35 35
5 35, 195
5:1–11 5
6 35
6:1 5
6:3 211
6:8–7:60 313
7:51–52 313
7:54–56 313
7:59 313
7:60 313
8:12 4
8:26–40 80
8:27 5
8:29 53
8:39–40 53
9 57
9:1–6 71
9:1–19 228, 307
9:3–6 53
9:10–19 72
9:25–30 54
9:36–41 5
9:39 5
9:41 5
10 53, 80, 109
10:10–20 4
11:26 57
11:30 35
12:1–23 309
12:2 309
12:12 5
12:13 5
13 57, 108, 177
13:1–4 80

13:2 4, 58, 59
13:3 210, 211
13:14 211
13:42–44 211
14:1 210
14:22 4
14:27 54
15 6, 35
15:5 211
15:29 210, 211
15:36 35
16:1–40 4
16:5 35
16:6 4
16:6–7 106
16:6–10 80
16:8–10 53, 54
16:9–10 53
16:13–15 5
16:16–18 5
17:4 5
17:12 5
17:34 5
18 57, 151
18:2–3 5
18:3 175, 351, 352
18:9 53
18:18 5, 211
18:24–26 260
18:26 5, 175, 352
19:1–41 4
19:8 4
20 35
20:25 4
20:27 35
20:33–35 175
21:8–9 260
21:9 5, 257
22:17–21 53
23:11 53
24:17 35
24:24 5
25:13 5
25:23 5
26:30 5
28:17–30 309
28:23 4
28:31 4

Romans

1:7 60
2:17–29 198
4:1–25 106
5:3–5 68
8:14–17 78
8:30 60
12:1–2 71
13:8 211
15:20 35, 160, 348
16 257
16:1 257
16:5 175, 352
16:7 35

16:16 210

1 Corinthians

3:10 35
4:12 175, 351
5 35
7 268
7:27 211
9:7 170
9:19 198
10:27 211
11:5 211, 260
11:8–9 258
11:10 210
11:11–14 257
11:12 258
11:14 211
11:24 210
11:34 35
12:8 54
12:26 303
13 238, 248
14:5 211
14:16 211
14:35 210
14:40 49
16:1 211
16:9 54
16:19 175, 257, 352

2 Corinthians

1:3 178
2:12 54
3:18 71, 74
5:17 74
7:2 350
8:9 328
10:16 35
11:7–9 176
11:13 35
11:28 35
12:12 53

Galatians

2 109
2:9 210
3:28 257
4:6–7 78
5:22–23 70

Ephesians

2:18–19 107
3:18 303
6:5 210
6:10–18 65, 311
6:10–20 68
6:18–19 69
6:19 35

Subject Index